BRIAN BORU AND THE BATTLE OF CLONTARF

BRIAN BORU AND THE BATTLE OF CLONTARF

SEÁN DUFFY

Gill & Macmillan

Gill & Macmillan
Hume Avenue, Park West, Dublin 12
with associated companies throughout the world
www.gillmacmillanbooks.ie

© Seán Duffy 2013
978 07171 5778 5

Index compiled by Gráinne Farren
Typography design by Make Communication
Print origination by Síofra Murphy
Printed and bound by ScandBook AB, Sweden

This book is typeset in Minion 12/15 pt.

The paper used in this book comes from the wood pulp
of managed forests. For every tree felled, at least one
tree is planted, thereby renewing natural resources.

A CIP catalogue record for this book is available from
the British Library.

5 4 3 2 1

For Linzi and Sadhbh

CONTENTS

LIST OF ILLUSTRATIONS   IX

PREFACE   XIII

INTRODUCTION: VIKING AGE IRELAND   1

PART I: BRIAN BORU'S WORLD

1.   The family of Brian Boru   61

2.   Brian's rise to power   92

3.   Emperor of the Gael   125

PART II: CLONTARF

4.   Clontarf in the Irish annals   167

5.   Cogadh Gáedhel re Gallaibh   198

6.   Clontarf through others' eyes   223

CONCLUSION: THE LEGACY OF BRIAN AND

     CLONTARF   239

ABBREVIATIONS   280

REFERENCES   282

BIBLIOGRAPHY   301

INDEX   334

LIST OF ILLUSTRATIONS

Maps

1. Ireland at the start of the Viking Age (after F. J. Byrne, 1973). *Irish Kings and High Kings* by F. J. Byrne; reprinted by kind permission of Four Courts Press. 10

2. The lands of the Southern Uí Néill, c. 800 AD (after F. J. Byrne, 1973). *Irish Kings and High Kings* by F. J. Byrne; reprinted by kind permission of Four Courts Press. 17

3. In Fochlae (the North), including lands of the Northern Uí Néill, Ulaid and Airgialla, c. 800 AD (after F. J. Byrne, 1973). *Irish Kings and High Kings* by F. J. Byrne; reprinted by kind permission of Four Courts Press. 22

4. Connacht, including Bréifne, c. 900 AD (after F. J. Byrne, 1973). *Irish Kings and High Kings* by F. J. Byrne; reprinted by kind permission of Four Courts Press. 28

5. Leinster, c. 900 AD (after F. J. Byrne, 1973). *Irish Kings and High Kings* by F. J. Byrne; reprinted by kind permission of Four Courts Press. 32

6. Munster and Osraige, c. 900 AD (after F. J. Byrne, 1973). *Irish Kings and High Kings* by F. J. Byrne; reprinted by kind permission of Four Courts Press. 36

7. Killaloe: conjectural map of Killaloe and district by the twelfth century (after John Bradley, 'Killaloe: a pre-Norman borough?' *Peritia*, 8, 1994, 170–79). Courtesy of John Bradley and Donnchadh Ó Corráin. 68

8. Battle of Clontarf (conjectural, based on material compiled by Seán Duffy). (Design Image) 203

Genealogical tables

1. Brian's remote ancestors of Dál Cais, from the mythological Mug Nuadat to Tairdelbach, c. 8th century AD. 40

2. Brian's immediate kinsmen of the Uí Thairdelbaig branch of Dál Cais.   63

3. Brian's wives and offspring.   100

4. Some of Brian's known and conjectural familial relationships.   147

Plates

1. Killaloe from the air.

2. Bél Bóraime (Béal Bórú).

3. The interior of Béal Boru today. (photograph: Seán Duffy)

4. St Molua's Oratory, Killaloe. (photograph: Seán Duffy)

5. St Flannán's Oratory, Killaloe. Commonly known as Brian Boru's Vault. (photograph: Seán Duffy).

6. St Flannan's Cathedral, Killaloe.

7. Mag Adair. (photograph: Seán Duffy)

8. Craicliath (the townland of Craglea, near Killaloe).

9. Inis Celtra (Holy Island), Lough Derg. (photograph: Seán Duffy)

10. Tuamgraney Church, Co. Clare. (photograph: Seán Duffy)

11. Rock of Cashel, Co. Tipperary. (photograph: Seán Duffy)

12. Dún na Sciath, Co. Westmeath.

13. Bleanphuttoge, on the shores of Lough Ree in Co. Westmeath. (photograph: Seán Duffy)

14. V-shaped landing-place, revetted in stone, on the side of the lough at Bleanphuttoge. (photograph: Seán Duffy)

15. Dún Delca, the hill fortress nowadays called Castletown Mount, about 2 km west of Dundalk.

16. Book of Armagh (Trinity College Dublin, MS. 16, fol. 16v).

17. Tailtiu (Teltown, Co. Meath), one of the complex of monuments in the vicinity, Rath Dubh.

18. *Cogadh Gáedhel re Gallaibh*, the Book of Leinster (Trinity College Dublin, MS. 1339, fol. 309).

19. The Curraghmore Sword.

20. Engraving from 1723, frontispiece of Dermod O'Connor's English translation of Keating's *Foras Feasa ar Éirinn*.

21. Battle of Clontarf, painting of 1826 by Hugh Frazer from Dromore, Co. Down (1795–1865).

22. Depiction of the Battle of Clontarf, drawn by Henry Mac Manus ARHA and litho-mezzotinted by W. H. Holbrooke of Dublin (National Library of Ireland).

23. Armagh, plaque on the wall of the Church of Ireland cathedral church of St Patrick.

24. Bully's Acre, Kilmainham, Dublin, early nineteenth-century water-colour by the Yorkshire artist Thales Fielding (1793–1837) (copyright John R. Redmill).

25. Shrine of the Stowe Missal.

26. Church of Santo Stefano, Rome. Burial plaque far left.

27. Burial plaque of Donnchad mac Briain, Church of Santo Stefano, Rome.

PREFACE

One of the landmark works of scholarship in the field of Celtic Studies in Ireland in the nineteenth century was the publication of the near-contemporary romantic biography of Brian Boru known as Cogadh Gáedhel re Gallaibh ('The War of the Irish with the Vikings'). In the introduction, its editor, the remarkable Trinity College scholar James Henthorn Todd, made a plea for the publication of critical editions of the mediaeval Irish annals, stating:

> Until these and other original sources of history are made accessible, it is vain to expect any sober or trustworthy history of Ireland; the old romantic notions of a golden age, so attractive to some minds, must continue to prevail; and there will still be firm believers in 'the glories of Brian the brave,' the lady who walked through Ireland unmolested in her gold and jewels, and the chivalrous feats of Finn Mac Cumhaill and his Fenians.[1]

Happily, in the century and a half since, great strides have been made in editing and making available the annals and a large volume of other documentary source material for mediaeval Ireland; and, indeed, thanks to the ground-breaking 'CELT' project of University College, Cork (Corpus of Electronic Texts, available at www.ucc.ie/celt/), anyone anywhere in the world who has a computer and an internet connection can gain access to a vast digital archive of this material, free of charge and almost instantaneously, in the comfort of their own home.

The publication of these primary sources has led to an explosion of secondary scholarship—books and articles written by professional historians and Celtic scholars—on the subject of mediaeval Ireland, grounded in the professional interrogation of these same source documents. And Todd's hopes for a 'sober or trustworthy history of Ireland,' freed of 'old romantic notions,' have largely been realised.

But his misgivings about what he sarcastically called 'the glories of Brian the brave' stemmed from a belief that the popular image of Brian Boru was at variance with the reality. This is Brian the all-conquering, Viking-vanquishing champion who died in his hour of victory at the Battle of Clontarf, a victory seen as possibly the most glorious achievement by any Irishman through the ages. This is Brian the hero-figure who led his people to victory over their would-be Norse conquerors and secured their freedom from foreign oppression—as one respected author unequivocally put it, the leader of the Irish Resistance Movement.[2]

Brian Boru's pre-eminence in Ireland's royal pantheon is starkly obvious from the fact that of the fifty or so high-kings who reigned from the dawn of Irish history until the institution went into abeyance in the aftermath of the English invasion of the late twelfth century he is, sad to say, the only one who has wide name-recognition to this day. The Battle of Clontarf is similarly one of the few Irish battles—and the only mediaeval one—fixed in the public imagination and its date, 1014, one of the very few mediaeval dates that resonate for Irish people in a way that Hastings and 1066 do for our neighbours. Todd was writing a full half century before the 1916 Rising, but the Irish of his day viewed 1014 much as a later generation would view 1916: if the bloody execution of the leaders of the Easter Rising represented lives sacrificed in the cause of Ireland, so the Battle of Clontarf, taking place on Good Friday, had associations with Christian martyrdom in the form of King Brian's death in his hour of victory over the heathen Norse.

Todd hoped for a more dispassionate assessment, which would scrape away later folklorish residues and get to the 'real' Brian. But progress since has been patchy, because, while historians continue to refine our understanding of the subject, theirs is a constant battle with the force of the dictum that when *the* legend becomes fact one prints the legend. And in the Google age, in the age of on-line wargame videos, of battle re-enactment mania, of the television and Hollywood historical drama, and in the age of the instant self-publishing novel, the legend of Brian has never been more alive.

The antidote to legend and folklore about Brian lies in Máire Ní Mhaonaigh's admirable recent biography, *Brian Boru: Ireland's Greatest King?* (2007), as there is no greater authority on contemporary Gaelic literature. As to Clontarf—the millennium of which is now upon us—in twenty years of teaching mediaeval Irish history in an Irish university the one question the writer has been asked more often than any other is the innocuous-sounding 'So what really happened at the Battle of Clontarf?' What follows is a long-winded attempt at an answer.

It is a straightforward political narrative. It situates Brian in the politics of Viking Age Ireland. It tells the story of the rise from relative obscurity of his North Munster dynasty of Dál Cais, of his own rapid ascent to national dominance and of the political transformation he wrought. It charts the inter-provincial struggle for supremacy that fed into his final great battle on Good Friday, 1014, in which he lost his life. And it examines the international context—the Second Viking Age—in which Clontarf was fought, when England was being conquered by the Danes under the family of King Knut, and the Norse of Dublin made their fatal gamble on breaking free from Brian's overlordship. It examines the evidence to see what was at stake in 1014 and how it can be that Brian was victorious at Clontarf yet lost his own life.

———

As this book goes to press within weeks of the millennial anniversary of the Battle of Clontarf, it is a pleasure to acknowledge the contribution of Dublin City Council to its production. The City Heritage Officer, Charles Duggan, has encouraged the project from its inception and obtained funding to enable me to secure additional leave in which to complete it. I am indebted to the City Archaeologist, Ruth Johnson, to Paul Clegg and Margaret Geraghty of Dublin City Council's Culture, Recreation and Amenity Department, and to Elaine Mulvenny of the North-Central Area Office, who have also generously contributed funding. The then head of the Department of History at Trinity College Dublin, David Ditchburn, kindly facilitated teaching leave as the deadline loomed. Eoin O'Flynn and Denis Casey read a large chunk of the manuscript, spotting blunders and recommending changes. Fergal Tobin of

Gill & Macmillan was all carrot and no stick on this outing, which seems to have done the trick. Field-trips to Brian's home place were memorable and enjoyable in the company of Linzi Simpson and Sadhbh Duffy (who will be disappointed to find only passing references to her inspiration, Sadb iníon Bhriain, of whom she has heard much and expected more). Both women put up with my crankiness for months on end: I dedicate the book to them and promise to make amends.

INTRODUCTION

VIKING AGE IRELAND

Brian Bóraime (anglicised Brian Boru) was born in the second quarter of the tenth century into a kinship dynasty of which not a great deal had hitherto been heard and from which only the most far-seeing can have expected much. Brian's people, who lived in the south-east corner of what is now Co. Clare, were the Uí Thairdelbaig, who were a branch of the Déis Tuaiscirt, better known as Dál Cais, who were a branch of the Déis Bec, who were a branch of the Déisi of Munster. Déisi means 'vassals': thus Brian's people were a branch of a branch of a branch of a branch of people who were in any event only vassals of the kings of Munster.

It was not a great pedigree. True, promoters of Brian's dynasty concocted a family tree to feign descent from the ancient kings of the province, but, to begin with at least, it cannot have fooled many. Yet Brian, and his brother Mathgamain before him, made themselves kings of Munster—quite an achievement. What is more, no king of Munster before Brian had gained general acceptance throughout the country as king of all Ireland, and yet he did—a truly remarkable achievement. To get the measure of that achievement we must consider the Ireland into which he was born.

EARLY IRELAND

The Celtic-speaking people who would eventually emerge into the light of history as the Irish arrived in the island perhaps only a few hundred years before the birth of Christ. Regrettably, these Iron Age people have left us nothing in writing until the fifth century AD, when we begin to find inscriptions using a system of symbols called *ogham* that takes the form of a series of lines and notches on standing-stones used as territorial markers or to commemorate the burial place of great men.[1] The majority of the four hundred or so that survive are found stretching from the Dingle Peninsula through south Kerry, Cork and Waterford to Co. Carlow, but there are quite a number of Irish ogham stones in Wales, particularly south Wales, with lesser concentrations elsewhere, such as Devon and Cornwall.

While the ogham alphabet may have been derived from that of Latin, the language of the ogham inscriptions is Irish (although ogham stones from Wales have inscriptions in both Irish and Latin), and therefore they testify to Irish settlement in western Britain—presumably involving the conquest of territory and the military subjugation of peoples—and to Irish contact with this most western frontier of the Roman Empire. So, while Late Iron Age Ireland was not conquered by Rome and remained economically underdeveloped—it had no Roman roads, bridges or towns—it was by no means cut off from the outside world.

It is not surprising, therefore, that in the early years of the fifth century there were Christians in Ireland. We should perhaps expect this, given the extent of Ireland's communication with western Britain, where there had been a Christian presence for several generations. The Irish colonies in Wales in particular were an obvious conduit if, say, some of those *Laigin* (Leinstermen) who gave their name to the Llŷn peninsula in west Wales converted and brought their new religion home, or if British Christians, perhaps with a knowledge of the Irish language from Irish settlers among them, ventured across the Irish Sea to spread the Word.

And of course the most famous of these early Christian missionaries was the Briton Patrick. To the evidence that we have of Irish colonies being established in this age on the west coast of Britain—from Argyll in the north to Cornwall in the south—we can add Patrick's testimony that his own first encounter with Ireland was at the receiving end of Irish aggression when he was taken prisoner by Irish raiders from his father's estate and brought as a captive to Ireland 'with many thousands of people (*tot milia hominum*).'[2]

While others evangelised in the south of Ireland, Patrick's mission was in the northern half of the island, and by the seventh century Armagh was gaining a position of prominence in the Irish church because of its purported foundation by Patrick: its churchmen argued that if Patrick was the Apostle of Ireland, and he chose Armagh as his special church, then the head of the church of Armagh was *comarbae Pátraic* (St Patrick's heir) and Armagh should be the special church for all Ireland.[3] Other churches, such as St Brigit's great monastery at Kildare, might dispute this, but, armed with the best propagandists and allied to the dominant political dynasties, the claims of Armagh ultimately won out; and although its fortunes might fluctuate in line with those of its political sponsors, it gradually impressed its sense of its own primacy on the Irish in general.

Hence the fact, as we shall see later, that Brian Bóraime, a Munster king we should expect to find promoting the primatial claims of a Munster church, aligned himself closely to Armagh—and when he visited it in 1005 the great Book of Armagh, a collection of writings by and about Patrick, formed part of the pageant—even though Armagh lay firmly in the territory of his northern rivals. A man who would be king over all the Irish required a national ecclesiastical capital.

One of the Irish churches that vied with Armagh for pre-eminence was Iona, founded by St Colum Cille (Columba) in 563.[4] As Iona is not actually in Ireland—it is a small island off a larger island (Mull) off the Atlantic seaboard of Scotland—this might at first seem surprising, especially given our modern tendency to regard the sea as something that cuts off rather than links up. But Colum Cille is also said to have founded the monastery of Derry, and it would have taken him a lot less time to travel by boat from there to Iona than overland from Derry to the third of his great foundations, at Durrow (Co. Offaly).

Neither should we think of Iona as being somehow foreign to Ireland. As no more than a dozen miles separate the Mull of Kintyre in Scotland from Fair Head in Ireland, we must envisage both land masses as having always shared populations. Furthermore, in the early Middle Ages a people called Dál Riata with a base in the north-east corner of Antrim came to dominate Mull and its neighbouring islands (including Iona) along with Islay and *its* neighbouring islands (including the Kintyre peninsula), as well as the adjacent parts of Argyll on the mainland. (The very name Argyll comes from *Airer Goídel*, 'the coast of the Irish').[5] When, therefore, Colum Cille settled in Iona he was admittedly not in Ireland—in what the Irish called Ériu and Latin writers Hibernia or Scotia—but he was in Irish territory. He was a Goídel among his fellow-Goídil or, as Latin writers would have put it, a Scottus among fellow-Scotti, which explains how it was that when that Irish colony eventually smothered its Pictish neighbours to the north and east, and its British neighbours in Strathclyde to the south, and gained ascendency throughout northern Britain, it became the land of the Scotti, i.e. Scotia, and hence Scotland.

And hence too, as we shall see, the inscription written into the Book of Armagh to mark Brian Bóraime's visit to the primatial city in 1005 records his title not as *Rí Herend*, 'king of Ireland', and not even as 'emperor of Ireland' but as *Imperator Scotorum*, 'emperor of the Goídil', who, of course, were not confined to the island of Ireland.

THE SHAPE OF SOCIETY

One of our brightest windows into early mediaeval Irish society is provided by a large body of law tracts, often called Brehon laws, from *breithem*, 'a judge', which survive from the late seventh, eighth and ninth centuries.[6] These and other sources make it clear that in early Ireland individuals did not hold their land in their own right but rather as members of their kindred-group or *fine*. And at the time when the law tracts were being written the group that inherited and farmed land was not the modern conjugal family but a four-generation group called the 'certain kindred (*derbfhine*)', comprising the male descendants, in the male line, of a common great-grandfather. Females were not entirely unaccounted for: daughters could inherit movable goods, and they could also get a life interest in the family land if their father had no sons. The *derbfhine* held land jointly—and this was marked off from that of the neighbouring kin-group by fences and boundary stones—each member having an equal share of the family land; and with the passage of every generation the land was repartitioned between the surviving members so that each had an equivalent portion of good and bad land, arable, pasture, bog and so forth.

As we move closer to the time of Brian Bóraime it is likely that inheritance was confined to a closer male descent-group, the 'bright kindred (*gelfhine*)', comprising a man, his sons, and his sons' sons. In either case the idealised image of early Ireland that is sometimes presented, with vast numbers of people holding land and property communally, is not valid: the *gelfhine* property-owning group of first cousins might only have two or three adult males and the *derbfhine* perhaps double that.

Early mediaeval Ireland was a hierarchy of aristocrats, their dependants, and their slaves. Slavery was common—so common that a female slave or *cumal* was a standard unit of value. A person could be born into slavery or condemned to such a life as punishment for a crime, or—which was how St Patrick ended up in Ireland—could find himself or herself enslaved as a consequence of war or rapine. Viking involvement in the slave market may have coloured attitudes to the practice among the Christian Irish, and formal slavery must surely have been in decline by Brian's day, although contemporary sources from the period continue to lay heavy emphasis on the enslavement of people captured in war, and commentators on Ireland as late as (the admittedly biased) Giraldus Cambrensis in the late twelfth century still thought of it as a recent phenomenon.[7]

Needless to say, a slave owned no land, and the demands upon him or her were arbitrary and onerous, unlike the middle category of society, the commoner or non-lordly class, sometimes called the *grád Fhéne*, comprising those who owned or aspired to own land. An obsession with the classification of people by status meant that the laws prescribed different ranks of commoners—eight according to the law-tract on status called *Crith Gablach*—but it is not always clear that these are not just a lawyer's insistence on rigid distinctions where the reality was more fluid. The disparity between individual grades was given definition by assigning to each an 'honour price (*lóg n-enech* or *eneclann*)', measuring the compensation payable for a legal offence against them, which was considered an insult to their *enech* ('honour', literally 'face'). Thus, the *mruigfher* ('man of cultivated land'), who may have been the equivalent of a well-to-do farmer, had an honour price of three milch cows, the honour price of the slightly less prosperous farmer in the *bóaire* ('cow-freeman') category was two-and-a-half milch cows, and that of a low-ranking *fer midboth* ('between-house man'), who was in transition from being dependent on his father to acquiring his own place, was a two-year-old heifer.

A clear distinction was made between these commoners and a *flaith*, someone, like Brían Bóraime, of noble or princely rank—although barriers were to some extent porous, so that upward or downward mobility was possible over a number of generations. What distinguished them, while binding them together, was the institution of clientship (*célsine*). When we imagine the workings of feudalism in mediaeval Europe we think of a system in which lords held all the land and granted portions of it as fiefs to their vassals in return for rent or military aid or help with the harvest. In the Irish system the *céle* ('client') tended to have his own land by inheritance, and therefore what the lord gave him instead was usually cattle or other livestock and a promise of protection. In return the lord could expect his clients to render him a portion of the profits, in the form of meat or butter or cheese, or grain for his bread and ale, and to fulfil limited farm duties (the work not done by slaves and the semi-free) in, for instance, the lord's reaping-party or *meithel*, and also to entertain the lord and his entourage at feasting times, especially during the lean months.

Within this system the preoccupation with hierarchy and status dictated that there were two levels of client: the 'free' client (*sóerchéle*) and the 'base' client (*dóerchéle* or *céle giallnaí*). Both were freemen, but the *sóerchéle* could choose when to terminate the relationship with his lord by handing back his stock, and in any event it was for a seven-year term, whereas the *dóerchéle*'s relationship of dependence normally ended only with the lord's death; and if the base client predeceased his lord (or lords, as he could have more than one) the bond of clientship passed to his heirs.

And there were different grades of lord, whose status was determined by the number of clients they had. Thus the lowest-ranking lord, called 'lord of vassalry (*aire désa*)', had a minimum of five free and five base clients, whereas the lord of highest rank, called the 'lord of superior testimony (*aire forgill*)', had at least forty clients. Such an individual was considered *nemed*, a member of a privileged or sacred class, a class that also included clerics, poets and all those whose status was derived from their learning or skills, known collectively as *áes dána* ('people of craft').

Rank mattered here to the same if not a greater extent. There were seven grades of churchmen, from novices to bishops (the latter having the same honour price as a king), and there were seven grades of poet—based on the number of years spent mastering the different types of poetic metre—all the way up to the *ollam* or master poet, who likewise had an honour price equivalent to a king.

KINGSHIP AMONG THE IRISH

There are few subjects more critical to an understanding of the politics of mediaeval Ireland than the matter of kings and kingship, and few more complex or, consequently, more controversial.

The first point to grasp is that, as in all walks of life, nothing ever stays the same: the role and powers of Irish kings in the tenth century, when Brian was born, had changed considerably since the dawn of the historic age five centuries earlier. But the second point to grasp is that, again as in all walks of life, sometimes change comes slowly and sometimes dramatically. And Irish kingship, and therefore every facet of life affected by it (and that was most), changed dramatically and irrevocably during and because of Brian's career.

All political communities have leaders, by popular acclamation or hereditary succession, and in early mediaeval Europe the leaders of even relatively small communities might be styled *rex* ('king'), and might be chosen by their people. But powerful leaders have a vested interest both in establishing the hereditary principle and in denying grand titles to subordinates and potential rivals; and so over the centuries in Europe the term 'king' came to be restricted to the greater polities, usually national monarchies operating to a defined order of succession. The same forces are apparent in Ireland, although movement was slower.

The word used in Ireland for the basic unit of local political organisation was *túath* (Latin *plebs*); the population groups occupying the river valleys and the fertile plains and the major forest clearances throughout the land were *túatha*. Because of Ireland's size and low population, and because stable farming communities do not encourage mobility, it would not be surprising if there were many ties of blood linking such communities, but it is important to note that the *túath* might have many strangers living within it, and it was not therefore a tribe. What makes it *appear* tribal is the complex Irish system of naming *túatha* and other territories after an apical ancestor-figure, which gives the impression that everyone within that political lordship was linked by common descent to the ancestor celebrated in its very name. Thus, for example, Brian Bóraime's dynasty was called Dál Cais because it claimed to be the *dál* ('section, division') of a supposed ancestor called Cass. But Dál Cais was the name of both the lineage and the territorial kingdom over which the lineage ruled, and by no means everyone in the territory was of that lineage.

When he was growing up, Brian's territorial neighbours to his west, in mid-Clare, were a parallel descent-group called Uí Chaissíne, who, their name shows us, believed themselves to be the *uí* (grandsons, and by extension descendants) of the eponymous Caisséne. Just west of them were their kinsmen Cenél Fermaic, where *cenél* means that they were the 'race' or descendants of an apical forebear called Fermac. Their neighbours to the west did not belong to Dál Cais, but their name, Corcu Bascind, preserves an ancestor-figure Baiscend of whom they were the *corcu*, the seed; and so on.

Ireland was dominated by political groupings calling themselves the *uí* of A or the *cenél* of B or the *corcu* of C or the *dál* of D or one of a variety of other population names.[8] Each, and the territory they occupied, was a *túath* (although, if they prospered, in due course they divided like cells into multiple *túatha*). But they were not tribes, and each had within it many people who were not related by blood to the dominant lineage. In addition, there are numerous examples through the centuries of lineages that expanded into neighbouring territory and embraced the name of the dynasty they displaced.[9] To give just one example, in the Boyne Valley there was a territory ruled by a people called the Ciannachta, whose name indicated descent from a man called Cian (just as the Connachta were descended from Conn and the Eóganachta from Eógan). When, therefore, the annals record the death in 748 of a man called Indrechtach, *rex* Ciannachte, we should expect him to be able to trace his ancestry to Cian, but in fact Indrechtach was of the great dynasty of Uí Néill, which had expanded into the Ciannachta's territory and confined them north of the Boyne in what is now Co. Louth but kept their dynastic name for their own new territory.[10]

Frequently the community and territory known as a *túath* had its own bishop, and the laws recommended that it have its own church, its own ecclesiastical scholar, and its own poet, and that it should be ruled over by its own king (*rí*), who was therefore called a *rí túaithe* ('king of a people'). There were as many of these 'kings' in early mediaeval Ireland as there were political communities who thought of themselves as a *túath*, and there were surely at least a hundred of the latter. The laws, of course—fascinated with the classification of society—liked to grade kings according to status: so, if there was such a thing as a *rí túaithe* there would need to be a king on a higher rung of the ladder, and then another type of king who was higher up still, each having an honour price commensurate with his rank.

The surviving law tracts are not consistent in the names they give these different grades of kings, but one arrangement has the *rí túaithe*, as king of a single petty kingdom, coming below the *ruirí* ('overking'), who would have been the superior of several petty kings, in turn coming below the *rí ruirech* ('king of overkings'), who was at the top of this pyramid. If one were imagining them ruling in modern Ireland (bearing in mind that there is often little relationship between modern administrative divisions and mediaeval territorial units) the *rí túaithe* might rule something the size of a barony, the *ruirí* something like a county or a diocese, and the *rí ruirech* an entire province or archdiocese. But this was a theoretical framework: it might have had some validity at a very early date (although many would doubt it) but in the real world into which Brian Bóraime was born it probably counted for little. By then the leaders of local communities had stopped pretending to be kings, and contemporaries refer to them instead as a *toísech* ('leader') or a *tigern* ('lord'), words that acknowledge their noble rank but deny them kingly prestige.[11]

NATIONAL CONSCIOUSNESS

What this pyramid of kingship, conjured up in the law tracts, did not allow for was a king operating at a higher level than a province-king, i.e. a high-king of Ireland. But this does not mean that no such notion existed: it occurs occasionally in legal texts and is a commonplace in historical texts and in literature.[12] A kingship of all Ireland presumed a sense of Ireland as representing a whole, and such a sense certainly existed. Another name for the highest rank of king, the *rí ruirech* ('king of overkings'), was *rí cóigid* ('king of a fifth'), from the assumption that the island had been, or should be, divided into five provinces—though in the historic era there were always more (see map 1)—and of course the concept of a fifth presupposes a whole of which it was a part.

Furthermore, mediaeval Ireland's *de facto* political fragmentation was in stark contrast to its jurisprudential uniformity. True, the surviving Brehon law texts can be shown (by passing mentions of people and places) to emanate from regional locations—for example, the group called *Bretha Nemed* ('Judgements of privileged persons') has a Munster provenance, while the best-preserved collection, known as *Senchas Már*

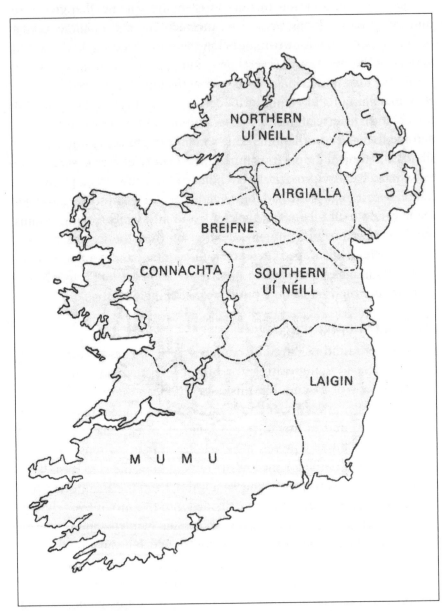

Map 1. Ireland c.800 AD.

('The great tradition'), comes from somewhere in the north-eastern quadrant of the island; but the laws themselves apply throughout the entire island. There is one law, and that is the law of Ireland. We find reference to *béscnu ínse Érend* ('the law-practice of the island of Ireland'), and whatever the regional focus of the people called the Féni (a trace of whom is later found in Finn mac Cumaill's legendary warrior-bands, the Fianna), their law, called *fénechas,* is used to mean the earliest customary law of all Ireland.

And the language of the laws—like all materials written in Old Irish—betrays no dialectal variations: there was a standardised grammar and a standardised orthography throughout the Irish-speaking world, which must have had an evocatively cohesive effect. This was achieved, no doubt, because the law was developed by professional jurists, members of the *áes dána* (like the poets and medics and historians and high-status craftsmen), whose authority transcended local boundaries: a *túath* might have its own *brithem* (legal expert) in the same way that it had its own poet or bishop, but when such men of learning ventured into another *túath* they did not cease to be a bishop or poet or judge. The men of learning practised their craft throughout the Irish world, and because they were the jurists who shaped the laws of that world or the poets who sang the praises of its heroes or the historians who recorded the deeds of its royal lineages, they were a potent and persuasive unifying force.

What comes across most strongly is the Irish sense of themselves as a single people, a remarkably precocious self-awareness that reflected itself in many different ways. Among them is the early development of a national origin-myth, versions of which were in circulation by AD 800 if not sooner and that culminated in *Lebor Gabála Érenn* ('The book of the taking of Ireland'), compiled from earlier materials in the decades following Brian's death. This recounts the succeeding waves of invaders of Ireland from the time of Cessair, the daughter of Noah's son Bith, to Partholón, who fought the Fomorian demons, to Nemed the Scythian, to the Fir Bolg (who may be related to the Continental Celtic tribe Belgae), to the magical Túatha Dé Danann ('the peoples of the Goddess Danu'), the climax coming with the arrival of the Milesians. These latter are the Irish, and the invasion-myth had them descend from the daughter of an Egyptian pharaoh; her name Scota, the myth-makers claimed, gives us the Latin name of the island, Scotia, while her son, Goídel Glas, gives his

name to the people (the Goídil) and their language (Goídelc). The truth
seems rather different, however. It is common enough for early peoples
not to have a name for themselves until they need one with which to
distinguish themselves from strangers, and it seems the Irish borrowed
theirs from that given to them by the Welsh, Gwyddyl.

The Irish had an exceptional pride in their language—which they
boasted Goídel Glas (or his ancestor Fénius Farsaid) selected from
the best bits of all the other languages scattered throughout the world
from Nimrod's Tower of Babel—and it is indeed remarkable how early,
in western European terms, the Irish were in developing a written
literature in the vernacular in addition to, or instead of, Latin. Banished
from Egypt, their wanderings brought them to Spain, and it was the
sons of Míl (i.e. Milesius) of Spain who led them to Ireland, doing battle
with the Túatha Dé Danann and proceeding to Tara, where the three
goddesses Banba, Fótla and Ériu won the right to have the island named
after them.

This bravura compendium was a long time in the making and
contains (while struggling to reconcile) many fabulous contradictions,
but its Irish audience down through the generations found it powerfully
convincing. By tracing the Irish back to Noah it found a place for them
in the biblical history of the world, it provided an explanation for
their presence on the island, it offered a justification—when that was
required—in their struggle to retain possession of their homeland, and
above all else it served to emphasise the ancestral links between all the
Irish (including the Irish of northern Britain who became the Scots):
they were of one *natio* (birth), a nation.[13]

The emphasis on preserving (or inventing) these links led to a
preoccupation with the spinning of webs of genealogical data that
mapped out the descent of the political lineages, great and small. Irish
men of letters were greatly influenced by the Bible and hence therefore
by the latter's fascination both with vertical lines of descent (as when
Matthew opens his gospel by linking Christ back to Abraham) and with
horizontal relationships between peoples (as when the First Book of
Chronicles lists how the various tribes of Israel came to occupy their
lands by virtue of descent from their eponyms). We therefore still
possess a great corpus of genealogical material from mediaeval Ireland
that tends to be of two kinds: either a simple pedigree, called a *genelach*

(from Latin *genealogia*), tracing an individual's ancestry ascending upwards in the paternal line (A son of B son of C son of D, etc.) or a more ambitious lateral project, sometimes called a *cráeb coibnesa* ('branch of relationship'), which might begin at the apex of the pyramid and work down, tracing the parallel lines of dynastic descent as far as the point at which individuals break off from the main line and found new lines, and then trace these in turn.

Undoubtedly here the exercise is about more than just tracing one's ancestors as an antiquarian pursuit: by showing the connectedness between lineages that might have seemed unconnected, the genealogy plays a powerful role in dynastic solidarity. It is for determining the relationships between peoples, it is for proving one's status by virtue of pedigree, it is for enabling individuals to stake claims, it is for saying who belongs and who does not. It is therefore about society and about politics. And for that reason one should be wary of assuming that genealogies are always an honest attempt at recording the dynastic links between peoples: as the genealogy has a social and political job to do, while it will usually tell us what its compiler and his patron believed to be true, occasionally it tells us instead only what they *wanted* to believe, or wanted *us* to believe.[14] And, as we shall see later, no dynasty was more culpable in this matter than Brian's.

THE KINGSHIP OF TARA

The Hill of Tara—a ridge in east Co. Meath that is a full 2 km in length but never more than about 150 m high and yet affords views as far north as the Mourne Mountains and as far south as Slieve Bloom—preserves monuments dating from the late Stone Age. There are also extensive remains from the Bronze Age and the Iron Age, but there is very little archaeological evidence for occupation or use during the Middle Ages.

The glory days of Tara, therefore, lay in prehistory, and it is not surprising that it features prominently in early Irish mythology. Tara was thought to have been connected with the gods of ancient Ireland, and hence the story in the *Lebor Gabála*, mentioned above, that when the sons of Míl—the ancestors of the Irish—first set foot in Ireland they confronted the supernatural Túatha Dé Danann at Tara, before defeating them in battle at nearby Tailtiu (Teltown, Co. Meath). Clearly the point is that the Milesians now hold Tara and therefore have the right to rule over Ireland because of their triumph at Tailtiu. The latter was the site of *Óenach Tailten* ('the Fair of Tailtiu'), the assembly that only the king of Tara could convene.

The greatest of the Celtic gods, Lug—on whose August festival of Lugnasad the *óenach* was held—is associated with both Tara and Tailtiu. One tale has him gaining the kingship of Tara while another says that he celebrated his *banais rígi* ('wedding-feast of kingship') at Tailtiu. Lug is said to have appeared at Tara to Conn Cétchathach—ancestor of the peoples who gave Connacht its name and also of the great dynasty of Uí Néill, who came to dominate much of Ireland—accompanied by a beautiful young woman, whom he introduces as *flaith Érenn* ('sovereignty of Ireland'), who then gave a drink of ale to Conn and all his successors until the Day of Judgement. The idea here is that she is the sovereignty goddess who bestows entitlement to rule on the rightful aspirant and is therefore confirming the claim of Conn's descendants to the rule of Tara and of Ireland. The Irish called this concept *fír flathemon* ('truth of a ruler'), and in other texts she becomes the wife or lover of the rightful king. She represents the land and people, and through his marriage with the goddess the legitimate king is confirmed as temporal ruler of her territory, under whom the land flourishes and the people prosper.

On the hill of Tara there is a stone called the *Lia Fáil* ('Stone of Destiny'), which, the literature tells us, cries out like an oracle beneath the feet of the rightful king of Ireland. This tells us a little bit about the idea of the kingship of Tara. It was about the legitimation of a right to rule. Tara was not a kingdom, or the capital of a kingdom, ruled over by a king who, when he died or was overthrown, was replaced by the next in line. Sometimes there was no *rí Temro* ('king of Tara'), and usually the king of Tara lived nowhere near it. From the point when we begin to get a glimpse of events in Ireland in the fifth century until the middle of the seventh century, members of various dynasties—from the present-day provinces of Connacht, Ulster and Leinster—claimed the kingship of Tara, which shows that it was not the preserve of any one dynasty. Granted, it did not mean that the individual concerned ever managed to exercise a kingship over the whole island, as there was no centralised monarchy either in prehistoric or early mediaeval Ireland; but the fact is that the special status of the king of Tara was (at least sometimes) recognised throughout the island.

Later, however, this changed. From the middle of the seventh century and for the next three hundred years or more, until Brian came along at the end of the tenth century, the kingship of Tara was monopolised by the Uí Néill, one great dynasty with many sprawling branches. While there may have been a lingering memory of Tara's special place in the Irish polity, the term *rí Temro* came to be equated with the overking of the Uí Néill and with the attempts by the latter to claim hegemony throughout all Ireland.[15]

THE EMERGENCE OF THE UÍ NÉILL

Muirchú, who wrote a Life of St Patrick about the year 700, describes the celebrated historical or pseudo-historical figure Niall Noígiallach ('Niall of the Nine Hostages') as 'the one from whom was descended the royal stock of almost the entire island (*origo stirpis regiae huius pene insolae*).' It is a great exaggeration, but it sums up the contemporary reality of Muirchú's day, when so many of the dominant lineages in at least the northern half of Ireland seemed to trace themselves back to Niall.

Assuming he was a real person, Niall may have lived in the fifth century and is said to have descended from Conn Cétchathach ('Conn of the Hundred Battles'), who was believed to have lived seven generations before Niall, in the late Iron Age. Conn is much less likely to have been a historical figure, but the theory was that Conn gave his name to the people called Connachta (remembered in the province of Connacht), and it does seem quite likely that Niall's kin originated west of the Shannon.

The genealogies depict Niall as the father of more than a dozen sons (although the *Uí* of Uí Néill literally means 'grandsons' and hence descendants of Niall and therefore does not apply until we are two or more generations removed from him), each of whom went on to found a lineage of his own, which carved out a territorial presence. Even if this picture of a remarkably fertile and fortunate family were true, it is likely that many so-called Uí Néill lineages were nothing of the sort but that, as Uí Néill power grew over the centuries, other population groups grafted themselves onto the Uí Néill family tree by claiming that their ancestor had been one of Niall's sons. If some of these dynastic founders were actual sons of Niall, among the genuine articles may be Cairpre, Lóegaire, Fiachu, and Conall Cremthainne, from each of whom prestigious dynasties in the midlands, known collectively as the Southern Uí Néill, claimed their descent, while others of Niall's sons, who founded the north-western dynasties known collectively as the Northern Uí Néill, were Eógan and Conall Gulban (assuming Niall had two sons called Conall, a not unheard-of custom).

We do not know for certain when any of these individuals lived. Muirchú says that when Patrick came to evangelise Ireland in the fifth century Niall's son Lóegaire was 'emperor of the barbarians ruling in Tara, which was the capital of the Irish (*imperator barbarorum regnans in Temporia, quae erat caput Scotorum*)'; but he was writing more than two hundred years later, and his is not a work of history but of hagiography and ecclesiastical propaganda. The most we can say for certain is that the basic framework of the Northern and Southern Uí Néill dynasties was in place by the sixth century, at which point they were certainly attempting to stake a claim to Tara, and that they had made the kingship fully their own by the middle years of the following century.

The title *rí Temro* ('king of Tara') having being appropriated, it came to be used as an honorific attaching to the highest-ranking king among the Uí Néill. Then, for a period of a quarter of a millennium from the reign of Áed Allán (died 743) until the accession of Máel Sechnaill II in 980, the title 'king of Tara' alternated (with only one exception) between the Northern and Southern Uí Néill. Thus, when Áed Allán of the Northern Uí Néill died in 743 the title 'king of Tara' did not go to his northern successor but instead reverted to the foremost dynast of the Southern Uí Néill, Domnall Midi; and then, at the latter's death in 763, the northern leader Niall Frossach (died 778) obtained the title, after whom a Southern Uí Néill dynast, Donnchad Midi (died 797), secured the honour, and so on.

When we weigh up the impact of Brian, among the most important considerations to have regard to are his interruption of this system of rotation and his undermining of so prestigious a title.[16]

SOUTHERN UÍ NÉILL

When we use the term Southern Uí Néill (map 2) it is only as a convenient shorthand for what were a number of competing dynasties—all claiming descent from Niall Noígiallach—which occupied a broad swathe of territory stretching from north-east Connacht to just north of Dublin,

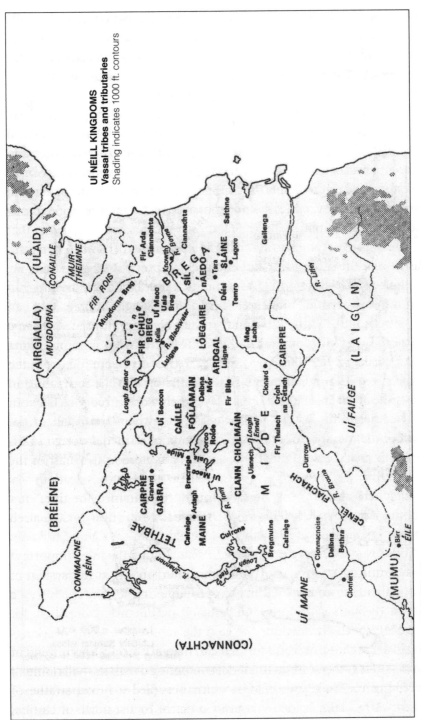

Map 2. Southern Uí Néill c.800 AD.

with their hub in the present-day counties of Meath and Westmeath. The most successful of them were descended from Niall's son Conall Cremthainne through the children of his grandson Diarmait mac Cerbaill (died 565), the last man known to have presided over the pagan fertility rite called *Feis Temro* ('the feast of Tara').

One of Diarmait's sons was Colmán Már, the founder of *Clann Cholmáin Máir* ('the children of Colmán the Elder'), which provided kings of Mide (literally 'the Middle') in present-day Co. Westmeath and adjacent parts of Cos. Longford and Offaly. Another son was Áed Sláine, ancestor of *Síl nÁedo Sláine* ('the seed of Áed of Slane'), which provided kings of Brega in Co. Meath and, at one time at least, south Co. Louth and north Co. Dublin.

When they first emerge into the light, in the seventh century, Síl nÁedo Sláine were the more successful and provided several kings of Tara, i.e. overkings of the Uí Néill. But by the middle of the eighth century they had split into two separate branches, a kingdom in northern Brega that had its centre at the prehistoric tumulus at Knowth in the Boyne Valley and a southern Brega kingdom that had as its royal palace a crannóg at Lagore near Dunshaughlin. This splintering of Síl nÁedo Sláine corresponded to the rise of Clann Cholmáin. Based in the west of the province, and sometimes bearing the title 'king of Uisnech'—from the sacred hill in Co. Westmeath thought to be the umbilical centre of Ireland, meeting-point of the five ancient provinces—their royal residences were at Dún na Sciath near Lough Ennell and on a crannóg called Cró-inis on the lake itself.

After 728 no king of Brega claimed the kingship of Tara and overkingship of the Uí Néill—with the solitary exception of Congalach Cnogba ('Congalach of Knowth'), who died in 956—as Clann Cholmáin of Mide grew ever more prominent.

It is during the reign of Donnchad Midi (died 797) that Clann Cholmáin assumed truly national importance and we find them trying to turn their kingship into an all-Ireland dominance. Donnchad, for instance, repeatedly attempted to gain the submission of the overkings of Leinster and Munster and formed marriage alliances with the kings of Ulaid in east Ulster. Although his death coincided with the beginning of the Viking Age, his grandson Máel Sechnaill I (died 862) copperfastened the dynasty's claim to national pre-eminence by his successes against the Viking offensive. In 845 Máel Sechnaill captured the Viking chieftain Turgéis and had him drowned in Lough Owel; in 848 he slew seven hundred Vikings in a battle in the same area; and in 849 he overran the new Viking ship-camp at Dublin. His success in championing this national effort enabled him to throw his weight around among his contemporaries. In 854 and 856 he took the hostages of Munster—the first king of Tara to do so—meaning that the province submitted to his overlordship. And in 858 he again entered Munster, accompanied by 'the men of Ireland'—the annalist's way of saying that Máel Sechnaill was the king of Ireland on campaign, accompanied by his military vassals—and brought the province to its knees, so that he gained an unprecedented acknowledgement of his superiority.

In the following year Máel Sechnaill convened a *rígdál* ('royal conference') at Rahugh, Co. Westmeath, the astonishing conclusion of which was that 'the Osraige were alienated to Leth Cuinn, and Máel Gualae, king of Munster, warranted the alienation.' Leth Cuinn was the name for the northern half of Ireland; the Osraige were a people who inhabited the Nore Valley in the southern half, which was dominated by the king of Munster. What Máel Sechnaill was doing was high-handedly transferring the overlordship of the southern kingdom of Osraige from Munster to himself, the Clann Cholmáin king of Tara.

Admittedly, our perception of the greatness of Clann Cholmáin is moulded by a historical record that they themselves helped to shape. Their great monastic church was Clonmacnoise on the banks of the Shannon, where Máel Sechnaill's celebrated son and successor Flann Sinna ('Flann of the Shannon') (died 916) has left us the magnificent Cross of the Scriptures commissioned by him and whose scriptorium was unceasing in recording the deeds of its kings and promoting their claims to national hegemony.

Flann's munificence to Clonmacnoise may have been in thanksgiving for success over Munster. Following years of opposition from the ambitious Cormac mac Cuilennáin, and punitive expeditions in 905 and 906, Flann's forces were overcome by Munster at the Battle of Mag Léna in 907, but he eventually defeated and killed Cormac, in alliance with the kings of Leinster and Connacht, at the bloody battle of Belach Mugna (Ballaghmoon, Co. Carlow) in 908. These conflicts, a century before the horrific Battle of Clontarf, are proof that bloodletting in Irish warfare was nothing new and that inter-provincial enmities had been intensifying in recent generations—proof, of course, that there was much at stake.

For Flann's son Donnchad Donn (died 944) the threat came from the newly restored power of the Norse of Dublin, whom he defeated heavily in 920. Then he burned the town in 936, while in 938 he laid the Vikings under siege, ravaging their territory from Dublin to Áth Truisten (near Castledermot, Co. Kildare). Donnchad Donn managed to achieve the latter success because he was now allied to his erstwhile rival of the Northern Uí Néill, Muirchertach son of Niall Glúndub—although which of them had the upper hand is a moot point. With Muirchertach's support, Donnchad was able to entertain ambitions in the southern half of Ireland, taking the hostages of Leinster and Munster in 940, while in 941 he achieved the notable success of securing the capture of the overking of Munster, Cellachán Caisil.

But in the confusion that followed the deaths of both Muirchertach in 943 and Donnchad Donn in 944 the kingship of Tara was seized by the audacious head of the rival Southern Uí Néill line, Congalach Cnogba of Síl nÁedo Sláine of northern Brega. In 944 Congalach and the Leinstermen sacked Dublin. By 945 Congalach had swapped sides and now allied himself with Amlaíb Cuarán, the Norse king of Dublin and York; and although they were defeated by a Northern Uí Néill rival at Slane in 947 they triumphed together against the same foe in 950.

Secure in his possession of the kingship, Congalach Cnogba repeated the efforts of his Uí Néill predecessors to press his advantage in the southern half of Ireland. Indeed in 956, having subdued Leinster, he proceeded to celebrate the Óenach Colmáin ('Fair of Colmán'), an assembly that took place on the Liffey plain and whose convening was the sole prerogative of the king of Leinster. It was an astonishing break with convention and may have played a part in stirring the rebellion against Congalach that then took place, by which the north Leinster dynasties joined his former allies, the Norse of Dublin, and ambushed and killed him at Tech Giugrann, near Dublin.

It is worth noting that Congalach's predecessor as king of Tara, Donnchad Donn, had taken as one of his four wives Brian Bóraime's sister Órlaith. Now, in the reign of Congalach Cnogba, that engagement continued apace. In 950 Congalach invaded the territory of Dál Cais and killed two of Brian's brothers. All the indications were that Brian's family was beginning to make an impression on the national stage.[17]

NORTHERN UÍ NÉILL

The success of the sons of Niall—whether real or invented—in conquering the midlands is said to have been matched by a similar expansion into the north-west (map 3), although there is little or no contemporary evidence for it: indeed the theory of a northerly expansion from Connacht has been questioned and doubt cast on whether the peoples concerned were Uí Néill at all.[18]

According to the later traditions, however, two of Niall's 'sons' became ancestor-figures of extraordinary distinction. One was Conall Gulban (whose nickname means 'of Benn Gulban', i.e. Benbulbin, Co. Sligo), from whom were descended Cenél Conaill ('the kindred of Conall') and whose territory was Tír Conaill ('the land of Conall') in present-day Co. Donegal. The other was Eógan, whose name is preserved in Inishowen and Tyrone, i.e. Tír nEógain ('the land of Eógan'), home of his descendants, Cenél nEógain ('the kindred of Eógan'). For both groups, and for their less successful cousins, we use the term Northern Uí Néill as a shorthand; the paramount king among them bore the title 'king of the North (rí ind Fhochlai)'. They apparently gained their foothold first in Donegal, from which they began to expand eastwards into a province previously the domain of the people called Ulaid and Airgialla.

Cenél Conaill dominated at first, but after Áed Allán of Cenél nEógain secured the overkingship of the Uí Néill in 734 there began the long rotation of the kingship of Tara between his branch of the Northern Uí Néill and Clann Cholmáin of the Southern Uí Néill, with the result that Cenél Conaill's power declined and they remained confined to their Donegal homeland, while Cenél nEógain emerged into greatness.

At first based in the north-eastern corner of Donegal, with their headquarters at the great fort at the entrance to the Inishowen Peninsula known as the Gríanán of Ailech—and hence their ruler is often called rí Ailig ('king of Ailech')—they pushed eastwards across the Foyle into what is now Co. Derry and then south into what became, because of them, Tyrone; and, while they might claim to be kings of Ailech, their royal inaugurations later took place at Tulach Óc (Tullaghogue, near Dungannon). Needless to say, this area was not virgin territory when

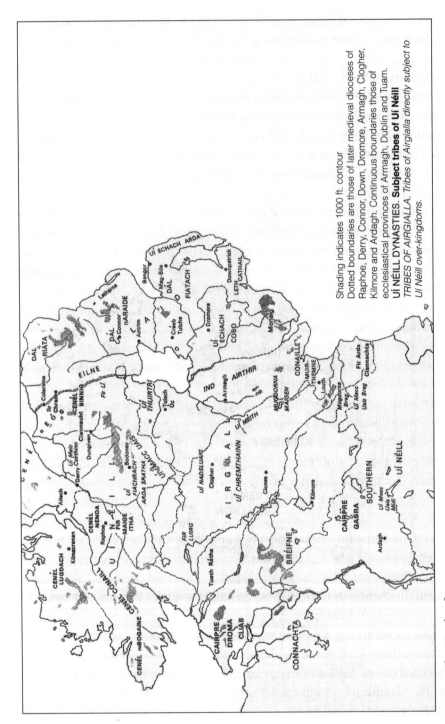

Map 3. The North c.800 AD.

Shading indicates 1000 ft. contour
Dotted boundaries are those of later medieval dioceses of
Raphoe, Derry, Connor, Down, Dromore, Armagh, Clogher,
Kilmore and Ardagh. Continuous boundaries those of
ecclesiastical provinces of Armagh, Dublin and Tuam.
Uí NÉILL DYNASTIES. **Subject tribes of Uí Néill**
TRIBES OF AIRGIALLA. *Tribes of Airgialla directly subject to
Uí Néill over-kingdoms.*

Cenél nEógain set their eyes on it. A huge chunk of what is now mid-Ulster was in the possession of a federation of kingdoms called the Airgialla (which means 'the hostage-givers', now Oriel). Their superiors may originally have been the Ulaid, but as Cenél nEógain pushed east and south of the Foyle the latter became the Airgialla's new masters. It is possible that the 'nine hostages' of Niall Noígiallach's sobriquet are nine *túatha* of Airgialla and that they were called the 'hostage-givers' because of their subordination to Cenél nEógain. The latter took possession of the Airgialla lands in Derry and Tyrone, pushing Airgialla's centre of gravity south to Fermanagh, Monaghan, Armagh and north Louth, its heartland later becoming the diocese of Clogher.

The great church of Armagh—which by the seventh century was already managing to convince many of its claim to be the primatial church of all Ireland—lay in Airgialla territory, and Airgialla dynasts were its patrons and supplied its leaders. At this time Uí Néill attachment lay elsewhere. Colum Cille came from an aristocratic Uí Néill background (he was of the Cenél Conaill), and therefore the great federation of churches subject to his monastery at Iona enjoyed the patronage and promoted the interests of the Uí Néill. But as the other great branch of the Northern Uí Néill, Cenél nEógain, increased its domination of Airgialla, so too Armagh fell under its sway, and as Armagh promoted its own cause it became the vehicle for the advancement of the claims of Cenél nEógain: if Armagh was to be Ireland's chief church, Cenél nEógain must supply its rightful kings. Their connection was such that when the annals record a murder taking place in the monastic city of Armagh in 870 they mention in passing that it happened 'in front of the door of the house of' Áed Findliath (died 879), the king of Cenél nEógain and overking of the Uí Néill. When one of Áed's grandsons died in 935 we are told that he was buried in Armagh 'in the cemetery of the kings (*in cimiterio regum*)', and Áed's great-grandson Domnall ua Néill died while in retirement at Armagh in 980.[19]

Propaganda produced at Armagh may have bolstered the position of these Cenél nEógain kings, but their successes in the world of politics and on the field of battle were their own. It was Áed Allán (died 743) who secured the exclusion of his collaterals Cenél Conaill from overkingship of the Northern Uí Néill and who triumphed over the Ulaid at the Battle of Faughart (Co. Louth) in 735 and over the Leinstermen at Áth Senaig

(Ballyshannon, near Kilcullen, Co. Kildare) in 738, having convened a remarkable *rígdál* (royal meeting) with the king of Munster, Cathal mac Finguine, the previous year—all testimony to the supra-provincial ambitions of Cenél nEógain by the eighth century.

Áed Allán's nephew Áed Oirdnide (died 819) was equally forceful in making his presence felt in Ulaid, and in the lands of the Southern Uí Néill and in Leinster. In 805 he deposed the king of Leinster, who was head of one of the three main lineages in the dynasty of Uí Dúnlainge, and partitioned the province between the heads of the other two lineages. And, his reign coinciding with the first wave of Viking incursions, he seems to have been effective in keeping them at bay.

Áed's son Niall Caille (died 846)—who finally subdued Airgialla to Cenél nEógain control—was equally firm in resisting Viking penetration of Northern Uí Néill territory and was very prominent on the national stage. He too deposed a Leinster king in favour of a protégé from a competing lineage but is most famous as the man who put paid to the most serious threat hitherto posed to the hegemony of the Uí Néill, that of Fedelmid mac Crimthainn (died 847), king of Munster. Niall's son Áed Findliath (died 879) was periodically allied to the Vikings, marrying his daughter to Amlaíb Find (Óláfr or Olaf the White), king of Dublin—an ally in Áed's ultimately successful bid for the kingship of Tara—although Áed was resolute in resisting attempts by the Vikings of Strangford Lough to strengthen their presence in the north.

On three occasions in the 870s the annalists had commented critically on the failure to hold the Óenach Tailten ('Fair of Tailtiu'), the calling of which was a prerogative of Áed Findliath as king of Tara, and it is noticeable that his son and successor Niall Glúndub (died 919) did just that immediately upon succeeding to the kingship in 916. This seems to have been a conscious revival by Niall of a symbolic occasion that had been drifting towards oblivion, and it is perhaps indicative of an attempt by Niall Glúndub to galvanise national opposition to Viking aggression. In 917 he marched south to support the attempt by the overkings of Leinster and Munster to halt the Viking occupation of Waterford and Dublin, in 919 becoming the first king of Tara to lose his life in conflict with Vikings when he suffered a major defeat in the Battle of Cell Mo-shamhóc, at Islandbridge, near Dublin. Moreover, Niall—from whom the later O'Neills of Ulster take their name—produced in his son Muirchertach (died 943) an even more inveterate foe of the Vikings. Known as Muirchertach na Cochall Craicinn ('of the leather cloaks'), apparently from the mantles worn by his soldiers in campaigning against them, his reign as king of the North (he did not live long enough to secure the kingship of Tara) again saw notable success in uprooting Viking attempts at settlement on the Ulster coastline. He is credited with a successful naval expedition to the Viking colony in the Hebrides and, like his father before him, lost his life in battle (at Clonkeen, Co. Louth) with the Viking king of Dublin. Muirchertach's career also testifies to the enduring national ambitions of the kings of Cenél nEógain. Although a poem celebrating his famous 'circuit of Ireland' in 941 can be shown to be a much later composition, the events at its core are historical and show a man campaigning far from his home base, marching through Mide and then south into Uí Failgi, Osraige and Déisi and capturing the overking of Munster, Cellachán Caisil, whom he brought back to his Southern Uí Néill overlord as a prisoner.

But Muirchertach's early death caused the first stutter in the Cenél nEógain advance. It led to an opening for the reigning king of the rival Cenél Conaill of Donegal, Ruaidrí ua Canannáin, to make a bid for power. Having secured the kingship of the North, Ruaidrí set his eyes on the kingship of Tara, now in the hands of the equally enterprising upstart Congalach Cnogba, king of northern Brega. Ruaidrí's efforts at outgunning Congalach are testimony to the persistent strength of the Dublin Vikings at this time. In 945 Ruaidrí was defeated in battle in Conaille Muirthemne (north Louth) by Congalach and Amlaíb Cuarán of Dublin; in 947 he again came south from Tír Conaill and this time defeated Congalach and Amlaíb Cuarán near Slane; and in 950 he turned again to the challenge of taking the kingship of Tara, setting up camp in Mide and in Congalach's lands in Brega for six months before facing the army of Dublin in the major battle of Muine Broccáin, in which, although two thousand of Amlaíb Cuarán's army are said to have perished, Ruaidrí lost his own life, and Cenél Conaill pretensions to the kingship of Tara rapidly disintegrated.

When Ruaidrí's death at the hands of the Dubliners was followed in 956 by Congalach Cnogba's in similar fashion it paved the way for the son of Muirchertach na Cochall Craicinn, Domnall ua Néill (he was literally Domnall ua Néill, i.e. Domnall grandson of Niall Glúndub), to reclaim Tara for his line, and it is noticeable that as soon as he did so he set about asserting military supremacy over the other provinces. In 962 he was in Mide and went as far as Munster to press his claims; in 965 he secured the submission of the overking of Connacht, Fergal ua Ruairc; and in 968 he was attacking Leinster and the Norse of Dublin. Although he suffered a major defeat at the hands of Congalach Cnogba's son and Amláib of Dublin in 970, in the following year, the annals tell us, 'he took revenge on them on that occasion for their opposition to him, for he erected a camp in every *túath* in Mide (*do-roine longport cecha tuaithe i Midhe*),' which seems to mean that he imposed garrisons on the inhabitants, perhaps representing an intensification of contemporary warfare.

But by now the great age of Cenél nEógain pre-eminence was coming to an end. By the time of Domnall ua Néill's death, in 980, Brian Bóraime was already beginning to make his mark, and the Uí Néill ascendancy was about to face its stiffest challenge.[20]

ULAID

Relations with one's neighbours can be fraught, and no neighbours were more constant in their antagonism than the Northern Uí Néill and the Ulaid, later Ulaidh. (*Ulaidh* + the Norse genitive *s* + *tír* ('land') = Ulster.) The enmity stemmed from the Ulaid's memory of former glory days, brought to an end by Uí Néill encroachment on their ancestral territory.

At the dawn of Irish history, in the fifth century, Emain Macha (Navan Fort, near Armagh) was remembered as the political focal point of the land of the Ulaid, but possession of it was lost when the Ulaid were driven eastwards by the Uí Néill and Airgialla from their dominant position in the centre of Ulster to a coastal remnant in Cos. Antrim, Down and Louth, a situation that had occurred by the eighth century. Strictly speaking, the mediaeval Ulaid were the people known as Dál Fiatach, whose capital was at Dún-dá-lethglas (Downpatrick) and whose territory stretched from Belfast Lough to Dundrum Bay in Co. Down. They were distantly related to the Dál Riata of the Glens of Antrim but did not have to compete with them for the overkingship of Ulaid, because by the sixth century Dál Riata were busy conquering Hebridean islands in the Islay and Mull groups and indeed, having overwhelmed much of mainland Argyll and Kintyre, founding what would become the kingdom of the Scots.

Of greater concern to the Dál Fiatach were the Dál nAraidi—descended from the Cruthni, who are sometimes thought to be connected to the Picts of northern Britain—whose kings lived at Ráith Mór (just east of the town of Antrim) in the fertile plain of Mag Line, around the valley of the Six Mile Water in south Antrim. During the Viking Age in particular Dál nAraidi enjoyed some success in outmanoeuvring Dál Fiatach for the Ulaid overkingship, perhaps because the latter's energies were dissipated in resisting Viking incursions into east Ulster and because of competition between Dál Fiatach and the Vikings for control of the Isle of Man, in which the Ulaid had a long-standing interest.

But Dál Fiatach remained the dominant force among the Ulaid. They were remarkably stubborn in their refusal to kowtow to Cenél nEógain imperiousness, for which they paid a price, as when the Cenél nEógain slaughtered the king of the Ulaid and many of their nobility at the battle of Craeb Telcha in 1004. One consequence of this catastrophe—apart from plunging the dynasty into a blood-spattered succession war—was that the Ulaid, who were normally happy to align themselves with Cenél nEógain's enemies and should therefore (as we shall see) have been ripe for enlistment by Brian in his great drive against the Cenél nEógain, proved to be of little benefit.[21]

CONNACHT

The western province is the land of the Connachta (map 4), a people said to descend from the Iron Age king Conn Cétchathach ('Conn of the Hundred Battles'), who is perhaps a product of legend. As with all the provinces, it was not that all those west of the Shannon were thought to be descendants of Conn, merely that the latter, having a dominant position, claimed the province as rightly theirs. They shared it with peoples many of whom were distantly related to population groups scattered far and wide throughout the island, such as the Ciarraige (related to those people who give their name to Kerry), the Luigne, Gailenga, Calraige, Grecraige, Partraige, Delbna, Sogain, and the Conmaicne (one of whose branches, Conmaicne Mara, give us the present-day Connemara). And the Connachta also shared their province with the Uí Maine (of east Co. Galway and south Co. Roscommon), who were significant enough

Map 4. Connacht c.900 AD.

to be supplied with a false genealogical link to the Connachta. By Brian Bóraime's day their main branch bore the surname Ua Cellaig (O'Kelly), and their king died alongside Brian at the Battle of Clontarf.

As for the true Connachta, they are all said to descend from three brothers of Niall Noígiallach: Brión, Fiachrae and Ailill. Ailill's progeny dwindled to local lordly rank (remembered today in the barony of Tirerrill, Co. Sligo). Brión's progeny, called Uí Briúin ('descendants of Brión'), were vastly more assertive and seem to have started from a base in the fertile plain of Mag nAí, where the province's ancient capital of Cruachu (Rathcroghan, Co. Roscommon), was situated.

As it prospered, over the course of time Uí Briúin splintered into branches. By far the most successful was the portion that remained in its Roscommon heartland in Mag nAí—they were thus called Uí Briúin Aí—from one of whose kings, Muiredach Muillethan (died 702), came the lineage known as Síl Muiredaig, which by Brian's time had adopted the surname Ua Conchobair (O'Connor) and throughout the rest of the Middle Ages provided kings of Connacht.

A second major branch of Uí Briúin was known as Uí Briúin Bréifne, having survived by pushing north-east into the badlands of what are now Cos. Leitrim and Cavan. From its leader Ruarc (died 898) it adopted the surname Ua Ruairc (O'Rourke), and by the time of Brian Bóraime it was beginning to make its presence felt on the wider national stage.

One final branch of the dynasty, that known as Uí Briúin Seóla, took its name from the plain east of Lough Corrib called Mag Seóla, although by Brian's day—at which point its main line had adopted the surname Ua Flaithbertaig (O'Flaherty)—it was no doubt beginning to feel the pressure that led to it being pushed west of the Corrib into Connemara.

Besides these descendants of Brión, the other great power among the Connachta was the reputed descendants of his brother Fiachrae, called Uí Fiachrach. To begin with they appear, if anything, even more successful than the Uí Briúin, at least up to the end of the eighth century. There were two separate arms of the dynasty, occupying opposite ends of the province. The northern Uí Fiachrach held the area surrounding Killala Bay and the valley of the River Moy and produced a number of overkings of the province until the beginning of the Viking Age, their decline from this point on perhaps hinting at destabilisation caused

by Viking activity in the region. The southern branch were called
Uí Fiachrach Aidne and held an area south-east of Galway Bay that
became the diocese of Kilmacduagh. Of the Connacht dynasties they
are arguably the one most closely involved in Munster affairs.

The Shannon had once formed the boundary between Munster and
Connacht, but the area south of the Slieve Aughty Mountains on the
Galway-Clare border had been seized by Brian's remote ancestors at
some point between the fifth and the seventh century. The Uí Fiachrach
king who came closest to claiming the lands stretching south to the
Shannon was the fabled Guaire Aidne (died 663), who fought a battle
in Co. Limerick against the Munstermen in 627 and whose family
remained closely associated with the great Thomond churches of
Inis Celtra (on Lough Derg) and Tuamgraney, Co. Clare. These long-
standing geopolitical links partly explain why Guaire Aidne's descendant
Máelruanaid Ua hEidin of Uí Fiachrach was one of the few non-Munster
princes to die alongside Brian at the Battle of Clontarf.[22]

LETH CUINN AND LETH MOGA

All these dynasties—the Connachta and Uí Néill, the Airgialla and
Ulaid—and the other unrelated descent groups and subject peoples
that coexisted around them and under them, were confined to the
northern half of Ireland. Its formal name was Leth Cuinn ('Conn's
Half'), from Conn Cétchathach, ancestor of the Connachta and
Uí Néill. The southern half of Ireland was called Leth Moga ('Mug's Half',
literally 'the half of the slave'), from Mug Nuadat, otherwise known as
Eógan, the ancestor-figure of the paramount dynasty in Munster, the
Eóganachta. The dividing line between the two halves, the learned men
of mediaeval Ireland said, ran along the course of the Eiscir Riada from
the ford called Áth Cliath over the Liffey at Dublin to the ford of the
same name over the river Clarin at Clarinbridge, Co. Galway.

The theory developed by the literati was that Ireland had originally
been divided in two between Éremón and Éber, the sons of Míl who first
settled the island, and that this division had been perpetuated in the
sharing out of the island between their descendants, Conn and Eógan. It
was probably an attempt to rationalise the political status quo at the time
of the theory's concoction, perhaps in the seventh or eighth century,
when the sphere of influence of the king of Tara coincided with these

northern provinces and the influence of the Eóganachta king of Cashel was restricted to Munster and, intermittently, its southern neighbours. But, given the fact that the Uí Néill king of Tara exercised somewhat more effective overlordship of the northern half—to say nothing of his authority beyond it, especially in Leinster—than the king of Munster did throughout the southern half, the claim that the two kings enjoyed equal status was weak, suggesting that it was originally dreamt up to bolster Munster's claims.

Despite this, the authenticity of the division was accepted by the Uí Néill. The term Leth Cuinn is used in literature associated with the Uí Néill, such as the Annals of Ulster (where it first appears as early as 748), and we have seen that in 859 Máel Sechnaill I convened a 'royal conference of the nobility of Ireland (*righdhal mathe Erenn*)' at Rahugh, Co. Westmeath, which presided over the short-lived alienation of the southern kingdom of Osraige from Leth Moga to Leth Cuinn, with the agreement (however reluctant) of the overking of Leth Moga, Máel Gualae of Munster.[23]

LEINSTER

The province of the Laigin (map 5), later Laighen, by the seventh century at the latest had shrunk to the area bounded by the Liffey, the Bog of Allen, the Slieve Bloom Mountains and the lower Barrow. (*Laighen* + the Norse genitive *s* + *tír* ('land') = Leinster.) It may have been geographically in the southern half, but the Uí Néill were wont to eye it up for Leth Cuinn.

There was a tradition that the Uí Néill were entitled to exact a *bórama* or cattle-tribute from them (a different *bórama* led to Brian acquiring his famous nickname), and the text called *Bórama Laigen* ('The cattle-tribute of Leinster') itemises what the Uí Néill kings of Tara demanded of the Leinstermen, as follows:

Thrice five thousand cows; thrice five thousand swine; thrice five thousand mantles; thrice five thousand chains of silver; thrice five thousand wethers; thrice five thousand cauldrons of brass; a great cauldron of brass into which twelve swine and twelve beeves would go in the house of Tara itself; thirty white, red-eared cows with calves of the same colour, and with ties of bronze and with tethers of bronze, and with their milk-pails of bronze in addition thereto.[24]

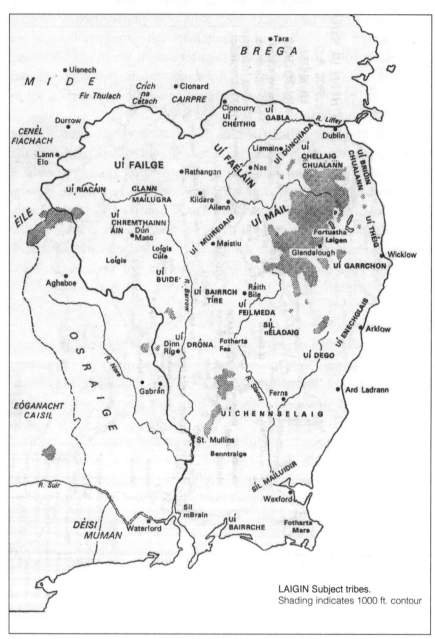

Map 5. Leinster c.900 AD.

This is literature, not history, but there might be a germ of truth in the basic point of the story, which is that the Uí Néill persistently sought the submission of the Leinstermen, something the latter strove to deny them.

It was probably pressure from the Uí Néill that had caused the contraction of Leinster in the first place, the Leinstermen remembering a time when their ancestors had ruled in Tara before it passed into Uí Néill hands. This annexation is the meaning behind those tales that feature an ancestor-figure of the Uí Néill mating with a Leinsterwoman—as when the legendary Cormac mac Airt abducts Eithne Thóebfhota, daughter of the king of the Laigin—as she is presumably a sovereignty figure who symbolises the kingship of Tara passing from the Laigin to the Uí Néill. It is not known whether the early Laigin settlements in Britain—which, as we have seen, we can trace from ogham inscriptions and place-names—were a response to this encroachment from the north, but they are a reminder that Leinster was a province that tended to maintain very close links with the world beyond St George's Channel.

As throughout Ireland, the geography of Leinster dictated settlement, and settlement dictated political allegiances. Thus the Wicklow Mountains were a dividing line between the northern part of the province in the fertile lands of the Liffey Valley and the plains of Kildare, dominated by the Uí Dúnlainge, and the southern part in the valleys of the Barrow and Slaney, dominated by Uí Chennselaig. The latter produced a few overkings of all Leinster up to the early eighth century—and were to do so again when the family of the infamous Diarmait Mac Murchada (Dermot McMurrough) came to the fore in the eleventh century—but in the interval the Uí Dúnlainge of north Leinster dominated.

Three brothers—Muiredach, Fáelán, and Dúnchad, who lived in the first half of the eighth century—each founded a lineage that became a substantial territorial kingdom within north Leinster, alternating the overkingship of the province between them. The descendants of Muiredach (died 760), known as the Uí Muiredaig, bore the title *rig Iarthar Liphi* ('king of the Western Liffey Plain') and maintained a grip on the dynasty's headquarters at Maistiu (Mullaghmast, Co. Kildare). From one of their more successful kings, Tuathal, who died in 958, they adopted the surname Ua Tuathail (O'Toole), and they were to remain a potent force in Dublin's southern hinterland for many centuries.

The same is true of the progeny of Fáelán (died 738), whose lordship was further north, based at Naas, and whose king bore the title *ri Airthir Liphi* ('king of the Eastern Liffey Plain'). Their king Máelmórda held the overkingship of Leinster at the time of the Battle of Clontarf and was Brian's principal Irish opponent in the battle, in which both men lost their lives. From Máelmórda's son Bran the dynasty adopted the surname Ua Brain (O'Byrne); and, while they (like their Uí Thuathail cousins) were later banished by the Anglo-Normans from the plains of Kildare to the wilds of Wicklow, they nevertheless went on to play a central role in later centuries.

The third line of the Uí Dúnlainge, descended from Dúnchad (died 728) and bearing the dynastic name Uí Dúnchada, was further north still (Dolphin's Barn, near Kilmainham, is said to be a corruption of Uí Dúnchada's Cairn) and had its headquarters at Liamain (Newcastle Lyons) on the border of Dublin and Kildare. By the eleventh century, when they had conquered the Cualu area of south Co. Dublin and north Co. Wicklow, they had adopted the surname Mac Gilla Mo-Cholmóc and after 1170 married into and merged with the Anglo-Norman conquerors of nearby Dublin.

It is possible that the Uí Dúnlainge gained supremacy in Leinster because they enjoyed the favour of the Clann Cholmáin kings of Southern Uí Néill; but as the Uí Néill consolidated their hegemony over Leth Cuinn their aspirations to impose themselves on Leth Moga set in. Donnchad Midi (died 797) invaded Leinster in 770—spending a week at the ancient hill-fort of Dún Ailinne (on Knockaulin Hill, near Old Kilcullen, Co. Kildare), a place of symbolic significance for the Leinstermen, and ten years later he also laid waste the land and churches of Leinster. Donnchad's successor as king of Tara, Áed Oirnide (died 819) of the Northern Uí Néill, devastated Leinster twice in one month in 804, and the following year he sought to undermine the province further by partitioning it in two between the heads of what would become the Uí Muiredaig and Uí Fáeláin lineages—an extraordinary demonstration of Uí Néill self-confidence and ambition. This same king of Tara was defeated by the Leinstermen at the Liffey in 808, partitioned the kingdom in two again in 818, and led one final invasion the following year in which he laid waste the province, from Cualu to Glendalough.

Áed's son Niall Caille (died 846) succeeded him as king of the Northern Uí Néill, and it is noticeable that after his assumption of the kingship of Tara in 833 he too intervened in Leinster to appoint a king of his own choosing, as if it were a right due him by virtue of his rank. But Leinster was part of Leth Moga, and Leth Moga was dominated by the kings of Munster; the latter therefore denied the right of the king of Tara to intervene there. This is why the celebrated king of Munster Feidlimid mac Crimthainn (died 847), entered Leinster in 841 and, though unsuccessful, did battle with the king of Tara, Niall Caille, somewhere in Co. Kildare. But the reason they came to blows was that Feidlimid had marched all the way from Munster to the place called Carman, where the kings of Leinster convened the *óenach* or assembly that was their sole prerogative; presumably he had been intending to celebrate the Óenach Carmain himself, to demonstrate that it was he, the king of Cashel, rather than the king of Tara who was Leinster's rightful overlord.[25]

MUNSTER

The province of Mumu (map 6), later Mumhain, was of course very much larger than Leinster. (*Mumhain* + the Norse genitive *s* + *tír* ('land') = Munster.) It was sometimes described, perhaps in an artificial attempt to mimic the division of Ireland into five fifths, as having five parts—north, south, east, west, and middle Munster (Tuadmumu, Desmumu, Aurmumu, Iarmumu and Medón Muman)—the first three of which have left an imprint in the area-names Thomond, Desmond and Ormond. The major fault-line in the province in the early period was between east and west, although the eventual triumph of Brian's dynasty reflected a north-south divide, with Brian and his descendants, the O'Briens, ruling Tuadmumu while the MacCarthys—*Meic Carthaig*, 'descendants of Carthach' (who flourished c. 1050)—the remnants of their vanquished predecessors, retained Desmumu.

The latter were the most successful survivors from a sprawling federation of dynasties claiming descent from the legendary Eógan Már—thus they were called the Eóganachta (similar to the descent of the Connachta from the prehistoric Conn). Their fabulous origin-myth tells of Cashel being 'discovered' by Eógan's descendant Conall Corc, whose mother, it was said, was British and who had spent a long exile

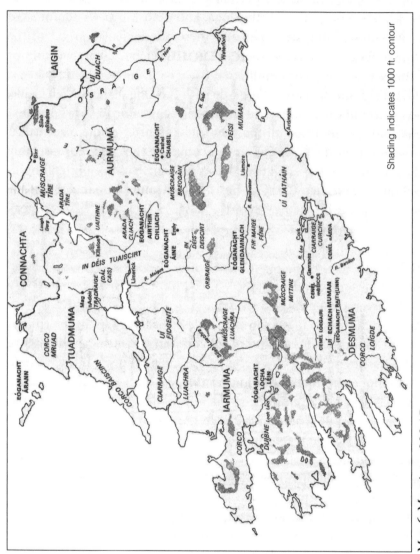

Map 6. Munster c. 900 AD.

Shading indicates 1000 ft. contour

among the Picts; and it is just possible that the origins of the Eóganachta lay in the expulsion of Irish colonists from their settlements in Wales (*Caisil* is an early borrowing from Latin *castellum*) which may have happened about the year 400 or so. The genealogists like to think of the Eóganachta as having seven branches, although in reality there were more, as, while some withered away over the generations, others prospered and produced successful offshoots.

In the earlier records a branch that features prominently is Eóganacht Locha Léin, whose name indicates a presence in the environs of Lough Leane at Killarney and who may have controlled the fertile lands northwards from there to the River Maine. While ruling this as their core territory they also claimed an overlordship of all Iarmumu (Cos. Clare, Limerick, Kerry and west Cork) but had gone into decline by the beginning of the Viking Age; and the loosening of their bonds of lordship was no doubt one of the factors that enabled Brian's dynasty of Dál Cáis to begin to assert itself. When the latter did so they found that it was another branch of the Eóganacht that offered stiffest rearguard defiance, the branch taking its name from Raithlend (near Bandon, Co. Cork): indeed the man who in 976 killed Mathgamain, Brian's brother and predecessor as king of Dál Cais, was the reigning king of the Eóganacht Raithlind, Máel Muad mac Brain, and the first major battle that Brian fought after his succession, the battle of Belach Lechta in 978, saw Brian wreak his revenge.

But the claim of Eóganacht Raithlind to the kingship of Munster during Brian's early years was a temporary interlude in the history of the sustained possession of the title by those branches of the dynasty based on the fertile plains of north Cork, east Limerick and Tipperary. The Eóganacht Glennamnach, ancestors of the Uí Cháim (O'Keeffes), have left a trace of their name in the village of Glanworth near Fermoy and held sway over the Blackwater Valley, producing a succession of kings of Munster—including one of its most illustrious, Cathal mac Finguine (died 742)—until decline set in in the early ninth century. From that point onwards, various lineages of Eóganacht Chaisil led the way, with a centre of gravity, as their name suggests, about Cashel (Co. Tipperary).

For some reason, though, the overkings of Munster drawn from the Eóganacht Chaisil do not show the same tendency as overkings elsewhere in Ireland to try to consolidate power in one direct line. For instance, if one were to trace the paternal ancestry of their two most remarkable kings of the Viking Age, Feidlimid mac Crimthainn (died 847) and Cormac mac Cuilennáin (died 908) one would have to go back to the time of St Patrick to find the common ancestor from whom both descend. This failure to concentrate power, and therefore material resources, in one pre-eminent lineage ultimately undermined them.

Besides, like all the great dynasties, the Eóganacht did not rule Munster after *removing* those who held land and power before them: rather, as the Eóganacht expanded they pushed others aside, taking their good lands and leaving the bad. But these peoples always had the potential to stage a recovery or pose a threat or side with an enemy. For instance, the kings of Cashel might claim overlordship of the Osraige, whose land was coterminous with the diocese of Ossory and who possessed at Belach Gabráin (Gowran, Co. Kilkenny) one of the few routes by which a land army could enter Munster; but Osraige pursued an independent strategy, tending if anything to align itself with Leinster, over which some of its more assertive kings could harbour ambitions.

Also, in the coastal valleys and in the peninsulas of the south-west there were other peoples who could be potential allies or foes. The Uí Liatháin, east of Cork Harbour, who no doubt had significant naval capacity, served with Brian at Clontarf, as did the kings of Ciarraige Luachra in north Kerry and Corco Baiscind in Clare. On the other hand, the Uí Fhidgeinti were an important dynasty who ruled much of the present-day Co. Limerick, who had poor relations with Brian and against whom he went to war soon after his accession to power. We shall hear more about such peoples later on.

The more embellished accounts of the Battle of Clontarf also report that among those killed by Brian's side in the encounter was the king of the Déisi, a Munster dynasty with a remote ancestral link to Brian's. Their various branches occupied a diagonal swathe running across Munster from Waterford to, eventually, Clare. Having splintered, the eastern segment, called Déisi Muman, can be found occupying Co. Waterford and a small part of south Co. Tipperary (it was their leader who fought alongside Brian at Clontarf); the western segment, which acquired the name Déis Bec ('Little Déis'), is the one from which Brian descends. That too ruptured with the passage of time, producing what became the lineages of the Déis Deiscirt ('Southern Déis') and the Déis

Tuaiscirt ('Northern Déis'), and Brian was of the latter. At some point, and certainly by the eighth century, they had breached the Shannon frontier and were in the process of acquiring their lands lying south of Slieve Aughty in east Clare. The brief notice in the annals for 744 recording 'Destruction of Corco Mruad by the Déis (*Foirddbe Corcu Mu Druadh don Deiss*)' is solid evidence of Brian's dynasty, the Déis, making effective war on the inhabitants of north Clare, the Corco Mruad.[26]

Brian's branch of the Déisi later adopted the dynastic name Dál Cais (literally, 'the share of Cas'), first recorded in 934, shortly before Brian's birth, at a time when they were making rapid strides in Munster at the expense of the Eóganachta. And it seems that, in a deliberate attempt to disguise their parvenu status, a learned promoter of Brian's dynasty produced a false pedigree concealing their humble origins among the Déisi vassals of the Eóganachta; instead, as the Eóganachta were said to derive from the eponymous Eógan Már, the genealogists invented a brother of the latter called Cormac Cass and claimed that Brian's people descended from him (table 1). Cormac Cass was made to have a descendant, about six generations later, called Cas (or Cass), son of Conall Echluaith, and this is the man from whom—it was claimed—Dál Cais took their name. This neat sleight of hand gave Brian's dynasty a position of collateral equality with the Eóganachta. It was needed only because Dál Cais were busy trying, as it were, to *become* the Eóganachta, trying to take their place as the rightful kings of Cashel and Munster; and this is what propelled them onto the national stage.[27]

MUNSTER'S ASPIRATIONS

The kings of Munster indeed had national ambitions. When Cathal mac Finguine (died 742) of the Eóganacht Glendamnach assumed the overkingship of Munster he did not just try to restrict Uí Néill intrusion into Leth Moga (the Southern Half): he took the war to the king of Tara when he and the king of Leinster invaded the east Meath kingdom of Brega in 721. The Munster Annals of Inisfallen claim that the king of Tara submitted to him, so that a later propaganda poem includes Cathal among the five Munster kings who 'ruled Ireland.' In 733 he invaded Mide and came to the site of the king of Tara's *óenach* at Tailtiu, defeating the Uí Néill at the symbolic hill of Tlachtga (the Hill of Ward, near Athboy), sites chosen no doubt because of their political

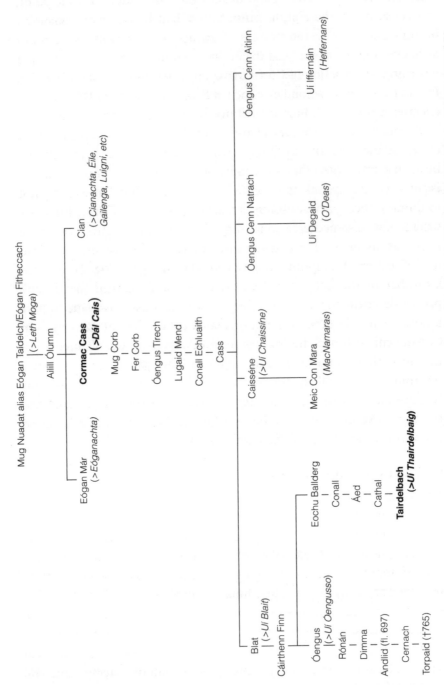

Table 1: Brian's remote ancestors of Dál Cais, from the mythological Mug Nuadat to Tairdelbach (c. 8th century AD)

significance. These were extraordinary testimony to Munster ambition. Indeed in 737 a *rígdál* took place between Cathal and the new king of Tara, Áed Allán, at Terryglass (Co. Tipperary) at which peace was declared between them (and the authority in Munster of the church of Armagh was acknowledged). Clearly Cathal was a remarkable man, and in addition to his contests with the kings of Tara his career is notable for his attempts to assert supremacy throughout Leth Moga.

Cathal was succeeded by his son or grandson Artrí, about whom the annals record that in 793 he underwent an ordination into the kingship of Munster (*ordinatio Artroigh maic Cathail in regnum Mumen*). This is the first time, so far as we know, that this had happened in Ireland (although Áedán mac Gabráin had long ago been ordained by Colum Cille as king of Dál Riata) and is surely evidence of an attempt by their overkings to enhance their prestige.

Indeed the next significant king of Munster, Fedelmid mac Crimthainn, was actually a cleric and was described in his obit as a scribe and anchorite, suggesting a man of learning, but it did not dim his ambitions for his kingdom. He sought to dominate Leinster and then, as the controller of Leth Moga, to compete with the king of Tara, taking part in a *rígdál* with him in 827. In 831 Fedelmid, with the Laigin, raided the Southern Uí Néill kingdom of Brega. In 838 he met the king of Tara, Niall Caille, in a *rígdál* at Clonfert (inside Leth Chuinn, the northern half), and the Munster record of the event claims that Fedelmid received the submission of Niall Caille. This record is biased in Fedelmid's favour; if there were any truth in it it would be an astonishing development. We know that Fedelmid launched an offensive against Uí Néill in 840, setting up camp at Tara—a pointed message to the Uí Néill.

The following year Fedelmid marched into Leinster, where he seems to have intended to convene the *óenach Carmain,* a privilege of the king of Leinster—again evidence of exceptional Munster ambition, although in this instance the king of Tara caught up with him and gave him a bloody nose. Fedelmid also saw the potential of Armagh's claim to primacy and tended to promote its interests, to mutual advantage; clearly he saw— as Brian was later to do—that one way of advancing his own national profile was by associating himself with Armagh's national objectives. This explains the unusually positive obit of Fedelmid recorded in the Annals of Ulster at his death in 847, which describes him as *optimus*

Scotorum ('the best of the Irish'). It was a not unworthy tribute, as Fedelmid mac Crimthainn, like Cathal mac Finguine a century earlier, had shown what Munster was capable of.

Only one of his successors before Brian came close to offering a challenge to Uí Néill, and that was Cormac mac Cuilennáin (also of Eóganacht Chaisil, although remotely related, and also reputed to be in clerical orders and very learned). Having obtained the kingship of Cashel in 902, he led Munster resistance to Uí Néill demands. When the king of Tara, Flann Sinna, invaded Munster in 904 and 905 Cormac was forced to hand over hostages, but in 907 he defeated Flann at the battle of Mag Léna (near Tullamore, Co. Offaly), and the Munster annals also claim that Cormac marched north at Christmastide the same year and took the hostages of the Southern Uí Néill and the Connachta.

There may be an element of wishful thinking here, but Cormac's threat to Uí Néill dominance was certainly real enough while it lasted. In 908 the Munster army was slaughtered by the Uí Néill forces at the battle of Ballaghmoon (near Leighlinbridge, Co. Carlow), and Munster's king, Cormac mac Cuilennáin, lost his life in the encounter. Although his death turned out to be a landmark in the decline of the Eóganachta, as regards the power of Munster, Cormac's career had at least demonstrated that kings of the southern province could question Uí Néill dominance. But the decline of the Eóganachta paved the way for Brian's emergence, and Munster's challenge resumed.[28]

THE HIGH-KINGSHIP

What these great and ever more inflammatory wars testify to is political ambition; and it was an ambition to hold power throughout Ireland. The Uí Néill started it. Of one of their energetic early kings, Diarmait mac Cerbaill (died 565), Adomnán of Iona had stated (writing as far back as the year 700 or thereabouts) that God had ordained him as 'ruler of all Ireland (*totius Scotiae regnatorem*)', while his son Áed Sláine (died 604) had 'the prerogative predestined by God, the monarchy of the kingdom of all Ireland (*a Deo totius Euerniae regni praerogatiuam monarchiae praedestinatam*).' Needless to say, the Uí Néill had no such predestined right, but they were more than happy to claim it. They claimed it through their possession of the kingship of Tara: because they were kings of Tara, it was said, they had rights throughout Ireland.

Thus Muirchú (the biographer of St Patrick), as earlier noted, says of one of the founding fathers of the Uí Néill, the pagan king Lóegaire, son of Niall Noígiallach, that he was 'emperor of the barbarians, living in Tara, which was the capital of the Irish (*imperator barbarorum regnans in Temoria, quae erat caput Scotorum*).' So, powerful rhetoric was flying around: Ireland was a kingdom (*regnum*)—indeed it was a monarchy (*monarchia*), and it had a capital (*caput*). That was the theory. The problem was putting it into practice.

We have seen that by the beginning of the Viking Age the Uí Néill had evolved a system whereby real power, to all intents and purposes, was confined to the Cenél nEógain of the north and Clann Cholmáin of the Southern Uí Néill. Both kept a tight grip on the reins of power, so that usually the succession followed in a straightforward way from father to son; and the overkingship (the kingship of Tara) rotated predictably between north and south. They did this in ever closer co-operation with the great monastic churches—especially Armagh for the Northern Uí Néill and Clonmacnoise for the Southern—which chronicled their glories and propagandised for their continuing ascent.

That concentration of political control, and the amassing of economic might that followed from it, enabled the Uí Néill to dominate the northern half of Ireland and intermittently to secure *bórama* (cattle-tribute) from the Leinstermen in acknowledgement of the latter's subordination to them. And we have seen the lengths to which they went in trying to secure Munster's submission. It was Máel Sechnaill I (died 862) who first succeeded in this great goal, startling his contemporaries when he secured the hostages of Munster in 854, 856 and 858, leading 'the men of Ireland' into battle and even alienating Osraige from Leth Moga to Leth Cuinn. And so it is not surprising that the high cross at Kinnitty (Co. Offaly) bears an inscription calling Máel Sechnaill *RIG HERENN* ('king of Ireland'), or that the annals should call him *ri h-Erenn uile* ('king of all Ireland') at the time of his death.[29] But these were partisan assertions rather than statements of undisputed fact, and other power centres sought to repudiate such claims and put forward claims of their own. Advocates of the kings of Munster in particular, it has been argued, directly expressed the superiority of the kingship of Cashel over that of Tara.[30] So, while Máel Sechnaill was an extraordinary man who came closer than any of his predecessors to instituting a high-kingship of

Ireland, it was a personal edifice that had to be reconstructed from the ground up by each of his successors. And by the middle of the tenth century this Uí Néill paramountcy had begun to wobble. What had seemed inevitable—that they would intensify their lordship to the point where it went unchallenged in Ireland—failed to come about. And that failure had much to do with the complications of the Viking Age.

THE VIKING ONSLAUGHT

Irish churchmen had been extraordinarily active on the Continent from the seventh century, beginning with Columbanus, one of the great figures of the early Middle Ages. Some of these *Scotti vagantes* ('wandering Irish') were certainly what we might call missionaries, although later they were teachers—men like Sedulius Scottus, the grammarian, classicist and poet, and John Scottus Eriugena, whose astonishing Greek scholarship made him the outstanding philosopher of the ninth century. Why they left Ireland, and how they went about securing positions for themselves, is shrouded in mystery, but one possibility is suggested by the chronicle known as the Annals of St-Bertin, in which it is stated of the year 848 that

> the Irish, descending upon the *Nordmanni* [i.e. Vikings], with the help of our Lord Jesus Christ were victorious, and expelled them from their borders, and thus the king of the Irish sent ambassadors of peace and friendship with gifts to Charles [the Bald] seeking right of passage to Rome.[31]

As Sedulius appears on the scene out of nowhere at this very point, it is quite possible that he was among the envoys sent by the king of Tara, Máel Sechnaill I, or perhaps by Ólchobor, king of Munster (southern forces having won two major victories over the Vikings in 848), to the court of Charlemagne's grandson. It is certainly a fact that the regular references in Sedulius's writings to the *Nordmanni* suggest that he greatly feared them, and perhaps the disruptive effect of the Vikings on the schools of Ireland was a factor in his removal and that of countless other Irishmen to the Continent in this period.

The great Dícuil, one of the most original thinkers of the age, was one such. We know nothing of his Irish background, but it is unlikely to be a coincidence that he arrived on the Continent just as the Viking incursions began in his homeland, after which he managed to join the ranks of the remarkable band of scholars, many of them Anglo-Saxon and Irish, attached to Charlemagne's court. His greatest work, completed in 825, is his *De mensura orbis terrae* ('On the measurement of the earth')—so far as we can tell, the first mediaeval geography. In it Dícuil informs his readers that Irish monks had travelled to Orkney, the Shetlands and Iceland: he states that thirty years earlier—before the Viking 'discovery' of Iceland—he spoke to Irish clerics who had stayed there from February to August and told him it was so bright all night around midsummer that they could pick lice from their shirts.

Dícuil personally had been to other north Atlantic islands: 'Near the island of Britain are many islands, some large, some small, and some of medium size; some of them are situated to the south and west, but the majority are to the north-west and north. I have lived in some of them and I have visited others'—perhaps suggesting that he had been a monk in Iona.[32] And he seems to have had the Faroe Islands in mind when he informs the world that 'for nearly a hundred years hermits sailing from our country, Ireland, have lived there, but just as they [the Faroes] were always deserted from the beginning of the world, so now, because of the Northman pirates, they are emptied of anchorites, and filled with countless sheep.'[33]

As Dícuil is a reliable writer, there is presumably some basis to his observation; but even if it is entirely groundless his words capture the essence of contemporary reality. The purported banishment of Irish hermits from the Faroes mirrors the thoroughly negative experience of churchmen elsewhere throughout much of north-western Europe in the ninth century when faced with the violence of Viking raiding; but their replacement by sheep reminds us that this Scandinavian expansion sometimes had as much to do with farming and colonising as with raiding and warring.

We do not know why the Viking Age began when it did. Scandinavians, of course, had never been cut off from the world, and there are traces of their activities further afield long before the age of large-scale raiding began. Their earliest ambitions seem to have been towards the east and south, into what is now Russia. This involved the importing into Scandinavia, and the onward dispersal, of large quantities of precious metal (especially silver from the Islamic world), the intensive trading of furs and skins acquired in places like Finland and northern Russia, and the cornering of the market for luxury commodities, such as amber and walrus-ivory and probably slaves, and their sale to western European merchants. Certain Scandinavian rulers accumulated wealth from this trade and gained power from their position of dominance over the peoples to the east whom they exploited for such produce. Increased trade required more shipping, and increased wealth facilitated *better* shipping.

The earliest Viking activity was essentially piracy, and the Baltic trading networks probably fell prey to pirates who were eventually tempted to venture out from the Baltic to the North Sea. Here they were undoubtedly hitting coastal targets for some time before such raids began to be noticed by writers whose reports have come down to us, and for geographical reasons it seems reasonable to imagine that northern Britain and Ireland would have felt the brunt of raiders from what is now Norway, while Danish raiders would tend, for the most part, to concentrate their energies on southern England and the lands on each side of the English Channel.

The first recorded raid took place in 793, when the monastery founded by Irish monks on Holy Island at Lindisfarne in Northumbria was attacked, the Anglo-Saxon Chronicle telling us that 'the ravages of heathen men miserably destroyed God's church in Holy Island, with plunder and slaughter.' That this was something new and unexpected is suggested by the same source's observation that the attack was preceded by 'dreadful forewarnings over the land of the Northumbrians, terrifying the people most woefully: these were immense sheets of light rushing through the air, and whirlwinds, and fiery dragons flying across the firmament.'[34]

The great English scholar Alcuin was similarly startled by the incident and wrote to the community of Lindisfarne shortly afterwards to commiserate, lamenting that

the pagans have desecrated God's sanctuary, shed the blood of saints around the altar, laid waste the house of our hope and trampled the bodies of the saints like dung in the street. I can only cry from my heart before Christ's altar: 'O Lord, spare thy people and do not give the Gentiles thine inheritance, lest the heathen say, "Where is the God of the Christians?"'[35]

Alcuin, outraged as he was by the desecration of this holy place, thought it must be some kind of divine retribution for the victims' sins, but he nevertheless offered to help. He was then attached to the court of Charlemagne at Aachen, and he adds:

When our lord King Charles returns from defeating his enemies, by God's mercy, I plan to go to him, and if I can then do anything for you about the boys who have been carried off by the pagans as prisoners or about any other of your needs, I shall make every effort to see that it is done.

This shows that the Vikings had begun as they meant to go on: they were already in the business of slavery.

The raiders were back in England the following year and attacked another North Sea monastery (although this time they met stiffer resistance),[36] and by now it seems that the Irish world was aware of the new crisis. We can only imagine what horror underlies the deceptively matter-of-fact remark of the writer of the Annals of Ulster for 794 in noting: 'Devastation of all the islands of Britain by heathens.' This speaks of something more than mere raids, rather a pervasive offensive against the inhabitants of isolated maritime communities; and if the annalist had in mind islands off Scotland's western coast it is possible that the raiders took possession of some of these Hebridean islands, because they were venturing further south the following year.

The Viking raids on Ireland are taken to have begun in 795, as in that year Rechru was burned by the heathens and its shrines broken and plundered.[37] Rechru was the Irish name for both Rathlin Island, off the Antrim coast, and Lambay, in the Irish Sea north of Dublin, and so the raid may have been on either. That it was the latter is suggested by the fact that a church on a nearby island, Inis Pátraic (St Patrick's Island), 10 km to the north, near Skerries, was also burned by the Vikings three years later, which may show that this part of the Irish Sea had become the object of their continuing attention.

What is more, the same entry for 798 tells us that they 'took the cattle-tribute of the territories (*borime na crích do breith*),' and then that this group of Vikings made 'great depredations in both Ireland and Scotland (*innreda mara doaib cene eiter Erinn & Albain*).'[38] Perhaps this was no more than casual 'rustling' of the livestock belonging to the hapless inhabitants of the area, but it smacks of something more formal and substantial; it certainly suggests a more complicated engagement with their victims than we tend to think of in this very early stage of the Viking campaigns and, at the least, more varied activity than the proverbial smash-and-grab raiding of churches. If there were Vikings in what is now north Co. Dublin in the late eighth century exacting tribute from its inhabitants, a tribute that was handed over in the form of cattle, which had to be managed by their new owners—even if it was only in preparation for their eventual slaughter—one would have to assume that they had secured themselves a camp nearby and might be thinking of staying put.

How well it fits in with the archaeological evidence that has recently come to light from nearby Dublin, where the long-standing assumption that a Viking presence came to be felt only in the 840s, has been thrown into doubt. The skeletons of several Viking warriors found at South Great George's Street in 2003 have been shown by radiocarbon dating to have a 95 per cent probability of dating from between AD 670 and 880 but with 'intercept dates' (which attempt to pinpoint the date of death) ranging between 770 and 782, while another warrior excavated in 2002 in nearby Ship Street Great produced dates ranging between 665 and 865, with an intercept date of 790.[39] Another Viking burial a little distance away, at Golden Lane, has dates ranging between 678 and 832, which would suggest an intercept date (though unfortunately we do not have one) similar to the other early burials.[40]

These were formal burials of young warriors, who seem to have met their death in conflict and who were buried beside their camp on the banks of the Poddle River, near where it joins the Liffey; and it seems they occupied this camp and lived and died in its vicinity in the very earliest days of the Viking Age.

It is still undoubtedly true that it was Irish churches that were falling victim from the beginning to piratical crews of Scandinavians. Although the Vikings are not mentioned, presumably they were involved in the orgun (ravaging) in 795 of Colum Cille's great monastery of Iona and of Inishmurray (off Co. Sligo) and Inishbofin (off north Connemara),[41] and they are specifically stated to have been responsible for burning Iona in 802 and again in 806, when sixty-eight of its community were killed; and we know that in 807 Vikings came round the west coast and again razed Inishmurray, off Sligo, and Roscam, at the inland end of Galway Bay.

But what is clear is that concentration on such acts of violence alone cannot capture the full dimensions of Viking-Irish involvement, even at that early stage. Annals are written in churches and are concerned with the affairs of churches—and of course it was an outrage that these places of devotion and of local and regional prestige were subject to unprovoked aggression—but there was much more going on than this.

When the fleet came to the area around Skerries in 798 and so overawed the population of the adjacent districts of what is now north Co. Dublin that they agreed to the payment of a consignment of beef (*bórime na crích*), we are seeing war and diplomacy in operation. And when in 821 the Vikings plundered the Howth peninsula and 'carried off into captivity a great number of women'[42] they were—unless there was a now-forgotten nunnery there—attacking a farming and fishing community rather than a monastery.

The evidence points to Irish political leaders, from the start, trying to come to terms with their new enemies and struggling to ward off inroads into their people's territory. We can surely conclude from the cryptic mention in 811 of *Strages gentilium apud Ultu* ('slaughter of the heathens by the Ulaid')[43] that the latter—probably the people known as Dál Fiatach in east Co. Down—were defending their kingdom rather than a church from Scandinavian aggressors. A measure of its significance is the fact that news of it (or a similar success, probably brought by an Irish migrant scholar) reached the court of Charlemagne in Aachen and is recorded in its chronicle.[44]

Connemara takes its name from the Conmaicne Mara, and in 812 they were slaughtered by a Viking force that was presumably making incursions into west Galway. Just north of it the Fir Umaill occupied the area around Clew Bay, which also seems to have been the focus of Viking attentions, because in that same year the inhabitants slaughtered some Vikings but then had to do battle with them again in 813 and this time lost their king in the encounter. Also in the latter year the annals tell us that the king of the Eóganacht of Loch Léin (based, as the name suggests, around Lough Leane and the other lakes of Killarney) slaughtered the heathens in Munster. These are local kingdoms going to war to protect their territory.

Assuming that these Vikings in west Munster were linked to those active off the Connacht coast that year—having travelled all the way down the western seaboard—it would cause one to wonder about the practicality of their doing so from their Scandinavian homelands. These look more like sustained offensives made possible because the aggressors, even at this early stage, were digging themselves in in coastal camps around Ireland, such as that excavated on the banks of the Poddle in Dublin, which, as we have seen, housed the burials of Viking warriors apparently from around the 790s, or the possible Viking Age enclosure and burials that have been found beside a bend in the Ballysadare River at Knoxpark, Co. Sligo.[45] The biography of St Patrick called the Tripartite Life, which may perhaps have been written about this time, says of the church of Killaspugbrone (about 10 km from Knoxpark on the Strandhill Peninsula) that Patrick prophesied that *Gentilibus desereretur locus ille,* which duly came to pass.[46] As the phrase implies that the Gentiles (i.e. Vikings) caused the church to be deserted, it may mean that they set up camp there.

While it is assumed that there were Scandinavians occupying permanent bases in western Scotland or the Isles within a generation or so of the beginning of the Viking Age, one wonders where the heathens were based who in 824 arrived at Sceilg Mhichíl, far out in the Atlantic off the Kerry coast, and captured and killed the leader of its hermits, or those who plundered the church of Beggerin and Dairinis Chóemáin in Wexford Harbour in 821, or Cork the following year, or Inis Daimle (near Waterford) in 825, or Lismore on the River Blackwater, which was attacked twice, in 832 and 833, or Kilmolash on the Suir not far to the north, which also fell victim in 833.

In 825 they were victorious in battle against the army of Osraige, the territory bounded by the Rivers Nore and Barrow in the Co. Kilkenny area; and it seems reasonable to assume that the battle arose from Viking activity on these inland waterways, just as their overthrow of the Fortuatha Laigen in 827 points to a Viking presence in their land in the coastal area around the later town of Wicklow. Further south, in Co. Wexford, lies the monastery of Taghmon, and the following year, 828, its community joined forces with the local king of the Uí Chennselaig in inflicting a heavy defeat on Vikings. Glendalough was attacked in 834 and Ferns and Clonmore (Co. Carlow) in 835.

This concentration of Viking activity in the south-east in those years surely allows us to suppose that they had a foothold nearby; indeed when Clonmore was attacked again in 836 it was on Christmas Eve, and such midwinter raiding is surely the work of 'local' Vikings.[47] It is possible that they were based in the great Viking encampment that has recently been discovered by archaeologists at Woodstown in Waterford Harbour.[48] Another possibility is an island in Wexford Harbour, especially given the fact of the attacks there in 821, suggested by the mention in the Tripartite Life of Patrick, written about this time, that shrines from 'the lesser island' there had been moved elsewhere, 'since it was taken by the heathens (*iarnagabail dogentib*).'[49]

But proof of a Viking base in the vicinity comes to light only for the year 836. For the first time since the Viking campaigns began, the annals name the site of one of their camps when they tell us that in this year the great monastery of Kildare was plundered by 'heathens from Inber Dée,' which is probably Arklow.[50]

By this time there were undoubtedly other bases around the coast—and many more were soon to follow—and the establishment of one such encampment in the Shannon Estuary is surely the context for the great victory over Viking forces obtained in 834 by the Uí Fidgente, a dynasty that controlled much of Co. Limerick; one imagines the magnificent chalices and brooches found at Ardagh in the heart of Uí Fidgente territory being anxiously buried in circumstances such as this.[51] The following year the monastery of Mungret, just south-west of what would become the city of Limerick, found itself under assault by Vikings, along with other churches of west Munster, just as the enchanting monastic island of Inis Celtra on Lough Derg to the north of Limerick was to do in 837. Evidently the Foreigners were functioning out of a centre of operations in the locality, and this was bound to have a traumatic effect on the whole region; quite how traumatic was demonstrated by a battle fought in 836 that resulted in the slaughter of the army of the Déis Tuaiscirt. This was the dynasty of Brian Bóraime.

THE IMPACT OF THE VIKINGS

In the early decades after their first descent on Ireland in the 790s the Vikings had perpetrated raids on coastal sites; and, while they are found looting the larger churches in particular, we can guess that they were also trying to secure a foothold in remoter outposts with a view to winning land. But, to judge from the epigrammatic documentary evidence, it was only in the 830s that Ireland, like England and the western territories of the Carolingian empire, was exposed to intensive Scandinavian assault. They began by raiding Leinster and Southern Uí Néill territory in Brega, and they had fleets operating on the Boyne, the Liffey, the Shannon, the Erne, and Lough Neagh, where they overwintered in 840/41. And it was in 841 that they built a *longphort* (ship-camp) at Dublin and another one at Linn Duachaill (Annagassan, Co. Louth), followed soon afterwards by an encampment on Lough Ree, from which bases they were able to wreak devastation over a wide area. In 845 they captured the abbot of Armagh himself and 'brought him to the ships of the Shannon Estuary (*a brith do longaibh Luimnigh*)', which may mean that they already had a base at or near Limerick.

And now that certain Vikings were stationed permanently in Ireland we see them immediately taking sides in Irish wars; and, equally, now that they had land armies on regular campaign throughout the country they became vulnerable to Irish resistance. The late 840s therefore saw a succession of Irish victories, and a record of military triumph over the Viking foe was no doubt a feather in the cap of aspiring leaders. Thus the extraordinary king of Osraige, Cerball mac Dúnlainge (who became celebrated in saga as far away as Iceland), made quite a name for himself as an opponent of Viking activity in the Barrow valley, slaughtering 1,200 Dublin Vikings in 847.[52] The following year Máel Sechnaill killed 700 in a battle at Skreen (Co. Meath), the combined forces of Munster and Leinster killed either 200 or (other sources say) 1,200 near Castledermot (Co. Kildare), the king of southern Brega killed another 1,200 somewhere in Co. Meath, the Eóganacht Chaisil killed 500 in their own territory, and the king of Munster destroyed Dún Corcaighe, apparently a fort established by Vikings at Cork.

It was a truly extraordinary year; little wonder that, as we have seen, the Frankish 'Annals of St-Bertin' record under the following year, 848, that a delegation arrived at the court of Charlemagne's grandson Charles the Bald bearing gifts from the *rex Scottorum* (presumably Máel Sechnaill), announcing the vanquishing of the heathens by the Irish (and requesting free passage for a pilgrimage to Rome by the same Irish king).[53]

These victories would not have been possible unless the Vikings' initial military superiority was now in question. If their earlier advantage over the Irish was their naval capacity, or the quality of their weaponry and armour, or their better tactical organisation, or their sheer force of numbers, or disunity among the Irish, or a combination of all these factors, something had happened to change that. And perhaps we can assume that by the late 840s—a full half century after the Vikings' first appearance in the West—the Irish had begun to adapt, had captured or otherwise acquired some of the Vikings' sophisticated troop-carrying vessels, were fighting fire with fire with better and more lethal weaponry, were beginning to professionalise their armies, and were opting to coalesce with former enemies in the face of this dreadful new menace.

No doubt too the Irish began recruiting Viking war-bands as mercenaries or political allies, for use against their own Irish enemies or other Vikings. Indeed at this point the Irish became attuned to the potential of exploiting disunity among the invaders, the annals recording for 849 that 140 ships of 'the people of the king of the Foreigners (*di muinntir righ Gall*)' arrived to subdue the Foreigners already there, and 'they disturbed Ireland between them.'

By 851 two groups are distinguishable to the Irish. In Dublin and at Annagassan there are *Findgaill* or *Findgenti*, foreigners or heathens who are *finn*, 'white, bright, fair', and in that year their fortresses were attacked by newly arrived *Dubgaill* or *Dubgenti*, dark or black foreigners. We tend to think of them as Norwegians and Danes at war with each other, although the distinction might mean nothing more than existing Ireland-focused Vikings versus a newly arrived British-based group, from York perhaps,[54] but whatever the meaning of the terms, the antagonism between them was ferocious. In 852 the Findgenti swooped in a flotilla of 160 ships on the Dubgenti naval camp in Carlingford Lough and battled it out for three days and three nights before admitting defeat and abandoning their ships to them. A new Viking chieftain, Óláfr the White—whom the Irish believed was 'the son of the king of Lochlainn (*m. righ Laithlinde*)' somewhere in the Scandinavian world—arrived in 853, so that the Foreigners of Ireland all submitted to his rule and the Irish even handed over tribute (*coro giallsat Gaill Erenn dó & cis o Goidhelaib*). But once he began to rule in Dublin—jointly perhaps with another Scandinavian, called Ívarr (died 873), sometimes equated with

Ivar the Boneless—he behaved much as an Irish king would, allied with or opposed to neighbouring kings as political advantage dictated and attempting to build up a power base in the Dublin hinterland rather than wreaking havoc, in Viking style.[55]

Despite this—and perhaps it partly explains why their Irish conquest ran out of steam—these Irish-based Vikings seem to have remained active overseas.[56] For some, who desired uncontested land for settlement, the discovery of Iceland was soon to offer a new prospect; others looked to Ireland's nearest neighbour. In 856 Horm (or Gorm), chief of the Dubgenti, was killed by the Welsh king Rhodri Mawr of Gwynedd, and years later, in 877, the latter was forced to seek refuge in Ireland from the Dubgenti, who were presumably attempting to conquer territory in Anglesey in the north-west of Rhodri's kingdom.

In 866 Óláfr and another Viking leader, Auisle, 'together with the Foreigners of Ireland and Scotland,' plundered Fortriu, the lands of the Picts in north-eastern Scotland, exacting tribute and taking hostages. In 870 they captured the great fortress of Dumbarton on the outer Clyde, and the following year Óláfr and Ívarr returned to Dublin with two hundred shiploads of captive 'Angles and Britons and Picts.'[57] The evidence is only sporadic thereafter, but in 918, for instance, there was a major battle on the banks of the Tyne between the leaders of the recently re-established Waterford Vikings and an army of Scots and perhaps the English of Northumbria.[58] This attention to the north of England explains how it was that, for a significant part of a long career that spanned the years from 941 to 981, Amlaíb (Óláfr) Cuarán of Dublin also ruled the kingdom of York.[59]

The Vikings may have had to channel their energies in other directions because of the success of the Uí Néill in preventing large-scale settlement in their territories. Áed Findliath launched a remarkable offensive against Viking bases from Lough Foyle to the Antrim coast in 866, although he does not seem to have challenged their base in the sensitive estuary at Strangford (a Norse borrowing: *Strangfjørðr*, 'rough fjord'),[60] which was active in 879 and saw a Norse fleet again in 924, while the Strangford fleet assaulted Dunseverick on the coast of north Antrim in 926. Strangford was of course in Ulaid territory, and one can well imagine the king of Cenél nEógain being indifferent to their plight; and in any event the major victory by local Ulaid forces against the Norse of Strangford in 943 seems to have been the nail in the latter's coffin.

The Cenél nEógain would have had greater concern about Viking activity on what was for them the vital waterway of Lough Foyle but do not seem to have been successful in removing the ship-camp there, which was still active in 898, as the Foreigners of Lough Foyle were engaged in local warfare as late as 943. It is possible that the Norse fleet reported to be on the Erne lakes in 924, 933 and 936 was more than just a predatory incursion from further afield, and that the Norse presence on Lough Neagh in 900 and 928 was converted into a fixed camp under the Jarl Torolb (Þórólfr) in 930; and although Torolb was killed by the combined armies of the kings of the Northern Uí Néill and the Ulaid in 932, the camp remained active for some time afterwards, until its fleet was finally destroyed by Domnall ua Néill in 945.

All in all, given that the north of Ireland was most vulnerable to sustained Viking assault, because of its proximity to their colonies in western Scotland and the Isles, the achievement of the Uí Néill in preventing permanent large-scale Viking settlement was remarkable indeed. Of course, as has been pointed out, in the long run this may have had as many economic drawbacks as it had short-term political advantages: after all, from Viking bases in one's hinterland came the possibility of hiring their fleet and their army, and from the trading emporia that the Irish-based Vikings developed came wealth. Perhaps in defeating the Vikings, the Uí Néill cut off their own nose to spite their face.[61]

The same was not true for the south. By 860 there seems to have been a Viking military camp at Waterford, whose fleet was destroyed in Osraige that year, while in 862 *longphuirt Rothlaibh*, the encampment of the Viking chief Hróðolfr (which may have been at Dunrally, Co. Laois) was destroyed by the king of Loígis in north-west Leinster.[62] They must also have been making their presence felt in the Shannon Estuary, because they killed the king of Corco Baiscind in south Co. Clare in 864, while Jarl Tomrar (Þórormr) of Luimnech—which at this time may still mean the Shannon Estuary rather than the later Viking base of Limerick—attacked Clonfert from his base in the estuary in 866, and the Foreigners of Luimnech were defeated by the Connachtmen in 887. A Viking fortress at Youghal was destroyed by the Déisi in 866, who followed this victory by killing the chief of the Cork Vikings the following year, while in 868 the king of Uí Bairrche Tíre in south Co. Wexford demolished the *dún* (fortress) of the Foreigners, presumably in his territory, although he died in doing so.

Nevertheless these regular triumphs over the Viking bases did not eliminate them from the south, and in 892 we hear of a battle against the combined Viking forces of Waterford, Wexford and St Mullins (Co. Carlow). And although a major split emerged among the Vikings of Ireland in 893, headed by those of Dublin, which led to a large-scale exodus from the country, they had in fact returned with some force within a year, by now heavily involved in slaving, as when they went to Armagh in 895 and brought 710 people away into captivity.[63]

But a mass expulsion of Vikings was effected by the king of Leinster in 902, when he drove them from their *longphort* at Dublin, and there is no record of Irish-based Viking activity—as opposed to sporadic encounters by Irishmen with Vikings from further afield—for more than a decade, until 914, when a great fleet landed at Waterford and established what would become a permanent base. This was undoubtedly perceived by the Irish as an urgent threat, and heavy emphasis is placed by contemporary writers on both the impact of the Viking restoration and the widespread and concerted Irish opposition they faced, led by the new king of Tara, Niall Glúndub—all the more so after they succeeded in re-establishing themselves at Dublin in 917.

As we have seen, Niall became the first king of Tara to die in battle with Vikings when he was unsuccessful in a critical confrontation with them at Cell Mo-shamhóc (at Islandbridge, near Dublin) in 919, revenge for which was obtained by his successor, Donnchad Donn, at the battle of Tigh-mic-nEthach (in Co. Meath) the following year.[64]

The Irish sources conceive of these conflicts in national terms. The Annals of the Four Masters describe the battle of Cell Mo-shamhóc as a victory 'over the Irish by the Foreigners (*for Ghaoidhealaibh ria n-Gallaibh*)'; the Annals of Ulster have something similar, saying that the heathens won a 'battle at Dublin against the Irish (*Bellum re n-gentibh occ Duiblinn for Goidhelu*)'; and the Annals of Inisfallen paint it as a defeat of 'the men of Ireland (*for firu h-Erend*).' When it was followed within a year by Donnchad Donn's slaying of large numbers of Norse at Tigh-mic-nEthach, the Chronicon Scotorum reports that 'slaughter was inflicted on them so that it was impossible to count them, but there were more Foreigners killed there than Irish killed in the preceding battle.'

Nearly a century was to pass before the Battle of Clontarf, but it is clear that the Irish had already begun to imbue these epic encounters with the Foreigner with more than a tinge of national sentiment, and to conceive of their champion in such contests as a national hero. This, of course, is the mantle that Brian was to assume.

PART I

Brian Boru's world

| THE FAMILY OF BRIAN BORU

W e must not think of Brian Bóraime as a man raised from the dust, a pauper-turned-prince. He was born into nobility. True, as we have seen, the wider dynastic group to which he belonged has a name, the Déisi, that means 'vassalry', but it does not imply non-noble status, merely a position subordinate to the main royal lineages of Munster, the Eóganachta.[1]

THE DÉIS TUAISCIRT
Brian belonged to a branch of the Déisi called Déis Tuaiscirt (Northern Déis), and they get honourable mention in public affairs as far back as the year 680 or thereabouts, when an ordinance was promulgated in west Munster called *Cáin Fhuithirbe* ('Fuithibre's Law'). This contains a catalogue of southern lords, among whom we find 'the king of the Déis Tuaiscirt,' although his name is not given.[2]

Some years later, in 697, a great gathering of the kings and leading churchmen of Ireland, Dál Riata and Pictland was held at Birr (Co. Offaly), at which the *Cáin Adomnáin* ('Adomnán's Law') was put into effect. Otherwise known as the *Lex Innocentium* ('Law of the Innocents'), it was a remarkable measure for protecting non-combatants—women, children, and clerics—from violence and the effects of war by means of a system of fines and guarantors. Included in the list of guarantors are ninety-one senior Irish and Scottish ecclesiastical and secular figures, and among the dozen or so Munster kings listed we find 'Andelaith, king of the Déis Tuaiscirt (*Andelaith rí in Deissi Tuaiscirt*)'.[3] This Andelaith, or Andlid, as the genealogists call him, had a brother who is credited with bestowing Inis Sibthonn (King's Island at Limerick) on St Mainchín or Munchin, which if true would prove that the dynasty ruled that area by the late seventh century.[4] And what the annals for 744 bluntly describe as 'Destruction of Corco Mruad by the Déis (*Foirddbe Corcu Mu Druadh don Deiss*)' was presumably a milestone on the advance of the Déis Tuaiscirt in Co. Clare, as this was the Corco Mruad's homeland. This would explain why Aindlid's grandson Torpaid, who died in the late 760s, is styled in one set of annals *tigherna na n-Déisi* ('lord of the Déisi') and in another *ríg Corc m-Drúad* ('king of Corco Mruad').[5]

UÍ THAIRDELBAIG

But Aindlid and Torpaid were not direct ancestors of Brian (see table 1).[6] They, and no doubt several of their heirs as kings of the Déis Tuaiscirt, were of the branch of the dynasty called Uí Óengusso, descended from Aindlid's great-grandfather Óengus (son of Cáirthenn Finn son of Blat), who lived about the year 600. Instead Brian's people were descended from Óengus's brother Eochu Ballderg, and their lineage name was Uí Thairdelbaig, from an eponym Tairdelbach who lived seven generations before Brian, some time in the eighth century. Tairdelbach had five sons, one of whom was St Flannán of Killaloe, which accounts for the family's patronage of this ecclesiastical site. If these traditions are true, and as Tairdelbach probably lived before the Viking Age, this area—very much the dynasty's later heartland—was presumably theirs already at that time.[7]

From another of Tairdelbach's sons, Mathgamain, the lineage traced its descent, through his son Anlón (see table 2). The latter, the genealogists tell us, had one son, Corcc, who in turn had only one son, Lachtna, who, rather remarkably, also had only one son—showing how fragile a lineage can be—and he was Brian's grandfather, Lorcán.

We do not know when and how Uí Thairdelbaig managed to outmanoeuvre their Uí Óengusso kinsmen and gain the ascendency. One possibility is that the latter were undermined by the Vikings of Limerick. We know from the annals that the year 836 witnessed a 'slaughter of

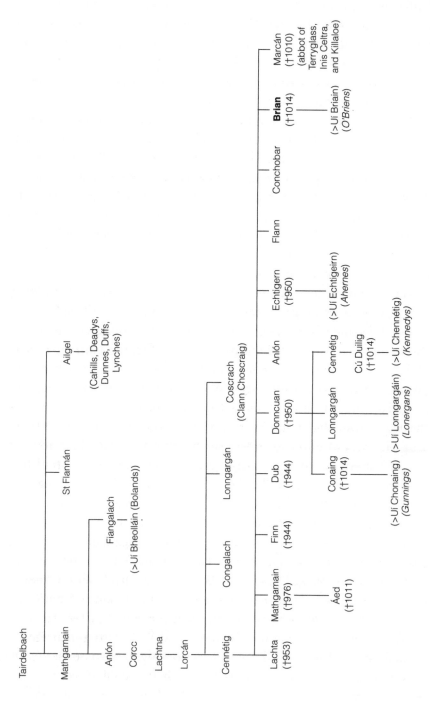

Table 2: Brian's immediate kinsmen of the Uí Thairdelbaig branch of Dál Cais

battle over the Déis Tuaiscirt by the heathens (*Ar catha forsin Dess Tuaisceirt o genntib*),[8] and the pseudo-historical tract called Cogadh Gáedhel re Gallaibh ('The war of the Irish with the Foreigners') places among the events of the following year a revenge victory by the Déis Tuaiscirt on Lough Derg,[9] although Limerick is not specifically mentioned in either account.

By 845, however, there was known to be a Viking fleet operating out of the Shannon Estuary. Its forces raided inland to capture the abbot of Armagh—then making a circuit of the district—at Cluain Comarda (Colmanswell, Co. Limerick) and brought him back a hostage to *longaibh Luimnigh*, the ships in the estuary at or near Limerick.[10] When this later became a permanent base the Viking fortress was on Inis Sibthonn (King's Island), and we have seen that this may previously have belonged to Uí Óengusso (if the tradition of their granting a church site there to St Mainchín is to be believed).

All we can say for certain is that by the time of Brian's grandfather Lorcán or even of his great-grandfather Lachtna the Uí Óengusso were in rapid decline and a transfer of power to Brian's line of the dynasty was in prospect. We can tell this from the very first recorded mention of Uí Thairdelbaig. It is in a version of the Tripartite Life of St Patrick that was possibly written some time after 900 or so, which, in describing Patrick's alleged journeys around Ireland, is careful to include encounters with all the people who matter. It is interesting, therefore, that the account of the saint's journey through north Munster has him at Saingel (Singland, just east of Limerick), where he met a certain Cáirthenn Finn, son of Blat. This man was the father of both Óengus (ancestor of the Uí Óengusso) and Eochu Ballderg (from whom the Uí Thairdelbaig descend).

If the Uí Óengusso were still on top we might expect some mention; instead Cáirthenn Finn is called simply 'ancestor of Clann Tairdelbaig (*sen Clanne Tairdelbaig*)', i.e. the Uí Thairdelbaig. What is more, we are told that before being blessed and baptised by Patrick all Cáirthenn's children were born deformed but that the saint worked a miracle that brought forth Eochu, who was given the nickname *Ballderg* ('red-spot' or 'red-member') in memory of the blood clot from which Patrick created him![11] Obviously, the author is working hard to prove that the rightful kings of the Déis Tuaiscirt are Uí Thairdelbaig.

BRIAN'S EARLIEST KNOWN FAMILY MEMBERS

The earliest members of Brian's family mentioned in the historical record (other than a later genealogy) are Connadar and Ainéislis 'of the Uí Thairdelbaig (*d'Uibh Tairdealbaigh*)', who are said to have been killed at the great battle of Belach Mugna (Ballaghmoon, Co. Carlow) in 908.[12] Brian's grandfather Lorcán was probably the head of the lineage at that point, and Connadar and Ainéislis may have been his siblings (and perhaps they were unknown to later genealogists because of their early death without issue). Belach Mugna was the battle in which the Uí Néill king of Tara, Flann Sinna of Clann Cholmáin, triumphed over the Eóganacht king of Cashel, Cormac mac Cuilennáin, but the Uí Thairdelbaig died fighting on the latter's losing side.

If true, this is potentially significant, because such an association with the Eóganachta might well help to explain how the Uí Thairdelbaig came to displace their Uí Óengusso kinsmen. The problem is that the story of the men's deaths is not preserved in the straightforward annalistic accounts of the battle but rather in the so-called 'Fragmentary' Annals of Ireland, a later narrative in which the bare contemporary record has been much embellished for literary effect. So perhaps we should not read too much into it. Interestingly, though, appended to the annal entry is a poem on the battle that also refers to Connadar and Ainéislis. It is ascribed to Dallán mac Móire, the earliest of the Irish court poets whose work survives in any quantity. He was the *ollam* or chief poet to the Uí Fáeláin king of Leinster, Cerball mac Muirecáin (died 909), and six poems survive that are generally thought to be authentic.[13] If Dallán's poem is genuine it would obviously serve to corroborate the annal account, especially as part of it (though unfortunately not the quatrain referring to Connadar and Ainéislis) is attested elsewhere, being preserved in the Annals of the Four Masters.

THE MAG ADAIR INAUGURATION SITE

As well as listing Connadar and Ainéislis among the dead in the battle at Ballaghmoon, Dallán refers to Connadar as being 'of Mag Adair (*Connadhar din Adhar-mhaigh*)' and to Ainéislis as 'of the Bórama (*Aineslis din Borumha*)'. Mag Adair (Moyare Park) is the plain between Tulla and Quin on which the dynasty's inauguration site was situated, and this flat-topped mound still survives (see plate 7), surrounded by a bank and ditch, not far from which is a stone pillar that may also have played a part in the inauguration of the king.[14] The site also had a sacred tree called a *bile*, which evidently played a role in the fertility rite that was part of the royal inauguration ceremony, during which at a later period, presumably reflecting an ancient ritual, the new king was conferred with a white wand called the 'rod of kingship (*slat na rige*)', which was doubtless cut from the sacred tree.[15]

The significance of this tree as a symbol of sovereignty is evident from enemy attacks on it. In 981, when the king of Tara brought an army south to counter the rising threat from Brian, 'the *bile* of Óenach Maige Adair was cut, after being dug from the earth along with its roots (*bile Aonaigh Maighe h-Adhar do thesccadh iarna tochailt a talmhain cona frémaibh)*,' presumably in an attempt to deny Brian his legitimacy; but another was apparently planted in its place, because we know that seventy years later 'the *bile* of Mag Adair was felled by Áed Ua Conchobair (*Bile Maige Adar do thascrad do Áed h-Ú Chonchobuir*)' when the latter king of Connacht invaded Munster.[16]

The mention in 981 that the sacred tree was in Óenach Maige Adair is also significant, because it shows that Mag Adair was not merely Brian's inauguration place but the site of his dynasty's *óenach*, the meeting-place for the assembly of its inhabitants, where public business was conducted, where the king might promulgate an ordinance in a time of crisis, where sporting contests took place between the communities, and where no doubt a market-place evolved (and thus in later Irish the word *aonach* came to mean a fair or market). Indeed the great Limerick antiquary Thomas Johnson Westropp visited the site in 1891 and reported that even then 'the older peasantry remembered its great meetings, held down to the time of the famine, no doubt a survival of the ancient fair, or merrymaking of Eanagh Magh Adhair.'[17]

BÓRAMA

The Ainéislis who died in 908 is referred to in Dallán's poem as 'of the Bórama (*Aineslis din Borumha*)'. The word *bórama* comes from *bó-rím* or *bó-ríme* ('cattle-counting') and came to mean 'cattle-tribute', but the 'Bórama' of the poem is a place, a place that presumably got its name because it was where cattle offered as tribute were gathered and counted.[18] And the place in question, sometimes called Bórama and sometimes Bél

Bóraime ('the mouth of Bórama', i.e. the entrance to Bórama), is an impressively large ring-fort on the west bank of the Shannon less than 2 km north of Killaloe (see plates 2 and 3). It may have taken its name from the ford at Killaloe on the Shannon (where the bridge is now), which is called Áth na Bóraime (plate 1; map 7), either because it was the ford that cattle-tribute was traditionally brought across or because it was the ford one crossed to get to Bórama. And presumably Ainéislis is referred to in Dallán's poem as 'of the Bórama' because of a belief that he resided in or was associated with the great ring-fort of that name.

This word *bórama*, of course, gives us Brian's famous epithet, generally anglicised as Boru. There has always been a doubt about whether he got the nickname because of a reputation for imposing cattle-tribute or because of an association with the place called Bórama or Bél Bóraime near Killaoe. In other words, is he 'Brian of the cattle-tribute' or 'Brian of Bél Bóraime'? The balance of the evidence favours the latter explanation. There is one piece of evidence that would point to 'Brian of the cattle-tribute', and that is a poem by the great twelfth-century historian and bardic poet Gilla na Náem Ua Duinn (died 1160), which refers to the Battle of Clontarf as 'the battle of Brian of the cattle (*cath Bhriain in buair*)'.[19] Evidently, if he was Brian of a *place* called Bórama rather than a *thing* called *bórama* (i.e. cattle-tribute) the confusion began early!

We must balance Ua Duinn's poetic reference against another in a poem (on the subject of three famous trees of Ireland) that is said to have been written by Brian's famous contemporary Cúán ua Lothcháin (died 1024), a man who would have known Brian well, having served at the court of his rival and predecessor as kigh-king, Máel Sechnaill mac Domnaill. In this poem the author specifically refers to him as 'Brian of Ireland from Bórama (*Brian na Banba a Bórumi*)'.[20] This strikingly parallels the poem ascribed to Dallán mac Móire that described Brian's putative ancestor Ainéislis as 'of the Bórama (*Aineslis din Borumha*)'. The historical tract on Brian called Cogadh Gáedhel re Gallaibh refers to Brian's dynasty as 'Dál Cais of Bórama (*Dail Cais Boruma*)', includes an elegy for Brian's brother Mathgamain in which the latter is styled 'fiery king of Bórama (*rí bruthmar Bóroimhe*)', and specifically includes Bórama among the fortifications of Munster that it claims Brian built (*do ronad ... Boruma*).[21] In an elegy allegedly written for Tadc Ua Cellaig, the king of Uí Maine who died fighting alongside Brian at Clontarf, the

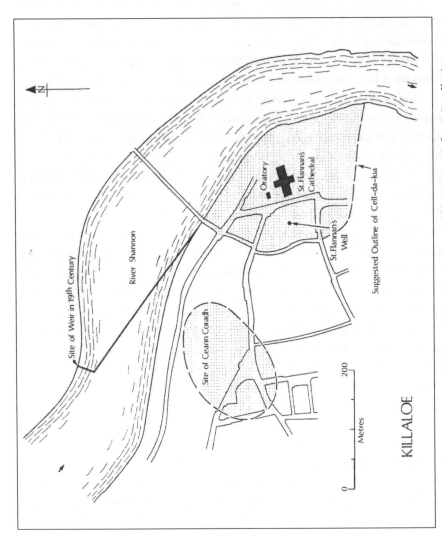

Map 7. Conjectural map of Killaloe and district by the twelfth century (after J. Bradley).

high-king is referred to variously as Brian Bóraime and Brian Bóirne; and as the latter refers to a place, the Burren in Co. Clare, it heightens the chances that the former does likewise, i.e. the ring-fort at Bórama or Bél Bóraime.[22]

If this poem, sometimes ascribed to Muirchertach mac Liacc (died 1014 or 1016), were genuinely of that vintage it would be the earliest occurrence of the famous soubriquet; but there are reasons for doubting it.[23] Likewise, he is called Brian Bóraime in an entry in the Annals of Tigernach for the year 992, but with annals one can never rule out the possibility that they have been tampered with at a later date; at least with a poem it was harder to do this, as the requirement for rhyme and alliteration minimises the opportunities to cut and paste. As against this we can be reasonably confident of the early date of the king-list preserved in the Book of Leinster, attributed to the eleventh-century historian and poet Gilla Cóemáin, which mentions 'the destruction of Brian Bóraime (díbad Briain Boroma)'.[24]

Other evidence suggests that there is every likelihood that Brian did have Bórama as one of his principal residences, along with Cenn Corad (usually anglicised as Kincora), which seems to have been slightly further south, overlooking Killaloe (plate 4; map 7). Bórama occurs as a site of importance as early as 879, when we are told that Flann Sinna, the king of Tara, caused 'the laying waste of Munster, from where Bórama is to Cork (Indreadh Mumhan ó tá Boraimhe co Corcaigh)'.[25] This Bórama may refer to the ford at Killaloe: the boundaries of the dynastic territory as listed in a tract preserved in a famous twelfth-century codex (known by its library shelf-mark as Rawlinson B502) include the area 'from the ford of Bórama, in the east, westwards to Loop Head (óthá Áth mBorrome anair siar co Léim Con-Caulaind)'.[26]

We can see the association of the residences at Bórama and Cenn Corad from, for example, the invasion of Munster that happened in 1116 under the rising king of Connacht, Tairdelbach Ua Conchobair, 'so that he burned and demolished Bórama and Cenn Corad (gur ro loiscc & gur ro mhúr Boromha & Cenn Choradh)'.[27] Little remains of the latter—it is said to have been where the Catholic church in Killaloe now stands—but Bórama is still a magnificent site (plate 3), which was excavated by archaeologists in 1961. Although the site was then (as it still is) heavily overgrown by trees, it was established that it comprised a typical ring-fort or rath, with a circular earthen rampart that was revetted in stone on the outside. A wooden building was unearthed, which measured internally about 4 metres by 2.5 metres, and it had a central hearth.[28] More importantly—in connecting Bórama with Brian's family—a silver coin was found inside this house, and another just outside it, both of which were minted in Dublin in the eleventh century, probably between 1035 and 1070, and were presumably captured or exchanged and brought south to Bórama when it was a residence of Brian's son Donnchad (died 1064) or grandson Tairdelbach (died 1086).[29]

DÁL CAIS

In 934 the death took place of a man called Rebachán mac Mothla, described in the Annals of Inisfallen as 'abbot of Tuamgraney and king of Dál Cais (*abb Tomma Grene & rí Dál Chais*)'. The news is remarkable in a number of ways. It is not particularly surprising that the person in question was both an abbot and a king. In the preceding hundred years or so there had been a series of prominent Eóganachta overkings of Munster who were also in holy orders, beginning perhaps with the celebrated Feidlimid mac Crimthainn (820–47), an ecclesiastic linked to the ascetic Céli Dé movement who variously obtained for himself the abbacies of Cork and Clonfert. Ólchobur mac Cináeda (847–51) of the Eóganacht Áine was king of Cashel and abbot of Emly, as was one of his immediate successors, Cenn Fáelad ua Mugthigirn (859–72) of Eóganacht Airthir Chliach. Cormac mac Cuilennáin (902–8) was famously both a bishop and king of Cashel, and his successor, the Múscraige king Flaithbertach mac Inmainén (914–22), was abbot of Inis Cathaig (Scattery Island) and the last king of Cashel to be in holy orders.[30]

So the fact that the Rebachán who died in 934 could hold down the abbacy of Tuamgraney and the dynastic kingship is not without precedent. What is new is his royal style, 'king of Dál Cais (*rí Dál Chais*)'. This term Dál Cais ('the share of Cas') survives in no earlier record. It is a term that would for ever afterwards be associated with Brian Bóraime and his descendants and with the area of north Munster from which he hailed, but—so far as we can tell—it is an entirely new concoction coined at this time for the peoples who were previously known as the Déis Tuaiscirt. They took their new name from a supposed ancestor called Cas or Cass, who was the fecund father of thirteen fecund sons, including Blat, father of Cáirthenn Finn, father of both Eochu Ballderg (from whom Brian's lineage of Uí Thairdelbaig descend) and Óengus (from whom their collateral rivals Uí Óengusso descend). From Blat and his busy brothers—collectively, Dál Cais—a whole army of conquering aristocrats claimed descent (table 1).

What is more, learned antiquaries of the kind who worked up this theory—no doubt to serve a political rather than a genuine historical purpose—went one step further and suggested that from the Cas who spawned Dál Cais it was but a hop, skip and jump back to an ancestor called Cormac Cas. This Cormac, it was now propounded, was one of the seven sons (there were a dozen others by other wives) that Ailill Ólum had with his wife Sadb. Sadb was the daughter of Conn Cétchathach, ancestor of the Connachta and Uí Néill. Such a pedigree in the female line brought no demonstrable legal or lordly advantage, but it was a nice injection of blue blood all the same. More importantly, Ailill Ólum was the founder of most of the leading royal lines of Munster. The Eógan Már who gave us the Eóganachta was his son; and now, by this newly fabricated theory, Cormac Cas, the supposed ancestor of Brian and his family, 'became' one of the many brothers of Eógan Már, on a par with the aristocrats who had ruled Munster since the dawn of history.

These are bold statements, and evidently they were concocted on behalf of the people who now called themselves Dál Cais for one purpose and one purpose only: to demonstrate that they were just as entitled as the Eóganachta to rule Munster.[31]

THE BREAKTHROUGH OF BRIAN'S FAMILY

In the 920s there seems to be a new vibrancy to Viking activity on the doorstep of Dál Cais. The Cogadh records that Þórormr (Tomrar) son of Helgi, 'king of an immense fleet (*rig longes adbalmor*)', took possession of Inis Sibthonn (King's Island) at Limerick and ravaged the greater part of Munster.[32] The annals—a version of which the author of the Cogadh is using—also tell us that in 922 this *jarl* of the Foreigners was 'on the Shannon Estuary (*Tomrair mc. Elgi, iarla do Gallaib, for Lumnech*),' that he plundered the islands on Lough Derg, including Inis Celtra (the Cogadh adding that they 'drowned its shrines, relics and books' and then attacked Terryglass, Lorrha, and Clonfert) and then sailed further up the Shannon and burned Clonmacnoise, proceeding on to Lough

Ree to ravage its islands, doing likewise in Uí Néill territory in Mide (and, the Cogadh says, in south Connacht), 'and took great booty in gold, silver and much treasure' back to the Shannon Estuary.[33]

It is at this point that the author of the Cogadh inserts his famous remarks about the *jarl* Óttarr the Black (Oittir Dub), who came with a hundred ships to Waterford and ravaged east and south Munster, put all 'under tribute and service to the Foreigners (*fo chain ocus fo geillsine gall uile iad*)' and levied his 'royal rent (*a chios riogda*)', so that

> the whole of Munster became filled with immense floods and countless sea-vomitings of ships and boats and fleets, so that there was not a harbour nor a landing-port nor a *dún* nor a fortress nor a fastness in all Munster without fleets of Danes and Foreigners (*loingeas Danmarccach ocus allmurach*) . . . And assuredly the evil which Ireland had hitherto suffered was as nothing compared to the evil inflicted by these parties. The entire of Munster, without distinction, was plundered by them on all sides and devastated. And they spread themselves over Munster and built *dúna* and fortresses and landing-ports over all Ireland, so that there was no place in Ireland without numerous fleets of Danes and Foreigners; so that they made spoil-land and sword-land and conquered-land of her throughout her breadth and generally; and they ravaged her *túatha* and her privileged churches and her sacred places; and they rent her shrines, and her reliquaries, and her books . . .
>
> In short, until the sand of the sea or the grass of the field or the stars of heaven are counted, it will not be easy to recount or to enumerate or to relate what the Gaídil all, without distinction, suffered from them: whether men or women, boys or girls, lay or clerics, freemen or serfs, old or young—indignity, outrage, injury, and oppression. In a word, they killed kings and lords, royal heirs, and the royal princes of Ireland. They killed the brave and the valiant, and the stout warriors, champions, and soldiers, and young lords, and the greater part of the heroes and warriors of the entire Gaídil; and they brought them under tribute and servitude; they reduced them to bondage and slavery. Many were the blooming, lively women, and the modest, mild, comely maidens, and the pleasant, noble, stately, blue-eyed young women, and the gentle, well brought up youths,

and the intelligent, valiant champions, whom they carried off into oppression and bondage over the broad green sea . . .[34]

Obviously we must take this with an even larger pinch of salt than usual, given that the sole purpose of this stirring overture is to set the scene for what follows, namely that Munster, and indeed Ireland, needed Brian's family to ride to the rescue. The Cogadh tells us:

There was, however, a certain gracious, noble, high-born, beautiful sept in Ireland, who never submitted to tyranny or oppression or unwonted injury from any other sept in the world, namely, the descendants of Lugaid son of Óengus Tírech [great-grandson of Cormac Cas], who are called Dál Cais of Bórama, one of the two pillars [along with the Eóganachta] of the nobility, and one of the two houses that always sustained the rule and sovereignty of Ireland . . . It was not therefore honourable to the mind or to the courage or to the nature of these . . . champions . . . who never brooked injustice or tyranny from any king of the kings of Ireland (and, not only that, but who never gave them pledges or hostages in token of obedience), to submit of their own accord to cruel slavery from Danes and from fierce, hard-hearted marauders.[35]

This is nothing short of propaganda on behalf of Brian's dynasty, but it contains at least one small germ of truth: Brian's immediate family did break through into the headlines at this very moment; and if they did not save the Irish from the heathen oppressor perhaps we can at least surmise that there is nonetheless some link, and that part of the explanation for the rise of Brian's family lies in their success in exploiting this new Viking energy for their own ends.

When they did come to the fore, in the 930s, their advance was dramatic and bloody. The abbot of Tuamgraney, Rebachán mac Mothla, who died as king of Dál Cais in 934, does not seem to have been a member of Brian's lineage of Uí Thairdelbaig: according to a later source he belonged to a branch of Uí Óengusso called Uí Chernaig.[36] But although his three predecessors in the kingship were also of Uí Óengussa, they were of a different branch. This suggests that Uí Óengussa were splitting into competing lines, and we must assume that what happened next is to be interpreted as Brian's family seizing their opportunity. In the same year that Rebachán died the annals report that his son Dub Gilla was killed in treachery by Congalach son of Lorcán (*Duibhghiolla mac Robacáin, tighearna Ua Corbmaic, do mharbhadh la Congalach mac Lorcáin trí tangnacht*).[37] The culprit here was one of the four sons—Cennétig, Coscrach, Lonngargán, and Congalach—of Brian's grandfather Lorcán (table 2), and evidently they were murderously paving their way to power.

Having performed the assassination, nothing much became of Congalach, but each of his brothers went on to found substantial lineages. Cennétig, of course, enjoys a place of honour in the history books as the father of Brian (and of other sons who went on to found successful lines of their own). But two other prestigious lineages of Dál Cais—Clann Choscraig and Uí Lonngargáin (unless the latter spring from Lonngargán, son of Brian's brother Donncuan)—traced their descent from the other two sons of Lorcán. This suggests—bearing in mind that any preferment among this sprawling family was soon to be swallowed up by the large and successful brood of Cennétig—that Coscrach's and Lonngargán's offspring were building on foundations laid before Cennétig's sons came of age. So the great leap forward for Brian's family would seem to have come about at a time when his grandfather Lorcán had sons who were politically active and before Cennétig's sons elbowed them aside.

BRIAN'S FATHER

If we were to believe the later king-lists it was only when Rebachán mac Mothla died in 934 that Lorcán himself succeeded as king of Dál Cais; but that seems rather late, given that within a very few years it is clear that his oldest son, Cennétig—Brian's father—is well and truly in charge. Another late source, *An Leabhar Muimhneach*, claims that Cennétig, who died in 951, had a reign of forty years—not that we can place much trust in this.[38] What little we know for certain of Cennétig shows us a man capable of mingling on the national stage. He took as his wife Bébinn, daughter of Aurchad son of Murchad, king of Iar-Chonnachta, to the west of Lough Corrib (it is from her nephew and Brian's first cousin Flaithbertach that the great dynasty of Uí Fhlaithbertaig or O'Flaherty descends).[39] Such a marriage indicates a political preoccupation—on the assumption that all such aristocratic alliances were political—focused as yet on the western seaboard.

With Bébinn (and with other unidentified wives) Cennétig had twelve sons (table 2), five of whom produced heirs (Brian, Mathgamain, Donncuan, Echthigern and Anlón) and seven of whom did not. From genealogies we know the names of Lachtna, Finn, Dub and Marcán; and another two, Flann and Conchobar, Brian's only full brothers, are recorded in the eleventh- and twelfth-century text called *Banshenchas* ('Lore of Women'), while the name of the final son is unknown.

Cennétig presumably also had a number of daughters, but we know of only one. Her name was Órlaith, and what we know is extraordinary. The *Banshenchas* includes her as one of the wives of the king of Tara, Donnchad Donn (died 944), son of Flann Sinna, but only the annals known as Chronicon Scotorum inform us that she met her death in 941 when Donnchad had her executed for sleeping with Óengus, his son from another marriage (*Orlaith ingen Cinneididh meic Lorcáin do bas la Donnchadh mac Flainn rí Eirenn iarna liudh for Aongus for mac*).[40]

This is the first time one of Brian's siblings appears in a contemporary record, and it is not a very auspicious beginning, but it does help to cast some light on these early stages of their ascent to national prominence. This kind of official execution is a rare phenomenon, and we must assume that it took place because Órlaith's offence was considered a grave slight to the high-king. The fact that she was killed rather than quietly repudiated does rather suggest that her life was taken because she was expendable, her family being of low rank relative to the king of Tara, and is therefore an indication that, although Brian's family had been rising through the ranks, they had some way to go. Órlaith may in fact have been a secondary wife or concubine to the high-king, given the prevalence of polygamy among Irish aristocrats. Her execution was in 941, and the last of Donnchad's four known wives died two years later, in 943, when she was at least in her fifties, which would suggest that the marriage took place years earlier, she perhaps being the senior wife at court when Órlaith arrived. If so, such secondary status would again point to the continuing subordinate role of Brian's family beyond their own locality.

Still, notwithstanding its ignominious end, the very fact that Donnchad Donn had taken a Dál Cais princess in marriage was an acknowledgement that Brian's family was in the ascendant.[41]

The marriage had presumably been intended to cement an alliance between the king of Tara and Órlaith's father, Cennétig. And the probable motivation for such an alliance was mutual animosity to the Eóganacht king of Munster, Cellachán Caisil (died 954), who had come to prominence in the late 930s, at precisely the same time as Cennétig. Cellachán had sacked the Uí Néill-sponsored monastery of Clonmacnoise in 936 and three years later plundered Uí Néill territory as far as Clonard, which prompted the king of Tara to invade Munster in 940 and take Cellachán's hostages; perhaps Donnchad Donn linked up with Cennétig of Dál Cais on that campaign, and the latter's daughter Órlaith may have been married off to the high-king as part of her father's diplomacy.

But Cellachán Caisil seems to have quickly reneged on his submission, because in 941 there was another Uí Néill invasion of Munster, which led to his capture and imprisonment. Cellachán was also at war in these years with Osraige and with the Déisi of south-east Munster,[42] and it is not hard to imagine Cennétig and his sons making the most of Cellachán's distractions by fomenting trouble for him and putting themselves forward as an alternative focus for the loyalties of the Munstermen.

We must conclude, therefore, that there was much going on behind the scenes in these years, of which we get only the occasional dramatic glimpse. Such was the case, for example, in 944 when we read in the Annals of Ulster that 'the battle of Gort Rotacháin was won by Cellachán against Tuadmumu, and many fell in it.'[43] This is surely the same confrontation that the Four Masters intend when they report for this year that 'a victory was gained by Cellachán Caisil, over Cennétig son of Lorcán, at Mag Dúin, where many were slain,' a calamity that lived so long in the memory of Dál Cais that when the great genealogical collections were being assembled two centuries later the list of Cennétig's sons lacks the names of some of those who died young but remembers that Finn and Dub 'were killed in the slaughter of Mag Dúin (*ro marbait i n-ár Maige Dúine*).'[44] We do not know where either Gort Rotacháin or Mag Dúin were—presumably the *gort* or cultivated field of Rotachán was somewhere in the *mag* or plain of Dún—but we can take it that this considerable setback for Cennétig denoted Cellachán's riposte to the challenge the Dál Cais king had begun to pose.

For that reason, despite the unhappy outcome for Cennétig and his family, we can nevertheless reckon it a mark of their arrival on centre-stage. For one thing, Cellachán Caisil, the Eóganacht overking of Munster, was at war with Dál Cais only because they had become at best errant vassals and at worst a threat to his kingship. (To the annalistic evidence we can add the less trustworthy testimony of *An Leabhar Muimhneach* that the Dál Cais under Cennétig defeated Cellachán in a battle at Inis Locha Saingleann, or Singland, near Limerick.[45])

More importantly, while the account of the Battle of Mag Dúin specifically cites Cellachán's opponents as Cennétig and his family, the account of what is probably the same event but under the alternative name of Gort Rotacháin has Cellachán doing battle with Tuadmumu. This is the first use of the term Tuadmumu ('North Munster', anglicised Thomond) in the annals.[46] A version of the Tripartite Life of St Patrick may have been written about this time, and it too has Cennétig's lineage of Uí Thairdelbaig ruling Tuadmumu.[47] It seems clear that the term was coined to designate the area over which Cennétig's family had lately come to hold sway, an area considerably greater than that of their dynastic lands, and it undoubtedly indicates that within Munster a regional rival had emerged to challenge the hegemony of the Eóganachta.

We have seen that the men of learning sometimes thought of Munster as being divided into five fifths (north, south, east, west and middle), and by that scheme the fifth of Tuadmumu over which Cennétig now held sway would not count for much (see map 6). But it was more common to view Munster as having only two parts; and, as we noted earlier, while in the early centuries the distinction was between east and west, this changed—because of the emergence of Dál Cais—to a north-south split. By the twelfth century it was normal to speak of 'the two provinces' of Munster, Tuadmumu and Desmumu (Thomond and Desmond), the former dominated by the descendants of Cennétig and Brian, the Uí Briain (O'Briens), the latter by Cellachán Caisil's descendants, the Meic Carthaig (MacCarthys). Evidently the reference to the victory of Cellachán 'over Tuadmumu (*for Tuathmumain*)' in 944 marks the emergence of this schism.

Perhaps it is for this reason that the twelfth-century tract known as *Caithréim Chellacháin Chaisil* ('The battle-career of Cellachán of Cashel'), which seeks to elevate the latter's successors, the Meic Carthaig, by emphasising the martial achievements of their ancestor Cellachán, nevertheless concedes that he and Cennétig came to share the kingship of Munster between them. According to the *Caithréim*, when 'the great hosts of the two provinces of Munster (*mor-shocraite dha choiced Muman*)' had gathered together to elect a king they were about to choose between Cennétig of Dál Cais and a certain Donnchad of Eóganacht Glendamnach, according to a system of rotation whereby the kingship of Munster was shared between the Dál Cais and the Eóganachta. 'The most senior man of the free kindreds (*an fer ba sine dona saer-clannaib*)' would succeed, and 'if the overking was of the Eóganachta, the position of heir-apparent would be held by Dál Cais (*Damad do Clainn Eogain in t-airdri in tanaistecht do clainn Cormaic Cais*),' and vice versa, but neither would succeed unless he were 'the best in knowledge and true learning, and princely honour (*bhudh fhearr fis & fir-leigenn & flaith-einech*).' At this point, however, Cellachán's mother intervened and reminded them of the rotation agreement that the ancestor of Dál Cais had made with his counterpart of the Eóganchta, adding that 'there is of Clann Eógain [the Eóganachta] a man more senior in age and knowledge than you, Cennétig, and he is a king in figure and appearance (*ata do Clainn Eogain fear as sine dh' aeis & dh' fis ina thusa a Cheinnédig & is ri ar deilbh & ar denam h-e*).' When Cennétig asked who she meant, she replied that it was Cellachán. Cennétig then retired from the gathering, but he would not 'break his brotherhood (*a bhrathairsi do bhriseadh*)' with the Eóganachta; both he and the other Eóganacht candidate withdrew from the contest because only the Vikings would prosper from a dispute over succession.

This, the Caithréim claims, is how Cellachán became king, and having waged war on the Vikings he went to Cashel (plate 11), where Cennétig and the nobles of Dál Cais already were, whereupon Cennétig 'was given the office of heir-apparent of Munster (*tucadh tanaisdeact Muman do*) and its kingship after Cellachán (*& a righi tar eis Ceallachain*).'[48]

Now, we know that until the middle of the tenth century the Eóganachta had reigned supreme in Munster, and therefore this myth that they had traditionally shared power with Dál Cais must be a creation of the latter. Indeed it occurs in the Dál Cais genealogies in the twelfth-century codex called Rawlinson B502,[49] and gets perhaps its first and most eloquent iteration in the Cogadh (which the author of *Caithréim Chellacháin* had undoubtedly read):

To them [Dál Cais] belonged the lead in entering an enemy's country, and the rear on returning; and besides this they had an equal inherited right to Cashel, viz., every alternate king in Cashel (*comduchus cirt Casil cach arfecht doibsin iarsin, i. cach re rí i Caisiul*). Whenever these conditions were not justly observed to them the king of Cashel had no legal claim to anything from them.[50]

At first sight, therefore, it seems surprising to find this Dál Cais claim to parity being conceded by the author of *Caithréim Chellacháin Chaisil*—which is, after all, a twelfth-century document written with a pro-Eóganacht agenda. But it is a testimony to the success of Dál Cais that the Eóganachta were forced to swallow their pride and accept this Dál Cais myth of their long-standing greatness. What, therefore, the author of *Caithréim Chellacháin* is doing in the passages above is accepting the reality of the Eóganachta's fall and of Dál Cais's pre-eminence and, on the principle that half a loaf is better than none, taking the opportunity to remind the descendants of Cennétig, the Uí Briain, that they should reciprocate and share Munster with Cellachán's heirs, the Meic Carthaig. The underlying premise, however, is that Dál Cais's greatness is to be traced back to the reign of Cennétig.

CENNÉTIG'S ACHIEVEMENT
We must therefore credit Cennétig mac Lorcáin with the establishment of Dál Cais as one of the two great provincial powers in Munster. *An Leabhar Muimhneach*, for what it is worth, describes him as the first king of Dál Cais to lead an army beyond his own territory, and mentions an expedition as far as Athlone (presumably by means of the Shannon), which led to a month-long assault on the Connachtmen.[51] Even if that particular episode is a fable, Cennétig may nevertheless have been able to make hay to the north, because of a crisis among the Uí Néill in those years. In 943 the death took place of the high-king Donnchad Donn of the Southern Uí Néill dynasty of Clann Cholmáin (Cennétig's son-in-law for a time until, as we have seen, he had his Dál Cais wife executed for adultery). His death propelled Clann Cholmáin into an upheaval that lasted for thirty years and involved no fewer than seven men enjoying seven brief and violent reigns as king of Mide until the emergence of the great Máel Sechnaill II in the mid-970s.

The removal of Donnchad Donn's iron fist—which had battered heavily on Munster—and the paralysis that gripped Mide thereafter surely allowed Cennétig's family unprecedented room for manoeuvre. Clann Cholmáin's centre of gravity was, after all, the western part of the present-day counties of Westmeath and Offaly, making them Dál Cais's near neighbours (and nearer neighbours still because of their competing exploitation of the Shannon passageway), especially as Dál Cais began to expand east of the Shannon into north-east Tipperary.

For many years Donnchad Donn's position as king of Tara had been coming under challenge from his Northern Uí Néill counterpart, the Cenél nEógain king of Ailech, Muirchertach na Cochall Craicinn, son of Niall Glúndub. Even while Donnchad lived, Muirchertach took an active interest in southern affairs, and indeed it was he who led more than one spectacular Uí Néill invasion of Munster towards the end of Donnchad's life (campaigns that later entered into Muirchertach's dynastic folk memory).[52] There was every expectation, therefore, that Muirchertach would succeed Donnchad Donn as king of Tara, which would have entailed further pressure on Munster; but in fact he predeceased the high-king by about a year or so when caught in a skirmish with the Norse of Dublin in 943. Therefore, when Donnchad Donn died there was no outstanding candidate for supremacy among the dominant lines, and the kingship of Tara was seized by Congalach Cnogba ('of Knowth') of the Southern Uí Néill dynasty of Síl nÁedo Sláine, none of whose ancestors had held the honour in more than two centuries; and Congalach's position as high-king was consolidated following the defeat and death in 950 of his northern challenger Ruaidrí ua Canannáin at the hands of the Dublin Norse under their king, Amlaíb Cuarán.

Congalach's ancestral kingdom of northern Brega in the Boyne Valley was a long way from that of Cennétig of Dál Cais, and yet no sooner had his position as king of Tara been secured than he committed himself to pursuit of the old Uí Néill goal of dominance over the Leth Moga (the southern half of Ireland) by invading Munster. In 950, we are told, Congalach led 'a hosting into Munster, so that he plundered Iarmumu.' This is the Co. Kerry area of west Munster, and so it is very surprising (unless Iarmumu is a mistake for Tuadmumu) to find that the most significant outcome of the assault was the killing of two of Cennétig's sons, Echtigern, progenitor of the Uí Echtigeirn or Ahernes, and

Donncuan, from whose sons we get families such as the Uí Chennétig (O'Kennedys), perhaps Uí Lonngargáin (O'Lonergans), and certainly Uí Chélechair (O'Kellehers) and Uí Ríacáin (O'Reagans).[53] Whether the invasion in 950 was of west or north Munster it was a direct challenge by the Uí Néill king of Tara to Cennétig's family and is remarkable testimony to the hostility between them.

The latter were surely the intended targets therefore when, in the following year, Congalach appeared with the full fleet of Leth Cuinn (the northern half of Ireland) on Lough Derg in the Shannon—very much Cennétig's back yard—and 'plundered all the islands of the lake, and obtained hostages and sway over Munster, after some opposition (*ro oirgset dno uile innsedha an locha & ro gabhsat geill & neart Mumhan iar na frith-bheirt friú*).'[54]

At some point in the same year Cennétig died, and it is fascinating to see the range of titles bestowed on him in the annals (assuming they have not been tampered with at a later date, which is always a possibility). Chronicon Scotorum calls him 'king of Dál Cais (*rí Dáil cCais*)'. The Annals of Ulster go one step further in geographical extent and call him 'king of Tuadmumu (*ri Tuathmuman*)'. But the Munster set called the Annals of Inisfallen applies the most ambitious style yet awarded to a member of Brian's family, recording simply '*Mors Cennétig m. Lorcain, rígdamna Cassil* (the death of Cennétig son of Lorcán, the *rígdamna* of Cashel)'.

Cashel in this context means the kingship of Munster. *Rígdamna* is a term that might on occasion mean nothing more than that a person was worthy of the kingship, but for this period it has been shown to be quite a technical term. When the kingship was held by the head of one dynastic line the term *rígdamna* was frequently applied to the head of the main, usually competing, dynastic line not in possession of the kingship.[55] If, therefore, the entry in the Annals of Inisfallen is contemporary it is a remarkable statement of the heights to which Cennétig had brought his lineage. This petty chieftain from Co. Clare had earned the honour of being the province's *rígdamna* because he had made his lineage the leading dynastic group not then in possession of the kingship. He was therefore worthy of being overking of all Munster, and his dynasty had an undeniably valid claim to the kingship should the opportunity to stake it arise.

LACHTNA MAC CENNÉTIG

Cennétig may have greatly advanced the fortunes of his lineage, but it was by no means plain sailing from this point onwards. The Cogadh—although written more than a hundred years later—claims that Cennétig was slain (*marbad*), as does the king-list in the twelfth-century Book of Leinster.[56] And although we are not told by whom, the context of the Cogadh's mention of it, in a list of Irish heroes who fell at Norse hands, suggests that the Vikings of Limerick played some part.[57] What seems to have happened then is that Cennétig's son Lachtna succeeded him in the kingship (although Lachtna is not given a royal style in the annals), who in turn was dead within two years, struck down by enemies of the family. The twelfth-century genealogies say that Lachtna was slain by Uí Flaind, and *An Leabhar Muimhneach* adds to them the Uí Chernaig.[58] Both were rival branches of Dál Cais, and the death of Lachtna at their hands therefore shows that Brian's family were by no means safe from competing aspirants to the kingship.

If Lachtna had lived he would no doubt have headed the family for a great many years, and his younger brother Brian would have been but a trusty lieutenant, but it was not to be so. Instead it is Lachtna who has all but vanished from history. When the genealogists were recalling the family tree of his father, Cennétig, a couple of centuries later the only additional detail they thought to record (apart from Lachtna's accession to the kingship after Cennétig's death and his murder at the hands of the Uí Flaind) was that there was still a place named after him, Grianán Lachtnai in Craicliath. This is now the townland of Craglea, near which the ring-fort of Bórama is situated (plate 8), and so presumably the *grianán* (which can mean a sun room or a bower or perhaps a sunny green) was a residence Lachtna had built for himself beside the main family fortress—perhaps it was built before his succession while his father was still alive and occupying nearby Bórama. In the early twentieth century the great Limerick antiquary Thomas Johnson Westropp published a detailed description of what he considered to be the site. At that date, he said, it was still known to local people as 'Greenaun'.[59]

MATHGAMAIN MAC CENNÉTIG

Fortunately for the dynasty, Lachtna's death led to no great crisis, because there were still at least three of Cennétig's dozen sons alive and able to step into the breach. One of these was Marcán, who indeed was to live for more than another half-century. He, however, was, or was to become, a churchman, who was temporarily installed as abbot of Emly in 990 and when he died in 1010 was described as 'head of the clergy of Munster (*cend cléireach Mumhan*)', by which point he was the pluralist abbot of Terryglass, near the north-eastern corner of Lough Derg, and of Inis Celtra (Holy Island) on the lough, and of the family's home church of Killaloe.[60] Presumably he had embraced the clerical life early and was not in the running to succeed Lachtna (although we have seen that it was not unheard of in Munster for men in holy orders to assume the kingship). If Marcán was the youngest of the three remaining sons, the middle one was undoubtedly Brian, who had to bide his time again as the kingship went to another of the brothers, Mathgamain.

Mathgamain got a lucky opportunity within months of his accession because of the death of the king of Munster, Cellachán Caisil, causing the Eóganacht overkingship to descend in a tailspin from which it never recovered. Although the Uí Chellacháin (O'Callaghans) take their name from him, and he was the direct ancestor too of the more successful Meic Carthaig (MacCarthys), descended from his great-grandson Carthach, Cellachán's immediate successors in the kingship of Cashel were ephemeral characters. Over the next decade four Eóganacht dynasts held the kingship in rapid succession, but all died violently, at least three of them at the hands of kinsmen.[61] The last of them was Cellachán's son Donnchad, whose grasp of the kingship was so faltering that he is not included in the lists of the kings of Cashel that have come down to us.[62] At the time of his death in 963, however, he was called 'king of Cashel' by the annalists, and even the author of the Cogadh, always anxious to exaggerate Dál Cais's claim to kingship, nonetheless has their enemy Donnchad as king.[63]

So Mathgamain can have become king of Cashel only at some point after Donnchad mac Cellacháin's death in 963, as the Eóganacht were dissolving into confusion. But if this calamity provided circumstances conducive to Mathgamain's rise to power, still the achievement was his. Although later overshadowed by his remarkable younger brother, Brian, Mathgamain mac Cennétig was no lightweight.

We know nothing about the early years of Mathgamain's active career, from 953 onwards, as head of his family and of the wider Dál Cais. Given that his brother and perhaps his father before him were murdered by internal dynastic rivals, these must have been years of bare survival. In fact it is only in 959 that he appears in the historical record at all, and yet by then he was in outwardly aggressive mode, launching an attack on the monastery of Clonmacnoise (presumably a waterborne assault from the Shannon).

Clonmacnoise, like all the great churches of the age, was a heavily politicised institution. Previously it had been closely aligned with the Clann Cholmáin kings of Mide, but it was now coming under the sway of the Síl Muiredaig of Uí Briúin Aí—at least it was now where their royal family chose to be buried, the family that would soon emerge, bearing the surname Ua Conchobair (O'Connor), as the most potent in Connacht. Whoever Mathgamain's aggression was aimed against it was certainly no mundane attack on a monastery but rather an offensive against a political opponent under whose protection Clonmacnoise then was. It therefore shows us that Mathgamain mac Cennétig was beginning to make an impact. What is more, we are told that the assault on Clonmacnoise was by Mathgamain 'and by the men of Munster (*& lá Fiora Mumhan*),'[64] the implication being that he was leader of the Munstermen by that time. He might not yet be king of Munster, strictly speaking; but the same year had seen the assassination of the latest Eóganacht claimant, Dub-dá-Bairenn (957–9), who was replaced by the very obscure Fergráid (959–61), who in turn was felled by his own kin, and it is certain that Mathgamain was exploiting their powerlessness in order to make inroads for himself by offering the men of Munster charismatic new leadership.

It is perhaps relevant that it is only at the death of the fourth of these weak Eóganacht overkings, Donnchad mac Cellacháin (961–3), that Mathgamain once more crops up in the headlines, and again he is at war with Shannonside opponents to the north. The king of Uí Briúin Bréifne, Fergal ua Ruairc—from whose grandfather Ruarc (died 898) the great lineage of Uí Ruairc (O'Rourkes) descends—had earlier secured the overkingship of Connacht, and now in 963 he triumphed over the Munstermen in a battle that took place on the Shannon at Catinchi, an island on the river to the south of Clonmacnoise.[65] Another source calls this a 'slaughter of the Tuadmumu on the Shannon, and they abandoned their vessels and were drowned.'[66] Having defeated the Munster forces there, Fergal continued south and ravished Dál Cais territory (*Dal Cais do orccain lais iarsin*).[67] The Four Masters seem to be weaving together two different records of these events, because, having told us about this raid, they add an account—as if it were a separate incident—of a slaughter inflicted by Fergal on Mathgamain, in which the latter lost 140 men, including 'three uí Lorcáin (*dú i t-torchair tri h-ui Lorcáin & secht fichet impu*).'[68] The Lorcán in question was Mathgamain's grandfather, whose three slain *uí* (grandsons) were of course Mathgamain's brothers or first cousins.

The later pro-Dál Cais source called *An Leabhar Muimhneach* also records a clash between Mathgamain and Fergal ua Ruairc, but if they are referring to the same event they manage to convert it into a great victory for Mathgamain.[69] Either way, the battle of Catinchi is significant for a number of reasons. It is evidence for the vitality of the Shannon, which was a contact highway for the province-kings. The manoeuvrability it offered made it possible to fight inter-provincial wars, and it is likely that the adoption by the Irish of shipbuilding craftsmanship and naval systems introduced by the Vikings led to a more intensive exploitation of the country's waterways. Surely Mathgamain and his family were rising to prominence at this point precisely because they had made themselves masters of the Shannon's potential.

Also, the site of the battle demonstrates that Mathgamain had ventured north out of his own territory, as he had done four years earlier, in 959, and this suggests that he had stabilised his power base at home. And, again, the battle was thought of as a contest between the king of Connacht and the Munstermen: Fergal ua Ruairc secured a *maidhm . . . for Muimhnechaibh* ('rout of the Munstermen'); and here again we see Mathgamain perhaps not yet formally king of the province but certainly its *de facto* overlord.

MATHGAMAIN AND THE KINGSHIP OF CASHEL

It seems to have been shortly after the death of Donnchad mac Cellacháin in 963 that Mathgamain made his bid for the overkingship of the province. The Cogadh, which thus far has been little more than a litany of Viking raids on Irish monasteries (assiduously culled, in rough chronological order, from the annals),[70] suddenly becomes specific about Norse activity on the doorstep of Brian's family. We are told that

a certain Ímar ua hÍmair (Ívarr grandson of Ívarr) had established a
Norse base on Inis Sibthonn (King's Island) at Limerick, from which the
Norse forced the Munstermen into abject servitude. But, we are told, in
the year following the death of Donnchad mac Cellacháin, Mathgamain
assembled the Dál Cais to ask advice on whether he should make war
on the Norse—because it pretends that his blatant usurpation of the
Eóganachta's kingship was a patriotic war against the Foreigners—
and of course his people said that 'they preferred meeting death and
destruction and annihilation and violence in defending the freedom of
their patrimony, and of their race, rather than submit to the tyranny
and oppression of Foreigners (*allmarach*), or abandon their country
and their lands to them.'[71]

Mathgamain agreed to do as they advised and leapt into action; but
what the Cogadh describes is not a war on Vikings but his agreeing to

> go to Cashel of the Kings, and to the Eóganacht also, for that was the
> chief residence of Munster, and the principal seat of the descendants
> of Ailill; very properly too, for it was the Ailech of Munster and the
> Tara of Leth Moga. It was also the place of their [Dál Cais's] origin and
> their ancient birthright. He said that it was better and more righteous
> to do battle and combat for their inheritance, and for their native
> right, than for land acquired by conquest and the sword; and that
> though they must necessarily sustain labour or loss in defence of the
> freedom of the chief seat of Munster, and the two sustaining pillars
> [the Eóganachta and Dál Cáis] of the government and sovereignty of
> Ireland, it was for that they ought to contend and seek.[72]

As we have seen, this assertion of Dál Cais entitlement to the
kingship of Cashel is baseless; but notwithstanding this we are told that
the Dál Cais army then invaded the territory of the Eóganachta—but
only to free it from the tyranny of the Norse. We are told that they
marched eastwards and were joined by the local Eóganachta and the
people called the Múscraige, 'from Dún na Sciath to Belach Achaille', i.e.
from Donaskeagh, about 13 km west of Cashel, to Ballycahill, which lies
about 20 km further north, just west of Thurles.[73] Then Mathgamain
went to Cashel and camped at Dún Cuirc, presumably on the Rock
(plate 11), and 'great plunders and ravages and conflicts were effected

by them on all sides throughout Munster, wherever the Foreigners and their people were.'

Opposition to Mathgamain was led, the Cogadh would have us believe, not by the Eóganachta but by Ímar ua hÍmair of Limerick, whom it depicts as 'chief king of the Foreigners of Munster and of the Irish at that time (*ardri Gall Muman ocus Goedel in tan sin*) . . . after his having made all Munster tribute-giving and hostage-giving to the Foreigners (*fo cain ocus fo geillsini Gall*).' It was Ímar who summoned a 'great muster and a great hosting of the men of all Munster, both Irish and Foreigners,' to invade Dál Cais and reduce its people to submission or death. What is more, the man who we know from other sources to have been the Eóganacht claimant to the kingship of Munster at this juncture—Máel Muad mac Brain of the Eóganacht Raithlind (from the Bandon area of Co. Cork)—is relegated in the Cogadh to being a mere lackey of Ímar's, as is Donnubán mac Cathail of Uí Chairbre (ancestor of the Uí Donnubáin or O'Donovans, a branch of the Uí Fhidgeinti based in Co. Limerick to the east of Sliab Luachra) (map 6). Together they marched on Dál Cais, Ímar of Limerick and this 'army of Munster both Foreigners and Irish (*Imar Lumnig co sluag Muman umi eter Gall ocus Goedel*).' Mathgamain was joined by the king of the Delbna, who claimed a genealogical link with Dál Cais[74] and from one of whose branches derives the name of the barony of Delvin, Co. Westmeath, and by Dál Cais warriors called home from service in the armies of the Uí Néill, and they proceeded to Sulchóit (Solloghod, about 6 km north-west of Tipperary), where Mathgamain had the first great victory of his reign.[75]

This Battle of Solloghod is no fiction concocted a century or more later by the propagandist author of the Cogadh. In the Annals of Inisfallen for 967 we read of the 'defeat of the Foreigners of Limerick by Mathgamain son of Cennétig, at Sulchóit, and Limerick was burned by him before noon on the following day (*Maidm for Gullu Luimnich re Mathgamain m. Cennetich oc Sulchuait, & loscud Lumnich dó ría medón laí arna bárach*)'; and if the other annals do not specifically mention Solloghod they certainly knew of Mathgamain's triumph over the forces of Limerick. The Four Masters report that he gained a 'battle-rout of the Foreigners of Limerick (*cath-raoineadh ria Mathghamhain mac Cindeidigh for Gallaibh Luimnigh*),' that he slaughtered them and burned their ships and plundered their King's Island fortress.[76]

Even shorn of the Cogadh's hyperbole, the scale of Mathgamain's victory over the Limerick Norse seems to have been exceptional, without parallel by any of his Dál Cais predecessors. The Cogadh has his forces marching all night after victory at Solloghod until they reached Limerick—30 km or so as the crow flies; and while we rightly mistrust the author's tendency to overplay its heroes' deeds, still it is worthy of note that the contemporary annalist specifically pointed out that Limerick was sacked *before noon* the next day, as if to emphasise that there was something unusually impressive about this feat of military dexterity.

At Limerick, Mathgamain's forces overran the Norsemen's fortress (*dún*) and slaughtered them 'on the streets and in the houses (*ar na srataib ocus isna taigib*),' and

they carried off their jewels and their best property, and their saddles beautiful and foreign; their gold and their silver; their beautifully woven cloth of all colours and of all kinds; their satins and silken cloth, pleasing and variegated, both scarlet and green, and all sorts of cloth in like manner. They carried away their soft, youthful, bright, matchless, girls; their blooming silk-clad young women; and their active, large, and well-formed boys. The fort and the good town they reduced to a cloud of smoke and to red fire afterwards. The whole of the captives were collected on the hills of Saingel [Singland]. Every one of them that was fit for war was killed, and every one that was fit for a slave was enslaved.[77]

Obviously this picture of the opulence of the town of Limerick, and of the fate that befell its citizens, is exaggerated for effect, but the basic proposition seems valid: this was a truly memorable milestone in the ascent of Dál Cais to national status and in the career of Mathgamain mac Cennétig. And therefore we note that when the Annals of Ulster record this great triumph over the Limerickmen they call Mathgamain 'king of Cashel (*ri Caissil*)',[78] as if these recent victories had propelled him into the office—although they might of course mean that he was now the overlord of the Eóganacht Chaisil, rather than that he was king of all Munster.

Other sources have preserved more evidence of how Mathgamain formalised his claim to the kingship. The Cogadh describes an assault by Mathgamain on the Uí Énda of Eóganacht Áine in east Co. Limerick, which is recorded in the Annals of Inisfallen for 968. The Cogadh also knows of a campaign against the Uí Énda's neighbours in the west of the county, the Uí Fhidgeinti, securing the hostages of the latter's king, Donnubán mac Cathail; and the Annals of Inisfallen note an expedition further west into north Kerry in 972, among the lands of the Ciarraige, many of whose fortresses he demolished, including Dún na Fithrech near Ballybunnion.[79] In addition, the Cogadh claims that Mathgamain enslaved the *suartletu* (perhaps from Old Norse *svartleggja* and here meaning billeted soldiers) that the Norse had quartered on the province,[80] allegedly defeating the Norse in seven separate battles, and forced Ímar to spend a year in banishment overseas. This occurred in 974, when his base on Inis Cathaig was attacked by Maccus mac Arailt and the *Lagmainn* (from Old Norse *Lögmenn*, meaning 'Lawmen') of the Isles, Ímar being brought overseas, from which he made his escape the following year.[81]

Most significant of all, though, the Four Masters report for 967 that Mathgamain led an army to Sciath ind Eccis, the Hill of Skea to the south of the River Bandon, 'so that he carried the hostages of Munster with him to his house, and expelled [Máel Muad] mac Brain, lord of Desmumu (*go t-tucc gialla Mumhan lais da thaigh, & go ro indarb mac Brain tigerna Deasmhumhan*).'[82] This assertion of lordship over Máel Muad is recorded by the Annals of Inisfallen as having taken place in 969, and it seems the Four Masters have got their chronology wrong here; indeed the same annals report a similar expedition along with the events of 969—and may therefore be duplicating accounts of the same development—to the effect that Mathgamain led an army to Desmumu and spent three nights at Cork, bringing home the hostages of Desmumu.

Likewise, the Cogadh tells us that Mathgamain took the hostages of Máel Muad mac Brain (whom Mathgamain captured, it says), so that he 'took the pledges and the hostages of all the men of Munster.' As we have seen, Máel Muad of Eóganacht Raithlind was Mathgamain's only real contender for the kingship of Munster, and when Mathgamain captured or banished him, and secured Munster's hostages, the Dál Cais king became the province's new overlord, the first of Brian's family to earn such distinction.[83]

We can see Mathgamain acting as king of Munster thereafter. In 969, when Osraige was invaded by the king of Leinster, Murchad mac Finn, it was Mathgamain 'and the men of Munster (*co Feraibh Mumhan*)' who sent him packing. Mathgamain's army included also Osraige, the men of Éli in north Tipperary, the Déisi from south-east Munster and the Norse of Waterford, indicating a wide range of support at least in that part of the province.[84]

His authority reached its peak in 972 when he presided over a major assembly of the southern nobility:

> The three ordinances were enacted in a council of the nobles of Munster (i.e. Mathgamain and Fáelán and the son of Bran and others), namely, the banishment of the *svartleggja* [Norse mercenaries], the banishment of the Foreigners from Limerick, and the burning of the fortress (*na trí cáne do dénam a comarle degdóene Muman, .i. Mathgamain & Foelan & mc. Brain &rl., .i. innarba na suaitrech & innarba na n-Gall a l-Lumniuch & in dún do loscud*).[85]

Mathgamain's two named associates in this assembly were the king of the Déisi and Máel Muad mac Brain of Eóganacht Raithlind, the man who would otherwise have been king of the province himself, and therefore his participation in this extraordinary convention—which seems to have had as its sole purpose the imposition of Mathgamain's authority over the Norse of Limerick—is a great tribute to Mathgamain's authority. And that prestige was on display the following year when the *comarba* of St Patrick (the abbot of Armagh) made a visitation of Munster, partly to impose an ecclesiastical tax that was objected to by the abbot of Emly (the great church traditionally associated with the Eóganachta); but 'Mathgamain, the king of Munster, made peace between them and they agreed on the right of [the *comarba* of] Patrick in perpetuity (*co n-derna Mathgamain, ri Muman, síd ettarru, & a n-oentu im chert Patraicc do grés*).'[86]

But Mathgamain's dominance did not last. In 974 we hear that one of the two joint convenors of the conference of 972, Máel Muad mac Brain, 'took the hostages of Munster from Limerick southwards, and marched against Mathgamain'; and the other joint convenor, Fáelán of the Déisi, must similarly have rebelled against him, because in 975 Mathgamain's army slew his son Cormac.[87]

What happened next was an act of betrayal that was widely condemned. In 976 one of Mathgamain's old enemies, Donnubán mac Cathail of Uí Chairbre (a branch of the Uí Fhidgeinti), treacherously captured and handed over Mathgamain—at the instigation, the Cogadh says, of Ímar of Limerick—to his old Eóganacht rival Máel Muad mac Brain, who put to death the 'chief king of all Munster (*áirdrí Mumhan uile*)', as the Four Masters call him, 'against the protection of saints and just men (*dar erthach naomh & fíreon*)' or, as the Annals of Inisfallen put it, 'in violation of the guarantee and despite the curse of the elders of Munster (*tar sarugud & tar mallachtain sruthi Muman*).'[88]

It was a catastrophe for the dynasty that had never before produced a scion of such undoubted capacity. What extraordinary good fortune for Dál Cais that, so many of Cennétig mac Lorcáin's fine sons having fallen at enemy hands, there was among the pair still alive a man who was, as the Cogadh puts it, 'not a stone in the place of an egg; and he was not a wisp in the place of a club; but he was a hero in place of a hero; and he was valour after valour'![89] This was Brian, whose extraordinary ascent to greatness would now begin.

Chapter 2 ～

| BRIAN'S RISE TO POWER

We cannot be certain when Brian Bóraime was born. The Annals of the Four Masters record his birth among the highlights of the year 927 (Chronicon Scotorum has it with the events of 924). But annals rarely if ever record births, and certainly not that of a person who at the time was someone of small consequence, and so we can assume that this is a later insertion. What the chroniclers are doing is working backwards from an account of the Battle of Clontarf in 1014, which states that at that time Brian was in his eighty-eighth year. If this is true he was indeed born about 927. On the other hand, the Annals of Ulster—for no stated reason and again retrospectively—report Brian's birth under 941, which would make him seventy-three at the time of his death at Clontarf.

There are arguments in favour of both dates. As we have seen, Brian's sister Órlaith died as the wife of the king of Tara in 941, and two of his brothers were killed in the battle of Mag Dúin in 944 when obviously of fighting age; as the latest that they can have been born is the mid to late 920s, a birth date for Brian of 927 would fit perfectly well (table 2). For what it is worth too, a poem inserted in the Dál Cais propaganda tract Cogadh Gáedhel re Gallaibh claims a role at the battle of Belach Lechta in 978 for Brian's son Murchad, and Brian is more likely to have had a son of fighting age at that date if he himself was a 51-year-old than a 37-year-old.[1] As against this, Brian had a son, Donnchad, who lived until 1064 and was old enough to succeed his father fifty years earlier, immediately after Clontarf (table 3). He was a product of Brian's marriage to the famous Gormlaith, which may have begun in the early or mid-980s; and if, therefore, we imagine Donnchad being born at that time, Brian would have been about sixty if his date of birth was 927 but only in his early to mid-forties if born in 941; and the latter date seems somewhat more credible.

One suspects that the portrayal of Brian dying in the Battle of Clontarf in his eighty-eighth year is a romantic notion from a later time, an idealised image of a wise old king whose long and glorious reign comes to an end in his hour of triumph. On the contrary—as we shall see—Brian's frenetic energy in the years leading up to Clontarf suggests a man of younger years, still possessed of the soldierly force and warlike vigour that made him one of the great military commanders of his or any era.

BRIAN'S NAME

Brian was presumably one of the youngest, if not the youngest, of his father's twelve sons. His mother, as noted before, was a Connachtwoman, Bébinn daughter of Aurchad son of Murchad, king of Iar-Chonnachta, to the west of Lough Corrib. We cannot say for certain how Brian's name was chosen.[2] After his own day the name became very familiar and has since grown to be extraordinarily popular throughout the world; but few of those who bear the name, or choose it for their children, can be aware that it seems to have been unknown in Ireland before him and that its popularity thereafter was due largely to his great celebrity. Presumably Brian's mother helped choose the name, and indeed the only one of Brian's contemporaries to bear it was Brian mac Máelruanaid, the king of Iar-Chonnachta who died in 1004, a younger kinsman of hers.

Bébinn was a member of a dynasty descended from a man called Brión (said by the genealogists to have been a brother of Niall Noígiallach, ancestor of the Uí Néill). But this is not quite the same name: for one thing, *Brión* has two syllables and the genitive is *Briúin* (hence Bébinn's dynasty was the *Uí Briúin*), whereas *Brian* is monosyllabic and has a different genitive, *Briain* (and hence Brian's descendants were the *Uí Briain*).[3] But the name *Brión* seems to have been declining in popularity by the tenth century, and it is possible that nothing more significant than fashion caused its displacement by the name *Brian* and that our Brian's renown simply hastened the displacement of one by the other thereafter (indeed by the twelfth century copyists would regularly replace *Brión* with *Brian* when transcribing manuscripts).

There is one outside possibility that should, however, be mentioned. At the time when Brian was born—as we have seen, some time between 927 and 941—the only place in which the name Brian is found is not Ireland but Brittany. (And, incidentally, the occasional occurrence of the name in later mediaeval England derives not from our Brian or from Ireland but from landed connections between England and Brittany arising from the Norman conquest in 1066.)[4] The reign of Brian's father, Cennétig (934–51), closely overlaps that of Alan II, Duke of Brittany (936–52), and both men spent their lives at war with Vikings, and sometimes the same Vikings. Indeed following the death of Alan's grandfather, Alan I, in 907, the Vikings had overrun Brittany and the young Alan sought refuge in exile in England at the courts of Edward the Elder and his son Æthelstan, where he seems to have remained until he invaded Brittany with the English king's aid in 936 and expelled the Vikings.[5] While Alan was in exile, in 913, a Viking fleet from Brittany led by the jarls Hróaldr and Óttarr appeared in the Bristol Channel and raided around the Welsh coast, but its further advance was repulsed by the men of Hereford and Gloucester, at which point part of the fleet, led by Jarl Óttarr, made for Ireland and established a Viking base at Waterford.[6] This man is one of the arch-villains of the Cogadh, which famously says of him, as we have seen above, that

> the Earl, Oiter Dubh, came with a hundred ships to Waterford, and the east of Munster was plundered by him, and the south; and he put all under tribute and service to the Foreigners; and he levied his royal rent upon them. The whole of Munster became filled with immense floods, and countless sea-vomitings of ships and boats and fleets, so that there was not a harbour nor a landing-port nor a *dún* nor a fortress nor a fastness in all Munster without fleets of Danes and pirates.[7]

However, the Cogadh says there was one 'gracious, noble, high-born, beautiful sept in Ireland, who never submitted to tyranny or oppression, or unwonted injury, from any other people in the world.'[8] These were of course Dál Cais under the sons of Cennétig mac Lorcáin, Mathgamain and Brian, who now set about freeing the Irish from this oppression.

The fact that the name Brian occurs regularly among the families of the Breton nobility in this age but is hitherto unknown in Ireland suggests the possibility—but no more than that—that a political alliance against a common Viking enemy (or even a trading relationship between the two regions) led to the adoption of this Breton name by Cennétig for one of the youngest of his many sons.

BRIAN MAC CENNÉTIG'S EARLY YEARS

Brian appears for the first time in contemporary records in the year 977, the Four Masters adding, after their record of the event, *Brian caogad bliadhain d'aois an tan-sin* ('Brian was fifty years of age at that time').[9] As we have seen, there is a strong chance that he was in fact only thirty-six, but still this is quite late in life for so famous a person to have to wait before being noticed. The reason of course is that the annals confine their interest overwhelmingly to the affairs of kings and high-ranking clerics, and it is decidedly unusual for royal kinsmen to get a mention, apart from their obits. Brian was one of at least thirteen children, none of whom is mentioned in the annals other than to have their death recorded, apart from his brother Marcán (who, as a senior churchman, crops up once or twice) and the two other brothers who preceded Brian in the kingship, Lachtna and Mathgamain (and even Lachtna goes entirely unnoticed until his untimely death).

It is no surprise, therefore, that contemporary writers are silent about Brian. It does not mean that he was a nonentity until he reached middle age, merely that it was not the job of annalists to write about the son of a king or the brother of a king: that would have taken from the aura of the member of the family who held the kingship. And for this reason it is quite likely that had Mathgamain not been murdered we would know nothing whatsoever of Brian until the time came to record an epigrammatic obit, if anyone bothered.

But that does not mean that later writers—naturally aware of the strange twist of fate that meant that Brian managed the highly unusual feat of becoming the third son of his father to succeed—did not revisit the earlier part his life and write him into the story. The author of

Cogadh Gáedhel re Gallaibh, for example, lived at a time when everyone knew it was Brian rather than any of his siblings who had gone on to great things—indeed he probably wrote at the behest of one of Brian's heirs—and therefore it was necessary to give him a leading role even before his succession. Thus, having begun his story with a litany of atrocities committed by the Vikings against the Irish, the writer turns to the subject of the one Irish dynasty who can defend the people— Dál Cais—at a time when we know it was ruled by Brian's brother Mathgamain. But that is not quite how the writer sees it:

There were then governing and ruling this sept two stout, able, valiant pillars, two fierce, lacerating, magnificent heroes, two gates of battle, two poles of combat, two spreading trees of shelter, two spears of victory and readiness, of hospitality and munificence, of heart and strength, of friendship and liveliness, the most eminent of the west of Europe, viz., Mathgamain and Brian, the two sons of Cennétig son of Lorcán son of Lachtna son of Corcc son of Anlón son of Mathgamain son of Tairdelbach son of Cathal son of Áed son of Conall son of Eochu Ballderg son of Cáirthenn Finn son of Blat son of Cass son of Conall Echluaith son of Lugaid Mend son of Óengus Tírech son of Fer Corb son of Mug Corb son of [Cormac] Cass son of Ailill Ólomm son of Mug Nuadat who divided Ireland with Conn Cétchathach.[10]

The long genealogy is to show the blue blood flowing in the veins of Mathgamain and Brian, but to all intents and purposes theirs is a joint rule, or so the author of the Cogadh would have us believe.

Seeing 'the bondage and oppression and misrule that was inflicted on Munster and on the men of Ireland in general,' jointly Mathgamain and Brian chose not to submit to it and so brought their peoples and their chattels westwards over the Shannon (into Co. Clare) and dispersed themselves among the forests and woods of the peoples living there. From this base, the Cogadh tells us, Mathgamain and Brian waged a kind of guerrilla war of resistance, plundering and killing the Vikings, neither side offering or receiving quarter. And when eventually both sides had tired of conflict and a truce was agreed between them, it was the initiative of Mathgamain, now styled 'king of Dál Cais'. Not so his brother:

But as regards Brian mac Cennétig, he was not willing to make peace with the Foreigners, because however small the injury he might be able to do to the Foreigners, he preferred it to peace; and though all others were silent he would not be. Brian, however, after that, and with him the young champions of the Dál Cais, went back again into the forests and woods and wastes of Tuadmumu [North Munster]. He began then immediately to plunder and kill, and retaliate on the Foreigners. When he did not inflict evil on the Foreigners in the daytime, he was sure to do so the next night; and when he did it not in the night he was sure to do it on the following day.[11]

The Cogadh therefore paints Mathgamain as something of an appeaser, a dove to Brian's hawk. Camping out in makeshift huts in the woods and deserted places and caves of Dál Cais, Brian and his men wasted the land from Lough Derg in the east to the River Fergus in the west and from the Slieve Aughty mountains (on the Galway-Clare border) to Tratraige (the area around Bunratty). Then 'the Foreigners of all Tuadmumu' built a *dúnchlad,* a kind of earthen ditch, around Tratraige, proposing to turn it into a fortress (*dúnárus*) and to conquer all Tuadmumu and Uí Chonaill Gabra (a branch of the Uí Fhidgeinti in west Co. Limerick). But Brian killed them 'in their twos and in their threes and in their fives and in their scores and in their hundreds,' and fought numerous conflicts with them, suffering 'hardship and harm and bad food and bad bedding in cooking-huts in deserted places and on the hard, bumpy, wet roots of the soil of his native land,' with the Foreigners killing his people, his retainers and his foster-brothers until, it says, the historians record that he had but fifteen followers remaining.

The Cogadh then has it that Mathgamain, hearing of his brother's plight and dreading that he would die at the hands of the Vikings, sent messengers to him and arranged to meet. And when they did, Brian reproached Mathgamain for conceding a truce to the Foreigners while they occupied his rightful inheritance, the patrimony of his father and his grandfather, saying that the latter, Lorcán son of Lachtna, would never have made such a peace, just as Lorcán—so the author says, displaying a very poor sense of chronology—had never submitted to the Uí Néill king of Ireland, Máel Sechnaill I (died 862), or to any of the five provinces of Ireland. Mathgamain's defence was that he did not possess the power to resist the Foreigners, especially because of the number of their warriors, with their breastplates and swords and other arms, and did not want to lead the Dál Cais to their deaths, as Brian had. But Brian won the argument with a stirring riposte:

> Brian said that he [Mathgamain] was wrong to say that, because it was hereditary for him to die, and hereditary for all the Dal Cais, for their fathers and grandfathers had died, and death was certain to come upon themselves; but it was not natural or hereditary to them to submit to insult or contempt, because their fathers or their grandfathers did not submit to it from any one on earth. He said also that it was no honour to their courage to abandon, without battle or conflicts, to grey Foreigners and black mighty Heathens (*do Gallaib glasa ocus do Gentib gorma gusmara*), the inheritance which their fathers and grandfathers had defended in battles and conflicts against the nobles of the Irish.[12]

And so when Mathgamim put the matter to a gathering of the men of Dál Cais they were unanimous in declaring for war against the Foreigners.

It was this war that won Mathgamain the kingship of Munster from his Eóganachta opponents; and yet the Cogadh, in noting that the Eóganachta and their allies were marching to oppose Mathgamain, nevertheless has it that 'this news reached *Brian* and Mathgamain and the nobles of Dál Cais when they were at Cashel of the Kings,' as if Brian rather than Mathgamain were in charge, although when they assemble all the Dál Cais before them it is Mathgamain who asks what they wish him to do—perhaps because he is the king taking counsel but with more than a suggestion that he is back to his old vacillating ways.[13]

The outcome of their deliberations was the march to Solloghod that led to Mathgamain's famous victory over the Vikings in 967 and his storming of Limerick the following morning. But the Cogadh has Mathgamain after the Battle of Solloghod asking Brian for an account of it, as if the latter led Dál Cais on the day while Mathgamain remained aloof from proceedings. It is only after the overthrow of Limerick that Mathgamain comes into his own in the Cogadh, but his moment in the sun is brief before his assassination in 976, which thrusts Brian back into the limelight.

BRIAN'S WIVES AND CHILDREN

We know of nine of Brian's children, six sons (Murchad, Domnall, Donnchad, Tadc, Conchobar and Flann) and three daughters (Sadb, Sláine and Bébinn) (table 3). The evidence suggests that he was something of a serial monogamist, if not a polygamist. We know of four wives—all, one assumes, political contracts rather than love matches—and although we do not know the sequence of the marriages, the temptation is to try to match them up with political needs at particular junctures in Brian's career. If he was born in 941 his first marriage was probably arranged for him by the late 950s, at a time when his older brother, Mathgamain, was trying to hold on to the kingship of Dál Cais in the face of the internal rivalry that had led to the assassination of their brother Lachtna. A marital alliance with a neighbour who could offer assistance and protection was therefore a desideratum for the family, and so it was probably at this point that Brian married Mór, daughter of Eiden mac Cléirig of the South Connacht dynasty of Uí Fiachrach Aidne.[14]

It was not the most prestigious house, as none of its members had held the overkingship of Connacht for 250 years, but Mór's father, Eiden, and grandfather Cléirech were significant figures as regards lineage: from Eiden are descended the Uí Eidin (O'Heyne or Hynes) and from Cléirech are derived the Uí Chléirig (O'Clery or Clarke).[15] That the marriage with Mór came early in Brian's career is also apparent from the fact that of the three sons we know to have been children of the marriage—Murchad, Conchobar and Flann—the best-known of them, Murchad, who was killed at the Battle of Clontarf in 1014, was old enough to have had a son (Tairdelbach) who also fought and died there. If Murchad was only, say, forty at this time (and one dubious source says he was sixty-two)[16] he would have been born in or before 974.

In any event we must assume that the end of the marriage (perhaps only because of Mór's early death) did not lead to a breakdown in relations between Brian and his erstwhile in-laws, because one of the few non-Munster kings to die alongside him and his son Murchad at Clontarf was Máel Ruanaid ua hEidin of Uí Fiachrach Aidne, who was Mór's nephew and Murchad's first cousin.

It we try to piece Brian's other marriages into a sequence dictated by politics we might imagine that he next married the most famous of his

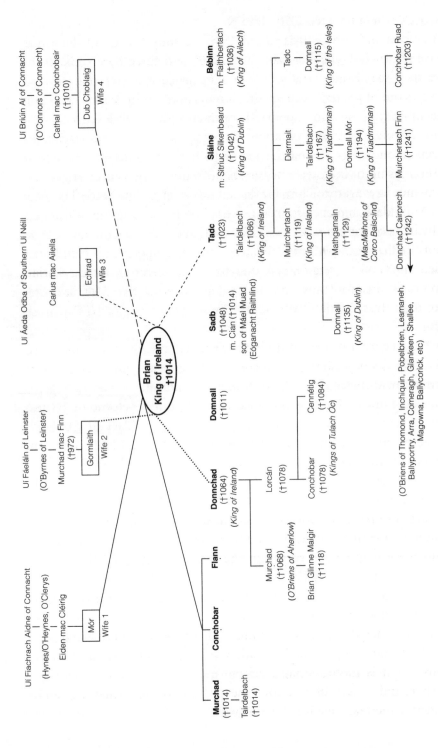

Table 3: Brian's wives and offspring

wives, Gormlaith (died 1030). She had been married to Amlaíb Cuarán of Dublin and York, who died in Iona in 981, at which point she would have returned to Ireland (table 4; see below, page 147). A year later (as we shall see) Brian, now secure as king of all Munster, marched his armies out of the province for the first time and launched an assault on neighbouring Osraige, and a Leinster alliance might have proved useful at this point. Gormlaith's father, Murchad mac Finn, was head of Uí Fáeláin, one of the three branches of Uí Dúnlainge that alternated the overkingship of Leinster between them; he had died as overking of the province in 972, at which point the kingship went to the second branch, Uí Muiredaig, and then in 978 to the third branch, Uí Dúnchada, after which the conventional expectation was that the next overking would be Gormlaith's brother Máelmórda. But when the Uí Dúnchada incumbent died in 984 Máelmórda failed to secure it for his line (although Brian eventually installed him as king nearly twenty years later). It seems not unlikely, therefore, that Gormlaith was married off to Brian at her brother's insistence in the early 980s as part of the jockeying for position by these Leinster princes and at a time when Brian was trying to expand his authority beyond the confines of Munster. As we have seen, she had one son with Brian, Donnchad, who was of fighting age at the time of the Battle of Clontarf and who died in Rome as a very old man in 1064. If we imagine him about eighty then, he would have been born in 984.

Although the Cogadh has Gormlaith still residing at Brian's court in 1013 in the immediate prelude to the Battle of Clontarf (and helping to initiate it, as we shall see, by urging her brother Máelmórda to rebel), it seems more likely that they had parted ways by then. Norse sources in fact, also painting Gormlaith as a malign force, have her becoming embittered with Brian following the proverbial acrimonious divorce.[17] And there may be something to this; at least it may be that Brian's marriage to Gormlaith did not last long. This is because Brian probably married the third of his wives, Echrad, not long afterwards (assuming that these marriages did not overlap), as their son Tadc (died 1023) had himself fathered a son (the future high-king Tairdelbach ua Briain) by about 1009, suggesting that Tadc was born at the latest in the early 990s. What is more, because Echrad came from an undistinguished background it is probable that the political alliance that no doubt underlay the marriage was formed well before Brian's ascension to the high-kingship. Her father was Carlus son of Ailill Fiach of the little-known dynasty of Uí Áeda Odba.[18] So obscure were they that we cannot say for certain where they were situated, although it was somewhere within the lands of the Southern Uí Néill, and perhaps the alliance was formed at about the time that Brian first began to bring pressure to bear on the king of Tara, Máel Sechnaill mac Domnaill, when he invaded Southern Uí Néill territory in 988.

The fourth of Brian's known wives was Dub Choblaig (died 1009), daughter of Cathal mac Conchobair, king of Connacht since 973, and one possible occasion for such a union would have been about 992, when Brian can be found acting as protector of the Connachtmen, retaliating against the aggression of the king of Tara; however, as Cathal mac Conchobair was openly opposed to Brian as late as 1001, the marriage may in fact have sealed a *rapprochement* the following year when Brian finally secured the high-kingship and obtained, among others, the hostages of Connacht.

It is more than likely—as has been the case around the world and through the ages—that these women, however aristocratic, were treated as a political vouchsafe by the men who had charge of their destiny. And, just as Brian took wives to seal deals and to ensure good will and secure the peace, he did precisely the same with his own daughters. We only know of three, but doubtless there were more.

We have seen that Brian's brother Mathgamain had been treacherously murdered in 976 by Máel Muad mac Brain of the Eóganacht Raithlind (from the Bandon area of Co. Cork); and although Brian obtained revenge and killed Máel Muad in battle two years later, nevertheless Sadb (died 1048) was later given in marriage to Máel Muad's son, Cian, in order to secure the peace. Later, in 999, Brian slaughtered the Norse of Dublin in the great Battle of Glenn Máma; and when their king, Sitriuc (son of Brian's former wife Gormlaith), became Brian's vassal shortly afterwards he was given Brian's daughter Sláine as wife to seal the deal. And it was presumably after Flaithbertach Ua Néill, the recalcitrant king of Cenél nEógain, finally succumbed to Brian in 1010 that he acquired as his wife the third of Brian's known daughters, Bébinn, to ensure good will between contemporary Ireland's two polar points of attraction.

BRIAN AS KING OF DÁL CAIS

Although we cannot be certain, it is likely that Brian stepped into his brother's shoes immediately on the death of Mathgamain in 976, murdered by his old Eóganacht rival Máel Muad mac Brain, having been delivered to him as a captive by Donnubán mac Cathail of Uí Chairbre, both acting, the Cogadh says, at the instigation of Ímar of Limerick.

The picture the Cogadh presents of Brian and Mathgamain at loggerheads, at least in relation to strategy, might at first arouse a suspicion that Brian rejoiced at—or even was complicit in—his brother's overthrow: regicide was, after all, the oldest story in the book among the Irish. And yet the evidence shows that all three who took part in his brother's murder now became Brian's declared enemies, and he was ruthless and unflinching in wreaking his revenge. The Cogadh indeed comments that although his reign 'at length became bright, placid, happy, peaceful, prosperous, wealthy, rich, festive, giving of banquets, laying foundations,' the beginning was 'full of battles, wars, combats, plundering, ravaging, unquiet.'[19]

Within a year of his brother's death Brian pursued the first of his enemies, Ímar of Limerick, to the new haven he had secured for himself on the monastic island of Inis Cathaig (Scattery), near the mouth of the Shannon. Brian's forces stormed the island—which a contemporary chronicler considered a violation of ecclesiastical sanctuary—and killed Ímar and his two sons, Amlaíb (Óláfr) and Dubcenn (the latter an Irish name found among the Dál Cais, indicating their interconnection, despite the Cogadh's depiction of black-and-white enmity between them).[20] In the same year, 977, Brian fought the first actual battle of his reign when he led an army against the second of his enemies, Donnubán mac Cathail of Uí Chairbre, and against the Norse of Limerick, and slaughtered the latter. The Cogadh adds the details that this battle was fought at a place called Cathair Cuan, which is unidentified but was somewhere in the territory of Uí Fhidgeinti in Co. Limerick, and that Donnúban was killed in it, along with Aralt (Haraldr), son of Ímar of Limerick, to whom Donnúban had offered refuge when Brian defeated and killed his father.[21]

And then the following year, 978, Brian was victorious in his second battle as king, the Battle of Belach Lechta, fought in the Ballyhoura Hills in north Cork,[22] which therefore shows Brian still on the offensive.

Before the battle, according to the Cogadh, Brian sent Coccarán, his confidential officer (*giolla grádha do Brian*), as a messenger to Máel Muad mac Brain, the man who had murdered his brother, seeking the *éric* or compensation payment that he owed Mathgamain's kindred for dishonourably killing an unarmed king, and challenging Máel Muad to appear at Belach Lechta in a fortnight and a day with a full muster of his army.

Máel Muad duly appeared, with disastrous consequences for himself and his dynasty, because he was roundly defeated by Brian's army. The battle was significant not just because Máel Muad mac Brain was the man who had murdered Mathgamain and that Brian's defeat of him at Belach Lechta therefore was the culmination of his efforts to avenge his brother's assassination: more importantly, Máel Muad was the leading contemporary figure among the Eóganachta, who would have considered Mathgamain a usurper of the kingship of Cashel that his own Eóganachta ancestors had monopolised for half a millennium (although his own particular line of descent was undistinguished, to say the least). Therefore, having killed Mathgamain in 976, Máel Muad undoubtedly thought of himself as overking of all Munster, and is credited as such in the king-lists and in his obit in the Annals of Inisfallen and even in the Cogadh (although the other annals call him merely king of Desmumu or king of the Uí Echach branch of Eóganacht Raithlind).

But Brian did not only defeat Máel Muad at Belach Lechta: he killed him and slaughtered his army (to the number of 1,200, the Cogadh claims), and in doing so he killed off any chance of an Eóganacht revival.[23] He then took the hostages of the province of Munster as far as the very sea, as the Cogadh puts it; and thus, within two years of his succession as king of Dál Cais, Brian had made himself overking of all Munster. And when Máel Muad's son Cian was later given Brian's daughter Sadb (died 1048) in marriage, the acquiescence of the Eóganacht in the new Dál Cais supremacy was complete.[24]

BRIAN AS KING OF MUNSTER

Brian presumably was the unopposed king of Munster from 978 onwards, but contemporary sources are strangely quiet about his activities for the next four years. The author of the Cogadh heard of a third battle, against the Norse, fought at an unidentified place called Fan Conrach, which does not seem to be mentioned in any of the surviving annals; but all is otherwise silent.[25] We can assume he was strengthening his hold on the province and dousing what resistance remained to his new hegemony. And after four years of consolidation, Brian was ready to make his mark beyond Munster.

If his ambition was to make himself supreme in the southern half of Ireland, Leth Moga, he needed to force or otherwise win the submission of the Laigin, the peoples of the great province of Leinster, and of their ambitious neighbours, the Osraige (map 6), who were the meat sandwiched between them and Munster. It cannot therefore have come as too great a surprise to contemporaries when in 982 Brian marched his armies out of Munster for the first time and launched an assault on Osraige. It was not too successful: he took a 'great prey (*préid móir*)' from it, presumably in the form of cattle, but even the Munster Annals of Inisfallen admit that he lost a number of his men.[26]

However inauspicious a start this was to Brian's interprovincial career, it seems to have got the attention of the new king of Tara, Máel Sechnaill II (Máel Sechnaill mac Domnaill), head of the Clann Cholmáin branch of the Southern Uí Néill.[27] This is the man Brian would eventually topple from the high-kingship, but not before the lengthiest of rearguard actions over the next two decades. In 982, however, the shoe was still on the other foot and Máel Sechnaill, having succeeded to the overkingship of the Uí Néill only two years earlier—and having enjoyed some spectacular successes in the interval against the Norse of Dublin in particular—was determined to make a statement to Brian that Dál Cais pretensions to power were just that: pretensions. He therefore marched south from his base in Co. Westmeath—or perhaps sailed down the Shannon—and, entering Dál Cais territory, made for Mag Adair, the plain west of Tulla in Co. Clare in which the Dál Cais held their *óenach* or assembly.

Here, on an ancient site—perhaps a prehistoric burial mound (plate 7)—the dynasty also inaugurated its kings. As we have seen, as part of the inauguration ceremony a rod known as *slat na ríge* ('the rod of kingship') was cut from the *bile* or sacred tree there, and the handing over of this wand to the king during the enkinging ceremony symbolised his new sovereignty. Six years earlier, when Brian succeeded to the kingship, he would have received just such a symbol of office cut from the sacred tree, and the theory was that without receiving such a wand at the beginning of his reign the king of Dál Cais had no authority to rule. It is highly significant, therefore, that the only detail of Máel Sechnaill's plundering expedition into Munster in 982 recorded in the annals is his action in regard to this tree. The Four Masters say that 'Dál Cais was plundered by Máel Seachnaill mac Domnaill, and the Tree of Óenach Maige Adair was cut, after being dug from the earth with its roots (*Dal c-Cais d'orccain do Maol Sechlainn mac Domhnaill & bile Aonaigh Maighe h-Adhar do thesccadh iarna tochailt a talmhain cona frémaibh*).'[28] The Annals of Inisfallen have simply: 'The Tree of Mag Adair was broken by Leth Cuinn (*Bile Maige Adar do brissiud do Leith Chuind*).'

It is an extraordinary insight into the vestiges of arcane symbolic belief still living and breathing in late tenth-century Ireland. Just when we begin to think of these men as mere warlords bent on political advantage and answering to no imperative other than personal aggrandisement, we are brought back to another kind of reality, in which one warlord attempts to put manners on another not by way of the battlefield, not by ransacking his estates, not by making off with his cattle or his hostages, but by chopping down a tree, a sacred tree from which his opponent draws his sovereignty, in the process seeking to deny his legitimacy to rule.[29]

BRIAN AS OVERKING OF LETH MOGA

If that was Máel Sechnaill's expectation it was to no purpose. The sacred tree was regrown and, as we have seen, the *bile* of Mag Adair had to be cut down again by another invading army seventy years later.[30] The least Máel Sechnaill might have hoped for was that Brian would now know not to meddle beyond his own bailiwick. But seldom can a message have been more impudently disregarded; for the campaigning seasons that followed were ones of astonishing ambition on Brian's part. In 983, utterly ignoring the fact that his invasion of Osraige had been the *casus belli* that brought Máel Sechnaill down on top of him, he again re-entered Osraige, captured its king, Gilla Pátraic (ancestor of the Meic Gilla Pátraic or Fitzpatricks), harried the territory, and took its hostages as a sign of his overlordship.

Not only that but the Annals of Inisfallen say that Brian had first of all taken the hostages of the Leinstermen. If this is true (and it has been doubted)[31] it was a major development. It should be stressed that it is not recorded in the other annals and may just be Munster wishful thinking; but then, especially at this early stage in his career, non-Munster sources have a tendency to ignore and play down Brian's achievements. The fact that the episode is explicitly stated to have taken place in Mag nAilbe in Co. Carlow—not the most prominent of places—adds a little more colour to what might otherwise appear to be a mere concocted formula. The Cogadh, needless to say, picked up the Inisfallen account and duly noted that this alleged submission by the men of Leinster, following that of Osraige, meant that 'Brian was thus king of Leth Moga (*Amlaidh sin ba ri Lethi Moga Brian*).'[32]

One could dismiss this as propaganda, except that the Cogadh then appends the credible detail that two kings of Leinster 'came into his house' (i.e. submitted to Brian), namely Domnall Clóen and Tuathal, *rig Iarthar Liphi* ('king of the Western Liffey Plain'). This act rings true, although Tuathal is an error for Dúnlaing mac Tuathail. Tuathal (ancestor of the Uí Thuathail or O'Tooles) died as king of Uí Muiredaig and overking of Leinster in 958. As we know, the convention was that the title 'king of Leinster' rotated among three different branches of the great dynasty of Uí Dúnlainge, and so after Tuathal's death it went first to an Uí Dúnchada prince and then to an Uí Fáeláin claimant before it reverted to Tuathal's son Augaire in 972; and when Augaire was killed by the Norse of Dublin in 978 the title went to Domnall Clóen of Uí Dúnchada (map 5), the man who, the Cogadh claims, submitted to Brian in 983.

That Domnall Clóen might have felt compelled to do so is not in the least remarkable. He had only a brief and troubled reign: he was captured by the Norse of Dublin in 979 shortly after assuming the role, and his son Bróen was also captured and then killed by them in 980. He secured his own release from captivity when Dublin was stormed by Máel Sechnaill in 981. But in the very year in which he made his supposed submission to Brian, Domnall Clóen (allied with the Norse of Waterford) was roundly defeated in battle by Máel Sechnaill (allied with the Dublin Norse). Presumably it was his vulnerability that led him to submit to Brian that year, in the hope of some protection.

And if Domnall Clóen had been allied with the Waterford Norse in 983 while Máel Sechnaill was linked to those of Dublin, it is surely relevant that the following year Brian too was in Waterford, forming an alliance aimed at an attack on Dublin. In other words, if Brian and Domnall Clóen shared allies (the Waterford Norse) and enemies (Máel Sechnaill and the Dublin Norse), it is not in the least unlikely that Domnall Clóen had become Brian's man. Domnall, however, was murdered by other rival Leinster dynasts, including the Uí Chennselaig of South Leinster, in 984, and it is perhaps not coincidental that Brian launched an invasion of Leinster at this point, co-ordinated with a strike by the Waterford Norse on Uí Chennselaig—retribution, perhaps, for their slaying of Domnall Clóen.[33]

Also—bearing in mind the regular tripartite alternation of the overkingship—because Domnall Clóen was of Uí Dúnchada, and because his immediate predecessor had been Augaire mac Tuathail of Uí Muiredaig, the man who would have considered himself the *rígdamna*, the next in line, was Máelmórda mac Murchada of Uí Fáeláin, the king of Leinster who died opposing Brian at Clontarf. In such circumstances one can imagine the Uí Muiredaig claimant, Dúnlaing mac Tuathail, throwing in his lot with Brian, on the off chance of inheriting the title himself. It was indeed the Uí Muiredaig representative who, according to the Cogadh, joined Domnall Clóen in submitting to Brian in 983, which seems far from improbable. And if we are to believe this, then perhaps it is more reasonable to accept than to reject the contention by the Inisfallen annalist that the weak and exposed kingdom of Leinster did indeed submit to Brian in 983, and perhaps we should imagine that it was at this point that Brian secured as his new wife Gormlaith, the recently widowed sister of Máelmórda of Uí Fáeláin (table 3).

EARLY MOVES AGAINST LETH CUINN

The implications are great. Within seven years of succeeding his brother as king of Dál Cais—and with a career of more than thirty years still ahead of him—Brian had done what none of his ancestors before him had done, becoming overking of all Leth Moga. The Annals of Inisfallen certainly looked on Brian as the champion of the Southern Half facing into a contest with Ireland's Northern Half. Máel Sechnaill's invasion of Dál Cais in 982 is summed up as simply the sacred tree of Mag Adair being 'broken by Leth Cuinn (*do brissiud do Leith Chuind*).'

And if Brian did become the master of Leth Moga in 983 it would provide a context for his most daring manoeuvre yet. In that year Brian took the war into Leth Cuinn. He brought what the annals call a 'large fleet (*coblach mór*)' up the Shannon and launched an offensive against the Connachta, although not for the first time the results were mixed. Among the casualties on his side were Máel Sechnaill, a son of Brian's uncle Coscrach, and Lochlainn mac Maíl Shechnaill, the *rígdamna* of Corco Mruad in north Clare, and a certain Finn son of Dubchrón, whose father may be Dubchrón Ua Longacháin (died 989), king of the Uí Fhidgeinti lineage of Uí Chuanach.

Having disembarked, Brian sent his *suatrich*, his mercenary soldiers, overland into the territory of the Uí Briúin, perhaps as far north as Co. Leitrim, where they inflicted slaughter and had slaughter inflicted on them.[34] And this less than happy conclusion did not prevent him from venturing into Leth Cuinn the following year, for which the Four Masters report that Brian undertook 'the ravaging of Western Mide (*Orgain Iarthair Mídhe*).'[35] If this is true—and it is not recorded in any other annal—the significance is that this was the heartland of the high-king, Máel Sechnaill mac Domnaill (map 2), and it was a most daring act. Brian having been at the receiving end of just such an assault two years earlier, the victim was now the aggressor.

The year 984 is also the one in which we first hear of Brian having anything to do with the men by whom he would eventually meet his end, the Norse of Dublin. That year a great fleet led by the meic Arailt (Haraldssons) arrived in the Hiberno-Norse town of Waterford, where they were joined by Brian. These men had a background in some unidentified islands off Britain's coast, probably the Western Isles of Scotland, although there is considerable evidence for their involvement in the Isle of Man and in Anglesey in north Wales.[36] In 974 one of the brothers had been responsible for the capture and abduction overseas of Ímar of Limerick, the enemy of Dál Cais whom Brian later killed immediately after his succession to the kingship, and so it is not altogether surprising to find the meic Arailt turning up as friends of Brian in Waterford. And in 984 they 'exchanged hostages there as a guarantee of both together providing a hosting to go to Dublin (*coro chloemclaiset giallu and & mc. Cennetich im imthairec sluagid do dul ar Áth Cliath*).'[37]

The Hiberno-Norse town of Dublin was of course in Leinster, being situated on the south bank of the Liffey, which formed the province's northern frontier at this time, but Máel Sechnaill had comprehensively overpowered the Dubliners at the Battle of Tara in 980 and had successively laid siege to their town the following year, so that it was now very much in his pocket. Undoubtedly Brian, as the new master of Leinster, regarded Dublin as subject to his overlordship, and the proposed expedition would have given effect to this, although no such assault seems to have materialised. Instead we are told that the Munstermen assembled their army and marched to Mairc Lagen (in which was situated Sliab Mairce, the hilly plateau of Slievemargy, Co. Laois), and—in what seems to have been a co-ordinated strike— the Foreigners overcame Uí Chennselaig, and 'they went over the sea (*coro fortatar in Gaill h-U Censelaig & co n-dechatar dar muir*).'[38] It is just possible that this means that the vanquished forces of the Uí Chennselaig were banished overseas, perhaps to a refuge in Wales, but it is more likely to mean that the meic Arailt returned to their Insular home after this campaign. In any event it looks as though Brian, having gained the submission of the North Leinster princes the previous year, was now also lord of those in the south of the province.

The same annals go on to report that Brian's army devastated Osraige that year, laying waste its churches and fortresses along with those of Leinster, and that Brian released their king, Gilla Pátraic (whom he had captured the previous year), doubtless because he was now pledged to be Brian's faithful adherent.

INTERNAL OPPOSITION

By 985 Brian mac Cennétig had enjoyed nine years of extraordinary success as king of Dál Cais. While one or two of his more overconfident adventures had led to the needless loss of valued lieutenants, he had nonetheless firmly established his dominance over the now humbled Eóganachta, appearing supreme throughout Munster, with control of the Viking-founded towns of Limerick and Waterford, whose fleets, more so than indigenous Dál Cais naval capacity, were ferrying his armed forces into campaign. He had displayed little mercy towards a recalcitrant Osraige, although we must treat as a manifest indication of character his decision to imprison rather than execute its king, and to free him when circumstances were right: this is surely suggestive of the wisdom and magnanimity that wins loyalty as opposed to the overbearing brutality that leads only to begrudging obeisance.

He had extended his sway into Leinster by a mixture of war and diplomacy, choosing allies carefully and identifying and dealing militarily with those who were less amenable. And he had even begun to test the possibilities of broadening his sphere of influence by despatching an expeditionary force into north Connacht, and it seems that he taunted even the great overking of the Uí Néill, Máel Sechnaill mac Domnaill, by sending a raiding party into his mensal lands in Mide, hitting him where it hurt.

It was all astonishingly successful. But then, in the mid-980s, we begin to see signs of vulnerability, weakness and danger. It began in 985 when the people known as the Déisi Muman, in Co. Waterford and south Tipperary—who, as vassals of the king of Munster, should now have been loyally subject to Brian—launched a raid on 'Brian's mercenaries (*amsu Briain*)', making off with three hundred cows. There must have been more to it than this jejune entry reveals, because Brian's response was a full-scale invasion of Déisi territory in revenge (*indrestar Brian na Désse da dígail*), 'so that he chased Domnall son of Fáelán as far as Waterford, and the whole of the Déisi was destroyed (*& coro loitte na Désse uile*).'[39] The Cogadh is evidently speaking of this incident—as it reproduces some of the same language—when it adds of Domnall, king of the Déisi and ancestor of the Uí Fháeláin (Phelans and Whelans), that Brian banished from Waterford 'the man who had forced the war on him.'[40] This, then, was no mere cattle-rustling raid by the Déisi but a rebellion, which had required suppression.

The Cogadh then adds, as if it happened immediately thereafter, that Brian took the hostages of all Munster and of the main churches of Munster, 'that they should not receive outlaws or robbers in the churches (*ro gab bragti airdcell Muman na fagbaitis merlig na foglaigi adin sna cellaib*).' But this is the episode that is recorded in the Annals of Inisfallen as occurring two years later, in 987, to the effect that there was 'a hosting by Brian mac Cennétig across Desmumu, and he took the hostages of Lismore, Cork, and Emly, for the banishment of robbers and lawless people from them (*Sluaged la Brian mc. Cennetich for Des Mumain co tuc giallu Lis Móir & Corcaige & Imblecha Ibair fri innarbu foglaide & aessa escána essib*).'

It is not entirely clear what this was about. These churches were hugely powerful institutions. They had extensive estates, populated by their own tenants, and they were not beyond putting armies into action to protect their interests. They were also heavily politicised and aligned with secular factions that acted as patrons and protectors, with the result that the enemies of a great church's political friends were that church's enemies too. In the case of Lismore, Cork and Emly in 987, Brian may simply have been acting as a responsible secular leader, anxious to ensure that church sanctuary was not being exploited, to society's disadvantage, by undesirables.

But even this terse annal entry makes it clear that Brian had come to Desmumu (South Munster) at the head of an army, and in some respects as king of Tuadmumu (North Munster), butting in where he might not have been welcome. And if an army was needed for this business, and hostages had to be extracted from the churches as an earnest of their future good conduct, it begins to seem likely that these three great churches were bastions of opposition to Brian, sheltering opponents of his regime, and that Brian was in the business of crushing dissension. When, therefore, we read in the same annals three years later that 'Marcán son of Cennétig took the abbacy of Emly' we might see in it more than a bit of run-of-the-mill church news. Emly was the most prestigious church in all Munster, very closely associated with its former Eóganacht kings, but even so it is very rare for the annals to announce the election of its abbot. In this case, however, the new abbot was Brian's brother, and this therefore is a political appointment if ever there was one. Evidently Brian was ensuring that it never again became a focus of dissent by handing over its governance to someone on whom he could rely.

Not that he was entirely free from threats from within his family at this stage in his career. As we know, the only reason Brian made it to the kingship of Dál Cais is because his older brother, Mathgamain, was murdered while king in 976. Mathgamain had his own family, and had he lived longer he would no doubt have groomed a successor from among them, leaving Brian and his sons as mere *rígdamnai*, men eligible for the kingship but denied it by circumstance. One can imagine therefore the bitterness felt by Mathgamain's son Áed—who did indeed die in 1011 with the prestigious honorific title of *rígdamna Chaisil*—that his father's early death gave Brian and his offspring the opening to grab the title for themselves, denying Áed the succession probably because he was not yet of age. But when Áed came of age that resentment seems to have spurred him to work to undermine his uncle's rule, because we hear that in 986, a full decade after the death of his father, Mathgamain, Áed was taken into captivity by his uncle (*Aed macc Mathgamna do chumriuch la Brian mc. Cennetich*).[41] No further information is given, and we can do no more than speculate that Áed had become a thorn in Brian's side at this juncture, a time, as we have seen, when Brian's vulnerabilities were being exposed on more than one front.

Incidentally, one thing the episode does demonstrate is Brian's magnanimity. As in every other contemporary country, a normal way of dealing with familial opposition was to despatch the irritant to his Maker, and even lenient Irish kings would casually blind an opponent to render him unfit to rule. But no such fate befell Áed mac Mathgamna, who lived for another quarter of a century and, as noted, died as 'one eligible for the kingship of Cashel', in his own house, in 1011.[42]

RESUMPTION OF RAIDS AGAINST LETH CUINN

It may therefore have been with a new sense of self-confidence, having beaten off recent challenges, that Brian initiated a stunning new undertaking in 988. Again his eyes were on opponents to the north, and again he used his geographical advantage to the full, launching onto the Shannon at Lough Derg—from his very doorstep—an expeditionary river-fleet of some three hundred vessels, including the Norse fleet of Waterford, and directing their course northwards to Lough Ree. From there, the Annals of Inisfallen tell us (although the northern annals are again silent on this point), he set forth into Máel Sechnaill's kingdom of Mide, which his men harried, journeying on as far as the hill of Uisnech near Lough Ennell. The significance is not just that it brought Brian's army perilously close to Máel Sechnaill's own palace at Dún na Sciath, a large ring-fort on the western shore of the lough (plate 12), and his crannóg of Cró-inis on Lough Ennell itself, painfully exposing his vulnerability[43]: just as important is the fact that Uisnech, like other sites in the region, such as Tara, Tailtiu (Teltown, Co. Meath) and Tlachtga (the Hill of Ward, near Athboy), was a place of symbolic significance to the Irish (see map 2). Considered the dead centre of Ireland—Giraldus Cambrensis later called Uisnech the *Umbilicus Hibernie*—it was the focus of the May Day fire cult of Beltaine in pre-Christian times and had been at the heart of the Southern Uí Néill kingdom for centuries.

Like all his contemporaries, Brian knew this, and he went there for a reason. We see again and again in his campaigns through Ireland, throughout the course of his life, an awareness of tradition and symbolism and a determination to make bold statements about his own status by establishing an association with places of sanctity and sites from which power was thought to derive. His journey to Uisnech in 988 was one such statement of intent.

The annals then report that a squadron of Brian's 300-strong river-fleet was sent into Connacht after harrying Mide, and in an encounter with the defending Connachtmen they killed one of Connacht's princes, Muirgius son of Conchobar; but it was otherwise disastrous for Brian's fleet, whose crews were massacred. Among those killed fighting for Brian was Dúnlaing, described as *rígdamna Muman,* because his father, Dub-dá-Bairenn, had been a short-lived king of the province in the late 950s. What is interesting is that Dúnlaing was head of the South Munster dynasty of Eóganacht Raithlind (as had been Máel Muad, the killer of Brian's brother Mathgamain) but was now a loyal adherent of his upstart Dál Cais overlord.[44] Indeed Brian's status as protector of the people of South Munster was now such that when the monastery of Rosscarbery—in the very south of the province, between Clonakilty and Skibbereen—was plundered by Norsemen in 990 and its 'scholar (*fer légind*)' was taken prisoner by them and brought to the quarters they had set up on Scattery Island, Brian intervened and paid the ransom to secure his release.[45]

Brian's apparent reverse in Connacht in 988 was followed the next year by a successful siege of Dublin by the high-king, Máel Sechnaill, and perhaps these two happenings combined to hand temporary initiative to the latter, so that in 990 he was emboldened enough to enter Leth Moga and face the people of Tuadmumu in battle. However, none of the annals mention Brian in connection with this, the only named fatality on the Tuadmumu side being the king of Múscraige Tíre, who ruled the Co. Tipperary lands to the east of Lough Derg, which suggests that Dál Cais themselves went unscathed.[46]

In fact Brian was on the march again in Leinster in 991,[47] and it becomes clear from the events of the following year that his ambitions in Connacht had come closer to being realised than one might have suspected, and that he had gained some measure of overlordship. In

992 Máel Sechnaill crossed the Shannon into Connacht, so that 'he took a prey of cattle, greater than a king ever took (*co t-tucc brat-bhóromha as móamh tuc rí riamh*)'; but Brian responded by invading Mide and reached as far east as Lough Ennell, although 'he took neither cow nor man, and left like a fugitive (*co n-deachaidh ass a coír n-éludha*).' So say the non-Munster annals, as ever taking a dim view of Brian's actions, but even these admit that when he invaded Mide it was at the head of an army comprising the men of Munster *and* Connacht. (Incidentally, the Annals of Tigernach use for the first time his famous nickname in describing this campaign, *Brian Boroma co feraib Muman & Connacht*.)[48]

It seems that Brian was here acting as protector of the Connachtmen, retaliating against the aggression of the king of Tara, and it is evident that at least some of them were now his subjects. However negligible the return on the campaign's investment, it was nevertheless a significant landmark on Brian's path to national supremacy. He was now master of all Leth Moga and of at least part of one of the great provinces of Leth Cuinn. The balance was beginning to tip against Máel Sechnaill.

Brian's new dominance in Connacht saw him muster his fleet again in 993 and sail far up the Shannon, beyond Áth Liag, to attack all Bréifne (map 4).[49] This is not Athleague on the River Suck on the Galway-Roscommon border but the stony ford across the Shannon at the northern end of Lough Ree, crossed now by the bridge at Lanesborough, Co. Longford, and in this attack on Bréifne we see Brian attempting to boost his authority throughout the province, suggesting that his successes so far had been confined to the Connachtmen further south. Although the high-king marched into Leth Moga in 994, burning the church of Nenagh and defeating Brian and the army of Munster,[50] it seems to have had limited effect. The Munster annals ignore it completely and instead accentuate the positive: we hear of Brian building a fortress in 995 at Cashel and another on an island on Lough Gur, a long way to the south in the heart of Co. Limerick, a third at Inis Locha Sainglend—presumably at Singland, just east of the Norse town of Limerick—'and many structures besides (*Cumtach Cassil & Inse Locha Gair & Inse Locha Sainglend & dentai imdai archena*).'[51]

Then the same source states that in 996 Brian 'took the hostages of Uí Chennselaig and of Iarthar Liphe,'[52] meaning that he received the submission of the king of south Leinster and of the Uí Muiredaig king of

the Liffey plain in south Co. Kildare (map 5). On the face of it, as neither
of these held the overkingship of Leinster (which was then held by the
king of Uí Dúnchada, Donnchad son of Domnall Clóen), this does not
seem like a hugely significant development, but it may have been one of
a series of incremental steps in Brian's elevation that tilted the balance of
power in his direction and undermined the credibility of Máel Sechnaill's
claim to the overlordship of all Ireland. At least that is the only conclusion
to be reached from the momentous events of the following year.

THE BLEANPHUTTOGE ACCORD (AD 997)

In 997 an event occurred that, among the chronicles, only the Annals of
Inisfallen bother to mention, unquestionably because it was a thrilling
development for devotees of Brian mac Cennétig but bad news for the
high-king, Máel Sechnaill, and those who supported his hegemony:

> Brian mac Cennétig, with the princes of Munster about him (*co
> rigraid Muman imme*), and Máel Sechnaill mac Domnaill, king of
> Tara, went to Port dá Chaineóc, and they divided Ireland between
> them into two (*coro rannsat h-Erind ettarru i n-dó*), viz. Leth Cuinn
> to Máel Sechnaill and Leth Moga to Brian; and the hostages of the
> Leinstermen and of the Foreigners, which Máel Sechnaill had, were
> given to Brian.[53]

It is no surprise that Cogadh Gáedhel re Gallaibh, delighting as it
does in all Brian's achievements, also records this agreement, in not
dissimilar terms:

> Brian now made a great naval expedition (*Da ronad dan mórcoblach
> la Brian*) to Plein Pattogi, where Máel Sechnaill came to meet him,
> so that they concluded a peace there (*ina comdail, co ndernsat sith
> and*), viz., such hostages of Leth Moga as Máel Sechnaill had, i.e.,
> the hostages of the Foreigners and of the Leinstermen, to be ceded
> to Brian, and the hostages of Uí Fiachrach Aidne and of Uí Maine to
> him [Máel Sechnaill?]; and the forfeiture of Leth Cuinn henceforth
> to Máel Sechnaill without war or trespass from Brian (*ocus dilsi Leth
> Cuind o hin amach can coccad cen fogail ó Brian do Maelshechlaind*).[54]

Obviously there are slight variations in the two accounts, and in particular the contemporary annals make no mention of the hostages of Uí Fiachrach Aidne and Uí Maine. It is not entirely clear from the Cogadh whether they were to go to Brian or Máel Sechnaill under the accord: the text's nineteenth-century editor has them going to Brian, but as both these south Connacht kingdoms were within Leth Cuinn, their hostages now undoubtedly belonged with Máel Sechnaill, and presumably the point was that Brian had obtained the hostages of Uí Fiachrach Aidne and Uí Maine by his recent exploits in war and diplomacy, and the terms of the peace worked out between the two parties required their transfer to their rightful northern master.

Also, the two accounts differ about the site of the conference. The Cogadh has Pléin Pattogi, now Bleanphuttoge, on the eastern shore of Lough Ree on the Longford-Westmeath border (plates 13 and 14), whereas the annals have Port dá Chaineóc, a place whose exact position has not been definitely identified. There is a reference in another set of annals to a bishop of Clonfert drowning on the Shannon at Port dá Chaineóc in 1171,[55] and it is assumed to be on the riverbank somewhere south of Lough Ree in the direction of Clonfert. A site on the eastern side of the Shannon here, to the south of Banagher, near the present-day Offaly-Tipperary border, would indeed make a suitable venue, as it was on the very frontier between Leth Cuinn and Leth Moga. But it seems like an extraordinary decision by the author of the Cogadh (who uses the same or a very similar source as the Munster annalist) to alter the venue of the meeting for no good reason—and to a place that was, then as now, far from being a household name—and especially to alter it in such a way as to deny the conference a neutral setting on the border and move it to within Leth Cuinn, indeed to within the lands of peoples directly subject to Máel Sechnaill as king of Mide. Presumably, therefore, we should incline ourselves to believe its author on this point.

Wherever the venue of the meeting, it was of great significance. It is not that such rígdála (royal conferences) were unprecedented: we have already mentioned the great rígdál that took place at Terryglass, Co. Tipperary, in 737 at which peace was declared between the king of Tara, Áed Allán, and another remarkable Munster king, Cathal mac Finguine (died 742). And then there was the royal conference convened by Máel Sechnaill's great-great-grandfather, Máel Sechnaill I (died 862), at Rahugh, Co. Westmeath, in 859, which had attempted to transfer Osraige from Leth Moga to Leth Cuinn.

So it was not the calling of such a conference that was unprecedented but rather the circumstances and purpose behind it. A high-king might call together a *rígdál* in order to arrange matters to his liking or to dictate the terms of a settlement to men acknowledging their subordination to him; but that is not what happened in 997. Before the meeting Brian had been Máel Sechnaill's inferior; however unenthusiastic he was about it, that is how contemporaries perceived their relationship. But Brian came away from Bleanphuttoge with an agreement that saw him as the equal of his former lord. Ireland was to be divided into two equivalent spheres of influence (whether or not the two halves were equal in area is largely irrelevant, as contemporaries treated them as such), and the king of Tara was now no longer king of Ireland—or, if he was, Brian was to be joint king.

It was a startling development. And it is extraordinarily difficult to comprehend how it came about. Nothing in the build-up to it gives wind of what lies ahead. It can only be that Máel Sechnaill's status had become greatly enfeebled by recent proceedings, largely hidden from us. And they are hidden because our main sources, the annals, are a deplorably inadequate record of day-to-day events. Annals will frequently ignore altogether, or only grudgingly admit, happenings inimical to the compiler's political proclivities and concentrate instead on developments that buttress them. Even then, however, they are described in a manner so cryptic and so lacking in detail that telling the important items from the trivial is nigh on impossible. But there seems to have been nothing trivial about the Bleanphuttoge accord. A record of it is absent from almost all the surviving annal collections (put together later but drawing on largely the same body of evidence)—not because it did not matter but precisely because it did, because it augured so ill for their hero, Máel Sechnaill, and the Uí Néill generally. Munster sources played up its significance because for their hero it was a triumph, and it is beyond doubt that, in Brian's march to national power, it was the point of no return.

The incumbent claimant to lordship over all the Irish—with the force of upwards of half a millennium of convention, propaganda and popular belief behind him—was in terminal decline. The Uí Néill high-kingship of Ireland—which admittedly had never been as all-embracing as later generations of nationalists wished to believe (but neither was it the *ignis fatuus* to which modern revisionists have sometimes relegated it)—was falling asunder, and doing so, ironically, in the hands of one of its more effective recent incumbents. Bleanphuttoge was therefore a bitter pill to swallow that bought Máel Sechnaill some time, but few can have thought it a permanent resolution.

BRIAN AS JOINT KING OF IRELAND

The failure of the non-Munster annals to mention the peace of Bleanphuttoge is all the more grievous—and surely confusing for their readers—in the light of what the same annals tell us happened next. The Four Masters, in an account only slightly more elaborate than the version preserved in the Annals of Ulster and Chronicon Scotorum, have as a highlight of the year 998 the following account:

> An army was led by Máel Sechnaill and Brian, so that they obtained the hostages of the Foreigners, as a guarantee of good behaviour towards the Irish (*co t-tuccsat gialla Gall fri suabhais do Ghaoidhelaibh*). Máel Sechnaill, with the men of Mide, and Brian, with the men of Munster, collected immediately to Dublin, and carried off the hostages and the best part of their valuables from them.[56]

These two men, who for so long had been at war, were now partners, and not a word of explanation from the annalist about how this may have come about. *We* know, however, that this represents the working out of the Bleanphuttoge deal between the two kings, and by its terms we can assume that when the Dublin hostages were surrendered they were given into Brian's hands, Dublin being in Leth Moga, over which he was now the mutually contracted lord.

The Annals of Ulster then tell us that in the same year, 998, Brian launched an invasion of Leinster and ravaged it—again this was in accordance with Bleanphuttoge, and he had Máel Sechnaill's imprimatur in so doing—and they say that Máel Sechnaill did likewise in Connacht. Máel Sechnaill had accompanied Brian in seeking to secure the submission of Dublin, and so their new partnership required a *quid pro quo* in regard to Connacht. So Chronicon Scotorum has it that 'Brian with the men of Munster and Máel Sechnaill with the men of Mide [went] to Connacht and took their hostages (*Brian go feroib Mumhan & Maolseclainn go fferoib Midhe go Connachtaibh go ttugsat a ngialla*).' And what happened to the hostages is revealed by the Annals of Inisfallen:

> Brian mac Cennétig [went] to Áth Luain so that he took the hostages of the Connachta in one week, and handed those hostages over to Máel Sechnaill (*Brian mc. Cennetich co Áth Luain cora gaib giallu Connachti n-óensechtmain co tuc na giallu-sein do Mael Sechnaill*).

Áth Luain is of course the famous ford over the Shannon where the town of Athlone later grew up, and evidently Brian, basing himself there, had to wage a week-long campaign against the Connachtmen before they acknowledged their subjection and handed over hostages to prove it, but the new deal between the northern king and the southern king required that one partner hand them over to the other.

THE BATTLE OF GLENN MÁMA (AD 999)

The Bleanphuttoge accord was soon put to the test. When Brian brought his army into Leinster in 998 he possibly secured the submission of its overking, Donnchad son of Domall Clóen of Uí Dúnchada—although no source confirms this. At some point in 999, however, Donnchad was taken captive by the Norse king of Dublin, Sitriuc son of Amlaíb Cuarán (Sigtryggr Silkiskegg or Sitric Silkenbeard) and by Donnchad's rival for the Leinster overkingship, Máelmórda of Uí Fáeláin. Donnchad was apparently deposed for the time being, and Máelmórda took the title in his place.[57]

We do not know how Brian viewed this development, but the probability is that he opposed it. When, therefore, we read in the annals that Máel Sechnaill launched a raid on Leinster that year,[58] the most likely explanation is that he did so on Brian's behalf, chastising these errant vassals of his new political partner rather than launching an initiative of his own in Leth Moga. If so, Bleanphuttoge was still working well.

Later the same year Brian decided to intervene himself by undertaking a major military advance that culminated in the Battle of Glenn Máma— as far as we know, the first major field battle he had had to face since Belach Lechta in 978. The Cogadh claims that 'the Leinstermen and the

Foreigners of Dublin became disobedient to Brian and were bursting out in war (*batar Lagin ocus Gall go hamriarach do Brian ocus batar ic tobruchtad coccaid*).' It adds that Brian therefore marched 'against the Leinstermen and against the Foreigners, i.e. to attack Dublin until the Foreigners should submit (*co Laignib ocus Gullu, i. do gabail for Ath Cliath no co riaraigtis Gaill*).'[59] It seems odd that if Brian's principal opponents were the Leinstermen the solution should lie in besieging Dublin and forcing the submission of the Dubliners. And perhaps the explanation is that the real power in the region was the Norse king of Dublin, and that the local Irish kings were puppets who were answerable to him and whose fortunes were intertwined with his.[60] So the Cogadh can proceed to say that the

Leinstermen and the Foreigners came (*tancatar Lagin ocus Gaill . . .*) . . . to meet Brian and into his presence, viz. to Glenn Máma. They met there, Brian and the Munstermen, and the Foreigners accompanied by the Leinstermen (*ocus Gaill co Laignechaib leo*).

One sentence implies that the Leinstermen were the primary foe; the next has them merely accompanying the Norse, and that is the message too of the Annals of Ulster, which have Brian marching to Glenn Máma, where 'the Foreigners of Dublin came to attack him, and the Leinstermen along with them (*co tangadur Gaill Atha Cliath dia fhuabairt co Laignibh imaille friu*).'[61]

The emphasis in both sources on Brian's march on Dublin suggests that it was his primary target, the Leinstermen acting as the city's allies, just as one would expect if the campaign was a response to the recent overthrow of the Leinster king, Donnchad—in which, after all, the prime mover had been Sitriuc of Dublin (even if the main beneficiary had been his faithful assistant, and maternal uncle, Máelmórda of Uí Fáeláin) (table 4). Perhaps, therefore, Donnchad had submitted to Brian as king the year before, and come under his protection, so that his overthrow was considered an act of aggression, warranting the sternest of rebukes, and hence Brian mustered a great army and marched in the direction of Dublin to punish the culprits.

There certainly seems to have been a great degree of urgency about this campaign, which might point to an immediate crisis (and an anxiety, no doubt, to ensure that the Dubliners could not avail of reinforcements from the Isles, as they had before the Battle of Tara in 980 and were to do again at Clontarf). Brian made a forced march in the depths of winter, reaching the battle site at Glenn Máma— somewhere south of Liamain (Newcastle Lyons on the Dublin-Kildare border), perhaps between Rathcoole and Kill, where the Naas Road still runs[62]—on 30 December 999, suggesting that they had been on the move since Christmas, if not before.

By all accounts, the battle that followed was the greatest triumph of Brian's career thus far, and the slaughter seems to have been immense, on both sides, including at least one member of Sitriuc's family— although we can disregard the Cogadh's assertion that four thousand of 'the best of the Foreigners who were in Ireland (*do neoch as fearr baoi do Gallaibh a nErenn*)' lost their lives. So great a victory was it, and so elevated might Brian have appeared to his contemporaries after it, that three sets of annals that consistently take a pro-Máel Sechnaill stance— Tigernach, the Four Masters and Chronicon Scotorum (all, it should be said, ultimately drawn from a single Clonmacnoise source)—make the victorious army a joint command, led by Máel Sechnaill. The text on the Christian kings of Ireland (*'Do Fhlaithesaib Hérend iar Creitim'*) in the Book of Leinster, which is very grudging about Brian and effusive about Máel Sechnaill, similarly has Glenn Máma as a battle 'by Brian and Máel Sechnaill against the Foreigners (*Cath Glinni Mámma la Brian & Mael Sechnaill for Gallaib*).'[63]

As against these accounts, the often slightly more reliable Annals of Ulster, and the pro-Munster sources, the Annals of Inisfallen and the Cogadh, have it as a purely Munster affair. This may not be the entire truth either but is perhaps somewhat closer to it. That is to say, under the Bleanphuttoge pact Dublin and Leinster were within Brian's sphere; if they rebelled they rebelled against Brian, and if that rebellion was to be confronted, Máel Sechnaill's role can only have been in support of Brian. While it is possible that the army that prevailed so magnificently at Glenn Máma consisted solely of the forces of Munster, it would be quite wrong to rule out Máel Sechnaill's presence as an auxiliary.

After victory on the battlefield Brian's army—or the army of Máel Sechnaill and Brian, as the pro-Máel Sechnaill sources insist—stormed the *dún* of Dublin on New Year's Day 1000, the Cogadh adding that Brian entered its market (*Tanic iarsin isin margadh*), obviously considered one of its more remarkable assets.[64] They spent a week in the town, the annals saying that they 'carried off its gold and silver and captives,'[65] burned the *dún*, delighted in using as firewood a place called Caill Tomair ('the wood of Þórormr'), which may have been a special site for the Dubliners, and expelled their king, Sitriuc Silkenbeard. He had been present at the battle but now fled by ship, up along the eastern coast until he arrived in the east Ulster kingdom of Ulaid, expecting to find refuge there; but, the Annals of Inisfallen tell us, he 'found no protection for himself in Ireland until he handed over his hostages to Brian mac Cennétig.'

All the annals report this latter event as one of great significance. Sitriuc and his men, having fled before Brian from Dublin, negotiated a return only by making formal submission to the king of Munster, whereupon, as the Annals of Inisfallen tell us, 'Brian gave their fortress to the Foreigners (*co tarat Brian a n-dún dona Gallaib*).'[66] Sitriuc was reinstated as king of Dublin, but he was now Brian's vassal and owed him military service. And Dublin was to prove a deadly addition to Brian's arsenal.

WAR RESUMES AGAINST MÁEL SECHNAILL

The Bleanphuttoge accord was a compromise, and compromises rarely satisfy either side. One could argue that both kings were frustrated with the arrangement—Máel Sechnaill because his erstwhile paramountcy had been compromised by someone he would no doubt have considered a usurper, and Brian because his ambition had for now to be curtailed—but the initiative was unquestionably with Brian, especially after the fall of Dublin.

This was followed, the Cogadh says with some credibility (however unreliable its precise detail), by the submission of Leinster. It claims that on the day after the Battle of Glenn Máma, Máelmórda of Uí Fáeláin was captured, hiding in a yew tree, and dragged from it by Brian's son Murchad—his first mention in any text. Brian then kept Máelmórda in captivity until he received the hostages of all Leinster, at which point he was freed and set up as king in place of Donnchad son of Domnall Clóen, and the Leinster hostages were given into his charge (although the Annals of Inisfallen, drawn from a source similar to that used by the author of the Cogadh, place Brian's deposition of

Donnchad and ceding of the hostages of Leinster to Máelmórda three years later, in 1003).[67]

Whatever about the small print of the Cogadh's account, about which we always have to be cautious, and its slightly cavalier approach to chronology, the gist seems sound. At some point after the Battle of Glenn Máma, Brian succeeded also in reasserting overlordship over Leinster, and we shall soon see him extracting the military service of the armies of Leinster. His position was now so unassailable that it was inevitable that he would dispense with the Bleanphuttoge compromise and make a bid to topple Máel Sechnaill.

The Annals of Tigernach insert into their account of the year 1000 the terse statement that it saw 'the first revolt of Brian and Connacht against Máel Sechnaill the Great, through treachery (*Cét-impodh Briain & Connacht for Mael Sechlainn Mór tre mebail*).' The Four Masters and Chronicon Scotorum have the same pithy comment, but their compilers deferentially omit the reference to treachery. In truth, the accusation of treachery is understandable (although Tigernach's use of the epithet *Mór* to describe its hero suggests that this is a retrospective entry). There had been a formal pact between Brian and Máel Sechnaill—these two big beasts of the contemporary Irish scene—to divide the spoils evenly between them. It was a gentlemen's agreement perhaps, rather than a legal one, and faint hearts were no doubt in scarce supply in Ireland in these early days of the second millennium. Brian therefore abided by its terms only so long as it suited him to do so, and when he emerged triumphant from what appears to have been a do-or-die confrontation at Glenn Máma, and utterly overpowered Dublin in its aftermath— which probably meant that he was now the commander of all Ireland's Norse armies and fleets—he seems to have been unstoppable.

Ireland's was a warrior society. Arguably, the Irish prided their kings more for their martial endeavour than for any other quality, believing that fortune favoured the brave, perhaps even the reckless; it is doubtful if many of Brian's contemporaries would have thought any honour was to be gained from spurning the opportunity that now fell to him for the sake of persevering with an arrangement such as Bleanphuttoge, forged in circumstances that had since been transformed. Máel Sechnaill's days as king of Ireland were numbered, and Brian's hour had come.

Chapter 3 ~

| EMPEROR OF THE GAEL

In the early weeks of the year 1000, when the dust had settled on the Irish political landscape after the crushing of the Dublin army in the fields around Glenn Máma, it was clear for all to see that the balance had shifted. The king of Tara was vigorous still, but he was no longer supreme: Máel Sechnaill mac Domnaill, the Clann Cholmáin king of Mide, was being made to look unremarkable by his audacious southern adversary.

In theory, he and Brian mac Cennétig of Dál Cais were still about equal. Máel Sechnaill claimed to be the overlord of all Leth Cuinn, the northern half of Ireland. That meant he was king of all the peoples known collectively as the Southern Uí Néill, from the Shannon to the Irish Sea. As king of Tara he also claimed suzerainty over the Northern Uí Néill and their Airgialla vassals, extending his claim of overlordship to all of present-day Ulster west of the Bann. A titular claim—however feebly asserted—to the lands of the Ulaid east of the Bann was part of the package, and the whole thing was completed by an assertion of lordship over Connacht, such as had resulted in his acquisition of its hostages in 998, as we have seen (map 1).

At first sight, Brian's position seems the lesser, as his claim to overlordship of the southern half, Leth Moga, extended his authority beyond Munster only as far as Osraige (the Nore valley lands of

Co. Kilkenny and the western half of Co. Laois) and Leinster south of the Liffey.

Of course, with fewer provincial kingships to dominate, Brian's mastery over Leth Moga was the more easily obtained and maintained. More importantly, it is only in Leth Moga that the Vikings had successfully sustained a presence, and by the early years of the eleventh century theirs was an urban world. Their coastal enclaves might have been established to provide safe harbour for seagoing and river craft, but we have no reason to doubt that many of those who came to Ireland from their Scandinavian homeland did so to settle down. The population of their military bases engaged with their Irish neighbours—both aggressively, laying claim to the hinterland, so that their camps expanded to become small territorial kingdoms on Irish soil, and amicably, cornering the market on markets and internationalising Irish trade.

Beginning at Dublin (indeed north of it, perhaps, at Howth) and stretching all the way around the coast of Leth Moga—through Wicklow, Arklow, Wexford, Waterford, Cork and on to Limerick—there were communities of Norse extraction whose focus was no doubt substantially agricultural but who seem to have exploited their maritime position more determinedly than their Irish precursors. If the smaller of these bases merely possessed a cluster of Nordic-style fishing skiffs it nonetheless enabled them to thrive, while the larger of them—and particularly Dublin, Waterford and Limerick—had fleets rigged for the ocean. We know from the certain evidence of archaeological excavation that they brought into their cities—for that is what they were in process of becoming—goods that originated throughout northern and western Europe, and the outward leg of such voyages must surely have carried cargoes of Irish produce for sale or exchange.[1]

Towns generate trade, and trade generates wealth. We must always treat warily the more bombastic statements in Cogadh Gáedhel re Gallaibh that are not copied from annals, but at the very least it can tell us what contemporaries *expected* to be found in the Viking-founded towns of Ireland. It states that, after the Battle of Glenn Máma, Brian marched on Dublin and made off with its treasures, including, it claims, human booty, and 'they left not a treasure under ground that they did not discover'—presumably hoards of coins and other valuables buried for safekeeping. Then it says:

It was in that one place were found the greatest quantities of gold and silver, and bronze, and precious stones, and carbuncle-gems, and buffalo horns, and beautiful goblets. All these valuables were collected by them to one place. Much also of various vestures of all colours was found there likewise ... Many women also, and boys and girls, were brought to bondage and ruin by them [Brian's army] ...

It was bad luck for the Foreigners when that youth was born, viz., Brian son of Cennétig; for it was by him they were killed, destroyed, exterminated, enslaved, and bondaged. So that there was not a winnowing sheet from Howth to Tech Duinn [in Co. Kerry], in western Ireland, that had not a Foreigner in bondage on it, nor was there a quern without a female Foreigner. So that no son of a soldier or of an officer (*mac oclaig no octhigirnd*) among the Irish had to put his hand to a flail or any other labour on earth; nor did a woman have to put her hands to the grinding of a quern, or to knead a cake, or to wash her clothes, but had a male or female Foreigner to work for them ...

Brian now returned to his home after this, cheerfully, in good spirits, victoriously and triumphantly, as was his wont. Men of learning and historians (*lucht fesa ocus senchusa*) say that there was not a yeoman (*urraidh*) of the men of Munster on that expedition who had not received enough to furnish his house with gold and silver, and cloth of colour, and all kinds of property in like manner.[2]

The temptation is to dismiss this talk of enslaving the Norse; but then, a little more than a decade later, the death took place of a man called Gilla Mo-Chonna mac Fogartaig, who was king of Southern Brega, right on Dublin's doorstep, about whom even the normally sober Annals of Ulster say that 'by him the Foreigners were yoked to the plough, and two of them made to harrow after them and sow from their satchels (*Leis do-rata na Gaill fon arathar & da Ghall ic foirsed asa tiaghaibh 'na n-diaigh*).'[3] So perhaps Brian did indeed inflict a similar punishment on the Dubliners after Glenn Máma.

And when the Cogadh says of Dublin that Brian 'was there encamped in the town (*a ffoslongport isin mbaile*) from Great Christmas to Little Christmas,' there is a reason why it adds that 'he came then into the market (*isin margadh*) and the whole fortress (*an dún uile*) was burned by' his men.[4] It seems that when the writer thought of Dublin he thought of its two great fixed assets: its *dún*—which a poem in the twelfth-century Book of Leinster describes as one of the seven wonders of Ireland[5]—and its *margad,* its market-place. The very term was new to the Irish language, having been borrowed from the Old Norse *markaðr,* presumably because the concept differed strikingly from such trading-places as existed in Ireland previously.

And because of this domination of Ireland's import and export trade, and monopolisation of its internal commerce, the man who was the overlord of towns like Dublin, Waterford and Limerick had an income-generating capability without peer in Ireland. There were certainly coastal settlements in the Northern Half that engaged in trade—perhaps the vestigial remains of former Viking hubs in the sea-loughs of Ulster and among the peoples of Connacht's western seaboard, who had a vibrant seafaring tradition—but Leth Cuinn had nothing that resembled a town.

And thus, not to put too fine a point on it, the overking of the north of Ireland was poor because he lacked the prospect of taxing or otherwise creaming off the profits of towns and their trade. In contrast, the new markets of the southern port towns were what Brian came to dominate when he gained ascendency throughout Leth Moga. What is more, while the archaeological record reveals that these towns were—as one would expect—absorbed in trade, the documentary evidence will not allow us forget the large numbers of soldiers, including cavalry forces, that they could put into the field, or the regularity with which their erstwhile trading vessels could be employed (if they were one and the same) for carrying troops to war, or the superiority of their weaponry.[6] These ships too turn up in archaeological excavations, and of course the Irish acquired them or copied them, and Irish shipwrights must have harnessed the skills of their Norse counterparts in trying to reproduce Viking-style ships in all their magnificence.

But if one was lord of the Norse towns one did not have to bother with this. By the early days of the year 1000 all the Norse warriors of Ireland were the vassals of Brian Bóraime. They paid a pecuniary tribute to him in acknowledgement of his overlordship, their soldiers owed military service in his army, and their deployment and that of their warship-fleets was his prerogative alone. In such circumstances the reigning king of Tara, Máel Sechnaill mac Domnaill, for all the self-assurance that his traditional pre-eminence and blue blood provided, was powerless to stand in the way.

BRIAN'S SEIZURE OF THE HIGH-KINGSHIP

Within months, if not weeks, of Máel Sechnaill having stood shoulder to shoulder (if his own annals are to be believed) with Brian at the great Battle of Glenn Máma, Brian had turned against his former superior and recent collaborator and launched an invasion of Leth Cuinn.

To undermine Máel Sechnaill it helped if his subordinates could be detached from him, and so we are told that Brian was joined in the expedition by the men of South Connacht, perhaps the men of Uí Fiachrach Aidne (to which his first wife had belonged) and Uí Maine (map 4)—both part of Leth Cuinn—whose backing for his offensive he had no doubt solicited. Brian's supremacy throughout Leth Moga is implicit in the breadth of the coalition he now commanded. He led the army of Munster, which was joined by those of Osraige and Leinster and by the newly subdued Foreigners of Dublin; all were marching to war in the service of their new lord.

It is surely significant that the sources say this army set out for Tara. It was of course the traditional 'seat' of Máel Sechnaill as overlord of all the Uí Néill; but it seems highly unlikely that any king of Tara of the historical era ever resided there. While its ceremonial and symbolic role continued, large-scale occupation of the site by any prestigious political power had ended in prehistory. In fact, even though Máel Sechnall was 'king of Tara', Tara itself lay beyond his patrimonial lands. He was king of Clann Cholmáin, the hub of whose kingdom of Mide was the present-day Co. Westmeath, and his real heartland was the lands around Lough Ennell—indeed he lived in a crannóg on the lough. Tara was a long way to the east in the kingdom of Southern Brega, over which Máel Sechnaill claimed a kind of indirect lordship as supreme king among all the Uí Néill (map 2).

When, therefore, it was announced that Brian was marching on Tara, Máel Sechnaill had little to fear with regard to his personal safety. But that was not the point. Throughout his career Brian attached a great deal of importance to symbolism. Even if only sheep were grazing the celebrated Hill of Tara, it was the symbol *par excellence* of the extraterritorial kingship that Máel Sechnaill claimed: after all, he asserted not only that he was king of Clann Cholmáin but that, by virtue of his possession of the kingship of Tara, all Ireland was his. So this notional claim to Tara mattered, and therefore, in proclaiming his intention to challenge Máel Sechnaill for the kingship of all Ireland, Brian set forth for Tara.

But this first great challenge to the high-king went awry when a 'raiding party of horsemen (*crech marcach*)' from the army of Norse Dublin broke from the ranks and advanced alone into Mag mBreg (the plain between the Boyne and the Liffey), where Máel Sechnaill caught up with them and slaughtered them. Brian marched on until he came to Ferta Nemed (perhaps Fertagh, near Moynalty, north of Kells), although he eventually withdrew, the Annals of Ulster (biased in favour of Máel Sechnaill) saying that he 'retreated without battle or laying waste— by the Lord's insistence (*Do-luidh Brian tra fora chulu cen chath ce(n) indriudh, cogente Domino*).'[7] But there was probably more to it than that.

The Annals of Inisfallen (which give us Brian's viewpoint) are missing an account of these events, and so we are relying on annals that tend to make light of his achievements. But the Cogadh, even though it is exaggerated and biased, is based on a Munster source similar to that used by the Inisfallen annalist, and if we use it judiciously and make allowance for its propagandist tendency it can fill in some of the picture. And what it says might well explain why Brian eventually chose to withdraw on this occasion:

> A great expedition of all Leth Moga, both Foreigners and Irish, was afterwards made by Brian, until they reached Tara of the Kings; and messengers were sent from them to Máel Sechnaill mac Domnaill, king of Tara, and they demanded hostages from him, or battle should he refuse hostages, and Máel Sechnaill was given his choice of these. Máel Sechnaill, however, requested a month's delay to muster Leth Cuinn; and that delay was granted to him, during which no plunder or ravage, no destruction or trespass, or burning, was to be inflicted upon him. And Brian remained encamped during that time in Tara.

Who is to know for certain that this did not happen?—because we have to presume that lost in the exceedingly synoptic prose of the annals is the detail of the conventions of war and diplomatic engagement that accompanied the military manoeuvres on which the annalists chose to concentrate. We must give the Cogadh, therefore, the benefit of the doubt on this point.

It proceeds to describe Máel Sechnaill's response—a not unlikely one—when word reached him of the threat he now faced. It says he sent a poet called Gilla Comgaill ua Slebinn and another messenger as emissaries to the other three great kings of Leth Cuinn—Áed Ua Néill, king of Ailech (the Northern Uí Néill), Eochaid mac Ardgail, king of Ulaid, and Cathal mac Conchobair, king of Connacht—to ascertain whether they were willing to do battle with Brian and Leth Moga 'and contend the freedom of Tara with them (*ocus sairdecht Temrach do cosnum riu*),' or otherwise he would give hostages to Brian, 'because he did not have the power by himself to meet Leth Moga.' The author quotes from the poem that he asserts was addressed by Gilla Comgaill to Áed Ua Néill urging him to respond:

> For the sake of the Gaídil take thy shield
> Against that one man who injures all;
> Let not the Hill of Tara come into Brian's house—
> With those who now possess it let it be for ever . . .
>
> Let Eochaid bring—long the march—
> All the Ulaid—a noble company;
> Let Cathal, the warlike, the just, bring
> The province of the illustrious men of Ólnécmacht [i.e. Connacht] . . .

But it fell on deaf ears. Áed—who had little to gain from propping up Máel Sechnaill in the kingship of Tara, on which he had his own designs—responded that when his dynasty, the Cenél nEógain branch of the Uí Néill, had held Tara they had defended its freedom (*ra cosainset a shaoiri*), as was expected of those who held it, and therefore Áed 'would not risk his life in battle against Dál Cais defending the kingship of any other man (*nach tibred a anmain i cend catha fo lamaib Dalcais do cosnam rigi do neoch ele*).' At this point, if we are to believe this version of events, Máel Sechnaill realised the depths of his own plight and went in person to Ua Néill, offering to give hostages to him rather than to Brian if he would defend Tara, 'for I would rather be yours than Brian's (*is ferr lem beith accatso na beith ic Brian*), for we cannot avert going into Brian's house [i.e. submitting] if you do not come with me at the head of the battle, and the nobles of Leth Cuinn also.'

Áed Ua Néill assembled the nobles of Cenél nEógain, explained Máel Sechnaill's offer, and asked them to go into secret council to consider it, but they were suspicious of the high-king's *bona fides* and would come to Máel Sechnaill's aid only if he ceded half Mide and half the lands of Tara (i.e. half of Brega?) to them, an offer he was certain to reject.

The Cogadh does not supply dates for the events it relates, but it seems to ascribe this supposed crisis for Máel Sechnaill to the aftermath of Brian's incursion into Mag mBreg and Tara in 1000. It then describes—and again this is unique to it and therefore unverifiable—that Máel Sechnaill returned to his home among Clann Cholmáin, where his men advised him to submit to Brian. He travelled, it tells us, with a party of 240 horsemen and arrived at Brian's tent without any guarantees for his own safety beyond the word of Brian and Dál Cais. He explained his plight—stressing that, had he been able, he would have done battle but did not have the military strength to do so—and therefore would submit to Brian and give hostages.

Brian at first refused the vanquished high-king's hostages and offered him a truce for a year, during which time he proposed to seek the submission of the kings of Cenél nEógain and Ulaid himself if Máel Sechnaill stayed at peace; but Máel Sechnaill advised Brian to return home, 'because his [Brian's] expedition was sufficiently successful since he [Máel Sechnaill] had come into his house.' Then, and 'because they were at the end of their provisions,' Brian's men agreed that this was sound advice. So Brian offered Máel Sechnaill a steed each for the 240 men in his party, as *tuarastal,* the ceremonial stipend a vassal would receive following submission to his lord; but the men declined to accept them, and Máel Sechnaill passed them instead to Brian's son Murchad, 'who had given his hand into his hand on that day, for he was the only *rígdamna* [one eligible for kingship] of the men of Ireland who had not previously been in alliance with Máel Sechnaill.' Then both sides departed in peace and returned to their homes.[8]

This romantic gathering is a far cry from the grudging, not to say mocking, account of Brian's Tara campaign that the annals preserve for 1000, and there is no reason to treat what the Cogadh has to say as anything other than imaginative fancy. It is important to emphasise again, though, that there is usually a germ of truth in its narrative, and it is possible that, if Máel Sechnaill did not actually submit to Brian, he may at least have entered into some kind of negotiation towards a settlement. It is hard otherwise to explain the insistence of even the pro-Máel Sechnaill annalistic accounts that Brian left Tara in 1000 without having either given battle or engaged in raiding. If he had the vast army of all Leth Moga with him, why would he decline the opportunity to plunder? And perhaps therefore there is something to the Cogadh's claim that Brian agreed to withdraw for a year—after which he would obtain Máel Sechnaill's submission—for even the pro-Máel Sechnaill Chronicon Scotorum states inscrutably for the following year, like a bolt out of the blue, that 'Brian begins to reign (*Brían regnare incipit*),' while the related Annals of Tigernach (referring to him by his nickname) have 'Brian Bóraime reigns (*Brían Boroma regnat*).'[9]

In 1001, therefore, some great change came over the Irish political firmament, and perhaps it had become clear to all that Brian mac Cennétig's great expedition to Tara in 1000 had sounded the death-knell of Máel Sechnaill's high-kingship, and that Máel Sechnaill's eventual submission to his Munster adversary was but a matter of time.

Máel Sechnaill had not quite given up yet, however. In 1001 he joined forces with the king of Connacht, Cathal mac Conchobair, and together they constructed what most of the annals call a *tóchar* across the Shannon at Áth Luain (Athlone); the Four Masters have another *tóchar* being built half way across the Shannon at Áth Liag (Lanesborough).[10] This word usually translates as 'causeway' or 'passage' and survives in many place-names, where it typically denotes a trackway through bog.[11] It might seem, therefore, that the two kings—whose territory straddled the Shannon—were engaged in a noteworthy feat of engineering to bridge their two kingdoms: lacking the capacity to build a bridge, one can imagine them laying a timber pathway across the great river's famous ford at the site.

But to think this would be to form an entirely wrong impression of what the two men were up to, as the fortunate survival in the Annals of Inisfallen of an alternative account of these engineering works makes plain. This version records the placing of what it calls 'a great obstruction on the Shannon (*mórimme mór for Sinaind*) at Áth Luain by Máel

Sechnaill and by the king of Connacht and by all Leth Cuinn *against* the men of Munster (*fri firu Muman*),' from which it is clear—and there can be no better indication of Brian's dependence on the Shannon for transporting his troops northwards—that the purpose was to forestall the advance of the Munster fleet. Evidently it was widely known that Brian's army would be on the march again soon, and this barricade on the Shannon was a novel if desperate—and doomed—attempt to inhibit it.

And just how futile it was is demonstrated by the brief admission by the annals that in the following year, 1002,

> Brian made a hosting to Athlone and took the hostages of the Connachta and of the men of Mide (*Slogad la Brian co Ath Luain co ruc giallu Connacht & fer Midhe*).[12]

We know a little bit more about this pivotal event from other accounts. The Four Masters, for example, note that Brian's forces comprised the armies of Munster, Leinster and the Norse.[13] The Annals of Inisfallen add that Brian also led an expedition into Connacht, and this version is amplified by the author of the Cogadh, who confirms that, the main force having sailed up the Shannon to Athlone, this land army was busy throughout Connacht (*sluagh ar tír ar fud Connacht*) and secured its hostages after a week. Perhaps the settlement included Brian's acceptance in marriage of Dub Choblaig, daughter of the king of Connacht, Cathal mac Conchobair (table 3). The Cogadh then adds that Máel Sechnaill offered his hostages that same day and that, when all the hostages were conveyed to Athlone, Brian immediately returned home with them.[14]

All the annals also note that in the same year the king of Ailech, Áed Ua Néill, led an army to Tailtiu (Teltown, Co. Meath; see plate 17)—the traditional setting for the *óenach* or assembly of the king of Tara (although it had gone into abeyance in recent times)—but returned home in peace, we are told, and he also led an invasion of Connacht. Evidently both campaigns were his angry rejoinder to the decision of the kings of Tara and Connacht to submit to Brian.

Yet none of the accounts have anything to say in recognition of the significance of the submission of the king of Connacht (including, oddly enough, the Cogadh, presumably because it sees the real transformation as occurring after Brian's Tara expedition in 1000). The dozen words used by the annals to describe the Athlone expedition of 1002 disguise a development of enormous significance in Irish history. The Uí Néill high-king of Ireland had become the vassal of Brian Bóraime (as had the king of the great province of Connacht). Brian mac Cennétig was now king of Ireland, in the sense that, even if there were other kings of Leth Cuinn who had yet to yield to the inevitable, there was no-one in Ireland with a better claim to the title. Máel Sechnaill would remain as king of Tara, but as he was no longer king of Ireland this meant that the link that had existed for centuries between the kingship of Tara and the kingship of Ireland was broken.

We have entered a new phase in Ireland's history. And so it was that when, later that year, Brian set out on a grand expedition to Dún Delca in Conaille Muirthemne (the hill fortress nowadays called Castletown Mount, about 2 km west of Dundalk, which takes its name from it; see plate 15) to extend his extraordinary new hegemony throughout the island, all the annals describe him marching at the head of 'the men of Ireland (*co feraib Erenn*).'

BRIAN AS KING OF IRELAND

What an extraordinary transformation in his fortunes Brian mac Cennétig had effected over the preceding quarter of a century, since he had been propelled from near-anonymity by the murder in his prime of his older brother Mathgamain! The Annals of the Four Masters say he was in his seventy-sixth year at the time,[15] because they believed him to have been born in the mid-920s; but, as we have seen, it is more likely that he had recently turned sixty. Whichever is true, he showed the most extraordinary drive for his years.

The annals tell us that the great national army Brian led to Dún Delca in 1002 included the men of Munster and Leinster and the Norse of Dublin and Waterford, joined now by his new subordinates, the men of Connacht and the men of Mide, under Máel Sechnaill's personal command. (Presumably the Norse of Limerick were there too, but by now they were considered a natural constituent of Brian's own forces and do not get separate billing.) Their decision to converge on Dún Delca is striking, bearing in mind that the Annals of Inisfallen describe it as a manoeuvre 'against the Ulaid to take their hostages (*co Ultaib do gabáil a n-giall*).' This is because Dún Delca was anciently associated with Cú Chulainn, whose role in single-handedly defending Ulster from Medb's invading army of Connacht is at the core of the epic tale *Táin Bó Cúailgne* ('The cattle-raid of Cooley'), which was rapidly acquiring the status of a national epic. Dún Delca therefore guarded the very entrance into the kingdom of the Ulstermen, the Ulaid, and it is quite possible that Brian's decision to make it the destination of his grand excursion was not just because it was on the traditional route northwards into Ulster but was a self-conscious manipulation of the site's epic associations.

There then came towards Dún Delca the Dál Fiatach king of Ulaid, Eochaid mac Ardgail, and Áed Ua Néill of Ailech (called by the Four Masters *rígdamna Érenn*, to show that he was now Brian's chief contender for the high-kingship), along with the latter's Cenél nEógain followers from Cos. Derry and Tyrone, as well as Cenél Conaill of Co. Donegal and the Airgialla of mid-Ulster (map 3).

It is not clear whether we should envisage two hostile armies facing each other at Dún Delca across a potential battlefield, or a high-powered conference between kings meeting to thrash out a new beginning in this new age of Brian. All sources state that Brian sought hostages from Áed and Eochaid, in acknowledgement of his overlordship, the Cogadh adding what goes unsaid in the annals, that 'otherwise war would be proclaimed against them if they would not give them,'[16] a threat under which they refused to buckle. There must have been some kind of stalemate, because the annals are clear that the northern kings 'did not permit them to advance further (*connár leigsidar secha-sin*),' but all sources are agreed that the two sides parted under a truce, Brian having failed, however, to secure hostages or sureties (*cor scarsat fo ossudh cen giall, cen eteri*).[17]

Perhaps too there is something in the Cogadh's insistence that the terms of the truce gave the northern kings a year in which to decide whether to opt for war or give hostages, during which time they undertook not to attack Máel Sechnaill or the Connachtmen.[18] The reason for thinking so is that, if we assume—as we must—that the Dún Delca expedition came in the latter part of 1002, a year's truce would explain why the annals record no action by Brian in regard to the north in 1003. The only notice of his actions is in Leinster, where he deposed its king, Donnchad son of Domnall Clóen, and set up in his place Máelmórda of Uí Fáeláin, on whom Brian bestowed the hostages of Leinster as a sign of his new lordship.[19]

The Cogadh then goes on to state:

A great expedition of all the men of Ireland, both Irish and Foreigners, of all who were from Sliab Fuait [in South Armagh] southward, was made by Brian at the end of a year after that against the Ulaid, and he took the hostages of all Ulaid since Áed [Ua Néill of Ailech] failed to give him battle.[20]

The implication here seems to be that, as Áed Ua Néill claimed to be overking of all the North (In Fochlae or In Tuaiscert), and entitled therefore to the Ulaid's hostages, the onus was on him—when the year's truce had expired—to resist Brian's overtures on the field of battle or to accept the consequences. His failure to meet the challenge meant that the Munster king could claim the hostages of the Ulaid, and these Brian now obtained.

If this account is true, Brian obtained the hostages of the ancient kingdom of Ulaid, probably at some point in the latter half of 1003. The problem is that it is not recorded in the surviving annals—which, it must be admitted, have very little to say about *anything* in 1003. This is another of those instances where the Cogadh's version of events cannot be proved but seems credible.

And there are one or two reasons for giving credence to its account. For one thing, in the following year, 1004, Brian headed north again. If he had not already received the anticipated submission of the Ulaid he would doubtless have come knocking again. Instead of heading to the north-east, however, he and Máel Sechnaill led a great army up into northern Connacht, reaching as far as Tráig Eóchaille, the strand of Trawohelly on Ballysadare Bay, Co. Sligo, where they obviously halted before attempting a crossing of the famous ford at Es Dara (from which Ballysadare gets its name), which would take them into Uí Néill territory—and indeed the annals report that they intended to 'go around Ireland (do dhol timcheall Ereann).' But the Cenél nEógain had got word of their plans, mustered an army, and prevented them passing any further.[21]

And another reason for thinking that the Cogadh may be correct in suggesting that Brian secured the hostages of Ulaid from under the nose of Áed Ua Néill in 1003 is that within months Áed went to war with Ulaid. His invasion culminated in the devastating Battle of Cráeb Tulcha, near Glenavy, Co. Antrim. (Presumably this site was chosen because of its symbolism, being the inauguration-place where Eochaid and his ancestors had been made kings of Dál Fiatach; see map 3.) It was considered a victory for Áed Ua Néill's army of Cenél nEógain, because the Ulaid were slaughtered in their droves and their king, Eochaid mac Ardgail, was slain; but in the counter-attack Áed himself—a rising star on the political scene, still only in his late twenties—lost his life.

IMPERATOR SCOTORUM

The Battle of Cráeb Tulcha was a traumatic affair. Cenél nEógain had to find new leadership, and it emerged in the person of Áed Ua Néill's nephew Flaithbertach, who in time would marry Brian's daughter Bébinn (table 3). As for Ulaid, it descended into a bloodbath as the princes of Dál Fiatach—the dynasty that tended to monopolise the overkingship—butchered each other for the chance to win the prize while also having to make war on their jealous rivals of Dál nAraidi.[22] Whatever relationships Brian had been building up with the northern kings on the eve of Cráeb Tulcha, they were set at naught.

Still, the instability must have undermined the north's ability to withstand Brian's demands. Therefore in 1005 he set out on a grand expedition to the north. The Four Masters—still rather damning in their faint praise—say that he led 'the men of the *south* of Ireland (*co f-Feraibh Deisceirt Ereann*),' but other annals have it as an army of Ireland, and the Annals of Ulster say that Brian travelled in the company of 'the royalty of Ireland (*co rigraidh Erenn ime*).'[23] This source, on the other hand, says nothing of the political objectives of the campaign, which the Four Masters and Chronicon Scotorum record as being to take the hostages of the new kings of Ulaid and Cenél nEógain (the Annals of Inisfallen have instead Cenél nEógain and Cenél Conaill). The army headed first for Tailtiu in Co. Meath, where, we are told, Brian stayed for a night (plate 17). The point of this was undoubtedly to exploit the significance of the site, that of the ancient *óenach* of the kings of Tara.

From there Brian marched north to Armagh, and the Annals of Inisfallen tell us that he camped at Emain Macha (unless they are talking about a second northern campaign that year, as their account of the year 1005 twice mentions perambulations to Armagh—the second, one suspects, a duplicate of the first). Emain Macha (Navan Fort) is about 3 km to the west of the primatial city, and undoubtedly the establishment of Brian's temporary royal headquarters there was another attempt to milk symbolism for all it was worth. In Irish literary tradition Emain Macha was the capital of Conchobar mac Nessa's kingdom of the Ulaid, whose heroic deeds are 'remembered' in the Ulster Cylce, of which the *Táin* is the best-known tale. We do not know if King Conchobar was a real person or whether Emain Macha—long since deserted by Brian's day—had ever been a royal fortress, as opposed to a place of prehistoric religious ceremony;[24] but Brian undoubtedly *believed* that Emain had formerly held great political significance for the Ulstermen, and he pitched his royal camp there in 1005 to let the men of the north know who was boss and to make the point that he was king in the mould of the kings of yore.

From Emain Macha he skirted around the eastern shore of Lough Neagh until he came to Ráith Mór (Rathmore, near the town of Antrim), the palace of the king of Dál nAraidi in Mag Line (the valley of the Six Mile Water), and there he did indeed accept the submission of the kings of Dál nAraidi and Dál Fiatach.

In political terms, this was a substantial achievement. But what all the sources regard as the highlight of the campaign was Brian's week-long visit to Armagh, during which he laid a gift of twenty ounces of gold on the altar.[25] Again this visit had much to do with symbolism. Armagh had long claimed primacy over the Irish church. It was a claim based on a supposed connection with St Patrick, which depended on believing that Patrick was the most noble of the saints of Ireland and that Armagh was the most noble of the churches he founded. As Patrick's status as the Apostle of Ireland became more firmly established over the centuries, the churchmen of Armagh strove ever harder to claim their right to be Ireland's first church and to extend Armagh's authority (and its revenue-collecting capability) throughout the Irish world.

Although Armagh lay within the territory of the Airgialla, it had for many generations been closely associated with their superiors, the kings of Cenél nEógain, and one might have expected the abbot of Armagh in 1005 to stand with the new king of Cenél nEógain, Flaithbertach Ua Néill, in resisting the unheard-of demands for supremacy of his future father-in-law, the Dál Cais upstart. Instead the abbot of Armagh accepted a very generous gift of gold from Brian, and it is clear that this was only the beginning of it, and that the two had done a deal: the abbot needed the collaboration of the king of Ireland—irrespective of his background—in asserting his own ecclesiastical hegemony throughout the island, and Brian of course knew that his own claim to political supremacy would be all the more persuasive if it came with the imprimatur of the country's leading ecclesiastic.

Armagh had in its possession a collection of early works by and about St Patrick, bound together, along with a set of the Gospels and a Life of St Martin of Tours, in an early ninth-century vellum manuscript called the Book of Armagh. Not a single artefact survives today that we can say for certain was touched, or even seen, by Brian Bóraime, with the exception of this manuscript (now preserved in the library of Trinity College Dublin). And we know that Brian saw it in 1005, because on folio 16v is written the following note (plate 16):

Sanctus Patri[ci]us iens ad Cœlum mandavat totum fructum laboris sui tam baptismi tam clausarum quod elemoisinorum deferendum esse Apostolicae Urbi que Scotice nominatur Ardd Macha. Sic reperi in bebliothicis Scotorum.

Ego scripsi id est Calvus Perennis in conspectu Briani Imperatoris Scotorum et que scripsi finituit pro omnibus regibus Maceriae.

St Patrick, going up to Heaven, commanded that all the fruit of his labour, as well of baptisms as of law-cases and of alms, should be carried to the Apostolic City which is called in the Scotic language Armagh. Thus I have found it in the libraries of the Scoti.

I have written [this], that is, [I], Calvus Perennis, in the sight of Brian, Emperor of the Scoti, and what I have written he determined for all the kings of Maceria.

The person who inscribed this important statement calls himself Calvus Perennis, meaning 'eternally tonsured one,' which is a literal translation into Latin of his Irish name, Máel Suthain. When he died in 1031 he was described in one version of his obit as 'venerable senior of

Ireland (*sruithsenóir h-Erend*),' but another reveals the vital intelligence that he was Brian's *anmchara,* a term that literally means 'soul-friend' but implies that he was his confessor, or royal chaplain.[26]

There can be little doubt, therefore, that this inscription in the Book of Armagh is an authentic record of Brian's visit in 1005—although he may have been in Armagh again the following year, when he is reported to have granted 'the full demand of the community and successor of Patrick (*co tarait oighreir samhtha Patraicc & a comharbai*),' or in 1012, when he 'gave complete immunity to Patrick's churches on that hosting (*co tuc og-shoere do chellaib Patraicc dont shluagad-sin*),'[27] and it is just possible that the inscription dates from one of those later visits.

Either way, it would be wrong to view this brief note as akin to something a passing dignitary might inscribe in a visitors' book. While the Book of Armagh was one of the great monastic city's most valued treasures, and indeed was part of the insignia of the abbot of Armagh, who regarded himself as the heir of St Patrick (*heres Patricii* or, in Irish, *comarba Pátraic*), what made the Book of Armagh so valuable was what it contained. Besides the text of St Patrick's *Confessio,* then believed to have been written in the saint's own hand, it contains Bishop Tírechán's *Collectanea* on churches associated with Patrick, the *Additamenta* or additions to Tírechán, Muirchú's Life of St Patrick, and the *Liber Angeli* ('Book of the Angel'), in which an angel is said to have decreed that Armagh would have primacy over the Irish church.[28] In fact the phrasing of Máel Suthain's inscription echoes the language of the *Liber Angeli,* and it seems certain that this great statement of Armagh's rights was placed before or read out to Brian on the occasion, so that he might see and hear for himself on what unimpeachable authority Armagh rested its claims. The memorandum is therefore not a million miles removed from an *inspeximus* (literally, 'We have inspected') or exemplification whereby a king views a charter of lands or rights granted by one of his predecessors and confirms them in his own name. In this instance Brian has seen for himself Armagh's claim to certain privileges, 'as well of baptisms as of law-cases and of alms,' and he is formally confirming these rights.

In theory, as king of Ireland, he should be able to impose Armagh's claims on the entire country, but he seems to be giving legal force merely to the extension of Armagh's prerogatives to Munster, which had been fitful in the past, hence the statement that this is what he 'determined for all the kings of Maceria.' (This term is undocumented elsewhere, but the great nineteenth-century Celtic scholar Eugene O'Curry, noting that *maceria* is Latin for a stone wall, suggested that it probably meant Cashel, whose name *Caisil* itself comes from Latin *castellum,* a stone fortress.)[29]

If the agreement in effect acknowledged the right of the church of Armagh to raise revenue and to enforce its church law in Munster, it was effective immediately. Two years later the death took place of a person called Tuathal ua Máelmacha, who hailed from the Armagh area and is described as 'scholar and successor of St Patrick in Munster (*saoi & comhorba Pháttraicc i Mumhain*)' and who seems to have been the first in a line of individuals holding the office of *máer* ('steward') of Armagh throughout Brian's province.[30]

The memorandum is important too for its description of Brian as 'Emperor of the Scoti (*Imperator*[*is*] *Scotorum*).' As we have seen, Máel Suthain was something of a pedant, who rejoiced in giving new names to familiar things, so that he himself became Calvus Perennis and Caisel (Cashel) or Mumu (Munster) became, instead of the usual Latin forms Cassel(ensis) and Momonia(e), the outlandish Maceria(e), which has caused some scratching of heads ever since. It is possible, therefore, that he concocted the formula *Imperator Scotorum* for Brian entirely off his own bat and that we should not read too much into it.

But it was another writer, the man who wrote the account of the Battle of Clontarf preserved in the Annals of Ulster, who likened Brian to Rome's first emperor when he called him 'the Augustus of the whole of north-west Europe.' Admittedly this term was later applied to a few kings, such as the great Tairdelbach Ua Conchobair (died 1156) and Muirchertach Mac Lochlainn (died 1166), but its first occurrence in the annals is to describe Brian—whom the Cogadh likewise dubs, using Augustus's original name, 'the beautiful, ever-victorious Octavian'; and perhaps both these writers did so being aware of some grand imperial ambition on Brian's part.[31]

Besides, this inscription was written into the Book of Armagh in Brian's presence, in a formal instrument that was intended to have something resembling legal force. At the very least we can assume that Brian was happy with the form of words and that it therefore reflected his own view of his status. And, that being so, it has something to tell us.

As has been pointed out before, the formula *Imperator Scotorum* is reminiscent of the title *Imperator Romanorum* used by the German king Otto III (died 1002) after he became Holy Roman Emperor some years earlier.[32] The Irish—especially the Irish of Munster—were very familiar with Germany because of the vibrancy of Irish Benedictine monasteries or *Schottenklöster* at such places as Erfurt, Würzburg, Nürnberg, Regensburg, Eichstätt and Vienna.[33] An educated churchman like Máel Suthain and a Christian king like Brian would of course know that the Frankish and German kings had been given the imperial title by Rome in expectation that they would act as protector of the church, and such a role was certainly implicit in Brian's new commitment to Armagh. But of course when the German king claimed to be emperor he did not cease to be king: rather the emperor was a king who believed himself the superior of all other kings; and there can be little doubt that, in claiming that he too was an *imperator*, Brian intended all to know, both at home and abroad, that among the many kings of Ireland he was supreme. He was therefore trying to give expression to a new reality: that while Ireland would continue to have many lesser kings, he—by compulsion or persuasion—was to be king over all the rest.

And if the Irish were familiar with the Frankish empire they were a great deal more familiar with contemporary England. Brian reached political maturity at a time when Edgar, king of the English (959–75), was displaying quasi-imperial tendencies. In 973, towards the end of his reign, Edgar held a strangely late consecration of himself as king, perhaps inspired by the imperial splendour of the marriage and the coronation as empress of Otto II's queen at Rome the previous year. It is probably relevant that Edgar's celebration took place at the Roman city of Bath. Immediately afterwards Edgar 'took his whole naval force to Chester, and six kings came to meet him, and all gave him pledges that they would be his allies on sea and land.'[34] Another account tells us that 'all the kings who were in this island, Cumbrians and Scots, came to Edgar—once eight kings on one day—and they all submitted to Edgar's direction.'[35] Later sources imagined that Edgar steered a boat on the River Dee that was rowed by the other kings, and they list them as including kings of Gwynedd (north Wales) and Deheubarth (south Wales) and of elsewhere in Wales, the king of Strathclyde and even the king of Scotland, Cináed son of Máel Coluim.

Also among them was Maccus mac Arailt, described as 'king of many islands (*plurimarum rex insularum*)'. The extraordinary thing about Maccus is that his family and Brian's had a long-standing alliance (as we shall see), which had begun at about the time of his submission to Edgar at Chester; and within a year Maccus was collaborating with Dál Cais to oust the Limerick Norse from their retreat on Inis Cathaig (Scattery).[36] This alliance continued for nearly a hundred years until Maccus's grand-nephew Echmarcach mac Ragnaill (died 1005) mic Gofraid (died 989) sailed off in exile to Rome with Brian's son Donnchad in 1064.[37]

A year before Edgar's assembly at Chester, Brian's brother Mathgamain had presided over a novel assembly of the nobility of Munster at which 'the three ordinances (*na trí cáne*)' were passed for the banishment of the *svartleggja* (Norse mercenaries), the expulsion of the Norse from Limerick, and the destruction of the latter's fortress,[38] and undoubtedly Edgar's Chester assembly the following year would have startled by its unprecedented scale and would have inspired by its sheer ambition.

BRIAN AND THE SCOTS

In the memorandum Brian is called emperor not of Ireland but of the *Scoti*. In one sense this just means 'the Irish': it is simply a Latin equivalent of *Goídil* ('the Gaels'); but then again the *Goídil* included the entire Gaelic-speaking world of Scotland, the Western Isles, and the Isle of Man. In fact in this very period the term *Scoti* (or *Scotti*) was beginning to acquire its restricted application to descendants of the early Irish colonists in northern Britain.[39] There was a way of making it clear that Brian was claiming to be emperor of the inhabitants of Ireland alone, and that was by using the word *Hibernici*, the people of Ireland. Everyone knew this, such as the amanuensis of the chronicler Marianus Scotus, who, writing in Mainz in 1072, clarifies the matter lest there be any doubt about his place of birth by pointing out in a marginal note that 'I have written this book out of affection for you and for all *Scoti*, that is, Irish (*Hibernensibus*), because I myself am Irish (*Hibernensis*).'[40] The failure to make the same distinction in the title given to Brian in the Book of Armagh is probably sheer indifference: one can imagine the Irish of what they considered the mainland, Ireland, routinely forgetting their provincial cousins across the North Channel.

Still, the title was adopted at Armagh, and Armagh did not forget Scotland, with which it had very firm links. When Dub-dá-leithe, *comarba* of Patrick at Armagh, undertook the headship of the Columban family of churches in 989 he did so 'by the counsel of the men of Ireland and Scotland.'[41] When Dubthach Albanach ('the Scotsman') died at Armagh in 1064 he was described as 'chief confessor of Ireland and Scotland.'[42] And when the most illustrious of all Patrick's successors, St Malachy, died in 1148 he was described as 'head of religion of all Ireland and Scotland.'[43]

Irish kings like Brian, therefore, who became benefactors of Armagh were associating themselves with what was a centre of religion and learning for the people of both Ireland and Scotland, the classic illustration of which was the gesture made in 1169 by the then king of Ireland, Ruaidrí Ua Conchobair, to provide a perpetual grant of 'ten cows every year from himself, and from every king [of Ireland] that should succeed him, for ever, to the lector of Armagh, in honour of St Patrick, to instruct in learning the students of Ireland and Scotland.'[44]

And while Brian's new title of Emperor of the Scoti was adopted when he was in Armagh on ecclesiastical business, the context, as we have seen, was a grand procession to the north-east corner of Ireland to seek the acquiescence of all those willing to 'come into his house', as the annals might put it. It would not be in the least bit improbable if some Irish—for that is how they were viewed, and viewed themselves— of Gaelic Scotland and the Isles took the opportunity to attend Brian's court and, at the very least, make the acquaintance of this new power in the land. Some may have sought his protection.

Just then turbulent things were happening across the North Channel. In the same year as Brian's Armagh campaign—and almost in the same sentence in the annals—it is reported that there took place 'a battle between the men of Scotland themselves, in which fell the king of Scotland, i.e. Cináed son of Dub (*Cath eter fhiru Alban immoneitir i torchair ri Alban, .i. Cinaedh m. Duibh*).'[45] Another account has it that 'Cináed son of Dub son of Máel Coluim, king of Scotland, was killed by Máel Coluim son of Cináed.'[46] This individual then succeeded as King Máel Coluim II (died 1034),[47] and it is said of him in the so-called 'Prophecy of Berchán' that he was the 'son of a woman of Leinster . . . son of the cow that grazes upon the countryside of the Liffey (*Mac mna Laighen . . . mac bo bronn as bruigh Life*).'[48] If this is true, his father,

Cináed II (died 995), had married a Leinster princess and presumably therefore formed a political alliance with a king of Leinster at some point during his reign (see table 4). There were four men whose reign as king of Leinster overlapped with Cináed's, but it is worth mentioning that when Cináed succeeded as king of Scotland in 971 the reigning Leinster king was Murchad mac Finn of Uí Fáeláin (died 972), father of the famous Gormlaith who was later to marry (and be divorced by) Brian, and of the Máelmórda whom Brian had allowed to succeed to the kingship of Leinster in 1003.

If another of the siblings was the 'woman of Leinster' who gave birth to King Máel Coluim II of Scotland we should perhaps allow for the possibility that when Máelmórda rose in rebellion against Brian in 1013, initiating the events that would lead to the great Battle of Clontarf, he may have looked for assistance to his putative nephew on the throne of Scotland.

Incidentally, Máelmórda murdered a rival in 999, which the Book of Leinster claims he did at the instigation of the then high-king, Máel Sechnaill mac Domnaill.[49] When, in 1007, Máel Sechnaill revived the ancient Lammas assembly known as Óenach Tailten the poet Cúán ua Lothcháin commemorated the occasion with a poem in which he claimed that an unbroken truce prevailed throughout Ireland and Scotland while it lasted.[50] This may just be poetic licence and surely does not require us to think that either Brian as Emperor of the Scoti, or Máel Sechnaill himself, exercised sufficient authority over Scottish affairs to be able to enforce such a peace; but it may be worth pointing out that Máel Sechnaill had a son who was called simply 'the Scotsman (In tAlbanach)' in one set of annals and in the Cogadh when he was killed in 1013,[51] and perhaps he got the nickname because this family of Brian's predecessor as high-king had indeed some notable connection with Scotland: perhaps he was fostered there, which territorial and dynastic nicknames are often used to indicate.

It is just possible, therefore, that when Brian was in the north of Ireland in 1005 one or more of the Scottish lords contending for power at that time made an approach to him for assistance—bearing in mind that he now had at his beck and call the magnificent warrior fleets of all the Norse towns of Ireland—and that Brian's grandiose title of Emperor of the Scoti is intended to reflect some loose suzerainty over them;

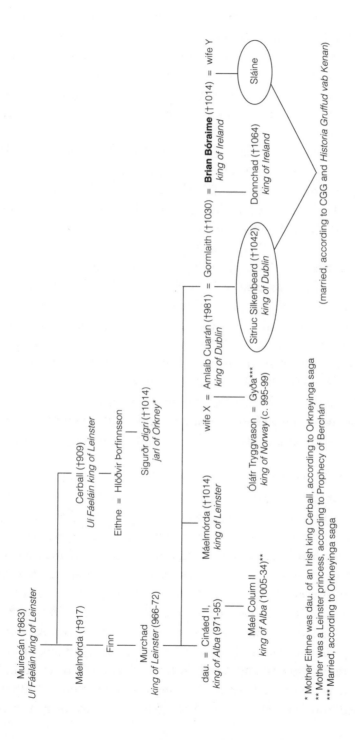

Table 4: Some of Brian's known and conjectural familial relationships

* Mother Eithne was dau. of an Irish king Cerball, according to Orkneyinga saga
** Mother was a Leinster princess, according to Prophecy of Berchán
*** Married, according to Orkneyinga saga

in which case it is interesting that, for the following year, 1006, the annals have an account of Brian's most elaborate and most successful northern expedition yet (as we shall see), followed immediately by a report of 'a battle between the men of Scotland and the Saxons, and the Scots were defeated and a great number of their nobles left dead (*Bellum eter fhiru Alban & Saxanu co remaidh for Albanchu co fargabsat ar a n-deghdhaine*).'[52]

The annals do not link the two events, probably for good reasons, but the Cogadh—which has hitherto proved to be fairly level-headed about Brian's campaigns, sticking tolerably closely to the annals from which it draws—suddenly bursts into what looks like fantasy, having described Brian's arrival at Cráeb Tulcha in Co. Antrim in 1006:

> He sent forth after that a naval expedition upon the sea, viz., of the Foreigners of Dublin and of Waterford and of Uí Chennselaig and of Uí Echach Muman, and of almost all the men of Ireland, such of them as were fit to go to sea; and they levied royal tribute from the Saxons and Britons and the Lennox and [or in?] Scotland and all Argyll, and [obtained] their pledges and hostages along with the chief tribute. Brian distributed all the tribute according to rights, viz., a third part of it to the king of Dublin; and a third to the warriors of Leinster and of the Uí Echach Muman; and another third to the men of learning and craft, and to every one who was most in need of it.[53]

This has tended to be dismissed as nonsense; but is it really so fantastic to imagine that when Brian was up in Co. Antrim, with a large fleet at his disposal, part of it was not given licence to wreak a bit of havoc among the coastal communities of Britain's north-western seaboard, and that these did not then buy them off with a payment of 'tribute' that was no more than a kind of blackmail? It smacks a little of an incident that happened four years earlier, when Brian was trying to force Ulaid into submission—and which was no doubt connected to it—in which his newly chastened and for now loyal vassal, Sitriuc of Dublin, 'set out on a predatory excursion into Ulaid, in his ships; and he plundered Kilclief and Inch [in Co. Down], and carried off many prisoners from both.'[54]

Sitriuc may well have been in command of the Cogadh's supposed naval expedition in 1006, which probably had a not dissimilar outcome.

If we imagine the communities mentioned in the Cogadh—the royal tribute of *Saxan ocus Bretan ocus Lemnaig ocus Alban ocus Airer Gaoidhel uile*—as being people of Anglian origin in the Lothian, the Cumbrians of Clydesdale, the Lennox a little to the north around Loch Lomond, and Argyll as being no more than the Cowal peninsula, we could in fact be referring to a rather confined area penetrated by putting some boats on the Clyde and Loch Lomond and therefore a modest enough achievement. Indeed it is reminiscent of what happened in 870–71 when Sitriuc's ancestors, having overthrown the fortress of Dumbarton—in precisely that area of the outer Clyde—returned to Dublin with two hundred ships bearing 'a great prey of Angles and Britons and Picts (*praeda maxima hominum Anglorum & Britonum & Pictorum*).'[55] This was not a vast pillaging of England, Wales and Scotland but rather a localised raid on the multi-ethnic communities who could be reached via the Firth of Clyde, and those same communities perhaps fell victim to Sitriuc's fleet when Brian was in Co. Antrim in 1006.

Furthermore, it may be worth pointing out that the Máel Coluim who had succeeded to the kingship of the Scots the previous year is described in the 'Prophecy of Berchán' as 'enemy of the Britons, battler of the Gaill, raider (?) of Islay and Arran (*biodhba Bretan, bádhudh Gall, loinnseach Ile agus Arann*),'[56] and perhaps this harks back to an episode of competition or co-operation (probably the former) between himself and Brian in the same region.

But all that is speculation. The fact is that we know for certain from other sources that Brian had strong links with the region. The family that provided kings—or claimants to the kingship—of the Western Isles at this time was the Meic Arailt (sons of Haraldr). In 971–2 Maccus and Gofraid (Guðrøðr) mac Arailt were trying to take possession of Anglesey, but in 974 they 'made a great hosting around Ireland (*co m-mórthinól mór timchell h-Erend*),' arriving into the Shannon Estuary in the company of the 'Lawmen of the Isles (*co l-Lagmannaibh na n-Innsedh*)', where they stormed the monastic site of Inis Cathaig, at which the Norse of Limerick had set up base, taking as prisoner overseas the latter's king, Ímar.[57]

As Ímar was a bitter enemy of Brian's family, whose war with them was to lead to the death of Brian's brother Mathgamain two years later, we can suppose that Dál Cais and the Meic Arailt of the Isles were already in alliance. In 980, shortly after Brian assumed the kingship, Gofraid mac Arailt was back in Wales, where he took sides in a succession dispute over the kingship of Gwynedd and ravaged Anglesey and Llŷn, while two years later he had turned his attentions to South Wales and attacked St Davids and Dyfed in general.[58]

It is another two years before we find direct evidence of the Meic Arailt's alliance with Brian. In 984 Brian travelled to the second great Hiberno-Norse town at Waterford, whose overlord he had become, and the annals describe an extraordinary rendezvous there with the Meic Arailt, who arrived with their fleet from Wales or the Isles. They had a formal exchange of hostages with Brian (*coro chloemclaiset giallu and & mc. Cennetich*) to act as collateral before a projected joint assault on the third and greatest of the Hiberno-Norse enclaves, Dublin (*im imthairec sluagid do dul ar Áth Cliath*). This did not materialise (although they did jointly wreak havoc on enemies in south Leinster),[59] and we hear nothing of the Meic Arailt for three years, until they fought a battle in the Isle of Man in 987, the same year as what seems to be a second operation by Gofraid mac Arailt in Anglesey—although Anglesey (*Môn*) and Man (*Mannin*) are easily confused—in which he took a massive prey of people.[60]

When Gofraid died two years later in Dál Riata (either in north Antrim or western Scotland) he is called 'king of the Islands of the Foreigners (*ri Innsi Gall*)', the first person ever to bear a title that would survive for centuries, and when his son Ragnall (*Rǫgnvaldr*) died in 1005 he too was styled 'king of the Isles (*ri na Indsi*)'. If he was still functioning as king in the Hebrides or the Isle of Man, or both, it is curious that another source tells us he died in Brian's province of Munster.[61] Presumably the family alliance with Brian was still intact. And 1005, of course, was the year of Brian's expedition to Armagh and of his adoption of his own new title, *Imperator Scotorum*, just possibly a nod in the direction of peoples in the wider Gaelic world.[62]

So, when Brian fought his last battle some years later at Clontarf, one of those who gave his life fighting alongside him was Domnall mac Eimin mic Cainnich Móir, the *mórmaer* ('great steward' or 'sea steward', later earl) of the Scottish province of Mar in Aberdeenshire.[63] What a Scottish earl was doing in the army of the king of Munster we can only guess at, and perhaps he was nothing more than a hired mercenary;

but even if he *was* a mercenary, Mar is in north-eastern Scotland, and Brian hailed from south-western Ireland: surely his ability to recruit to his banner someone from so distant a locality speaks volumes for his ties with the region. Besides, the earl of Mar is listed as one of the 'Irish' kings and noblemen who died alongside Brian, and it is most unlikely that he took part in the battle for payment. He was an ally of Brian; and perhaps—if there was anything to Brian's claim to be *Imperator Scotorum*—he was in fact his vassal.

BRIAN'S *SLÓGAD TIMCEALL ÉRENN* (AD 1006)

Brian now having become a patron of Armagh, it is noticeable that the Annals of Ulster (which give us an Armagh viewpoint on things) take a more benign view of his actions from this point on. They therefore decide that he had returned home from his 1005 campaign 'bringing the pledges of the men of Ireland with him (*co n-etire fer n-Erenn laiss*),' as if to suggest that his work was done and that he had now received the hostages, or pledges of the hostages, of all Ireland.

Even the Cogadh is more circumspect, noting that Brian acquired the hostages of Dál Fiatach of Ulaid and their neighbours of Dál nAraidi and of 'the North also [i.e. the lands of the Northern Uí Néill], except Cenél Conaill.'[64] But we come closer to the reality of the situation by considering the ambiguous way in which the Annals of Inisfallen record that Brian had come north 'to obtain the hostages of Cenél Conaill and Cenél nEógain' but then never quite say that it came to pass. And the reason is undoubtedly that these pro-Brian sources were concealing the unpalatable truth that (as the sceptical record of the Four Masters and the Chronicon have it) the net gains of the expedition were limited to the acquisition of the hostages of Ulaid, albeit both Dál Fiatach and Dál nAraidi. In fact the Four Masters tell us that in this year the king of Cenél nEógain, Flaithbertach Ua Néill, led an army into the Lecale district of Co. Down (Leth Cathail; see map 3), killing its king, and in a separate incident fought a battle at Loughbrickland, also in Co. Down, at which the heir-apparent to the kingship of the Uí Echach was slain. The people of Ulaid were being punished for their submission to Brian, to which Cenél nEógain were, it seems, vehemently opposed.

Indeed in the following year Flaithbertach widened his campaign of intimidation of Ulaid subject-peoples by launching an assault on the

Conailli Muirthemne of North Louth (although he seems to have come off the worst from it).[65] Therefore Brian's war would go on—if it is appropriate to call it a war, as, unlike Cenél nEógain's bloody aggression in Ulaid, the various accounts of Brian's northern campaigns thus far are entirely silent on whether as much as a single blow had been struck in anger.

It is this stubborn independence on the part of the Northern Uí Néill that compelled Brian to proceed north again in 1006. And this grand tour seems to have been quite extraordinary, even by comparison with the earlier exploits of this man, now probably sixty-five years of age. There seems to have been an air of majesty about it, which caught the contemporary imagination, so that the Annals of Ulster, in their coverage of more than a thousand years of Irish history, only once use the phrase *Slógad timceall Érenn* ('A hosting around Ireland'), and it is of this particular happening. Among the great historic campaigns throughout the length and breadth of Ireland, one that sticks out is the famous march in 941 by Muirchertach na Cochall Craicinn mac Néill, which entered into the folk memory of the Irish (certainly of the Uí Neill), and yet the account of it in the Annals of Ulster is by no means as elaborate as their description of Brian's expedition in 1006. (The annal that really goes to town on describing Muirchertach's campaign of 941 is that by the Four Masters, but it has clearly been embellished at a later date.)[66]

The fact is that for the period in which Brian was active—and presumably it is just a coincidence—the Annals of Ulster and other chronicles are unfailingly concise, to the point of being cryptic, and yet they burst into life to record the episode of Brian's march of 1006 and insist on documenting the great army's itinerary as it advanced in a vast clockwise manoeuvre around the island.

It was 'a great hosting of the men of Ireland (*Morsluaighedh ffer nErenn*)', according to the Four Masters and the Chronicon, and specifically, as the Annals of Inisfallen have it, of 'the men of Munster, the Leinstermen, the men of Mide, Máel Sechnaill, the Connachta, the Foreigners of Dublin, and the men of the whole of Ireland south of Sliab Fuait [in South Armagh].' They travelled first to Athlone (map 4), perhaps by boat up the Shannon, and from there to the famous plain of Mag nAí in north Roscommon, then up over the Curlew Mountains, between Lough Gara and Lough Key on the Roscommon-Sligo border, arriving we are told then into Tír nAilella (Tirerill) in south-east Sligo, then into Crích Cairpre (Carbury, Co. Sligo), before crossing over the Garvogue River, which runs from Lough Gill to the town of Sligo, and then—'keeping his left hand to the sea and his right hand to the land and Ben Bulben'—into the northern tip of Co. Leitrim, over the Duff River and over the Drowes (which flows to the sea just south of Bundoran), so that they came to the south Donegal plain called Mag Ene, between the Drowes and the Erne. They crossed the Erne near the famous falls of Assaroe, using the vital ford where the town of Ballyshannon has since grown up.

Now in the lands of the Cenél Conaill, whose submission Brian was seeking, the army traversed Tír Áeda (roughly the present-day barony of Tirhugh, which runs from the Ballyshannon area up past the town of Donegal), but they then inexplicably left Tír Conaill over the Barnesmore Gap into Cenél nEógain territory, nothing further being reported of their actions until they forded the River Bann at Fersat Camsa near Macosquin (south of Coleraine, Co. Derry)—a silence we can no doubt equate with lack of achievement.

They therefore headed into what had already proved happier hunting-ground in Ulaid (map 3), entering the lands of Dál Riata in the far north of Antrim, then into south Antrim, the lands of Dál nAraidi, then north Down, the Dál Fiatach patrimony, travelling all the way through Co. Down until they reached the borders of Co. Louth and the lands of Conailli Muirthemne—turning up, it seems, at their assembly (i n-oenach Conaille); or perhaps the point being made is that the army passed through the place where the Conailli traditionally held their assemblies. The great army finally disbanded around the feast of Lugnasad (the beginning of August) when they reached a place called Belach Dúin, which seems to be Castlekieran on the Blackwater west of Kells, Co. Meath.

The Cogadh tells us that Brian 'then dismissed the men of Ireland to their homes in all directions,' it and the Four Masters adding that 'the Leinstermen then proceeded southwards across Brega to their territory, and the Foreigners by sea round eastwards to their fortress. The Munstermen also and the Osraige and the Connachta went through Mide westwards to their territories.'

The whole enterprise seems to have been mesmerising to contemporaries in its scale and its splendour and in the sheer ambition that underlay it. But it is more than apparent that it failed. The total silence of the Annals of Inisfallen on the subject of whether the northern kings tendered their hostages speaks volumes. The Four Masters and Chronicon Scotorum expressly state that Cenél Conaill and Cenél nEógain refused to submit, although they concede that the Ulaid did give their hostages, and the Cogadh glamorises this triumph thus (providing, in passing, one of the earliest mentions of the word *baile*, from which Ireland's 'Bally-' place-names derive):

> Brian was then at Cráeb Tulcha, the Ulaid rendering food to him there (*aga biatadh ann*). They gave him twelve hundred beeves, twelve hundred hogs, and twelve hundred wethers; and Brian bestowed twelve hundred horses upon them, along with gold and silver and clothing. For no food-provider from any of their estates (*biatach aen bhaile díobh*) departed from Brian without receiving a horse or some other gift that deserved his thanks.[67]

It is at this juncture that the Cogadh places the expedition against Saxons and Britons and Scots (discussed above), and it is convinced that by this year, 1006, Brian had reached the pinnacle of his power:

> So Brian returned from his great royal visitation around all Ireland (*mórcuairt righ timchell Erend*) made in this manner; and the peace of Ireland was proclaimed by him, both of churches and people; so that peace throughout all Ireland was made in his time. He fined and imprisoned the perpetrators of murders, trespass, and robbery and war. He hanged and killed and destroyed the robbers and thieves and plunderers of Ireland. He extirpated, dispersed, banished, caused to fly, stripped, maimed, ruined, and destroyed the Foreigners in every district and in every territory (*Gullu gacha tire ocus gacha tuaithe*) throughout the breadth of all Ireland. He killed also their kings and their overkings, their warriors and strong soldiers, their men of renown and valour (*a riogha ocus a ruireacha, a ttreitill ocus a ttréin mhilid, a lathgaile ocus gaisccibh*). He enslaved and reduced to bondage their stewards and their overseers (*a maeir ocus a reachtairedha*), and

their mercenaries and hirelings (*a suaitreacha* [?*ocus*] *a namhais*), and their comely, large, cleanly youths; and their smooth youthful girls.[68]

We see here again the author's preoccupation with the Viking scourge and with Brian's supposed role in ending it. That aside, his point is that Brian ushered in an age of peace:

After the banishment of the Foreigners out of all Ireland, and after Ireland was reduced to a state of peace, a lone woman came from Tory [Island, off Co. Donegal], in the north of Ireland, to Clídna [Glandore Harbour, West Cork], in the south of Ireland, carrying a ring of gold on a horse-rod, and she was neither robbed nor insulted; whereupon the poet sang—
  From Tory to pleasant Clídna,
  And carrying with her a ring of gold,
  In the time of Brian, of the bright side, fearless,
  A lone woman made the circuit of Erin.
  (*O Thoraigh co Clíodhna cias* | *Is fail óir aice re a hais* | *I ré Briain taoibhghil nar tím* | *Do thimchil aoinbhen Erinn.*)[69]

It is a romantic notion that Brian brought such tranquillity and imposed such reverence for law and order that a woman could traverse Ireland from north to south on her own without hindrance; and we would expect nothing less of the naïve author of the Cogadh. Yet the same idea is in the Annals of Ulster. While its Armagh-focused author was most excited about the fact that in 1006, as he puts it, Brian granted 'the full demand of the community and successor of Patrick (*co tarait oighreir samhtha Patraicc & a comharbai*)'—which presumably means that Brian again met the abbot of Armagh and granted further privileges—the account of his bravura journey ends, like the Cogadh, by quoting a quatrain of verse:

It is remarkable that Sliab Cua [in the Knockmealdown Mountains] has no marauding-band,
That Foreigners do not row on the Eidnech [Inagh River, west Clare?],
That a lone woman crosses Luachair [Sliabh Luachra, west Munster],
That cows are without a herdsman, lowing.
—That is in Brian's time.

(Ingnadh Sliabh Cua cen choibden, | Gaill cen imram im Eidhnigh, |
Oenben do thecht tar Luachair, | Bai cen buachail ic neimleith
—Id est in tempore Briain.)[70]

This, of course, has more than a whiff of retrospection about it, and we may take it that it was not written contemporaneously; but it is interesting that it was inserted here, under the year 1006, precisely the same point at which the Cogadh places it. The Cogadh is not contemporaneous either but was written by someone who may well have lived through these last years of Brian's life and hence looked back on his childhood with rose-tinted spectacles.

Despite, therefore, the limited dividends he reaped in his stately circuit of Ireland in 1006, Brian had never been more dominant. His methods were undoubtedly not without precedent—indeed, so far as we can tell, his approach to power was entirely consistent with the long-established conventions for the assertion of lordship and the prosecution of war— but he realised the potential of the high-kingship more effectively than his predecessors and, having gained a position of ascendancy, was more committed to and more proficient at exploiting it to the full. By 1006 it was surely apparent to all that Ireland had never witnessed a more effective high-king.

THE HUMBLING OF CENÉL nEÓGAIN

But his work was not complete. Brian mac Cennétig could never justly consider himself king of all Ireland while the Northern Uí Néill remained recalcitrant. And when, in 1007, the Cenél nEógain king of Ailech, Flaithbertach Ua Néill, again demonstrated his intention of undermining Brian's efforts by heading an expedition to Ulaid, killing the Dál Fiatach king of Leth Cathail (Lecale) and taking seven of the Ulaid's pledges in acknowledgement of his overlordship, Brian had to respond if he was to salvage his own hard-won primacy.

Not surprisingly, the Four Masters and the Chronicon report only Flaithbertach's accomplishment in Ulaid, not Brian's retribution; indeed they delight in reporting that Brian's predecessor, Máel Sechnaill of Mide, revived the Óenach Tailten that year, as if to imply that it demonstrated true statesmanship on his part, whereas their reportage of news to do with Brian, by contrast, is confined to telling us that his son Murchad—his intended heir—was at the same time implicated in the treacherous murder of the South Connacht king of Síl nAnmchada.

It is the Annals of Inisfallen, therefore, that preserve a record of Brian's reaction. He led yet another 'great muster of the men of Ireland, both Foreigners and Irish (*mórthinol fer n-Erend la Brian eter Gullu & Goedelu*),' to Armagh and forcibly recovered the hostages of Ulaid from Flaithbertach Ua Néill.

Because of the Armagh connection the Annals of Ulster (which were probably being compiled there at this time) have a bit more detail. Brian led his expedition north towards Cenél nEógain, camping at Dún Droma 'beside Armagh'—which may be Dundrum, about 10 km to the south, near Keady—and 'took away ua Críchidéin, successor of Finnén of Mag Bile, who was a pledge in Cenél nEógain on behalf of the Ulaid.' This person was the abbot of Movilla, near Newtownards, Co. Down, who was obviously one of the seven pledges of the Ulaid secured by Flaithbertach in his earlier invasion of the kingdom, and we have to assume that the annalists' cryptic accounts omit to tell us that Brian threatened war on Cenél nEógain if the Ulaid hostages were not released, and that Flaithbertach buckled under whatever pressure Brian—and his army—was able to apply. Releasing the abbot of Movilla, therefore, was tantamount to surrendering the overlordship of Ulaid from Cenél nEógain to Dál Cais.

This campaign of 1007, therefore, merely restored the *status quo ante,* and the following year—for the first three months of which the country was paralysed by severe frost and snow[71]—brought no change. In fact by 1009—the year in which Brian's wife Dub Choblaig, daughter of the king of Connacht, died—Flaithbertach was attempting to assert lordship over the Southern Uí Néill, not, admittedly, by making war on the incumbent king of Tara (i.e. the overking of the Uí Néill), Máel Sechnaill mac Domnaill, but by raiding into Brega to Máel Sechnaill's east.[72]

But there was obviously more going on beneath the surface than the taciturn annals let on, because out of the blue, in 1010, Brian brought the army of Munster north to Armagh, as the Annals of Inisfallen have it, or, as the other annals report, to a place called Cláenloch of Sliab Fuait, somewhere in south Armagh (possibly Camlough). We know nothing of what his army did, whether war or diplomacy was the order of the day, but it culminated in the surrender of the greatest power in the north of Ireland, Flaithbertach Ua Néill, the Cenél nEógain king of Ailech, who, the Annals of Inisfallen tell us, 'gave to Brian his demand in full, and Brian brought Ua Néill's hostages to Cenn Corad (*co tuc h-Ua Neill a lánréir do Brian & co tuc Brian leis giallu h-Ui Néill co Cend Corad*).'[73]

It was an extraordinary achievement. Even the grudging Four Masters and Chronicon Scotorum admit it (adding that Brian also took the hostages of Ulaid), and his admirer behind the Annals of Ulster has him taking 'the pledges of Leth Cuinn', that is, the submission of all the northern half of Ireland—although this is an exaggeration, as Cenél Conaill remained non-compliant.

BRIAN'S BUILDING BLITZ

The hostages were brought back to Cenn Corad, which is mentioned here in a context that suggests that it was Brian's official residence. Tragically, and rather extraordinarily, the site is now unknown but is assumed to be where the Catholic church in Killaloe now stands, overlooking the town (plate 4).[74]

This reference in the Munster Annals of Inisfallen for 1010 appears to be the earliest to Cenn Corad. (Although it occurs in the poem celebrating Muirchertach mac Néill's famous campaign of 941, this has been shown to be of later vintage.[75]) Subsequently, mentions become regular, suggesting the possibility that it had only recently been constructed by Brian. He was certainly engaged in a programme of fortification in his later years. The annals usually do not mention construction work, other than occasionally at church sites, but the Annals of Inisfallen were impressed enough to report for the year 995:

> The fortification (*cumdach*) of Cashel, Inis Locha Gair, and Inis Locha Sainglend, and many structures (*dentai imdai*) besides, by Brian.

And again in 1012:

> Many fortifications (*daingne imda*) were made in that year by Brian, viz. the fort (*cathir*) of Cenn Corad, Inis Gaill Duib, Inis Locha Sainglend, and the fort (*cathir*) of Cnoc Fochuir.

Presumably the mention of Cenn Corad here refers to continuing works, bearing in mind that it must already have been Brian's official residence two years earlier when Ua Néill's hostages had been brought there. As to the other fortifications, it is not entirely clear where some of them were. Brian apparently built a castle on the old Eóganacht site at Cashel, Co. Tipperary, and the family certainly had a 'house (*tigh Uí Bhriain h-i c-Caisseal*)' there eighty years later.[76] Inis Locha Gair is presumably a crannóg on Lough Gur in Co. Limerick. Loch Sainglend was probably a lake that has since dried up at Singland, near Limerick, on which Brian perhaps constructed another crannóg. Inis Gaill Duib is where the poet Muirchertach mac Liacc, closely associated with Brian, died in 1016, his obit in Chronicon Scotorum stating that he died 'in Inis Gaill Duib on the Shannon (*i n-Inis Gaill Duiph for Sinainn*),' and perhaps therefore it was the new name for the island formerly called Inis Sibthonn before the Vikings captured it and that is now King's Island, the site of the later castle at Limerick. Cnoc Fochuir is also unidentified, but as *cathair* normally implies a stone fortress we may assume that at the very least the earthen banks of it and of Cenn Corad were strengthened by being revetted in stone.

The Cogadh inserts a similar statement about castles in its account of Brian's actions in these years:

By him were strengthened also the duns and fastnesses and islands and celebrated royal forts of Munster (*dúin ocus daingni ocus inseda ocus rigpuirt aireda na Muman*). He built also the fortification (*cumdach*) of Cashel of the Kings, and of Cenn Abrat, and the island of Loch Cend, and the island of Loch Gair, and Dún Eochair Maige, Dún Cliath, and Dún Crot, and the island of Loch Sainglend, and Inis an Ghaill Duibh, and Rosach, and Cend Corad, and Bórama, and the royal forts (*rigpuirt*) of Munster in like manner.

Clearly the author is here drawing on the same or a similar source as the Inisfallen annalist, but if so he omits the *cathair* at Cnoc Fochuir and adds a further seven. There is a tendency to assume that the writer dreamt up much of this kind of detail; but as he was writing for a Munster audience, and writing at a time when these structures would still have been standing and when a rough knowledge of when they were erected was probably still vivid in contemporary memory, it is reasonable to suppose that he could not have got away with much invention and that he is therefore passably accurate in suggesting that they were constructed by Brian or around his time.

One or two of his additions are, of course, famous even today. Bórama is the large ring-fort just north of Killaloe that seems to have given Brian his nickname (plates 2 and 3), and so it is more than likely that he was involved, if not in constructing the original edifice, certainly in making out of it a residence fit for a king of Ireland. Dún Eochair Maige was at Bruree, Co. Limerick; Dún Cliath (or Dún Cliach) may have been at Áine Cliach, now Knockainy, about 5 km east of Bruff, Co. Limerick; Cenn Abrat (or Cenn Febrat) is near the Ballyhoura Hills on the borders of Cos. Limerick and Cork; and Dún Crot is certainly Dungrud in the Glen of Aherlow on Limerick's border with South Tipperary. Various suggestions have been made for the site of Loch Cend, one of which is that it too was a now dried-out lake north of Knockainy, Co. Limerick, although there were certainly other places of the same name; and Rosach is unidentified, unless it is Russa, near Ennistimon, Co. Clare.[77]

The Cogadh would also see Brian crowning a glorious career in these latter years by acting as a patron of learning:

> He sent scholars and masters to teach wisdom and knowledge (*saoithe ocus maighistreacha do theaccascc eccna ocus eolais*); and to buy books beyond the sea and the great ocean; because their writings and their books in every church and in every sanctuary (*a screptra ocus a liubhair in gach cill ocus in gach neimedh*) where they were, were burned and thrown into water by the plunderers (*diberccachaibh*), from the beginning to the end; and Brian, himself, gave the cost of learning and the cost of books (*luach foghlama ocus luach leabhar*) to every one separately who went.[78]

Of course it is all a little idealised and romantic, but it may be that the description in the same section of the Cogadh of Brian commissioning other works, especially ecclesiastical architecture of note, has more to recommend it, as again—as with his fortresses—the Cogadh's audience comprised individuals in a position to contradict it if it were inaccurate:

By him were erected also noble churches in Ireland and their sanctuaries . . . Many works, also, and repairs were made by him. By him were erected the church (*tempull*) of Killaloe, and the church (*tempull*) of Inis Celtra, and the bell tower (*cloictheach*) of Tuamgraney, and many other works in like manner. By him were made bridges and causeways and roads (*drochait ocus dochair ocus sligedha*).[79]

Elements of each of the three churches named here survive today that are credibly datable—in so far as this can be established—to Brian's time. In Killaloe the cathedral built by Brian's great-great-great-grandson Domnall Mór Ua Briain in the late twelfth century is on the site of an earlier church, whose beautiful Romanesque doorway is preserved in its south-west corner (plate 6). The building also houses a remarkable stone on which is carved both a Viking runic inscription and an ogham inscription requesting a prayer for its maker, Þorgrímr (Thorgrim), presumably of Norse extraction, perhaps a Limerick mason. And in the grounds of the cathedral can be found St Flannán's Oratory—sometimes known as 'Brian Boru's Vault'—which has another fine Romanesque doorway, assigned to the twelfth century, perhaps in a remodelling of works undertaken under Brian's patronage in the previous century (plate 5).

Brian's brother Marcán died in 1010 as 'head of the clergy of Munster (*cend cléireach Mumhan*),' and among the various positions he had captured for himself was that of *comarba* or superior of Killaloe and of Inis Celtra;[80] and indeed it is harder to imagine Brian *not* presiding over the construction or re-edification of churches at these sites than his doing so.[81]

Inis Celtra has one of Ireland's most magnificent assemblages of mediaeval ecclesiastical remains,[82] including at least four churches, dedicated to St Michael (now almost gone, and perhaps the oldest of them), St Mary (the largest and latest, dating perhaps from the thirteenth century), St Brigit (which has a Romanesque doorway and is therefore usually assigned to the twelfth century, although the door may be an intrusion), and St Caimmíne or Caimín (which also has a grand twelfth-century Romanesque doorway but parts of which may be earlier) (plate 9). The island also has a classic 'bell-house (*cloicthech*)' or round tower of the kind that were constructed, typically under royal patronage, from the middle of the tenth century onwards. The Cogadh does not mention this but instead credits Brian with building a round tower at Tuamgraney, where none now survives. But here again the Cogadh is certainly at least partly vindicated, because we know that such an edifice did once exist there, for when the annals record the death in 966 of its *comarba,* Cormac ua Cillín, they add that 'by him was built the great church of Tuaim Gréne, and its bell-house (*as aige do ronadh tempul mor Tuama Grene et a claigtec*).'[83]

Although this was not during Brian's reign but rather that of his brother Mathgamain, we must view all such buildings as composite works that each generation remodelled as circumstances (and fashion) required and as resources permitted; and one can well imagine Brian's massively more profitable career lending itself to far greater benefaction than Mathgamain might have managed. And it is a remarkable validation of the family's efforts that not only is the beautiful church of Tuamgraney still standing but it may be the oldest Irish church still in use (although now as a heritage centre); and although its many Romanesque features are classically twelfth-century in date, the western portion and extraordinary lintelled doorway may well be that through which Brian entered when visiting (plate 10).

THE FINAL PUSH

Of course individuals who advance as far in years as Brian now had will often spend longer in contemplation of the hereafter, and the carrying out of works for the glory of God is to be expected. For when we next see Brian on the national stage, in 1011, he was—even by a conservative estimate—seventy years of age. And yet, remarkable as it may seem, it was at this age that Brian finally realised his life's ambition.

It was a year of feverish activity, during which Brian appears to have launched two separate campaigns to force into submission the last of Ireland's dissenting powers, Cenél Conaill.

Prospects had improved dramatically since Flaithbertach Ua Néill of Cenél nEógain became Brian's vassal the previous year, and perhaps also his son-in-law, marrying his daughter Bébinn. So, in 1011 Flaithbertach joined in what the Annals of Inisfallen call the 'great muster of the men of Ireland by Brian mac Cennétig (*mórthinól fer n-Erend la Brian mc. Cennetich*)' that encompassed the armies of Munster and Leinster and the Southern Uí Néill of the Midlands. Together they launched a massive invasion of the Donegal area inhabited by Cenél Conaill and severely ravaged it.

What is noticeable is that for the first time the contemporary sources note that Brian took a back seat. He had certainly travelled north, but when they arrived in Cenél Conaill the army broke into two divisions, led (the Annals of Inisfallen tell us) by the most senior of Brian's sons, Murchad and Domnall. According to the Four Masters, Murchad joined Flaithbertach and marched to the far north of Donegal to attack the Cenél Lugdach (ruled by the Uí Domnaill or O'Donnells), and probably therefore his younger brother Domnall led the battalions that were active further south in the county making war on the reigning overking of Cenél Conaill, Máel Ruanaid Ua Máel Doraid (map 3).

The campaign was successful in terms of booty. Three hundred captives and many cows were taken, the latter at least being brought back to Munster, at which point we hear that 'Brian went after that to the lough (*co tanic Brian iar sein dond loch*).'[84] Frustratingly, we are not told what lough is intended. It may be one of his new palaces at Lough Gur or Inis Locha Sainglend, or it may mean that he withdrew to a lake in the vicinity of Donegal before another push to secure Cenél Conaill's submission.

That Brian may have set up such a temporary headquarters is suggested by an enigmatic little sentence in Latin and Irish in the Annals of Ulster for this year, placed immediately after his first Cenél Conaill campaign, to the effect that Brian and his predecessor and now faithful ally Máel Sechnaill mac Domnaill were *iterum in classi sua oc Enach Duib*, 'again in their fleet (or camp?) at Enech Duib,' which may be Annaduff, near Drumsna, Co. Leitrim. Here, near the upper reaches of the Shannon, which they had presumably navigated from their homes to the south, we can imagine the two elder statesmen holding court while their younger lieutenants took charge of the challenge of grinding down the notoriously independent Cenél Conaill.

And from there, as on his expedition in 1006, Brian now led an army north-westwards up through the gap between Lough Arrow and Lough Gara into Mag Corainn (the plain around Ballymote, Co. Sligo) and 'carried back (*co ruc leis*) the king of Cenél Conaill, i.e. Máel Ruanaid Ua Máel Doraid, in submission (*fria reir*) to Cenn Corad.'[85] How Brian's presence in Co. Sligo led to the capitulation of the king of the Donegal area goes unexplained here, but the Annals of Inisfallen add the crucial detail that this was a 'great hosting by Brian to Cenél Conaill both by land and sea (*sluaged mór la Brian co Cenel Conaill eter muir & tír*),' from which it seems that, as Brian's land army was knocking on Ua Máel Doraid's front door a fleet had been sent up along the west coast to put pressure on his rear, and that it was this extraordinary combination that finally brought Ua Máel Doraid to his knees.

The Annals of Inisfallen agree with the other annals that this impressive manoeuvre ended with the king of Cenél Conaill returning to Cenn Corad with the Dál Cais king, 'so that he accepted a large stipend from Brian, and made complete submission to him (*co ruc innarrad mór o Brian & co tuc a ogréir do Brian*).' The word used for the gift—*innarrad*—is synonymous with *tuarastal* and is the ceremonial gift from the lord that seals a vassal's submission.[86] Brian mac Cennétig, this king of Munster, was now therefore the overlord of the king of Cenél Conaill in the far north-west, an event without precedent in Irish history, and also the overlord of every one of his contemporaries throughout Ireland.

It had not been easy, and it had not been without a price. (Brian's son Domnall died shortly after returning from this Donegal campaign, perhaps from injuries or illness acquired on it.)[87] But it was a truly magnificent achievement. The author of Cogadh Gáedhel re Gallaibh would have us believe that Brian's greatest achievement was a mythical banishment of the Vikings from Ireland, and subsequent generations looked on his death in the course of a glorious victory at Clontarf in 1014 as surely his finest hour; but emphatically that summit was climbed three years earlier. Of course it did not last; but for one brief season in the year 1011 there was not a king or a lord of any standing in Ireland who had not formally submitted to Brian Bóraime mac Cennétig of Dál Cais, and never before in the history of Ireland—and almost certainly never again in the history of Ireland—was that the case.

PART II

Clontarf

Chapter 4

CLONTARF IN THE IRISH ANNALS

No king before Brian Bóruma had attained the personal hegemony over all Ireland that he had secured by the year 1011. Every one of his contemporary kings, either directly by his own submission to Brian or—we must assume, the sources being entirely silent on the subject—indirectly by means of the submission of his provincial overlord, had accepted Brian of Dál Cais as lord. And the greater kings, and perhaps also those beneath them on the pyramid of kingship, had come into Brian's presence and acknowledged his suzerainty, some travelling back with him to his palace at Cenn Corad to enter his house in person as a sign of submission, handing over hostages or pledges of hostages and tribute and accepting ceremonial wages, as vassals did of their lord.

But it was personal: it was an authority achieved by the imposition of military force, in person. After all, the only certain constituent of Brian's army was the muster of the men of Dál Cais. It is just that, as he established his dominion throughout Munster, erstwhile enemies incurred the military obligations that came with political vassalage, and his army swelled to include levies from elsewhere in the province. And as he imposed his supremacy beyond Munster, so these kings too who yielded before his juggernaut incurred obligations to provide their own military service. Thus it became cumulatively more difficult for each still-autonomous provincial overking to withhold submission.

But the problem for Brian mac Cennétig was that when that submission came it came at the point of a sword. Brian's was a military rather than an institutional hegemony. Each of his provincial counterparts in turn was pressured into submission by the presence of a large—and presumably marauding—army in his territory. Take that army away and the imperative to stay loyal weighed less urgently on such fiercely independent kings. Furthermore, each of Brian's counterparts as a provincial overking was a potential Brian—had the potential to do to others what Brian had done to him—and surely therefore his dominion could not last.

THE UNDERMINING OF BRIAN'S HEGEMONY

The most restive of Brian's new vassals was his son-in-law, Flaithbertach Ua Néill of Cenél nEógain. It is not surprising. The kings of Cenél nEógain had come to expect that they would exercise overlordship of all the Northern Uí Néill by asserting their power over Cenél Conaill and Airgialla, and that they could then secure dominion over all the North—*In Fochlae,* as it was called—by forcing the submission of the Ulaid (map 3).

These prerogatives had been undermined by Brian's intrusive overlordship, which Flaithbertach himself had been forced to acknowledge. But one can well imagine him bridling at the injustice of it. What is more, an Uí Néill overking of In Fochlae could traditionally contemplate establishing himself as king of Tara by forcing the submission of the Southern Uí Néill (map 2). But the kingship of Tara had been held now for nearly a third of a century by Máel Sechnaill mac Domnaill, who was firmly subordinate to Brian. This too is something Flaithbertach must have resented. The force of tradition dictated that, of the two halves of Ireland, it was Leth Cuinn (the northern half, taking its name from Flaithbertach's supposed ancestor Conn Cétchathach) that should dominate over the southern half, whose very name Leth Moga—derived from Mug Nuadat, ancestor not of Brian but of the Eóganachta—literally meant 'the half of the slave'.

In 1011, therefore—the very year in which Brian sealed his universal hegemony of the Irish polity by securing the submission of Cenél Conaill—Flaithbertach Ua Néill set about undoing the whole superstructure. He launched an invasion of Ulaid, marching to the ring-fort of Dún Echdach (Duneight, south of Lisburn), burning the *dún*

1. Killaloe from the air: Brian's line of Dál Cais were called Uí Thairdelbaig, from an eponym Tairdelbach who lived seven generations before Brian, some time in the eighth century. Tairdelbach had five sons, one of whom was St Flannán of Killaloe, and hence the dynasty's patronage of this local site. The photograph is of the Shannon, looking northwards, with Killaloe centre left and behind it the hills of Co. Clare where Brian grew to manhood. (*Courtesy of Clare County Library*)

2. Bél Bóraime (Béal Bórú): This photograph, taken more than a century ago, shows Lough Derg as it empties into the Shannon above Killaloe with (to the right of centre, shrouded in trees) the impressive ring-fort of Bél Bóraime, which is very probably the origin of Brian's famous nickname. (*Courtesy of Clare County Library*)

3. The interior of Béal Boru today: Excavations in the early 1960s found house remains and two eleventh-century Hiberno-Norse coins minted in Dublin in the decades after Brian's death.

4. St Molua's Oratory, Killaloe: It was moved from its site on Friar's Island in the Shannon when it was due to be submerged in the Shannon Hydro-Electric Scheme in 1929. A small church with a nave and an added chancel with stone roof, it may well have existed in Brian's day. It has been reconstructed in the grounds of the Catholic church on a hill overlooking Killaloe, considered to have been the site of Brian's palace of Cenn Corad (Kincora).

5. St Flannán's Oratory, Killaloe: Commonly known as Brian Boru's Vault, it is in the grounds of the cathedral and predates the latter but is unlikely to have existed in its present form in Brian's lifetime, as the Romanesque doorway is classically twelfth-century in date.

6. St Flannan's Cathedral, Killaloe: In its present form it is substantially a product of the patronage of Domnall Mór Ua Briain (d. 1194), grandson of the great Muirchertach Ua Briain (d. 1119), who was in turn a great-grandson of Brian. He is said to have built it in 1185 but on the site of an earlier church, whose fine Romanesque doorway (pictured) in the cathedral's south-western corner still survives, although even it is later than Brian's reign. What may, however, be earlier is the extraordinary carved stone in the foreground, which has both ogham and runic inscriptions requesting prayers for its maker, Þorgrímr (Thorgrim), presumably a mason of Norse extraction from nearby Limerick or its hinterland. (© *Getty Images*)

7. Mag Adair: A complex of monuments survives in a plain called Mag Adair (Moyare) in which Brian's dynasty of Dál Cais held their *óenach* or assembly, about 3 km east of the village of Quin in south-east Co. Clare. Among the surviving remains are the basin stone in the foreground, which presumably played some part in the inauguration ceremony of Brian, and of his predecessors and successors, which took place before his people gathered around the ceremonial mound in the background.

8. Craicliath (the townland of Craglea, near Killaloe): This rocky outcrop was the site of the *sídh* or Otherworld mound that was home to Aíbinn (or Óebinn) of the Dál Cais, the fairy woman who was said to have appeared to Brian before the Battle of Clontarf and who foretold his death there. Nearby is Grianán Lachtnai (Greenanlaghna), which, the twelfth-century genealogies tell us, is named after Brian's brother Lachtna. (© *Derek Ryan Bawn*)

9. Inis Celtra (Holy Island, Lough Derg): Brian's brother Marcán died in 1010 as 'head of the clergy of Munster'. Among the various positions he had captured for himself was that of *comarba* or superior of Killaloe and of Inis Celtra on Lough Derg. Of the several churches on the island, the photograph shows that of St Caimmíne or Caimín, which also has a grand twelfth-century Romanesque doorway but parts of which may be earlier. Also in the photograph is its classic Irish round tower or bell house (*cloicthech*), of the kind that was constructed, typically under royal patronage, from the middle of the tenth century onwards.

10. Tuamgraney, Co. Clare: Brian built a round tower at Tuamgraney, although it no longer survives. The abbot who built the surviving church, dedicated to St Crónán, died in 966, and we can therefore justifiably believe that Brian walked through the early doorway (pictured) on many an occasion.

11. Cashel: In Brian's day the Rock of Cashel, Co. Tipperary, lacked the magnificent assemblage of ecclesiastical monuments that survives today; its importance was primarily political, symbolising the kingship of Munster, which he and his brother Mathgamain before him were the first of their dynasty to obtain. Their father, Cennétig, had died in 951 as a mere *rígdamna* of Cashel, 'the makings of a king of Munster'.

12. Dún na Sciath, Co. Westmeath: This platform rath or ring-fort at Dún na Sciath, on the shores of Lough Ennell (where he also had a crannóg, at Cró-inis, on which he died in 1022), was the principal residence of Brian's predecessor as high-king, Máel Sechnaill mac Domnaill, the Clann Cholmáin king of Southern Uí Néill. The exploitation of Lough Ennell, fed at each end by the River Brosna, mirrors Brian's dependence on Lough Derg and the Shannon.

13. Bleanphuttoge, Co. Westmeath: After he became king of Munster, Brian's first great triumph came in AD 997 when, Cogadh Gáedhel re Gallaibh tells us, he 'made a great naval expedition to Plein Pattogi, where Máel Sechnaill came to meet him, so that they concluded a peace there,' dividing power in Ireland between them, Máel Sechnaill, who had formerly ruled all Ireland, ceding Leth Moga (the Southern Half) to Brian. The site of this great meeting was Bleanphuttoge, on the shores of Lough Ree in Co. Westmeath: the photograph shows the *blén* ('creek') from which Bleanphuttoge gets its name, now known locally as Blean-na-puttoga ('pudding-creek' or perhaps 'creek of the intestines').

14. The photograph shows the V-shaped landing-place, revetted in stone, on the side of the lough at Bleanphuttoge where Brian may have come ashore.

15. Brian's first action on gaining the submission of Máel Sechnaill in 1002 and now claiming the high-kingship of Ireland was to press his claim against the kings of the north, and so he led his armies to Dún Delca, the hill fortress nowadays called Castletown Mount about 2 km west of Dundalk (which takes its name from it). It was anciently associated with Cú Chulainn, whose role in single-handedly defending Ulster from Medb's invading army of Connacht is at the core of the epic tale Táin Bó Cúailgne ('The cattle-raid of Cooley'). (© 2005 *Louth County Council*)

16. Book of Armagh: In the bottom right-hand corner of the page, one of Brian's visits to Armagh, probably that of 1005, is recorded with this famous inscription in which his confessor Máel Suthain (here called Caluus Perennis) claims to write 'in the presence of Brian, Emperor of the Scoti', i.e. the Gaels of Ireland (and perhaps Scotland and the Isles). It is just possible to make out the words: *Caluus P[er]ennis i[n] con | spectu briani imp[er]ato | ris scotor[um]*. (*Courtesy of the Board of Trinity College, Dublin*)

17. As Brian's army headed north to Armagh in 1005 it stopped en route at Tailtiu (Teltown, Co. Meath), where, we are told, Brian stayed for a night. The point of this was undoubtedly to exploit the significance of the site, that of the ancient *óenach* or assembly of the kings of Tara. The photograph shows one of the complex of monuments in the vicinity (Rath Dubh, a flat-topped mound 3 to 4 m in height, with steeply sloping sides) that dominate the surrounding landscape. (© *Leo Swan*)

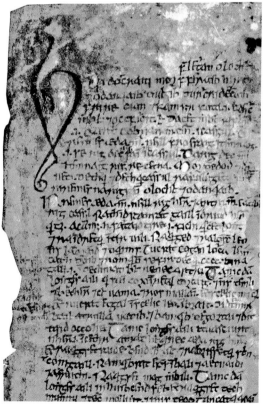

18. There is no more valuable source for the life of Brian Bóraime than Cogadh Gáedhel re Gallaibh ('The War of the Irish with the Vikings'), the earliest version of which was based on contemporary annals and, no doubt, local memory. The illustration shows the opening passage of the earliest surviving copy, transcribed in the middle years of the twelfth century into the Book of Leinster. (*Courtesy of the Board of Trinity College, Dublin*)

19. The beautiful Curraghmore Sword was discovered practically on Brian's doorstep on the eastern shore of Lough Derg at Curraghmore, Co. Tipperary. While it is unlikely that Brian himself ever held it—the best guess is that it was commissioned fifty years or more after his death—it was certainly the treasured possession of an aristocrat from this locality, someone like his grandson Tairdelbach (d. 1086) or great-grandson Muirchertach Mór Ua Briain (d. 1119). While it is in the Viking sword tradition, the intricate decoration on the hilt is in an Irish style. (*This image is reproduced with the kind permission of the National Museum of Ireland*)

20. Perhaps the earliest surviving depiction of Brian is this preposterous engraving that appeared as the frontispiece of Dermod O'Connor's 1723 English translation of Keating's *Foras Feasa ar Éirinn*. However bizarre the representation, it is significant that, of all the great figures from Irish history, Brian was chosen.

21. One of the finest artistic depictions of the battle is this large oil painting (2.5 by 1.7 metres), *Battle of Clontarf* (1826), by Hugh Frazer of Dromore, Co. Down (1795–1865). The artist has gone to considerable trouble to capture traditions associated with the battle, including Brian observing the battle from his tent and the single combat of his son Murchad with Jarl Sigurðr of Orkney (although the sun appears to be setting in the east over Dublin Bay!). This important work is now held in the Isaacs Art Center, Kamuela, Hawaii. (*Battle of Clontarf by Hugh Frazer, oil on canvas, 1826 © Hawaii Preparatory Academy*)

22. This depiction of the Battle of Clontarf, which features Jarl Sigurðr of Orkney and his raven banner, was drawn by Henry Mac Manus ARHA and litho-mezzotinted by W. H. Holbrooke of Dublin some time between 1821 and 1848.

23. Armagh: The extent to which Brian, the southern king, had become the patron of the great northern ecclesiastical centre at Armagh was made clear on his death at Clontarf when his body was brought north for burial there in the burial-ground hitherto favoured by the Uí Néill kings of Cenél nEógain. A plaque on the wall of the Church of Ireland cathedral church of St Patrick cannot be far from the actual site of Brian's burial. (© *Alamy*)

24. Bully's Acre, Kilmainham, Dublin: The Dubliner Richard Stanihurst, in his *Description of Ireland* (1577), states that, following the battle of Clontarf, Brian, his son Murchad, Tadc ua Cellaig, king of Uí Maine, and the other fallen Irish leaders were 'interred at Kilmaynanne over against the great cross.' While Brian and Murchad were certainly not buried at Kilmainham, there may be some grounds for the tradition that other Munster fatalities in the battle were brought from Clontarf for burial there, and the large decorated stone that still survives at Kilmainham may date from that period. It is illustrated here in an early nineteenth-century watercolour by the Yorkshire artist Thales Fielding (1793–1837). (*Courtesy of John R. Redmill*)

25. Shrine of the Stowe (or Lorrha) Missal, made for Mathgamain ua Cathail, abbot of Lorrha, Co. Tipperary (d. 1037). The inscription at the top reads 'OR[OIT] DO DONDCHAD MACC BRIAIN DO RIG HEREND ('A prayer for Donnchad mac Briain, king of Ireland'), indicating the claim by Donnchad (d. 1064) to have succeeded to the high-kingship at some point after the death of his father, Brian, at Clontarf. (© *Getty Images*)

26. Church of Santo Stefano, Rome: When Brian's grandson Tairdelbach ua Briain (d. 1086) ousted his uncle, Brian's son Donnchad, from power, the latter went off on pilgrimage to Rome, where he died in 1064 and is buried in the church of Santo Stefano on the Caelian Hill. The burial plaque is far left. (© *Corbis*)

27. The church contains a wall plaque of uncertain date but certainly several centuries old that features what is intended to be the crown of Ireland and, in translation, the following inscription: 'In the year of Our Lord 1064, Donatus O'Brienus, King of Cashel and Thomond, son of Brian Boru, Monarch of All Ireland, gave the royal crown as a gift to the Pope.' (*Courtesy of Vera Orschel*)

and demolishing its *baile*, the nucleated settlement around it, at which point he secured the pledge of the Dál Fiatach king of the Ulaid, thereby supplanting Brian as the latter's overlord.[1]

The following year he was back in Co. Down, raiding further still, all the way to the Ards Peninsula, from which he 'took the greatest spoils, both in captives and cattle, that a king ever took, though they are not counted.'[2] Also that year he marched twice on Cenél Conaill, taking a large prey of cattle on the first occasion and on the second occasion, when his energies were concentrated in the Co. Sligo area, defeating in battle Cenél Conaill's king, Máel Ruanaid Ua Máel Doraid.

This attempt by Flaithbertach to extend his authority throughout the northern kingdoms brought a response from the overking of all the Uí Néill north and south, Máel Sechnaill, who marched north while Flaithbertach was absent in Sligo and Donegal and burned the Cenél nEógain inauguration site at Tulach Óc in Co. Tyrone. Brian too expressed his apprehensiveness about the situation by marching north to Mag Muirthemne in north Louth but does not seem to have ventured into Cenél nEógain territory. In fact the Annals of Ulster, always interested in the affairs of Armagh, simply report that on this hosting Brian granted immunity to the churches subject to it, and the only activity in the north that it reports for the following year by or on behalf of Brian is a raid by Máel Sechnaill 'at the request of (*a forghaire*)' Brian and the abbot of Armagh. It was not directed against the Northern Uí Néill, however, but rather against the Conailli Muirthemne of north Louth for the profanation of Patrician shrines, including the breaking of Bachall Ísa, St Patrick's Staff.[3]

There are shades here of fiddling while Rome burns, because in the same year, 1013, Flaithbertach Ua Néill sought to build on his new northern dominance by leading an army into Southern Uí Néill territory. By the time his forces had reached a hillside in the vicinity of Kells, Co. Meath, Máel Sechnaill seems to have mustered to oppose him; but, not for the first time in Máel Sechnaill's career, he proved less than effective, the outcome being that he 'abandoned the hill' to Flaithbertach.[4]

THE REVOLT OF DUBLIN AND LEINSTER

By now Brian's authority was beginning to evaporate. We hear that in 1012 or 1013 he was busy fortifying palaces;[5] if this was ostentation the timing was bad, but perhaps Brian was instead readying himself to defend his home soil. The king of Cenél Conaill, Máel Ruanaid Ua Máel Doraid, who had so recently come into Brian's peace, launched an invasion of Connacht, the territory of another of Brian's vassals, slaughtered the Connacht army in battle, and devastated Mag nAí in north Roscommon (map 4).[6] This would not have happened if the Cenél Conaill had feared Brian's reaction; but they had no cause for fear, because this was the year in which a more widespread revolt broke out against him.

This rebellion was led by the Norse of Dublin and the Leinstermen, although it is not entirely clear which was the driving force. It was certainly considered momentous, all the annals applying the term *cocad* ('war') to it, which is hitherto very rarely used and usually only for major conflicts with the Vikings. In fact the word does not previously occur in the Annals of Inisfallen but is used for the first time in 1013 and then again for the traumatic events of 1014.

As far as the Annals of Inisfallen were concerned, the leading part was taken by the Norse: 'Great warfare took place that year between the Foreigners and the Irish (*Forcoemnactar cocaid móra isin bliadain sin eter Gullu & Goedelu*).' The Annals of Ulster and the Four Masters, on the other hand, have it that in 1013 'the Leinstermen and the Foreigners were at war with Brian (*Laighin & Gaill do chocadh fri Brian*).' This accords with the interpretation of the crisis found in Cogadh Gáedhel re Gallaibh, which at this point largely abandons its earlier approach— which was, to be fair to it, the generating of a muscular but substantially faithful narrative from the bare bones of an annalistic source—in favour of fiction. Thus it imagines an extraordinary set of events now unfolding. And here the villain of the piece is not a Norseman but Máelmórda mac Murchada, the king of Leinster, urged on by his sister Gormlaith, who, it envisages, was still Brian's wife in 1013. She was also, of course, the mother of King Sitriuc of Dublin from her marriage to Amlaíb Cuarán (died 981). So there was a tight nexus of conspirators here (see table 4; above, page 147).

But the Cogadh cannot be right in claiming that Gormlaith was still married to Brian in 1013. Even if we imagine him having a formal aristocratic wife at the same time as a secondary wife or concubine of less noble standing, it is hard to imagine Brian having two aristocratic queens concurrently (see table 3; above, page 100). The reason we can be certain that the Cogadh is drifting into unreality here is that, while it is true that in 1009 Brian became a widower when his then wife, Dub Choblaig, daughter of the king of Connacht, died, arguably freeing him to marry Gormlaith—which would neatly fit the Cogadh's belief that she was in residence at Cenn Corad in 1013—the fact is that by this time her son with Brian, Donnchad, was of fighting age, as we have seen, so that Brian's marriage to her must have preceded his marriage to Dub Choblaig, placing the Gormlaith union some time in the 990s, if not earlier.

In any event, this is a reminder not to take too seriously the Cogadh's claims for what happened in 1013. According to it, Gormlaith's brother Máelmórda set out for Brian's palace at Cenn Corad, bearing three pine masts for ships (*tri seolcrand giusaig*) cut from the trees of Fid Gaible (a forest on the borders of Kildare and Offaly, near Rathangan), one given by the local dynasty of Uí Failgi, another by the Uí Muiredaig of south Kildare, and the third by Máelmórda's own north Kildare dynasty of Uí Fáeláin (map 5). Presumably they represented tribute, which Máelmórda, as mesne lord of the peoples in question, was proffering on their behalf to their overlord.

Máelmórda was wearing a tunic with gold border and silver fasteners, earlier presented to him by Brian, but burst one of the clasps on the way, and therefore when he arrived at Cenn Corad he gave it for mending to his sister, Brian's wife Gormlaith. She, however, cast it into the fire and reproached Máelmórda for accepting a position of vassalage to Brian, which none of their ancestors would have tolerated.

Next morning, when Brian's most senior son, Murchad, and Brian's nephew Conaing were playing the board-game called *fidchell*, the Leinster king helped Conaing win. But Murchad then reminded Máelmórda that the last time he had offered advice was to the Norse at the time of their defeat—apparently in the Battle of Glenn Máma in 999—which caused Máelmórda to retort that he would do so again, and he therefore withdrew from Cenn Corad in anger, without Brian's permission. Brian sent a messenger, Coccarán, after him to call him back, as he had not brought with him his *tuarastal*, the ceremonial wages that a vassal accepts from his lord; but when the messenger caught up with Máelmórda—on the eastern end of the wooden bridge at Killaloe—Máelmórda lashed out at him with his horsewhip and then carried on northwards. Brian refused to compel him to return, as it infringed conventions of hospitality, saying that such compulsion should be applied on Máelmórda's doorstep, not Brian's.

That night Máelmórda was at the house of the king of Uí Buide at Senlis Abbáin (at or near Killabban, Co. Laois), and early next morning he arrived in Co. Kildare, at a place called Garbthamnach, home of Dúnlaing mac Tuathail, the king of Uí Muiredaig. There the nobles of Leinster met in convention (*comdail*), and when Máelmórda told them of the insulting words of Brian's son Murchad they decided to turn against Brian.

The Leinstermen allegedly then sent messengers to Flaithbrtach Ua Néill of Cenél nEógain, urging him to make war on Máel Sechnaill, the king of Tara, and on the Ulaid. The implication is that this aggression against others of Brian's vassals would be tantamount to rebellion against Brian. They sent similar messengers to the king of Bréifne, Fergal [correctly Niall] Ua Ruairc,[7] and to the king of Cairpre, Uallgarg Ua Ciarda, and 'all consented to turn against Brian.'

It is at this point that the Cogadh resumes weaving annalistic data into its tale and therefore records Flaithbertach's hosting into Southern Uí Néill territory, which, as we have seen, is noted in the annals under 1013. The Cogadh, however, adds the interesting detail that one of the casualties of this assault was a *fer gráda* or confidential retainer of Brian's by the name of Osli son of Dubcenn mac Ímair, who was *mormaer da maeraib,* meaning something like 'chief collector among his [Brian's] collectors of dues,'[8] and it would seem that, since Flaithbertach's raid was in what is now Co. Meath, Brian must have had officials stationed there to collect the revenue due him as the king of Tara's overlord.

There seems no reason to doubt the author's word on this, as this man's father is recorded elsewhere, Dubcenn mac Ímair having been one of the Norse of Limerick killed when Brian stormed their base on Inis Cathaig (Scattery Island) in 977, shortly after he succeeded to the kingship.[9] By the looks of things, after Brian was reconciled with the Norse they took service with him and he used them as tax-collectors, perhaps exploiting an established expertise in that field.

As to the events of 1013, the Cogadh then reports virtually word for word the account in the Annals of Ulster of a raid by Ua Ruairc and Ua

Ciarda on Gailenga, in which, however, the latter was killed by Máel Sechnaill. And, in common with the annals, the Cogadh describes Máel Sechnaill taking the initiative against Brian's rebels by leading an army into the Norse-controlled territory surrounding Dublin (which the Four Masters and Chronican Scotorum call Crích Gall and the Annals of Inisfallen call—for the first time on record—by the more familiar name Fine Gall, from which we get the modern Fingal).

If the object was to punish the rebels it is noticeable that Máel Sechnaill did not enter the territory controlled by Máelmórda south of the Liffey but rather burned Sitriuc's heartland in north Co. Dublin, all the way to the Hill of Howth. But it then went disastrously wrong for Máel Sechnaill. A contingent of his army was overtaken at Drinan, just south of Swords, by King Sitriuc of Dublin and by Máelmorda (in that order), the Annals of Ulster describing the full-scale battle that ensued as a defeat of Máel Sechnaill's army by 'the Foreigners and the Leinstermen (*ria n-Gallaib & Laighnibh*)'—again in that order—in which two hundred of Máel Sechnaill's men, including his son Flann, nicknamed 'the Scotsman (*in tAlbanach*)', were killed.[10]

At that point, it seems, it was the triumphant Norse who sought to press home their advantage by taking the war to Brian, although it is interesting that this assault on Munster is omitted for some reason in the Cogadh. The Norse of Dublin, the annals alone tell us, put to sea and sailed around the south coast, venturing up the narrow confines of Cork Harbour to attack the monastery of Cork—and presumably the little Norse trading settlement there, which may well have been an economic threat to them. Their forces were slaughtered, notwithstanding which they then travelled further till they reached Ireland's most southerly point at Oileán Chléire (Cape Clear); but again it proved ill-starred for them, Sitriuc losing a son, Amlaíb (Oláfr), and probably also a nephew by the name of Mathgamain (ironically, perhaps a name adopted in honour of Brian's brother of that name).[11]

Instead of this naval assault the Cogadh reports a land invasion of Mide by the Norse and the Leinstermen, who plundered as far as Fore in Co. Westmeath, taking an innumerable prey of cattle and captives from the monastic estate there. (The Four Masters and the Annals of Loch Cé have Termonfeckin, Co. Louth, instead of Fore and place this at the beginning of 1014.) In the aftermath of this assault the Cogadh has it that Máel Sechnaill sent messengers to Brian, complaining that his territory was being ravaged and his sons killed and praying Brian to prevent the Foreigners and Leinster, Bréifne, Cairpre and Cenél nEógain joining together to make war on him.

The Cogadh therefore paints what comes next as Brian's response to this request for protection from Máel Sechnaill. It claims that the men of Munster and Connacht, under Brian, undertook an expedition against Osraige and Leinster, and that Brian's son Murchad plundered Leinster, coming to Glendalough and burning the province from there to Kilmainham, to the *faithche* or green of Dublin.[12] This invasion of Leinster is confirmed by the annals for 1013, which have Brian camping out at Sliab Maircce (the plateau of Slievemargy, Co. Laois).

After Murchad had reached Dublin, Brian and the rest of their forces joined him, Brian setting up camp at a place called Áth in Cháerthainn (which is unidentified but is a ford on the Liffey or one of its tributaries), where he remained for more than three months, from the feast of St Ciarán (9 September) until Christmas, having 'made a siege and blockade around Dublin and an encampment there (*do ronsat forbasi ocus forcomet for Áth Cliath, ocus foslongport and*).'[13] The Annals of Inisfallen say of Brian's siege that 'he did not bring about peace (*ni tuc síd*)'; the Cogadh says instead that neither the Norse nor the Leinstermen (who seem to have remained with the Norse in Dublin) gave them a hostage or a battle or a peace overture (*coma*), and therefore, when his provisions were exhausted, at about Christmas, Brian retired home.

From the contemporary coverage of the situation—albeit with a strong tinge of retrospection—we are left in no doubt that all knew that both sides were heading for a major confrontation.

CLONTARF IN THE ANNALS OF INISFALLEN

The first thing that should be said about the Battle of Clontarf is that, such was its later notoriety, we cannot be certain that any of our annalistic accounts have not had later legend stitched into them. We have to be very cautious, therefore, not to accept later exaggerated detail as fact; but distinguishing one from the other is not easy.

Of all the accounts of the battle, that in the Annals of Inisfallen is the most unadorned, and there seems every likelihood that it was written quite close to the time of the event and that the facts it presents are accurate and the opinions—to the extent that it offers any—are reflective of contemporary reaction to what occurred. This is what it reports:

> A great war between Brian and the Foreigners of Dublin (*Cocad mór eter Brian & Gullu Atha Cliath*), and Brian then brought a great muster of the men of Ireland (*morthinol fer n-Erend*) to Dublin. It is after that (*Is íar sain*) that the Foreigners of Dublin gave battle to Brian (*doratsat Gaill Atha Clíath cath do Brian*) so that Brian mac Cennétig was slain, and his son Murchad, heir-designate of Ireland (*rigdamna h-Erend*), and the latter's son, namely, Tairdelbach, along with the royalty (*rígrad*) of Munster including Conaing mac Donncuain, and Domnall mac Diarmata, king of Corco Bascind, and Mac Bethad mac Muiredaig, king of Ciarraige Luachra, and Tadc Ua Cellaig, king of Uí Maine, and many others. There was also slain in that battle Máelmórda mac Murchada, king of Leinster, together with the princes of Leinster round him (*co rigraid Laigen imbi*), and there was a slaughter of the Foreigners of the Western World in the same battle (*ocus ar Gall iarthair domain isi[n] chath chetna*).

This is the extent of the annalist's commentary on one of the most famous battles in Irish history; but the sheer brevity is perhaps the surest sign of its contemporaneity.

If this was our only source of information on the battle, what could it tell us? As mentioned above, it is significant that for the events of this and the preceding year the author introduces into his lexicon the word *cocad* ('war') to capture a sense that this was in no sense a typical campaign. Of course he will have been aware that Brian fought very few full-scale field battles during his long life, and none since his last great confrontation with the Dubliners and Leinstermen at Glenn Máma nearly fifteen years earlier. And so perhaps it merited this word *cocad,* which, as earlier noted, the annalists had tended to reserve for conflict with the Vikings. Indeed that is very much how he perceives it.

Whereas some modern historians see the Leinstermen as Brian's primary enemy at Clontarf, the annalist was in no doubt that the enemy was the Norse of Dublin. In fact he has the same black-and-white picture of the opposing sides that we tend to think of as later legend, indeed as reflecting a later nationalist, if not xenophobic, outlook. After all, Brian—he would have us believe—commanded 'a great muster of the men of Ireland (*morthinol fer n-Erend*),' although the only evidence he offers to support the statement is the death of one non-Munster ally of Brian, the south Connacht king of Uí Maine. And this campaign was part of a 'great war between Brian and the Foreigners of Dublin (*cocad mór eter Brian & Gullu Atha Cliath*).' Brian prosecuted that war by marshalling an army that had only one destination: 'Brian then brought a great muster of the men of Ireland to Dublin (*morthinol fer n-Erend co Ath Cliath*).' There was more than one possible outcome of his arrival in the vicinity, but what transpired was that 'after that (*Is íar sain*),' after he challenged their contumacy, 'the Foreigners of Dublin gave battle to Brian (*doratsat Gaill Atha Clíath cath do Brian*).'

Admittedly the only one of Brian's opponents named as dying in the contest is Máelmórda of Leinster, along with 'the royalty of Leinster,' but evidently the writer felt that they had died serving the interests of Dublin, and one of the most notable outcomes of the day was the 'slaughter of the Foreigners of the Western World (*ocus ar Gall iarthair domain*).'

That, by the way, is as close as the author of the Inisfallen entry on Clontarf comes to describing it as a victory for Brian, and it is by no means certain that he viewed it as such. From his viewpoint—although he says it in a rather matter-of-fact way—by far the most considerable outcome of the encounter was the death of Brian. This loss was compounded by the death of Brian's most senior son, Murchad, who, as we know, had been his trusty lieutenant for many years and, as the annalist puts it, *rigdamna h-Erend,* someone he had assumed would seek to succeed his father as king of Ireland. Not only that but Murchad's own son, Tairdelbach, had died in the bloodbath (as had Conaing, son of Brian's brother Donncuan).

Aside from any sorrow the writer may have felt at the demise of the old king, he was surely conscious that the elimination of Brian and his intended heir, and his grandson, who might in turn have been the latter's heir (and bearing in mind that Brian's second most senior son, Domnall, had died less than three years earlier), cast a pall of confusion over the contemporary political landscape. Not only did it throw open again the struggle for the high-kingship but, from the author's Munster viewpoint, it meant that nothing short of chaos would reign in his kingdom until there was clarity within Dál Cais about which of the senior surviving members of Brian's family would gain from these most unlikely vacancies at the top and until, within Munster more generally, it was thrashed out by word or bloody deed whether Dál Cais would maintain its comparatively recent dominance or whether the previously ascendant Eóganachta might capitalise on this ill wind that had blown Dál Cais's way in so traumatic a fashion.

CLONTARF IN THE ANNALS OF ULSTER

If the Inisfallen annalist did not view Clontarf as a victory for Brian—and he could hardly think of it as an unqualified success, as the high-king himself lay dead at its conclusion—there is nonetheless a slight suggestion that the loss might almost be worth it, because of the 'slaughter of the Foreigners of the Western World in the same battle (*ocus ar Gall iarthair domain isi[n] chath chetna*).' And it is this aspect of the confrontation that other sources tend to emphasise. In other words, there is an undercurrent in all the other accounts of the battle that, great as the loss of their high-king was, the achievement by his army on the day was immense. This is how the Annals of Ulster report it:

A hosting by Brian mac Ceinnétig mic Lorcáin, by the king of Ireland (*la righ n-Erenn*), and by Máel Sechnaill mac Domnaill, by the king of Tara (*la righ Temhrach*), to Dublin. All the Leinstermen were assembled against them, and the Foreigners of Dublin, and a like number of the Foreigners of Lochlainn along with them, i.e. a thousand breastplates (*Laighin uile do leir i tinol ar a cinn & Gaill Atha Cliath & a coimlin do Ghallaib Lochlainne leó. .i. x.c. luirech*). A valiant battle was fought between them, the like of which was never [before] encountered.

Then the Foreigners and the Leinstermen first broke in defeat so that they were all completely wiped out (*Maidhis iarum for Gallu & for Laighniu i tosaigh corus-dileghait uile do leir*). In which battle there was killed on the side of the troops of the Foreigners (*In quo bello cecidit ex adhuersa caterua Gallorum*) Máelmórda mac Murchada, king of Leinster; and Domnall mac Fergail, king of the Forthuatha [of Leinster]; and there was in truth killed of the Foreigners (*cecidit uero a Gallis*) Dubgall mac Amlaíb; Siucraid mac Lodur, jarl of Innsi Orc;

and Gilla Ciaráin mac Glún Iairn, heir-designate of the Foreigners (*rigdomna Gall*); and Oittir Dub; and Suartgair; and Donnchad ua Eruilb; and Griséne; and Luimne; and Amlaíb mac Lagmainn; and Brotor who slew Brian, i.e. chief of the fleet of Lochlainn (*qui occidit Brian .i. toisech na loingsi Lochlannaighi*); and six thousand who were killed or drowned.

Of the Irish moreover there fell in the counter-shock (*Do-rochuir immorro a fritguin o Gaidhelaibh*) Brian mac Cennétig, high-king of the Irish of Ireland and of the Foreigners and of the Britons, the Augustus of the whole of Northwest Europe (*ardrí Gaidhel Erenn & Gall & Bretan, August iartair tuaiscirt Eorpa uile*); and his son Murchad; and the latter's son, i.e. Tairdelbach mac Murchada; and Conaing mac Donncuain mic Cennétig, potential-king of Munster (*rigdomna Muman*); and Mothla mac Domnaill mic Fáeláin, king of the Déisi Muman; Brian's three attendants (*tri coimthe Briain*), Eochu mac Dúnadaig and Niall ua Cuinn and [Cú Duilig] mac Cennétig; two kings of Uí Maine, [Tadc] Ua Cellaig [second name missing]; and Máel Ruanaid ua hEidin, king of Aidne; and Géibennach ua Dubagáin, king of Fernmag [recte Fer Maige]; and Mac Bethad mac Muiredig Cláein, king of Ciarraige Luachra; and Domnall mac Diarmata, king of Corco Baiscind; and Scannlán mac Cathail, king of the Eóganacht of Loch Léin; and Domnall mac Eimin mic Cainnich, earl of Mar in Scotland (*mormhaer Marr i n-Albain*), and many other nobles.

Máel Muire mac Eochada, successor of Patrick, with his venerable clerics and relics, came moreover to Swords, and brought away the body of Brian, king of Ireland, and the body of his son Murchad, and the head of Conaing and the head of Mothla, and buried them in Armagh in a new tomb (*i n-ailaidh nui*). For twelve nights the community of Patrick waked the bodies in honour of the king (*propter honorem regis*).

This is an extraordinary account, nearly twice as long as the next-longest entries before that date in the same annals, those recording campaigns by the Northern Uí Néill high-kings Áed Allán (his victory in battle against the Leinstermen at Áth Senaig in 738) and Niall Glúndub (his campaign against the Vikings in Munster in 917 and events surrounding the Battle of Cenn Fuait). This should alert us to the need for vigilance in accepting it at face value: there must be a possibility that parts of it were added to the contemporary record at a later date.

Two possibilities suggest themselves as explanations for the length of this entry. One arises from the fact that some at least of the contemporary content of this section of the Annals of Ulster was undoubtedly written at Armagh. We have seen that the partnership into which Brian entered with the clergy of Armagh in 1005 transformed the Armagh annalist from being at best neutral regarding his kingship ambitions to being an ardent advocate. Of course, therefore, Brian's death was considered by this writer a major event; and if it is true—as we have no reason to doubt—that Brian and his son Murchad were brought for burial to Armagh, surely even the commotion surrounding the great occasion would stimulate the resident annalist within their community to a more effusive obit than heretofore.

The other possibility arises from the fact (as we shall see) that there is a remarkable overlap between the names given here and in Cogadh Gáedhel re Gallaibh, to such an extent that it is quite likely that one was copied, directly or indirectly, from the other; and perhaps therefore the entry in the Annals of Ulster is so unusually long only because its author augmented it with names harvested from the Cogadh or a related source.

What we can say is that there is much in the entry in the Annals of Ulster that is corroborated by the apparently independent account in the Annals of Inisfallen, to the extent that all eight fatalities in the latter are also in the Annals of Ulster. We may take it as fact, therefore, that in addition to Brian and his son and grandson the dead on Brian's side at Clontarf included Domnall mac Diarmata of Corco Bascind in south-west Co. Clare and Mac Bethad mac Muiredaig of Ciarraige Luachra in north-west Co. Kerry, both seafaring communities, facing each other across the lower Shannon Estuary (map 6), whose vessels would no doubt have helped transport the Munster troops to Dublin. Tadc Ua Cellaig of Uí Maine in south Connacht was one of the few non-Munster powers who was there and also lost his life, which fired the poetic imagination of a later generation.[14]

Another certain fatality was Brian's nephew Conaing, son of his brother Donncuan (table 2). The Annals of Inisfallen do not give Conaing a title, although the Annals of Ulster call him *rigdomna Muman,* which in a case such as this cannot mean, as it sometimes does, 'heir-designate' but rather is an honorific to indicate that Conaing (ancestor of the Uí Chonaing or Gunnings and a number of other important lines) was a worthy elder statesman who had kingly potential and in other circumstances might have made it to the top. His brother Célechair was the first Dál Cais abbot of Terryglass, who died in 1008, a position he secured no doubt through Brian's influence.[15]

It is worth pointing out that, while we might imagine that, as Brian's nephew, Conaing was a young man in 1014, in fact his father had died as far back as 950, meaning that he would have been at least in his mid-sixties at the time of Clontarf. Perhaps therefore there is something to the claim of the embellished account of the battle in the later Annals of Loch Cé that neither Brian nor Conaing fought but were 'behind the battalions, chanting their psalms, and performing prayers (*Is ann boi an t-airdrigh .i. Brian mac Ceinneidigh & Conaing mac Duinn Cuan, ar cúl na cath ag cantain a salm & ag denam irnaide)*' when an unnamed Dane happened upon them and brutally beheaded both (*ro dhichend airdri Erenn & ros-dichend Conaing mur an cedna*). And sure enough the Annals of Ulster have it that when Brian was brought for burial to Armagh only Conaing's head was buried along with him, presumably because the rest of the body was not recovered, which would hardly be so if, as the Cogadh has it, Conaing died in hand-to-hand combat with Máelmórda of Leinster.[16]

It is also significant that neither the Annals of Inisfallen nor the Annals of Ulster refer to the precise site of the battle, or its date. That does not mean that this epic battle, which for centuries has been associated with the low-lying coastal district of Clontarf to the north-east of Dublin, did not take place there: we must believe it did, and it probably also occurred on the date assigned to it soon afterwards, Good Friday. But the point is that neither of these annal entries, which are the ones least tainted by later legend, actually says so. We shall discuss the scene of battle and the date presently, but for now the salient point is that had the account of the battle in the Annals of Ulster been markedly infected by supplementary 'facts' added in succeeding generations we might have expected it to incorporate also the pretty obvious information about the date and the site at Clontarf by which the battle later came to be known.

That it does not do so suggests that the original contemporary report on the battle has remained largely intact in the Annals of Ulster as they have come down to us.

The entry in the Annals of Ulster also echoes the Annals of Inisfallen in emphasising the primacy of the Norse as Brian's adversaries. It was a march on Dublin; although the Leinstermen are listed first among those assembled there (*Laighin uile do leir i tinol ar a cinn*), it is instead 'the Foreigners and the Leinstermen [who] first broke (*Maidhis iarum for Gallu & for Laighniu i tosaigh*)'; those Leinstermen who died were 'killed on the side of the troops of the Foreigners (*cecidit ex adhuersa caterua Gallorum*)'; and, having listed those of Brian's opponents who were killed, the author begins his inventory of the fatalities on Brian's side with the words 'Of the *Irish* moreover there fell in the counter-shock (*Do-rochuir immorro a fritguin o Gaidhelaibh*),' as if to suggest it was fundamentally a contest between the Irish and the Norse (although the latter too had Irish allies).

But whereas the Inisfallen annalist merely mentioned in passing the 'slaughter of the Foreigners of the Western World (*ar Gall iarthair domain*),' the Ulster annalist is much more talkative about the subject. The numbers of the Norse of Dublin who were present at Clontarf are matched by 'a like number of the Foreigners of Lochlainn, i.e. a thousand breastplates (*a coimlin do Ghallaib Lochlainne leó. .i. x.c. luirech*).' Whatever the origins of this term Lochlainn, which have been much debated by scholars,[17] the author here clearly intended somewhere in the greater Scandinavian world, as opposed to the Scandinavian enclaves in Ireland.

Incidentally, while the writer's insistence on telling us that Brian's Hiberno-Norse opponents were 'the Foreigners *of Dublin* (*Gaill Atha Cliath*)' might be taken to mean that the other major Norse forces in Ireland, from Waterford and Limerick, fought on Brian's side, this is not certain. The Limerickmen may have done so, as they seem to have been well and truly under Brian's thumb from his early years; but the Cogadh claims that the slain among Brian's opponents at Clontarf included Goistilin Gall and Amond mac Duibginn, 'two kings of Waterford' (although the former looks suspiciously like the Anglo-Norman name Jocelyn and may be a later invention).[18] And by 'breastplates' the Ulster annalist obviously intends to convey the sense that they were more heavily armoured or mail-clad than their Irish protagonists. He therefore imagines a force of a thousand armoured Scandinavians, and a similar number of Dubliners, and yet calculates that, of the Foreigners who fought at the battle, six thousand 'were killed or drowned'!

One explanation for what appears like very poor arithmetic may be that the author sought to imply that, while Dublin and its Scandinavian allies each provided a thousand armoured soldiers, there were in addition vast numbers of other unarmoured participants, and because many of the latter were also killed this brought the total up to six thousand. Of course another obvious explanation is that the figure of six thousand was added for effect by a later writer.

The other thing that the Annals of Ulster do regarding the Norse casualties is to provide names—the Annals of Inisfallen do not name a single one—and of the ten who are listed most if not all are credible and some identifiable.[19] The first one on the list—and therefore, we must assume, the one who was considered the most important or whose name resonated most with the writer—is Dubgall mac Amlaíb, who was probably a brother of the then king of Dublin, known to the Norse as Sigtryggr Óláfsson or Sigtryggr Silkiskeggi ('Silkenbeard') and to the Irish as Sitriuc mac Amlaíb. The second name on the list is Siucraid mac Lodur, jarl of Innsi Orc, who is Sigurðr Hlöðvisson or Sigurðr digri ('the Stout'), earl of Orkney, whose mother was apparently Irish and whose death at Clontarf is widely attested (table 4).[20] We shall discuss later what Sigurðr may have been up to, but for now the important point is that the Annals of Ulster are merely stating fact when they record him among the slain.

The third name is Gilla Ciaráin mac Glún Iairn, 'heir-designate of the Foreigners (rígdomna Gall)', and there is little doubt that he too was a prominent Dublin lord. King Sitriuc had a brother Glún Iairn (a Gaelicisation of his Norse given name, Járnkné, 'Iron Knee'), who preceded Sitriuc in the kingship until in 989 he was murdered while drunk by his own slave,[21] and the Gilla Ciaráin killed twenty years later at Clontarf was presumably his son. As the son of a former king of Dublin, no doubt having been too young to prevent his uncle Sitriuc from obtaining the crown when Glún Iairn was murdered, he was undoubtedly rígdamna Gall, one entitled to the kingship should political circumstances allow. (And, incidentally, his name Gilla Ciaráin, with its devotion to the founder of Clonmacnoise, is a reminder of how thoroughly Christianised and Gaelicised this family now were.)

From this point the names are less readily identifiable. Oittir Dub has the Norse name Óttarr and an Irish nickname, meaning 'the Black'. Assuming he was actually known as this, rather than having had his Norse nickname rendered thus by the Irish annalist, he came from somewhere in the Gaelic-speaking world. As to his identity, there is an outside chance, although there is a big gap between them, that his grandson is the 'Oittir, son of the son of Oittir, of the people of the Western Isles (*mac mic Ottir .i. Ottir do lucht Insi Gall*),' who seized the kingship of Dublin in 1142.[22] A cynic might suggest that a memory of this later Óttarr prompted the insertion of the name in Irish accounts of Clontarf, but there were other Óttarrs, and perhaps therefore it was a common name among the Hiberno-Norse. An Óttarr son of Járnkné was active in the Dublin area in the 880s, and there was a Jarl Óttarr operating from Waterford who was killed in England in 918.[23] Interestingly, the Óttarr who died in 918 becomes one of the villains of the Cogadh's account of Viking oppression, and it calls him Oittir Dub,[24] the same as the man allegedly killed at Clontarf. Assuming there were not two Ottir Dubs, we must reject one of them, perhaps giving the benefit of the doubt to the 1014 Oittir Dub rather than the Cogadh's 918 one (who is just plain Oittir in the annals). In other words, it seems slightly more likely that the author of the Cogadh added the nickname *Dub* to the 918 Oittir, having come across it in an annal-type record of Clontarf, than that the compilers of the Annals of Ulster liked the look of the early tenth-century Oittir Dub in the Cogadh and randomly added him to their account of Clontarf.

The Annals of Ulster then have among the Norse slain at Clontarf a certain Suartgair, which may be a Norse name Suartgarr or Suarfgeirr,[25] but if so it is very rare, which may add a hint of authenticity to it. Nothing is known of the man in question, whereas the next individual named, Donnchad ua Eruilb, is a little more familiar. His is an unlikely-looking name for a Norseman, and there is still uncertainty about whether his family was Norse or Irish, but the Clann Eruilb do at least occur in contemporary Irish sources, and this therefore is not a casual concoction by the author.[26] Then comes Griséne, whose name seems to be the Old Norse personal name Gríss but ending, it appears, with the

Gaelic diminutive *-ín,* suggesting that he too is from a Gaelic-speaking milieu. Next, Luimne might be Lambi, a relatively rare name that occurs a few times in *Landnámabók,* the Icelandic 'Book of Settlements', put together in its present form in the thirteenth century, which lists Viking colonists in Iceland from the late ninth century onwards.[27]

As for Amlaíb mac Lagmainn, his name is the very familiar Óláfr or Óleifr, and we may suppose that his patronymic derives from Old Norse *lögmaðr,* meaning 'lawman', and he may have been connected to the *Lagmainn na n-Innsedh* ('Lawmen of the Isles') who turn up in Ireland in the 960s and 970s. As far as the author of the Cogadh was concerned, however, he was one of the five chiefs of the Dubliners killed at Clontarf.[28]

Finally Brodor, the commander of this Scandinavian fleet, presumably has the Norse name Bróðir rather than the Irish name Bruadar; and Norse sources imply a background in the Isle of Man,[29] although the Cogadh implausibly considered him jarl of York and the north of England. In the Cogadh, though, he occurs alongside his uterine brother Conmael, and a person of this name was one of the Islesmen killed at the Battle of Tara in 980, suggesting, if the name runs in the family, an Insular background.[30] He is certainly a historical figure, whose leading role at Clontarf is chronicled in other accounts.

The author's insistence on recalling the names of these non-Irish high-status fatalities is important. They may be obscure to us now but they were obviously well-known figures in the Irish Sea region, whose participation in this anti-Brian coalition at Clontarf, and their deaths there, was big news. He is keen to emphasise that this was not just a Dublin army but was matched by 'a like number of the Foreigners of Lochlainn.' Hence, therefore, just as his list of the Irish who fell at Clontarf is given in order of seniority, beginning with Brian, his list of the deceased Norse commanders is headed by the king of Dublin's brother, Dubgall mac Amlaíb, followed by Sigurðr *Digri* of Orkney, because to him this was a joint command; and if, therefore, we are to give credence to his account we must think in similar terms. It was, after all, a view shared by the Inisfallen annalist, who thought of Clontarf as a 'slaughter of the Foreigners of the Western World.'

To complement his notion of a broad axis of Norse opposition the Ulster annalist must view Brian's army in national terms. Thus he captures the essence of the Annals of Inisfallen's 'great muster of the men of Ireland (*morthinol fer n-Erend*)' by telling us that the hosting to Dublin was led by both Brian, as king of Ireland, and Máel Sechnaill, as king of Tara. This is the first time that these two titles were applied to different individuals in the same sentence, showing how the writer had reconciled himself to the fact that they were no longer synonymous: one could be king of Ireland without being king of Tara, and vice versa. Máel Sechnaill's continued commitment to Brian's cause has been widely doubted, and he has been given a very bad press in later literary accounts of Clontarf, but the contemporary Ulster annalist thought he was one of the leaders of Brian's army for a reason. And that reason has to do with the Armagh author's knowledge of Máel Sechnaill's relationship with Brian. After he entered into Brian's allegiance in 1002 there is no evidence that he ever wavered in his duty.

Besides, Brian's enemies at Clontarf were Máel Sechnaill's enemies. At the beginning of that fateful year, 1014, while they waited for Brian and his allies to return—and no doubt to replenish their provisions before the impending assault—Sitriuc and Máelmórda made a foray out of Dublin into Máel Sechnaill's kingdom of Mide (along with Brega, as far as Termonfeckin in Co. Louth), from which 'they carried off innumerable cows and a great number of captives.'[31] Evidently they considered Máel Sechnaill as much an enemy as they did Brian. Furthermore, a text listing the kings of Ireland tells us that Máel Sechnaill fought in twenty-five battles, including the Battle of Tara and two battles at Dublin, which we must assume are Glenn Máma in 999 and Clontarf in 1014. (He successfully laid siege to Dublin on two occasions early on in his career, but neither counts as a battle.)[32]

And not only had Brian the forces of Mide with him but the casualty list shows that he had fairly wide-ranging backing. The Munster contingent in his army included such erstwhile Eóganacht enemies as Scannlán mac Cathail, king of the Eóganacht of Loch Léin, and Géibennach ua Dubagáin, the Eóganacht Glendamnach king of Fer Maige (not Fernmag, as the Ulster annals erroneously have, which is in Airgialla), both of whom lost their lives alongside Brian, as did Mothla mac Domnaill mic Fáeláin, king of the Déisi Muman, a people who in Brian's early years had been slow to rally to his cause (map 6). Indeed Mothla was considered such a part of Brian's inner circle that when his head was retrieved from the battlefield (presumably his decapitated trunk could not be identified, which says something for the mayhem that ensued) it was brought to Armagh for burial in the same tomb as the high-king and his slain family members (of one of whom, his nephew Conaing, as we saw, likewise only a severed head could be recovered).

And other Munster peoples were there in force too, if we are to judge from the fact that at least two more of their kings—the West Munster king of Ciarraige Luachra and the king of the Co. Clare people called Corco Baiscind—also fell with Brian. And his support extended beyond Leth Moga into Leth Cuinn. Not only had he the support of its most senior royal, the king of Tara himself, but a number of Connacht royals died fighting for his cause, including apparently two kings of Uí Maine, at least one of whom, as we have seen, was an Ua Cellaig (other annals confirm he was Tadc son of Murchad Ua Cellaig), and the king of Uí Fiachrach Aidne, Máel Ruanaid ua hEidin, nephew of Brian's first wife (table 3; map 4).

If these Connacht kings died we must assume there were others present who survived, and that means that the geographical spread was not inconsiderable. So significant was the compass of support, in fact, that a certain Domnall mac Eimin mic Cainnich, earl of Mar in Scotland (*mormhaer Marr i n-Albain*), also perished alongside Brian. We shall look again below at the involvement of this lord from north-eastern Scotland in this ostensibly Irish war. For present purposes, however, his death merely serves to emphasise that while the rebellion against Brian had been substantial (and others, no doubt, who did not rebel held aloof), still a wide spectrum of lordly power throughout the Gaelic world was willing to countenance death in support of Brian's objectives on that calamitous day.

Presumably it was the sheer unprecedented extent of the slaughter that motivated the formal removal of Brian's body for burial in Armagh (plate 23).[33] Of course he had become its patron, and one can well imagine the churchmen at Armagh being keen to pay their respects in this way, although equally there must have been one or two noses out of joint in Munster at losing him (which may account for the strange silence on the subject in the Annals of Inisfallen, material for which in this period was coming from the Dál Cais churches of Tuamgraney and Killaloe).[34] It would not have been an insurmountable operation to return his body home: the Cogadh claims that, after the battle, bodies that were recognisable as being followers of Brian among the 1,600 slain on his side were buried, presumably in a mass grave on or near the site of the battle, but that thirty other nobles who were killed were taken for burial to their own ancestral churches (*da cceallaibh dúthchusa féin*) in various places around the country,[35] and in any event the trek home to Killaloe was hardly more arduous or hazardous than that to Armagh.

Armagh, of course, long associated in particular with the Cenél nEógain of Northern Uí Néill, had a tradition of burying royalty, so that, for instance, in 980 Brian's predecessor but one as high-king, the great Domnall ua Néill, died in Armagh after penance (*post penitentiam i n-Ard Macha obiit*), and there are specific mentions in 935 and 1064 of other Cenél nEógain princes being buried *in cimiterio regum i n-Ard Macha* (in the cemetery of the kings in Armagh) and *in mausolio regum* (in the mausoleum of the kings) at Armagh.[36]

But ultimately the decision to inter Brian at Armagh must have been his own. Even when he first visited Armagh as high-king nearly a decade earlier he was in his mid-sixties and surely conscious of his mortality, and as the scene of his adoption of the title *Imperator Scotorum* it was intimately bound up with his own view of his national pre-eminence. He had embraced Armagh as ecclesiastical capital of his kingdom, and therefore it was surely he who considered it an appropriate home for his mortal remains. The Cogadh has him saying to his attendant when, before the battle, he had a premonition of his death:

Carry out my will (*mo thiomna*) after me, viz., my body and soul to God and to St Patrick, and I am to be carried to Armagh; and my blessing to [my son] Donnchad for discharging my last bequests after me (*mo bheannacht do Donnchadh ar mo cheinnaiti dic tar méis*), viz., twelve score cows to be given to the *comarba* of Patrick [the abbot of Armagh] and the community of Armagh; and its own proper dues (*a dhuthracht féin*) to Killaloe and the churches of Munster . . . Go tonight to Swords and tell them to come early tomorrow for my body and to convey it from there to Duleek; and then let them carry it to Louth; and let Máel Muire mac Eochada, the *comarba* of Patrick, and the community of Armagh come to meet me at Louth . . .[37]

And when his portent came true and he indeed lost his life, we are told that 'Brian was met as directed and he was taken to Armagh, and Murchad along with him, and Donnchad paid in full their bequests, and fulfilled Brian's will after him as he had himself directed.'[38] If we compare this with the following statement in the Annals of Ulster (repeated in generally similar terms in the later Annals of Loch Cé and the 'Cottonian' Annals of Boyle and by the Four Masters, all drawing on the same source used by the compiler of the Annals of Ulster[39]), it is clear that the annalistic record and the Cogadh are reasonably consistent:

> Máel Muire mac Eochada, the *comarba* of Patrick, with his venerable clerics and relics, came moreover to Swords, and brought away the body of Brian, king of Ireland, and the body of his son Murchad, and the head of Conaing and the head of Mothla, and buried them in Armagh in a new tomb (*i n-ailaidh nui*). For twelve nights the community of Patrick waked the bodies in honour of the king (*propter honorem regis*)

One may be borrowing from the other, or both may be borrowing from a now lost common source, but there is no very persuasive reason to think that either is making it up.

In 1832 George Petrie called attention to a monumental stone in Bully's Acre at Kilmainham (which still survives; see plate 24) that 'is still popularly supposed to be the tomb of the great and favourite Hero of our early history—that warrior Prince who died for his country in the arms of victory at the great battle of Clontarf.' He dismissed the tradition, on the grounds of the evidence in favour of Armagh in 'all our ancient historic authorities,' but added:

> ... it appears from the same sources that others of the Irish princes slain in that great battle were really buried at Kilmainham, and that this monument was erected to mark the place of their interment. The chief of these was the Prince Murrough, the son of Brian, who, according to the Munster book of battles, by Mac Liag, was buried at the west end of the chapel, with a long stone standing on one end of his tomb, on which has name was written. Of this inscription there

are now no legible traces, the stone being a coarse grained granite, and unfavourable to its preservation ...

There can be little doubt therefore that this cross, for such it was in its perfect state, was either the monument of Murrough, or of his son Turlough, who was slain in the same battle; and other circumstances corroborate this conclusion. About forty years ago [c. 1792], having fallen from its pedestal, it was again set up, on which occasion a number of coins of the Danish kings—the only minted money then generally in use—were found at its base; and with them a fine sword of the same period, which perhaps we are justified in calling the sword of Murrough O'Brian; it belonged at all events to one of his compatriots. This sword was deposited with the then commander of the forces, who had it placed in the hall belonging to his apartments, where it still remains, a highly interesting though hitherto unnoticed memorial.[40]

Despite what Petrie says, there is no genuinely mediaeval source that states that Murchad was buried at Kilmainham. A slightly later tradition is preserved by the Dubliner Richard Stanihurst in his *Description of Ireland*, published in 1577, who says that Brian, Murchad, Tadc Ua Cellaig and the other fallen Irish leaders were 'interred at Kilmaynnanne over against the great cross.'[41] But the same account has it that the Dubliners won, and it includes among the dead one Dúnlaing ua hArtagáin, who appears in the Cogadh as a supernatural being, who would hardly require burial.

It may be doubted, therefore, whether there is any substance to Stanihurst's assertion regarding the burials at Kilmainham. But that does not rule out the possibility that some of the fallen from Clontarf were buried at the site of the monastery there, near which Brian had set up camp for at least part of the proceedings—for instance, one might wonder why, if Brian and his son Murchad and nephew Conaing were brought to Armagh for burial, there is no mention of what became of Murchad's son Tairdelbach, Brian's grandson. But the fact is that there is no authentic documentary record of any casualties of Clontarf being buried at Kilmainham, and such a tradition must be regarded with scepticism.

CLONTARF IN THE LATER ANNAL COLLECTIONS

The version of these events preserved in the Annals of Ulster, a fifteenth-century manuscript, was copied quite faithfully into the seventeenth-century compilations usually called Chronicon Scotorum and the Annals of the Four Masters. They do, however, insert occasional morsels of information, and as ever the problem is knowing whether this came from another contemporary source, now lost, or whether it is no more than folklore. And it can be a complex story, because on the one hand both of these sources give if anything greater emphasis to the foreign component among Brian's opposition and yet provide additional names of Leinster lords who died in the conflict. Thus the Chronicon does not report the Leinstermen assembling against Brian but rather claims that 'the Foreigners of the world, such of them as were to the west of Lochlainn, gathered against Brian and Máel Sechnaill (*Gaill an domain do neoch baoi diobh o Lochlainn siar ro tionoilsit a n-aigidh Bríain & Maoileclainn*),' and by 'Foreigners' here it means Norse and by 'Lochlainn' it intends Scandinavia.

Similarly, the Four Masters have it that 'the Foreigners of Western Europe assembled against Brian and Máel Sechnaill (*Ro thionoilsiot Goill iarthair Eorpa i nd-aghaidh Bhriain & Maoil Sechlainn*),' and again these 'Foreigners of Western Europe' are confined to people of Viking origin. But both sources tell us that in addition to the Uí Fáeláin king of Leinster, Máelmórda mac Murchada, there also fell an Uí Muiredaig prince, Tuathal mac Augaire, who was a potential king (*rígdamna*) of Leinster, and the son of Brogarbán mac Conchobair, *rígdamna* of Uí Failge (map 5); and one presumes we can trust these new names, as there can hardly have been much incentive to concoct them at such a late date. They certainly seem to be historical figures, Tuathal presumably being a son of the Augaire who died at the battle of Bithlann in 978, while we have both annalistic and genealogical records of the family of Brogarbán, son of the Conchobar from whom the Uí Chonchobair Failgi (O'Connor Faly) descend.[42]

Interestingly too the Chronicon is faithful to its source to the extent that it does not record the date of battle and does not mention the place-name Clontarf. The Four Masters, on the other hand, are clear about both time and place: 'a spirited, fierce, violent, vengeful, and furious battle was fought between them, the like of which was not to be found in that time, at Clontarf, on the Friday before Easter precisely (*Feachar cath cródha, amhnas, aggarbh, aingidh, ainiarmartach, etorra da na frith samhail isin aimsir-sin, h-i c-Cluain Tarbh, isin Aoine ria c-Cáiscc do shonnradh*).' This is clearly information acquired from an alternative source, which does not of course invalidate it, as we shall see. But it seems unlikely that the compilers can be right in their belief that Brian was in his eighty-eighth year (as discussed earlier), or that his son Murchad was in his sixty-third. Admittedly Murchad had a son, Tairdelbach, who was old enough to die fighting in the battle, but a more likely estimate of the ages of all three would put Brian at about seventy-three, Murchad about fifty, and Tairdelbach not much more than a teenager (according to the Cogadh he was only fifteen when he died).[43]

A more substantial point of divergence between the account of the battle in both these sources, on the one hand, and the near-contemporary accounts in the Annals of Inisfallen and the Annals of Ulster is an implication that *after* the deaths of Brian and his lieutenants, and presumably therefore after an initial defeat,

The forces were afterwards routed by dint of battling, bravery, and striking, by Máel Sechnaill, from the Tolka to Dublin, against the Foreigners and the Leinstermen (*Ro mheabhaidh iaramh an cath tria neart cathaighthe, & crodhachta, & iommbuailte ria Maol Seachlainn ó Thulcaind co h-Ath Cliath for Gallaib agus Laighnibh*).

That is how the Four Masters put it. The Chronicon, which is partly illegible here, may omit Máel Sechnaill but nevertheless retains the sense that in the first stages of the confrontation, perhaps at Clontarf, Brian's forces were discomfited, but that in a secondary engagement further south, between the Tolka and the Liffey, perhaps led by Máel Sechnaill's contingent, the day was saved. Perhaps this suggestion of a rescue mission by Máel Sechnaill is special pleading by a writer who was never reconciled to the king of Tara being pushed aside by Brian, but nevertheless there may just be something to it.[44]

Whatever else, this has the merit of being feasible, which is more than can be said for the other great annalistic account of the battle, that preserved in the Annals of Loch Cé (and the related Annals of Boyle). The Annals of Loch Cé is in fact a book put together in Connacht in the sixteenth century, which intentionally begins with the events of the year 1014, omitting everything that happened in Ireland before that date, as its compiler evidently thought Clontarf ushered in a whole new phase in Irish history. And perhaps because he was beginning his book with it he wanted to begin with a flourish, and so he presents a dramatically embellished account of the battle.

Even though it is certain, therefore, that the contemporary notice from the Annals of Ulster underlies Loch Cé's account, the whole thing has been blown up into a piece of literature as much as of history. This is a pity—at least, it is to historians—as, when he is not indulging in flights of fancy, the Loch Cé chronicler has things to tell us. He was not persuaded, for instance, by those other voices that would see Brian mustering almost all Ireland to his banner. In fact he confesses that

> Brian assembled neither host nor multitude against this great army of the west of the world, and of Foreigners, but the men of Munster alone, and Máel Sechnaill with the men of Mide; for there came not to him the Ulaid nor the Airgialla nor the Cenél nEógain nor the Cenél Conaill nor the men of Connacht, save the Uí Maine and Uí Fiachrach and Cenél nÁeda; for there did not exist goodwill between Brian and Tadc in Eich Gil son of Cathal mac Conchobair, king of Connacht; and hence it was that Tadc refused to go with Brian to that battle of Clontarf (*Conidh aire-sin ro erig Tadhc dul la Brian isin cath sin Cluana Tarbh*).

This preoccupation with Connacht is accounted for, of course, by the book's provenance there, and perhaps the author knew something we do not know about the poor state of relations between Brian and Tadc ua Conchobair. The probability, though, is that the writer's conclusion that there was a dearth of support for Brian is based on nothing more scientific than a perusal of the casualty list in the standard annals. When, therefore, we see him describe how Brian—whom he calls by his famous nickname *Bóraime*—'set up camp in Clontarf in old Mag Elta, to the north of Dublin (*Gabhais Brían longport ig Clúain Tarbh, i sen-Muigh Ealta, ré h-Ath Clíath atthúaidh*),' it appears that he may have got his hands on some lost annalistic material, except that he adds:

To attack Dublin on this occasion was not to attack a 'neglected breach (*bearna bhaoil*)'. It was like putting a hand into a griffin's nest to assail it. It would not be evading conflict, but seeking great battles and contests, to advance against the multitude that had then arrived there; for the choicest brave men and heroes of the island of Britain had arrived there, from Caer Ebroc [York] and from Caer Eigist and from Caer Goniath. There arrived there, moreover, the principal kings and chieftains, knights and warriors, champions of valour and brave men of the north of the world, both Black Scandinavians and Fair Scandinavians, in the following and friendship of the Foreigners, until they were in Dublin with [Sitriuc] the son of Amlaíb, offering war and battle to the Irish (*etir Dhubh-Lochlonnach & Fhionn-Lochlonnach a sochraide & a m-báidh Ghall, go rabhadar a n-Ath Clíath ag mac Amhlaoíb, ag fritheólamh chogaidh & chathaighthe do Gaoídhealaibh*).

Thither came Síoghraidh Finn and Síoghraidh Donn, two sons of Lothar, jarl of Innsi Orc [Orkney], accompanied by the armies of Innsi Orc. Thither came, moreover, great hosts from Innsi Gall [the Hebrides] and from Manainn [Man] and from the Rhinns [of Galloway] and from the Britons and from the Flemings. There arrived there also Brodar, i.e. the Jarl of Caer Ebroc, with very great hosts, and Uithir the Black, i.e. the warrior of Eigist, and Grisine, a knight of the Flemings, and Greisiam from the Normans. There arrived there, likewise, a thousand bold, brave, powerful heroes of the Black Danars (*do Dhubh-Danaroibh*), with shields and targets, and with many corselets, from Thafinn (*ó tháfinn*). The great armies and famous young bands of the tribes of the Foreigners (*slóigh dhímhóra & gasradh óg allata fine Gall*) were also there, and the merchants who had come from the lands of France and from the Saxons and from Britain and from the Romans.

From this it is clear that the writer has ceased retelling what he knows to be fact and embarked on story-telling for the purposes of entertainment. Distinctions from a century or more before Clontarf between *Dubgaill* ('Dark Foreigners') and *Finngaill* ('Fair Foreigners') are resurrected to give us Black Lochlannachs and Fair Lochlannachs and a thousand Black Danars; and even Sigurðr, earl of Orkney, has become two contrasting bright-dark men, Síoghraidh Finn ('the Fair') and Síoghraidh Donn ('the Brown'). It will not do to have merely the familiar Caer Ebroc (York), it must be garnished with the obscure Caer Eigist and Caer Goniath. And it is not enough to have fighting men from York alone or from the Viking settlements in Orkney and the Hebrides, Galloway and Man: these must be glamorised by Welshmen and by Flemish and Norman knights and English, French and Roman merchants!

Again this is a pity, because hidden among these exotica are the men from the Scandinavian world who did indeed fight at Clontarf. And perhaps, therefore, in discarding this chaff we should take care to preserve some grain. Why would there not be men from York fighting alongside King Sitriuc of Dublin in 1014, as his own father had ruled the Viking fortress at York for many years in the middle of the tenth century?[45] Though it had been permanently lost to the Hiberno-Norse, his contacts with its fighting classes must have remained close. And why would there not be men from the Hebrides and the Rhinns Peninsula at the tip of Galloway and the Isle of Man, as Sitriuc's successors as kings of Dublin continued to exercise fitful lordship there for the next century or more?[46]

In other words, because the Annals of Loch Cé were put together by a family of professional hereditary historians who had access to materials that have not survived, what they tell us deserves proper consideration before being dismissed as mere legend. For instance, it is the only one of the surviving annals that maintains that Brian Bóraime was decapitated in the battle:

> The high-king, i.e. Brian mac Cennétig, and [his nephew] Conaing mac Donncuain, were behind the battalions, chanting their psalms and performing prayers, when a vehement, furious, Denmarkian escaped from the battle, avoiding death, until he came to the place where the king was. As soon as the Denmarkian perceived the king unguarded, he unsheathed his sword and beheaded the high-king of Ireland, and he beheaded Conaing likewise; and he himself fell in the mutual wounding of that fight (*Is ann boi an t-airdrigh .i. Brian mac Ceinneidigh, & Conaing mac Duinn Cuan ar cúl na cath ag cantain a salm & ag denam irnaide, con rus-terno fear dhian dassochtach Danmargach ar iomgabhail an bhaiss as an maidhm, go rainic gus an*

maighin a m-boí an ri. O dho airigh an Danmargach an rí a m-baogal ros-nocht a cloidhemh & ro dhichend airdri Erenn & ros-dichend Conaing mur an cedna, & torchuir féin a b-frithghuin in comhruic-sin).

Are we to believe this? It is surely quite likely that Brian, who was at least seventy-three years of age, did not take part in the fighting at Clontarf but directed events from a distance. And it is possible that a trusted lieutenant like the king's nephew stayed in his presence at all times. We do not know whether Brian, the man, was prayerful or profane. And we do not know how an elderly king in the early eleventh century would behave on such an occasion. But every member of Brian's family and every one of his extended kin who was of fighting age (and not in holy orders) would have been there before him on that day, risking life and limb for his cause, and he would have seen his son and grandson and many of the royalty of Munster and beyond cut down before his eyes in a battle that might go either way. Surely at some point in such a long and bloody day a Christian king turns to prayer? And it is not preposterous to think that a fleeing member of the opposing army might have happened upon Brian and his nephew at a remove from the action and—irrespective of whether they were praying or planning their next move—beheaded them both before he could be stopped.

The fact is that the contemporary annals do state that after the battle Conaing's head alone was brought for burial to Armagh, and we can assume therefore that he was indeed decapitated and that the rest of the body was not recovered. No source tells us that only Brian's trunkless head was brought north to Armagh from the battlefield; and while there is an outside chance that the explanation is that there was a kind of communal respectful denial of the awful truth of the situation, presumably the high-king's entire corpse was in fact retrieved. Nevertheless, there is nothing in the testimony of the more 'reliable' annal accounts that would cause us to dismiss definitively the contention of the Annals of Loch Cé that he died by decapitation; and it turns out that this version of events is corroborated in the most unlikely of sources.

As we shall see, an account of the battle found its way to the Norse world and is preserved in the Icelandic sagas; and this version also states that Brian was beheaded. It is slightly different, though: in this account Brian's companion is not also beheaded but loses an arm, which is reattached when Brian's saintly blood flows over the wound; and as for Brian himself, when his corpse is being laid out it is found that his severed head has similarly become reconnected to the torso!

The fact is that the Loch Cé annalist seems to have had access to a source of some antiquity originating in or around Brian's kingdom of Dál Cais. The reason for saying so is that his account of the Battle of Clontarf proceeds to tell two dramatic tales or visions seen the night before the battle. Neither is remotely historical, but both must come from a lost Munster source.

In the first *aisling* or vision, Brian's confidential retainer (*fer gráda*), Indéirge mac Uradáin, sees a group of praying clerics coming towards the camp, which turn out to be St Senán come to collect debts from Brian (*feich dlighes do Brian*) that were due on the day of the battle. When Brian is told of the vision he is greatly troubled, because 'thirty-seven years before that Friday night in which Brian was slain, this vision had been seen' by a man who 'had been at the killing of the Foreigners on Scattery Island (*ro boi-sium ag marbadh na n-Gall a n-Inis Cathaig*).'

We know from other sources that thirty-seven years earlier, shortly after assuming the kingship, Brian had indeed taken revenge on the Norse of Limerick who had been involved in the murder of his brother Mathgamain by following them to the monastery of St Senán on Inis Cathaig (Scattery Island) in the Shannon Estuary, where Ímar of Limerick had established a base. The Norse were presumably expecting the protection of sanctuary there, but Brian allowed them none and slaughtered them instead, the annals portraying this as a violation or profanation of the monastery (*Inis Cáthaigh do shárughadh do Bhrian*).[47]

This event replicated a similar slight to the community there three years earlier when Inis Cathaig was attacked by Maccus mac Arailt and the *Lagmainn* ('Lawmen') of the Isles—probably in collaboration with Dál Cais—as a result of which Ímar of Limerick was captured and brought overseas, making good his escape only in the following year, an affront that was likewise described as 'the violation of Senán (*sárughadh Senáin*).'[48] Obviously the point of the premonition witnessed the night before Clontarf was that St Senán would finally get retribution by Brian's death; but the story's effect is dependent on circumstantial knowledge. To get the point one needed to know that Brian and the clerics of Scattery had never since been close, and why that was; and therefore one needed to know what had happened in 977, a relatively inconsequential deed nationally but with sizeable implications locally. We can take it, therefore, that the source for the supposed vision was also local.

And this holds true for the second of these strange forebodings recorded in the Annals of Loch Cé. In this story Brian is visited the night before the battle by the fairy-woman Aíbinn, daughter of Donn Oilén from the *síd* or Otherworld mound of Craicliath (Craglea, near Killaloe; see plate 8), who tells him of his imminent death and that the first of his sons whom he would next see would be the one to succeed him. He therefore sends for Murchad, but it is Donnchad who first comes to him, to Brian's chagrin, who is then obliged to tell Murchad that 'that which I should wish, God has not permitted to you (*an ni ro bud mian lem-sa nir chedaigh Dia duit e*).' Aíbinn of Craicliath is a Dál Cais Otherworld figure, and we can assume a Dál Cais source for the story, someone who was perhaps not too pleased at Donnchad's succession.

Incidentally, a version of the story also occurs in a poem by the great Munster poet Gofraid Fionn Ua Dálaigh (died 1387).[49] And, sure enough, the story also occurs in Cogadh Gáedhel re Gallaibh (although only in the seventeenth-century manuscript, as this part of the narrative is missing in the earlier manuscripts), and surely therefore it originated within Dál Cais, relatively close in time to Brian's demise. The lesson to be learnt is not to dismiss out of hand even later romanticised accounts of Clontarf, as they may just contain important nuggets of information and inherited memories.

Chapter 5 ~

COGADH GÁEDHEL RE GALLAIBH

I t is Cogadh Gáedhel re Gallaibh that begins the process *par excellence* of bringing imagination to bear on events at and surrounding the Battle of Clontarf (plate 18).

It is often said that the Cogadh was written a century or more after the great battle, although the latest research suggests that it might be somewhat older than that.[1] The reason this matters is that there were still veterans of Clontarf alive fifty years after the battle, and there were yet more people alive who had lived through the cataclysmic years of Brian's high-kingship; and a text written by someone who had information supplied by such people is something of enormous value. Of course it must be taken with a pinch of salt, where its author forgets he is a historian and becomes a political propagandist (or we forget that he is primarily the latter and not a historian in the modern sense). But even at this remove it is frequently possible for us to detect such political points being made and therefore to disregard them and yet not make the mistake of throwing the baby out with the bath water.

The Cogadh tells us that Brian mustered for his campaign against Dublin and Leinster on St Patrick's Day (17 March) in 1014, but the Dubliners, hearing of it, sent messengers abroad in search of aid, and its list of those who flocked to the Dublin banner has quite a bit in common with that of the Annals of Loch Cé in particular:

They invited unto them Jarl Brodor and Amlaíb, son of the king of Lochlainn, i.e. the two jarls of Caer and of all the north of England. These two were the chiefs of fleets and outlaws and Danars of all Western Europe (*taisig longsi ocus inarbtaig ocus Danair iartair Eorpa uli*), having no reverence, veneration, respect, or mercy for God or for man, for church or for sanctuary, at the head of two thousand cruel, villainous, ferocious, plundering, hard-hearted, foreign, wonderful Denmarkians (*Anmargachaib*), selling and hiring themselves for gold and silver, and other treasure as well. And there was not one villain or robber of that two thousand who had not polished, strong, triple-plated, glittering armour of refined iron or of cool uncorroding brass, encasing their sides and bodies from head to foot.

They invited to them also Siucraid, son of Lotar, earl of the Orkney islands and the Isles also (*iarla Insi Orc ocus na nInsi archena*); with an assembled army of ignorant, barbarous, thoughtless, irreclaimable, unsociable Foreigners of the Orkney islands and of the Cat islands, from Man and from Skye and from Lewis, from Kintyre and from Argyll; and two barons of the Corr Britons and Corndabbliteoc of the Britons of Cill Muni (*do Gallaib Insi Orc ocus Insi Cat, a Manaind ocus a Sci ocus a Leodus, a Cind Tiri ocus a hAirer Goedel, ocus da barun a Corr Bretnaib ocus Corndabbliteoc a Bretnaib Cilli Muni*). They invited to them also Carlus and Ebric, two sons of the king of France, and Plat, a strong knight of Lochlainn, and the hero Conmael.[2]

Obviously there is a good deal of embroidery here. Amlaíb is described as 'son of the king of Lochlainn', by which is perhaps meant Norway, but he is then said to be a jarl in Caer (probably Caer Ebroc, York, but just possibly Chester) and the north of England. Presumably he is an invented figure and given the clichéd name of many a 'son of the king of Lochlainn' before him to appear in Irish waters, although what prompted it in this instance may be confusion (deliberate or otherwise) with the Dubgall mac Amlaíb, brother of Sitriuc of Dublin, killed at Clontarf. In fact if the Cogadh had called Amlaíb 'son of the king of the Foreigners' rather than 'of Lochlainn' it would have been right on the button, as King Sitriuc of Dublin had a son of this name (killed in England in 1034), and the family had indeed, as we have seen, a York connection.[3]

Otherwise the enlisting of Norse assistance from Orkney (the 'Cat islands' may be Caithness, but if islands are indeed intended it might be Shetland) and down along Scotland's western seaboard, from Lewis to Skye, to Argyll and Kintyre and to the Isle of Man, seems not only feasible but probable. Undoubtedly the 'two barons of the Corr Britons and Corndabbliteoc of the Britons of Cill Muni' is taking us into the arena of imagination, the former being perhaps Cornwall and the latter a Welsh chieftain from St Davids (although 'Corndabbliteoc' looks more like a place-name), assuming that Cill Muni is the 'church of Mymyw', where David built his monastery.

While these names seem fanciful, one needs to bear in mind that the contemporary Irish annals call Brian 'high-king of the Irish of Ireland and of the Foreigners and of the *Britons*,' and such titles invariably have a germ of truth in them. The claim being made, therefore, on Brian's behalf in the annals is that he had received an acknowledgement of overlordship from the Irish and the Hiberno-Norse, which we know is true, and from the Welsh, or some Welsh. We do not know the exact link, but the fact is that relations between Ireland and Wales were so close in this era that not only is it demonstrable that Irish kings entered into political arrangements with Welsh counterparts but an Irishman could even *become* king in Wales, as the mysterious Rhain was to do only eight years after the Battle of Clontarf.[4]

What is more, there is fairly solid evidence that the Norse of Dublin or the Isles, or both, had at least a foothold in Anglesey.[5] If the Norse claimed to be masters of some Welsh people, and Brian claimed to be master of the Norse, *ipso facto* he was master of those same Welshmen. In other words, there is nothing improbable about the annalist's claim that Brian was 'high-king of the Britons', i.e. had secured a declaration of fealty from at least one Welsh prince; and there was nothing remotely improbable about Sitriuc of Dublin looking to another Welsh lord for assistance against Brian at Clontarf, or gearing up for Brian's assault by drafting in reinforcements from his estates there.

We can afford to be rather more dismissive of the text's inclusion of Carlus and Ebric, 'two sons of the king of France'. An individual called Anrath mac Elbric, 'son of the king of Lochlainn', appears later in the text, and we may therefore imagine a Scandinavian background for Ebric/Elbric. Carlus may get his name and title from a casual association of the name (correctly Carolus) with Frankish royalty since the days of Charlemagne, but it is actually found among the Norse of Dublin, Carlus mac Amlaíb having died in 868. It has been suggested that the 'Sword of Carlus (*claidim Carlusa*)', which became a prized trophy, was his. Less likely, perhaps, is the Irish Carlus who was grandson of the Clann Cholmáin high-king Donnchad Donn (died 944) and who was murdered in Dublin in 960.[6] This, though, would explain why the sword first occurs on record as late as 995, when it was forcibly surrendered by the Dubliners to Carlus's first cousin, the then high-king Máel Sechnaill, along with the 'Ring of Þórir (*Fail Tomair*)'.[7]

In any event, the Carlus of the Cogadh, and his colleague Ebric, are certainly not 'sons of the king of France', but it is just possible that they were real people with some vague French connection, perhaps mercenaries from the Scandinavian colony in Normandy who arrived in Dublin in 1014 to help out in the city's hour of need.

As for Brian's forces in the battle, in fairness to the author of the Cogadh it must be said that he is very candid about the depleted nature of Brian's authority (though perhaps in an attempt to magnify his achievement). The only ones who assembled to join him, he tells us, were

> the two provinces of Munster [i.e. Tuadmumu and Desmumu] and Connacht and the men of Mide, but the men of Mide were not faithful to him, for he knew himself that they would desert him at the approach of that battle, although they came to the muster (*comthinol*).[8]

This, then, is the origin of the story that Máel Sechnaill proved disloyal to his lord, Brian, and perhaps there is truth in it; but, as we have seen, it is flatly contradicted by the statement of the Four Masters that, if anything, it was Máel Sechnaill who won the day for Brian's side, snatching a late victory from the jaws of defeat after Brian himself had fallen. It simply cannot be verified at this remove which side is telling the truth; nevertheless it is easy to imagine the Munster writer of the Cogadh finding it less painful to blame the death of his king on the fickleness of the king of Tara than to acknowledge that but for the latter worse things might have happened.

Having reached Dublin (see map 8), Brian's forces plundered the lands of Uí Gabla (north-east Co. Kildare) and Uí Dúnchada (south-west Co. Dublin) and Fine Gall, north of the Liffey, even sacking the monastic lands of Kilmainham and Clondalkin. Brian's son Donnchad was despatched with the forces of Dál Cais to attack the Leinster territories, while Leinster's armies were congregating at Dublin. And when the Foreigners saw Fine Gall and the area around Howth being set ablaze they came north from Dublin into Mag Elta, the coastal plain to which the Howth peninsula attaches, 'and they met and raised their battle-standards on high (*ros comraicset ocus tucsat a nidna catha os aird*).'[9] Brian meanwhile had pitched camp out on the *Faicthe Átha Cliath*, a green area possibly to the west of Dublin often thought to be in the vicinity of Kilmainham, in which case—which would seem unlikely—he was perhaps 10 km from where the Norse and Leinster army was assembling to counter those of his forces who were plundering Fine Gall. And there he met his chief lieutenants in assembly:

> Brian was then on the green of Dublin with the nobles of the Dál Cais in assembly (*ar Fachi Atha Cliath ocus mathi Dáil Cais in airechtus*), and with Máel Sechnaill and with Murchad and with Conaing and with Tadc son of Cathal, and with the nobles of Connacht together, and with the men of Munster and the men of Mide; but it happened that the men of Mide and Máel Sechnaill were not of one mind with the rest.[10]

If we are to believe this, Brian's leading advisers were Máel Sechnaill (whose motives, however, are suspect), Brian's senior son, Murchad, his nephew Conaing (both of whom were to die with him) and the king of Connacht, Tadc in Eich Gil ua Conchobair—although, as we have seen, the Annals of Loch Cé are adamant that Tadc did not join Brian on this occasion. Although it may only be an error for Tadc Ua Cellaig, who, we know from the annals, was one of Brian's leading allies to fall at Clontarf, caution is in order. Indeed the Cogadh, or rather one version of the Cogadh, proceeds to ascribe an important leadership position to Ua Ruairc of Bréifne, the only account that pretends any role for Bréifne at all in these events; and it is certain that this is a reverberation of an alliance dating from a hundred or more years later intruded into the narrative at this latter date.[11]

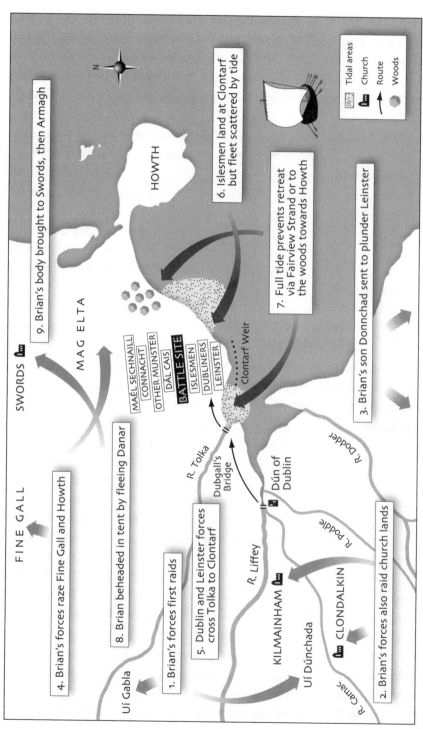

N

9. Brian's body brought to Swords, then Armagh

6. Islesmen land at Clontarf but fleet scattered by tide

7. Full tide prevents retreat via Fairview Strand or to the woods towards Howth

3. Brian's son Donnchad sent to plunder Leinster

Tidal areas
Church
Route
Woods

HOWTH

MAG ELTA

FINE GALL

SWORDS

MAÉL SECHNAILL
CONNACHT
OTHER MUNSTER
DÁL CAIS
BATTLE SITE
ISLESMEN
DUBLINERS
LEINSTER

Clontarf Weir

8. Brian beheaded in tent by fleeing Danar

4. Brian's forces raze Fine Gall and Howth

R. Tolka

Dubgall's Bridge

Dún of Dublin

R. Dodder

1. Brian's first raids

5. Dublin and Leinster forces cross Tolka to Clontarf

R. Poddle

R. Liffey

KILMAINHAM

Uí Dúnchada

CLONDALKIN

Uí Gabla

2. Brian's forces also raid church lands

R. Camac

Map 8. The Battle of Clontarf.

The Cogadh then gives a lengthy description of both sides as they prepare for battle, full of show-off alliterative adjectives—which, though tedious to modern tastes, one can imagine being read out with gusto to an assembled audience. Here is a small part of what it says of the Norse, for example (although it loses a lot in translation):

These had for the purposes of battle and combat, and for their defence, sharp, swift, bloody, crimsoned, bounding, barbed, keen, bitter, wounding, terrible, piercing, fatal, murderous, poisoned arrows (*saigti fegi, feochracha, fulecha, forderga, frithiri, frithbaccanacha, gera, goirti, gunecha, agmara, athi, acbeli, niata, nemhnecha*), which had been anointed and browned in the blood of dragons and toads, and water-snakes of hell, and of scorpions and otters, and wonderful venomous snakes of all kinds, to be cast and shot at active and warlike and valiant chieftains.[12]

As for Brian's forces,

these had for the purposes of battle and combat, above their heads, spears glittering, well riveted, empoisoned, with well-shaped, heroic, beautiful handles of white hazel (*slega suarci, semnecha, fithnasacha, fidcaimi, fianamla fir alli findchuill*); terrible sharp darts (*bera bodba biraithi*) with variegated silken strings (*co suathnemaib sita, sainemail*); thick set with bright, dazzling, shining nails (*tairngnib glana, glorda, glainidi*), to be violently cast at the heroes of valour and bravery . . . They had with them also, great, warlike, bright, beautiful, variegated shields (*sceith mora, mileta, etrochta, alli, illatacha*), with bosses of brass (*co comraidib cori creduma*), and elegant chains of bronze (*co slabradaib fir alli findruni*), at the sides of their noble, accomplished, sweet, courteous, eloquent clansmen. They had on them also, crested golden helmets (*cathbairr ciracha, fororda*), set with sparkling transparent brilliant gems and precious stones, on the heads of chiefs and royal knights.

    They had with them also shining, powerful, strong, graceful, sharp, glaring, bright, broad, well-set Scandinavian axes (*tuaga troma, taidlecha, trena, tolgda, taitnemacha, gera, gluair, glainidi, lethna, limtha Lochlannacha*), in the hands of chiefs and leaders, and heroes, and brave knights, for cutting and maiming the close well-fastened coats of mail (*lureach*). They had with them, steel, strong, piercing, graceful, ornamental, smooth, sharp-pointed, bright-sided, keen, clean, azure, glittering, flashing, brilliant, handsome, straight, well-tempered, quick, sharp swords (*claidmi cruadi, comnerta, colcda, coema, cumdachta, slemna, slipta, slisgela, gera, glana, gormglasa, luinecha lasartha, lainderda, dessa dirgi deocbrig emi*), in the beautiful white hands of chiefs and royal knights, for hewing and for hacking, for maiming and mutilating skins, and bodies, and skulls.[13]

Then the two armies were arrayed in battle order, and the Cogadh proceeds to describe their formation. The enemy was drawn up in three battalions, the foreign troops in the van, the Dublin army next, and the Leinstermen taking up the rear:

The Foreigners and the Leinstermen placed in the front the murderous foreign Danars (*Danairib diberchaib allmardaib*), under Bródar, jarl of Caer Ebroc, chieftain of the Danars; with Conmael, his mother's son, and with Siucaid, son of Lotar, jarl of Innsi Orc, and with Plait, brave champion of all the Foreigners (*tren milid Gall uli*), and with Anrath son of Elbric, son of the king of Lochlainn, and Carlus, and Torbenn Dubh, and Sunin [or Suimni], and Suanin, and the nobles of the Foreigners of western Europe, from Lochlainn westwards, along with them.

A line of one very great strong battalion was formed of all the Foreigners of Dublin, and it was placed after the above, that is after the Denmarkians. At their head were Dubgall mac Amlaíb and Gilla Ciaráin mac Glún Iairn mic Amlaíb and Donnchad ua Eruilb and Amlaíb [son of?] Lagmund mac Gofraid, four potential kings of the Foreigners (*cethri rigdomna Gall*). At their head also, were Oittir Dub and Grisin and Lummin and Snadgair, four viceroys of the Foreigners and four commanders of fleets (*cetri irrig Gall ocus cetri toisig longsi*), and the nobles of the Foreigners of Ireland along with them (*mathi Gall Erend aroen riu sen*).

A battalion was also formed of the Leinstermen and of Uí Chennselaig, and it was placed behind the above. And at the head of them were Máelmórda mac Murchada, king of Leinster, and Báetán mac Dúnlainge, king of Iarthar Laigen, and Dúnlaing mac Tuathail, king of Liphi, and Brogarbán mac Conchobair, king of Uí Failgi, and Domnall mac Fergail, king of the Fortuatha Laigen, and the nobles of Leinster likewise.[14]

We need not delay too long on these names, most of which we have seen before in the annal tradition. The problem, as usual, is that we cannot use the annals to verify the historicity of the Cogadh's account, because of the great chicken-and-egg question: did the author of the Cogadh incorporate them in his account having found them in a contemporary annalistic record of the battle, or did they get woven into the annals at a later date by a writer who had access to the text of the Cogadh? The second explanation seems slightly more likely; indeed a list of the fatalities at Clontarf based on that in the Cogadh was later in circulation, and a copy of it from the fourteenth century survives in a Connacht manuscript in Trinity College Dublin.[15] The best that can be said is that some of these names—especially those of individuals allegedly drafted in for the occasion from outside Ireland—are more than suspicious-looking but that up to half of them appear to be real, and their presence at Clontarf is historically credible, if not corroborated by any other source.

Precisely the same problem arises with the list of the Irish on Brian's side:

At the head of these was the matchless, ever victorious Hector of the many-nationed heroic children of Adam, namely Murchad son of Brian . . . Along with him were also Tairdelbach, his son, the best rígdamna (potential king) of his time in Ireland, and Conaing mac Donncuain, one of the three men most valued by Brian that were then in Ireland; and Niall ua Cuinn and Eochu mac Dúnadaig and Cú Duilig mac Cennétig, the three attendants (cometidi) of Brian; and Domnall mac Diarmata, king of Corco Baiscind, and the greater part of the men of bravery and valour of the Dál Cais along with them. One very strong and great battalion was also formed of the chosen hosts of all Munster and was stationed in the rear of the former. At the head of these was Mothla mac Domnaill mic Fáeláin, king of the Déisi, and Magnus mac Anmchada, king of Uí Liatháin, and the brave and heroic of all Munster along with them.

The battalion of Connacht also was led by Máel Ruanaid ua hEidin and by Tadc Ua Cellaig, king of Uí Maine, and by Máel Ruanaid mac Muirgiusa, king of Muintir Máel Ruanaid; and by Domnall ua Conchenainn, king of Uí Diarmada; and with Uallgarg mac Cerin, and with the nobles of all Connacht along with him. The ten *mormaír* ('sea-stewards'?) of Brian were drawn up with their Foreigner troops (*cona nGall socraitib*) on one side of the army. Fergal Ua Ruairc and the Uí Briúin and the Conmaicne were ordered to the left wing of the army. Also, Máel Sechnaill mac Domnaill, king of Tara, and the battalion of the men of Mide with him, were next; but he consented not to be placed along with the rest; because the counsel of the Foreigners on the preceding night was that he should put a ditch between him and the Foreigners (*clad etorro ocus Gaill*); and that if he would not attack the Foreigners, the Foreigners would not attack him; and so it was done, for the evil understanding was between them.[16]

More names are revealed as the action begins to unfold, principal among whom is Domnall mac Eimin, who enters the tale as if needing no introduction, even though we are casually informed later that his background was in north-eastern Scotland. We are told that Brian, seeing his son Murchad press too far ahead just before battle commenced, sent Domnall to order him to fall back: the implication is that Domnall was attached to Brian, occupying a leadership role. Murchad, however, rejected this as cowardly retreat, the Cogadh's author opining—critically, it would appear—that 'the reason why the nobles of all Desmumu were killed there was because they endeavored to follow Murchad to surround the Foreigners and the Denmarkians (*ic timcellad na Gall ocus na nAnmargac*).'[17]

Domnall mac Eimin then chided Murchad for his folly while praising his valour and offering to fight to the death, which was duly to occur. Then, when the contest between the two sides gets under way, it is this Domnall who sees first action, and now for the first time he is given a title: *mormaer Alban*, perhaps 'a sea-steward of Scotland.'[18] When his death is recorded in the annals they give him the more precise title of *mormaer* of Mar in Scotland, suggesting that the original annalist had another source of information in addition to the Cogadh, or personally perhaps knew something of Domnall's background. Either way, and despite his elusiveness elsewhere in the historical record, he seems to be an important figure.

In fact, according to the Cogadh, the very first action in the Battle of Clontarf did not involve any Irish person at all but rather a deathly duel between this *mormaer* of Mar and the Plait, 'son of the king of Lochlainn', whom we met in passing earlier:

> First then were drawn up there, Domnall mac Eimin, *mormaer Alban,* on Brian's side, and Plait, son of the king of Lochlainn, brave champion of the Foreigners (*tren milid Gall*). Because of Plait having said the night before that there was not a man in Ireland who was able to fight him, Domnall mac Eimin immediately took him up, and each of them remembered this in the morning. Then Plait came forth from the battalion of the men in armour, and said three times: '*Faras Domhnall,*' that is, 'Where is Domnall?' Domnall answered and said: 'Here, you wretch (*Sund, a sniding*),' said he. They fought then, and each of them endeavoured to slaughter the other; and they fell by each other, and the way that they fell was with the sword of each through the heart of the other; and the hair of each in the clenched hand of the other. And the combat of that pair was the first [of the battle].[19]

It is interesting to see the author of the Cogadh trying his hand here at a bit of Old Norse—*Faras* from Norse *Hvar es* ('Where is') and *sniding* from *níðingr* ('wretch', 'scoundrel')—which might suggest contact with the Hiberno-Norse settlement at Limerick. And while it is hard to imagine the Battle of Clontarf beginning with a bout of single combat between champions drawn from each side, what matters most perhaps is the prominent role ascribed to the *mormaer* of Mar. In a sense it does not matter if the story is true: what does matter is that the author thought it expedient to provide such a role. When individuals get a mention in the text it is usually for a reason, and if they crop up on Brian's side it is indicative of a political alliance. And we must bear this in mind when examining the broad context of Clontarf.

One version of the Cogadh then clumsily intrudes another episode, telling of the supposed great deeds accomplished by Fergal ua Ruairc and Domnall mac Ragallaig and Gilla na Náem ua Fergail, and the men of Bréifne and Conmaicne, in leading an assault on the forces of the Leinster prince Dúnlaing mac Tuathail of Uí Muiredaig, and on Uí Chennselaig. This engagement, we are told, led to mutual slaughter, both sides being almost entirely wiped out, and someone called Mac in Trin who was the 'household captain (*taiseach lochta taigi*)' of ua Ruairc allegedly cornered Dúnlaing mac Tuathail, beheaded him, and brought the head back in triumph to Fergal. The problem is that the story seems to be largely if not wholly fictional. Dúnlaing did indeed die in 1014, quite possibly of wounds received in the battle, but no other source places his death at Clontarf; indeed one version of the Cogadh later says of him that he 'received a wound of which he died,' which would go without saying if he had been decapitated.[20]

In fact there does not seem to have been a Fergal ua Ruairc at the battle, and the entire episode was probably concocted in the twelfth century to serve a contemporary purpose.[21] It is worth noting in passing, though, that when this interpolated passage has it that 'none of them paid any attention to any evil that was done at Cluain Tarbh on that day, excepting the evil and contention which they mutually occasioned against each other,' it is the first time the name of Clontarf is mentioned in the Cogadh and is therefore proof that the battle was known by this name by the twelfth century at the latest.

But it is only at this point that the account of the battle begins, and the author employs some remarkably purple prose to describe the smashing of bodies, the loud din of battle, the flashing of steel that ensued and the showers of sparks from the swords of the Dál Cais that struck their opponents' coats of mail, so that 'it was attested by the Foreigners and Foreigner women who were watching from the battlements of Dublin (*na Gaill agus na Gaillseacha batar uathib ac feithium ar scemlead Atha Cliath*), as they beheld, that they used to see flashes of fire from them in the expanse of air on all sides.'[22] Such was the ferocity, we are told—in words alleged to have been spoken by Máel Sechnaill—that within the time it takes to milk a cow no-one on either side could recognise even his own son or brother, except by voice, so covered were they in blood. Spears could not be raised above the head so clogged did they become with hair that floated in the strong, cold wind, having been hacked by swords and axes from the heads of the enemy.

When the men of Connacht took on the Dubliners, wholesale slaughter resulted, only a hundred of the Connachtmen surviving and twenty of the men of Dublin, 'and it was at Dubgall's bridge the last of these was killed, viz., Arnaill Scot, and those who killed him were the household troops of Tadc Ua Cellaig (*ic drochut Dubgaill ro marbad in fer maderead dib .i. Arnaill Scot .i. isiat ro marb e lucht taigi Taidg Ui Cellaig*).'[23] This person, called Arnaldr, was presumably prominent enough to be well known, and on the face of it his nickname points to a Scottish connection.

We do not know who Dubgall was, or where his bridge was, but he may be the Dubgall mac Amlaíb, brother of King Sitriuc, who commanded the Dublin forces at Clontarf, and perhaps also the Dubgall whose estate at Baile Dubgaill gives us the name of Baldoyle. His bridge was certainly a prominent feature. Almost a century later the king of Ailech, Domnall Mac Lochlainn, went south on a raid 'across Fine Gall, i.e. as far as Dubgall bridge (*Crech la Domhnall Ua Lochlainn tar Fine Gall, .i. co Droichet Dubhghaill*),'[24] and perhaps it is true, as is generally assumed, that this was the bridge over the Liffey (not far from the Four Courts) that separated the town of Dublin, perched on the south bank of the river, from its northern suburb of Oxmantown and its agricultural hinterland of Fine Gall. But a more likely site is a bridge straddling the Tolka at Ballybough (as John O'Donovan suggested),[25] which would fit if indeed Dubgall gave his name to Baldoyle, which one can reach to this day by the same general route (map 8).

We can imagine forces leaving the town of Dublin perched on the hill, where Christ Church and the Castle would later stand, heading over the Liffey bridge into the suburb of Oxmantown, which was already beginning to take shape north of the Liffey, then heading north-east through what is now Summer Hill and Ballybough and crossing the Tolka there by means of the bridge recently constructed by Dubgall mac Amlaíb to facilitate communication with his estate at Baile Dubgaill. It is interesting that a map as late as Charles Brooking's of 1728 calls the principal left turn in Fairview, reached after crossing the bridge, not by the present-day name Malahide Road but rather the 'Road to Boldoile'.

The Cogadh then presents a lengthy eulogy of Brian's son Murchad, who is described as the last man in Ireland who had equal dexterity in brandishing two swords: a Hector, a Samson, a Hercules, a Lug Lámfhada, who 'sprang over every obstacle, laid bare every brave head, and exterminated and expelled the Foreigners and overseasmen out of Ireland (*ro inarb Gullu ocus allmarathu a hErind*).'[26] When Murchad saw the Dál Cais being overwhelmed by 'the Danars and Denmarkians (*Danair ocus Anmargaigh*)' he rushed at the enemy—as is 'testified by his enemies after him, viz., the historians of the Foreigners and of the Leinstermen (*Forglit a escarit da heis .i. senchaidi Gall ogus Lagen*)'—so that he killed fifty with the sword in his left hand and another fifty with the right. He was accompanied in this charge by seven score kings' sons from his household (*ina theglach*), even the least noble of whom, we are told, was lord of a *tricha céd* (about the size of a present-day barony).

The people of Dublin were watching this scene unfold from their battlements (*daini Atha Cliath batar fors na scemlib*); and, likening the hair cut from scalps to sheaves of oats being reaped, Sitriuc of Dublin makes his first appearance (speaking, it would appear, in Irish):

> Whereupon mac Amlaíb, who was on the battlements of his watch tower watching them (*ar scemled a grianan fein aca fegad*), said, 'Well do the Foreigners reap the field,' said he, 'many is the sheaf they let go from them.' 'It will be at the end of the day that will be seen,' said Brian's daughter, namely, mac Amlaíb's wife (*Is maith benait na Gaill in gort, arse, is imda serrtlaigi leccait uathib. Ar dered lai is tecasta, ar ingen Briain, .i. ben meic Amlaib*).[27]

Later in the story they reappear when Sitriuc is angered by his wife's very vocal delight at imminent Irish victory. She jokingly remarked that the Foreigners were coming into their inheritance, and when asked by her husband to explain herself she wittily replied that the sea was a Viking's natural inheritance, and they were going into it! Whereupon he hit her a blow that knocked out a tooth.[28]

This is a remarkable glimpse of the contemporary political scene. If it is true, Sitriuc of Dublin did not himself take part in the Battle of Clontarf; perhaps his brother Dubgall (who was killed) led the Dublin contingent, Sitriuc remaining within the *dún* or fortress of Dublin to ensure that it did not fall into Irish hands, as it had to Brian after Glenn Máma. This, of course, was a most important role: Brian had marched north not simply to face down the rebellion against him but, as part of that offensive, to take Dublin; and even though the consensus is that his forces won the day at Clontarf, no account suggests that the victorious army followed up their triumph by marching on and taking the now defenceless town. Perhaps this is because, as the Cogadh suggests, Dublin was by no means unprotected, its king being in a position to repel any onslaught by Brian's greatly depleted forces.

The Cogadh later sums up the situation thus—providing a good excuse for Brian's failure to capture it:

> [Sitriuc] mac Amláib himself, king of Dublin, did not go into battle on that day, and that was the reason why he was not killed, for no Foreigner of any rank appeared in it who left it alive; and Dublin would have been attacked on that day also, were it not for Amláib's son and the party he had with him.[29]

But the most remarkable insight this vignette provides is the revelation that this mortal enemy of Brian's was in fact his son-in-law. We are not told the woman's name, and no other Irish source confirms this relationship, which at first sight seems improbable. One of the reasons why we might be suspicious of it is that we know that Brian had been married to Sitriuc's mother, Gormlaith, which would mean that Sitriuc married his (now divorced) mother's stepdaughter!

But perhaps it is not so improbable (see table 4). We already knew we were dealing with a remarkably tight nexus. We know, for instance, that Sitriuc was the son of Gormlaith's marriage to Amláib Cuarán but that Brian had a son with her too, Donnchad. Therefore, in 1014 Sitriuc found himself at war with his uterine brother, one of the leaders of the Munster army. Sitriuc's main ally was the king of Leinster, Máelmórda mac Murchada, but he was Gormlaith's brother and therefore Donnchad mac Briain's uncle.

With such a small coterie of aristocrats entwined together at the top of the social pyramid, a further tightening of the knot is normal with each generation and indeed with each political realignment. So when Brian crushed Dublin at the Battle of Glenn Máma in 999 and the following year accepted Sitriuc as his vassal, we can imagine them deciding to cement the new relationship with a judicious marriage. True, Brian had once been married to Sitriuc's mother, but Brian's daughters from other marriages had no blood tie to Sitriuc, and therefore nobody would have seen any impediment to Sitriuc taking one of them in marriage, as seems to have occurred.

And we do not have to doubt the word of the Cogadh on the subject, because confirmation of it comes from an entirely unconnected source. A text survives from Wales describing the life of the king of Gwynedd, Gruffudd ap Cynan (died 1137), who was born and reared in Dublin and whose mother was Sitriuc's granddaughter. This document—which is a work of propaganda written to glorify the Welsh prince's dynasty— proudly announces that Gruffudd is not only related to the kings of Dublin, by being the great-grandson of Sitriuc, but that, through Sitriuc's wife, he is also the great-great-grandson of Brian Bóraime. Not only that, but it goes one step further than the Cogadh and undertakes to tell us the woman's name: Sláine—a name that was by no means common but is one found among Brian's dynasty and indeed occurs among the Dál Cais for centuries afterwards.[30] It seems, therefore, that on this point at least the Cogadh is not only in the clear but is a demonstrably trustworthy source.

Allowing, therefore, for considerable exaggeration, we can perhaps take as a vaguely accurate picture of events the précis of the battle that it then preserves:

> ... they continued in battle array, and fighting from the time of rising till evening (*o trath ergi co iarnoin*). This is the same length of time the tide takes to go, and to flood, and to fill. For it was at the full tide (*lan mara*) the Foreigners came out to fight the battle in the morning, and the tide had come to the same place again at the close of the day, when the Foreigners were defeated (*in tan ro muid arna Gallaib*); and the full tide carried away their ships from them, so that they had at the end no place to fly to but into the sea after all the mail-coated Foreigners (*Gaill na lureach uli*) had been killed by the Dál Cais. An awful rout was made of the Foreigners and Leinstermen, so that they fled simultaneously; and they shouted their cries for mercy and whoops of rout and retreat and running; but they could only enter the sea because they had no other way of retreat as it was between them and the head of Dubgall's bridge and between them and a wood on the other side (*ocus ised ro thechsetar is in fairgi daig ni rabi accu*

let no techfetis cena, uair ro bas eturru ocus cend drochait Dubgaill ocus ro bas eturro ocus caill don leith eile). They retreated therefore to the sea, like a herd of cows in heat, from sun and from gadflies and from insects; and they were pursued closely, rapidly and lightly; and the Foreigners were drowned in great numbers in the sea, and they lay in heaps and in hundreds, confounded, after parting with their bodily senses and understandings, under the powerful, stout, belaboring, and under the tremendous, hard-hearted pressure with which the Dál Cais and the men of Connacht, and as many as were also there of the nobles of Ireland, pursued them.[31]

We have here a vivid picture of what happened at Clontarf as related perhaps to the writer of the Cogadh by a veteran. The Scandinavian fleet—whose arrival in Dublin is attested in a variety of sources—was in Dublin Bay, perhaps off the eastern (Fairview) end of Clontarf. These Scandinavians linked up with the Norse of Dublin and the Leinstermen, their vessels having availed of the full tide to make a landing. Battle began at first light and raged all day. But as the tide receded it drew the Scandinavian vessels with it and scattered them about the bay. By evening the Norse were compelled to retreat and would have made for the safety of Sitriuc's fortress at Dublin, or a wood that seems to have stood in the other direction (towards Howth). It is emphatically not stated that this wood is the famous Caill Tomair ('Wood of Þórormr'), part of which Brian had consciously set fire to in 1000 (as the Annals of Inisfallen put it, 'The men of Munster invaded Dublin, set fire to it and burned it, and they invested it on the Kalends of January; and they burned Caill Tomair as firewood').[32]

This event from fourteen years earlier is indeed referred to elsewhere in the Cogadh. When Brian first asks his attendant for news of the battle the reply is that the din is such that 'not louder in my ears would be the echoes of blows from Caill Tomair if seven battalions were cutting it down.' And when later Brian asks for a second time about the state of the forces on each side the attendant responds: 'They appear to me the same as if Caill Tomair was on fire and the seven battalions had been cutting away its underwood and its young shoots for a month, leaving its stately trees and its immense oaks standing.'[33] From these references we take it that Caill Tomair was a famously impressive tract of oakwood close to Dublin and highly prized by the Dubliners, perhaps where the Phoenix Park survives to this day.

However, the wood that features in the Cogadh's account of Clontarf is an unnamed and less celebrated grove, apparently to the east of the battle site. The problem for the enemy forces scattering before Brian's men was that they could not get to this wood because the incoming tide was between them and it. Similarly, on the west side of the battlefield, because of the high sea they could not get back to Dubgall's bridge. If this was over the Tolka at Ballybough, which seems likely from the context, they needed to reach it and cross it to escape to Dublin; but the tide was between them and the bridge.

On the present-day landscape we can imagine them being at the old heart of Clontarf—say, between Castle Avenue and Seaview Avenue— and to get to the bridge they would have to traverse Fairview Strand, except that the incoming tide had submerged it. In the other direction protection was offered by a wooded area that lay perhaps to the east of Vernon Avenue, but the inundation of the area around Oulton Road and Belgrove Road blocked off that route also, and so they had no option presumably but to position themselves with their backs to the sea and make a stand, which proved disastrous for them, many of them drowning as they were beaten back.[34]

The question of the tide on the day of the Battle of Clontarf is one that has intrigued scholars. As we have seen, according to the Cogadh there was a full tide early in the morning, before fighting began, and again after dark, when the battle had been fought to a close; but can this be taken literally? The Cogadh's remarkable nineteenth-century editor, James Henthorn Todd, set a challenge for his no less remarkable colleague at Trinity College Dublin, Samuel Haughton:

> It occurred to the Editor, on considering this passage, that a criterion might be derived from it to test the truth of the narrative, and of the date assigned by the Irish Annals to the Battle of Clontarf. He therefore proposed to the Rev. Samuel Haughton, M.D., Fellow of Trinity College, and Professor of Geology in the University of Dublin, to solve for him this problem:—'What was the hour of high water, at the shore of Clontarf, in Dublin Bay, on the 23rd of April, 1014?' The Editor did not make known to Dr Haughton the object he had

in view in this question, and the coincidence of the result obtained with the ancient narrative is therefore the more valuable and curious. Dr Haughton communicated the particulars of his calculation to the Royal Irish Academy in May 1861,[35] in the following words:—

'From twelve o'clock, noon, of the 23rd April, 1014, to the noon of the 12th December, 1860, allowing for the change of style and leap years, there were 309,223 real days. The synodical period of the moon is 29.630588715 days, and new moon occurred on the 12th December, 1860, at 47.6 minutes after noon. Multiplying the length of the synodical month by 10472 months, we find

$$29.530588715 \times 10472 = 309244.325 \text{ days.}$$

From which, subtracting the number of days from 23rd April, 1014, to 12th December, 1860, or 309,223 days, we find

21.325 days, or 21d 7h 48m.

It follows from this calculation that new moon occurred at

April   28d 0h 47.6m — 1014, A.D.

Minus   21d 7h 48m

Or, at   1d 16h 59.6m — April, 1014, A.D.

i.e., at 5 o'clock on the morning of the 2nd April.

Therefore full moon occurred at

April   1d 16h 59.6m

Plus   14d 18h 21.6m

16d 11h 21.2m

Therefore the astronomical, or true full moon, occurred at 21 minutes past eleven at night of the 16th April, 1014.

Calculating by the established rules, the calendar or ecclesiastical full moon occurred on the 18th April, 1014 (Sunday), which would therefore make Easter Day fall on the 25th April, and make the 23rd April, Good Friday, agreeable to the traditions of the Battle of Clontarf.

I shall now show that the calculation of the tides makes it quite certain that the date 1014 falls in with all the physical circumstances related of the battle.

It appears from the calculation that I have given already that:

The age of the moon at noon on the 23rd April, 1014, was 21.292 days, or

21d 7h nearly.

The tide was therefore a neap tide, and the moon in her third quarter. From the Academy's observations [on the tides round the coast of Ireland], it appears that on such a day of the moon's age, at the spring equinox, the tide at Kingstown [Dún Laoghaire] is full at

5h 22m in the morning,

from which it follows that the tide along the Clontarf shore, when not obstructed by embankments and walls, could not have differed many minutes on the 23rd April, 1014, from

5h 30m a.m.;

the evening tide being full in at

5h 55m p.m.'

The truth of the narrative is thus most strikingly established. In the month of April, the sun rises at from 5h 30m to 4h 30m. The full tide in the morning therefore coincided nearly with sunrise: a fact which holds a most important place in the history of the battle, and proves that our author, if not himself an eye-witness, must have derived his information from those who were. 'None others,' as Dr Haughton observes, 'could have invented the fact that the battle began at sunrise, and that the tide was then full in. The importance of the time of tide became evident at the close of the day, when the returned tide prevented the escape of the Danes from the Clontarf shore to the North bank of the Liffey.'[36]

It was a wonderful feat of mathematical detective-work, which confirmed Todd in his view that the Cogadh was a faithful record of all that happened at Clontarf. And when he produced his own magisterial edition of the Cogadh a few years later the ready availability of so valuable a resource led to numerous other investigations to see what a careful reading of the text could tell us of the event, studies such as Thomas O'Gorman's essay 'On the site of the Battle of Clontarf' (1879), Patrick Traynor's inquiry twenty years later entitled 'Where was the Battle of Clontarf fought?', Arthur Ua Clérig's study of 1905, J. H. Lloyd's two years after that, and Thomas J. Westropp's booklet *King Brian, the Hero of Clontarf* (based on a series of articles in the *Irish Monthly*), published in 1914 to mark the 900th anniversary.[37] And there have been many more before and since.

Apart from the fact that we rely on the Cogadh because beggars can't be choosers, the fact is that it has some extraordinarily enticing detail. It describes, for instance, the Irish assault in which Brian's fifteen-year-old grandson Tairdelbach lost his life:

> Tairdelbach son of Murchad son of Brian went after the Foreigners into the sea, when the rushing tide wave struck him a blow against the weir of Clontarf (*co tuc in bunni robarta bulli fair im carrid Cluana Tarb*), and so he was drowned, with a Foreigner under him, and a Foreigner in his right hand, and a Foreigner in his left, and a stake of the weir through him (*ocus cualli na carad trit*).[38]

And detail like this is bound to captivate. Needless to say, we simply do not know where this weir was. It was certainly near to the heart of the action, so near in fact that a list of the kings of Munster preserved in the twelfth-century Book of Leinster states that Brian was killed in 'the Battle of Clontarf Weir (*Cath Corad Cluana Tarb*)'.[39] The battle itself, therefore, was contested in the immediate environs of the weir. The Cogadh's editor, J. H. Todd, states that 'this ancient salmon weir is supposed to have been at the present Ballybough bridge, on the road from Dublin to Clontarf'.[40] This, however, is not strictly in Clontarf, and it is unlikely that a weir at this site would acquire the name 'Clontarf Weir'. It is possible, therefore, that the weir in question was not a barrier of wooden stakes across the River Tolka but was similar to the estuarine fish-traps found, for instance, in the Shannon Estuary and Strangford Lough, which sometimes have funnel-shaped fences of sharpened wooden stakes driven into the mudflats.[41] One could visualise one of these along the tidal shoreline at Clontarf and between the shoreline and Clontarf Island (which survived until the nineteenth century, now forming part of Fairview Park)[42] and young Tairdelbach being hurled by a wave onto one of its stakes (map 8).

Shortly after Tairdelbach's demise it was the turn of his father, Murchad. It was he personally, the Cogadh says, who slew Earl Sigurðr of Orkney, but in the act of beheading one of the earl's comrades-in-arms, mac Ebric (or Elbric), son of the king of Lochlainn, the latter drew his knife and 'gave Murchad such a cut that all his entrails were cut out and fell to the ground before him,' and he died eventually at about sunrise the next day.

Brian, who was in his tent praying, regularly asked his attendant, Laidainn, for news of the battle and specifically of Murchad's battle-standard, saying: 'The men of Ireland shall be well while that standard remains standing, because their courage and valour shall remain in them all as long as they can see that standard.' The first two times Brian asked, the attendant reported that Murchad's standard was flying high, but at the third time of asking he reported that the standard had fallen, and that Murchad was dead.

Then a version is told of the story preserved in the Annals of Loch Cé that Brian had been visited the night before by the fairy-woman Aíbinn of Craicliath, who had foretold his death and that whichever son he saw first would be the one to succeed him.

Just as Brian was saying this, Bródar and two warriors (*dias ócclach*) came towards them, whom Brian saw to be 'the Foreigners of the armour (*Goill na luireach*)', whereupon he unsheathed his sword. One of them, 'who had been in Brian's service (*robh ócclach do Brian féin e*),' recognised him and shouted, in what seems to be Old English rather than Norse (which would fit a background in York)—and again the author is showing off his linguistic prowess here: '*Cing! Cing!* this is the king (*as é so an rí*).' To which Bródar replied, '*Nó, nó, acht príst, príst*', adding: 'It is not, said he, but a noble priest (*ni headh, ar sé, acht sagart uasal*).'

But when the warrior insisted it was indeed Brian, Bródar approached him with his axe, and although Brian swung his sword at him, cutting off his left leg at the knee and his right foot and killing one of his two comrades, Bródar split Brian's head open with his axe, so that he died, causing the writer to proclaim:

There was not done in Ireland, since [the coming of] Christianity, excepting the beheading of Cormac mac Cuilennáin [in 908], any greater [i.e. worse] deed than this. In fact he was one of the three best that ever were born in Ireland; and one of the three men who most caused Ireland to prosper, namely, Lug Lámfhada and Finn mac Cumaill and Brian mac Cennétig. For it was he who released the men of Ireland, and its women, from the bondage and iniquity of the Foreigners and the overseasmen. It was he who gained twenty-five battles over the Foreigners and who killed and banished them as we have already said.

He was the beautiful, ever-victorious Octavian [i.e. Augustus Caesar] for prosperity and freedom of his patrimony and his sept (*a atharrdha ocus a chineoil*). He was the strong, irresistible, second Alexander, for energy and for dignity, and for attacks and for battles and for triumphs. And he was the happy, wealthy, peaceable Solomon of the Goídil. He was the faithful, fervent, honourable, gallant David of Ireland, for truthfulness, and for worthiness, and for the maintenance of sovereignty (*ar coimheitt flaiteimhnas*). He was the magnificent, brilliant Moses, for chastity and unostentatious devotion.[43]

Bródar (described as jarl of York) also fell, and along with him 'a thousand plundering Danars, both Saxon and Scandinavian (*.x.c. Danar dibeirgach Sacsanach ocus Lochlannach*).'

And when all the Foreigners were vanquished, the remnants of the Munster army regrouped and fell back to the *faithche* or green area near Dublin, where they waited for the return of Brian's son Donnchad, who—having been sent off foraging to Leinster before battle even began—rather incredibly did not return for two days, until Easter Sunday night, 'for it was on the Friday before Easter that the battle was fought, viz, the ninth of the Kalends of May.'

For this part of the story, unfortunately, we have only one version of the text (in a manuscript from the seventeenth century in the hand of Micheál Ó Cléirigh, one of the Four Masters), and so this story of Donnchad missing out on this most vital battle may be a later invention. But the statement that the battle took place on Good Friday—mentioned for the first time in the Cogadh only at this point—is attested at an earlier date. The Irish monk Marianus (Máel Brigte) Scottus wrote a chronicle while living in Germany in the decades before his death in 1082, and while he would have known in a general way of the great battle that had taken place when he was still a child, he also met in Germany an exiled monk from Inis Celtra, the island monastery on Lough Derg, of which, as we know, Brian was a prominent patron.[44] It is significant, therefore, that Marianus clearly states that Brian, the king of Ireland, was killed on the 9th of the Kalends of May, i.e. the 23rd of April, while preparing for Easter, having both 'hands and mind focussed on God (*Brian, rex Hiberniae, parasceue Paschae, feria vi, ix Kal. Maii, manibus et mente ad Deum intentus, occiditur*).'[45]

We therefore have an Irish source in Germany written within half a century or so of Clontarf that is clear about the Easter connection; and this is replicated in the Cogadh and in—presumably independent—Icelandic sources (as we shall see), which have it that Brian did not take part in the battle because he refused to fight on Good Friday, and the combination is surely unassailable evidence for the date. And this had become fixed certainly by the thirteenth century, when the well-known poem beginning 'Aonar dhuit a Bhriain Bhanba' ('To you alone, O Brian of Ireland') was written, which is attributed to Muiredach Albanach Ó Dálaigh (to which we shall return).

As for the assertion that Donnchad was absent from the fight, this may be intended to malign him, but it could perhaps be argued that it was included in the account by a writer favourable to Donnchad to explain away his very survival when so many of his family perished.[46] The fact is that the portrayal of Donnchad, who is now centre-stage in what is left of the story, is positive. We are told that he fulfilled the terms of his father's will and paid all bequests, as his father had asked. We are told that he had accumulated cattle from his raiding mission and now set about slaughtering them within sight of Dublin, at which point the men of Dublin threatened to come out from behind their defences and do battle with him. A messenger arrived from Sitriuc (Donnchad's uterine brother) offering to allow him to keep one in every twenty of the cattle, to which Donnchad replied that Dál Cais had never taken *tuarastal* (a vassal's wages) from the Foreigners and would not be starting now, 'for it appears to us that our hostility to each other is now greater than ever.' And so he proceeded to slaughter the remainder of the cattle, 'but the Foreigners declined the battle for fear of Donnchad and Dál Cais.'[47]

On the Monday they went to Clontarf and buried all those they recognised as their own people and made biers for carrying the wounded; presumably, therefore, somewhere in Clontarf there is or was a mass grave of these bodies (although, as we have seen, the later traditions are of burial at Kilmainham). Thirty nobles who had been killed were taken for burial to their patrimonial churches (*da cceallaibh dúthchusa féin*) in various places throughout Ireland.

Then began the long march home, Donnchad bravely meeting head-on a rebellion by the men of Desmumu (South Munster) and an attempted ambush by the men of Osraige and Loígis, both of whom drew back from combat on seeing the courage of Donnchad and Dál Cais. Truly, in the eyes of this author, he was his father's son.

And Cogadh Gáedhel re Gallaibh, this long narrative of Irish conflict with the Vikings, ends not with Brian's victory so much as with Donnchad's return to Cenn Corad—not altogether in triumph, perhaps, but certainly with Dál Cais pride intact, a dynasty that, under Donnchad mac Briain, lived to fight another day.

Chapter 6 〜

CLONTARF THROUGH OTHERS' EYES

G iven the number of people from overseas who took part in the Battle of Clontarf, it is not surprising that news of it spread not only throughout Ireland but into Britain and to south-western France and, less surprisingly perhaps, northwards to the Scandinavian world and Iceland, where the contemporary fascination with it meant that Clontarf became the stuff of saga and the death of the high-king so iconic that it was called simply *Brjánsorrosta* (Brian's Battle).[1]

Scotland lacks a tradition of chronicling in this age, and therefore there is no way of proving what we can probably take for granted, that the epic encounter at Dublin bent many an ear.

In England some months before the Battle of Clontarf a momentous event took place when the country was conquered by the Danes, a conquest that hung in the balance following Sveinn Forkbeard's death in February 1014. It is not surprising, therefore, that the Anglo-Saxon Chronicle can spare no thought for events across the Irish Sea. But Welsh writers were of a different mind.

CLONTARF AND THE WELSH *BRUT*

Although England was in the throes of revolutionary change at that precise moment, the Welsh annals have far less to say about it than about Clontarf: Clontarf is what interested them.

Nowadays we tend to think—for obvious historical reasons—of Wales being much more closely bound up with England than with Ireland; but in Brian's day it was quite the opposite, at least as regards the men of west Wales, bordering the Irish Sea. We have seen that Brian was described in his obit in the Annals of Ulster as, among other things, 'high-king of the Britons', i.e. the Welsh, and we have speculated that the explanation lies in dealings he may have had with one or more Welsh lords who had perhaps obtained his protection.[2] It is presumably no coincidence, therefore, that in all the preceding three hundred or more years covered by the Welsh annals known as *Brut y Tywysogyon* ('Chronicle of the Princes') there is not a single entry longer than its account of the Battle of Clontarf:

And Brian, king of Ireland, and Murchad his son, and many other kings, led hosts against Sitriuc, king of Dublin, son of Amlaíb, and against Máelmórda, king of Leinster. For those had allied themselves together against Brian. And Sitriuc hired long ships and pirate ships full of armed men to assist him; and the leader of those was called Bródar. And after there had been a hard battle between them and a great slaughter on either side, Brian and Murchad his son were there slain, and Bródar, leader of the ships, and King Máelmórda were slain.[3]

Perhaps there is not a great deal that is new here, but this is only because it presents an unadulterated factual account of what happened. There are some points of interest, though. As we can see from the account, while Sitriuc is described as king of Dublin and Máelmórda as king of Leinster, the writer does not call Brian king of Tuadmumu, or even Munster, but is in no doubt that he is 'king of Ireland'; he is therefore more than aware of, and fully accepts, Brian's claim to national primacy. This Welsh writer obviously also knew of Brian's son Murchad and considered it almost a joint command under father and son, presumably because he was aware of Brian's great age.

Clearly too he did not share the view that Brian was poorly served by allies, as he and Murchad led an army comprising 'many other kings'. They marched against Sitriuc mac Amlaíb of Dublin and Máelmórda of Leinster—in that order—because these 'had allied themselves together against Brian'; and Sitriuc certainly seems to be in the driving-seat, as we are told that it is he who 'hired long ships and pirate ships full of armed men to assist *him* (Sitriuc)' in his struggle.

In the hard battle that followed there was great slaughter on both sides, Brian, Murchad, Bródar and Máelmórda being slain. We are not told who won, and the impression is given that the battle was fought to a draw. This verdict apart, it is an account remarkably consistent with the Irish record, to the extent that Bródar is called 'leader of the ships (*a thywyssaoc y llogeu*)' in a phrase remarkably close to the Annals of Ulster's 'leader of the Scandinavian fleet (*toisech na loingsi Lochlannaighi*)'.

Of course the problem with the Welsh annals is that they took their present shape only in the thirteenth century, and it is impossible to say how contemporary this record is. It may tell us only what the thirteenth-century compiler *believed* happened and that, at that point, the writer thought of Clontarf as an event deserving a hitherto uniquely long entry. What it does not tell us is when people *began* to think of it as such. But presumably if, two centuries or more later, Clontarf was still considered immensely important in Wales, those living closer in time to it must have taken it every bit as seriously.

There is another, related Welsh tradition, preserved in the Latin chronicle called *Annales Cambriae*, which has a much briefer account of Clontarf, to the effect that 'Brian, king of Ireland, and his son, were killed by Sitriuc, king of Dublin (*B[r]ianus rex Hiberniae cum filio suo Ascuthin, scilicet rege Dulyn, occiditur*).'[4] But even this is notable for its insistence that Brian was Ireland's king and that his primary enemy was not his Leinster rival (who is not mentioned) but the Norse king of Dublin.

CLONTARF AND AQUITAINE

The chronicler Adémar of Chabannes, who lived in Angoulême in south-western France, lived through Clontarf and, rather remarkably, chose to write about it. We know that he put the finishing touches to his history a decade or so after the battle,[5] but we do not know from where his information was derived.

Angoulême, about 100 km from Bordeaux, is an ancient city on an important route, washed by the River Charante, which flows to the sea in the Saintonge at Rochefort, near La Rochelle. This is a region whose wine merchants have traded with Ireland through the millennia,[6] and it is most likely that such men returned from Ireland bearing news of the calamitous battle, which Adémar thought important enough to record for posterity in his famous history.

Interestingly, he precedes his account of the Battle of Clontarf by recording a raid on the port of Saint-Michel-en-l'Herm (about 25 km, as the crow flies, north of La Rochelle) by 'an infinite multitude of Northmen from the region of Denmark and Ireland with an immense fleet (*infinita multitudo Normannorum ex Danamarcha et Iresca regione cum classe innumera*). He tells us that, just as their predecessors had done, they tried to lay waste and capture all Aquitaine, and they dug themselves in in an encampment there, large ransoms eventually having to be paid for the recovery of captives. The raid, said to have been the last on the region in the Viking Age, has been dated to 1017 or 1018,[7] which would place it after Clontarf, although Adémar thought it came before it. Presumably, if we can believe the details of it, those involved were Danes and Hiberno-Norse, not unlike the composition of the non-Gaelic troops who fought at Clontarf.

Indeed Adémar begins his account of Clontarf by saying it was perpetrated by the same people, 'the aforesaid Northmen (*Normanni supradicti*)'. His commentary on the battle is more than a little confused, but he knows enough to know that Clontarf was a major event, with international implications, worthy of record:

> In this time the aforesaid Northmen did what their fathers had never dared (*quod patres eorum nunquam ausi sunt facere*), approaching the island of Hibernia, also known as Ireland (*Hirlanda*), with an innumerable fleet. They were accompanied by their wives, children, and enslaved Christians, hoping to exterminate the Irish and occupy their very rich land (*Hirlandis extinctis, ipsi pro eis inhabitarent opulentissimam terram*). It has twelve cities with bishoprics of the highest rank and one king and its own language, but Latin letters (*Quae xii civitates cum amplissimis episcopatibus et unum regem habet et propriam linguam sed latinas litteras*). The Roman Saint Patrick had converted this land to the faith and had become the first bishop. It is surrounded entirely by water and at the winter solstice there are scarcely two hours of daylight and at the summer solstice the same amount of night.

A battle ensued, lasting three days without interruption, and not one Northman survived. Their wives threw themselves into the sea with their children and drowned; those who survived were captured, then thrown to wild beasts to be torn apart alive. The king let one of the captives live because he knew him to be a Christian captive, and he gave him gifts.[8]

There is here (amidst the misunderstanding over how far north Ireland is) a certain basic knowledge of Ireland's Christian heritage, and an awareness of the existence of a high-kingship; and the writer has been accurately informed about the fact that central to the Clontarf story is the phenomenon of a mass drowning of Norse participants, as Cogadh Gáedhel re Gallaibh describes and as the Annals of Ulster have it when they baldly state that 'six thousand were killed or drowned (*ui. mile iter marbad & bathad*).' Adémar's statement that the battle raged for three days is an exaggeration, as it lasted only a single day, but we know that it continued from dawn to dusk, and that this was unusually long by contemporary standards, and so the essence of the idea is sound. And the conclusion of the account, with the statement that 'the king' allowed one of the Norse to live because he knew him to be a Christian captive, has more than an echo of the last sentence of *Njáls saga*'s account of Clontarf (discussed later), when one of the few Norse stragglers who survived Clontarf returned home and informed the chieftain Flosi that all the others were dead except for his brother-in-law Þorsteinn, who had been granted peace by Brian's foster-son Kerþjálfaðr [Tairdelbach?] and was staying with him.

At a more general level, Adémar is convinced that the Irish won and the Northmen lost. And from our point of view the most interesting element of the story is his perception that Clontarf amounted in effect to a Scandinavian invasion, and on an unprecedented scale: they were doing something their forefathers had not dared to do, and he had been told that they had brought their wives with them, obviously intent on staying. His account is therefore evidence that there were those far from Ireland's shores who thought that Clontarf mattered, not because of the death of the king of Ireland in it (Adémar was strangely unaware of this fact) but because it was a failed Scandinavian attempt to conquer Ireland. And, incidentally, Adémar's very next sentence begins on the subject of Knút's conquest of England, as if to suggest that they are, in his mind at least, linked.

ORKNEYINGA SAGA

Because of the importance of the Scandinavian component at Clontarf, it is not by chance that stories of it took root far to the north, particularly concerning the involvement of Jarl Sigurðr of Orkney. These stories, not surprisingly, found their way into *Orkneyinga saga*, written at the earliest about 1200. Despite its name, this saga originates in Iceland, and it contains little that is not elaborated on in the main Icelandic account in *Njáls saga* (to be discussed presently). This is what *Orkneyinga saga* has to say:

> Hlöðvir Þorfinnsson took the earldom [of Orkney] after Ljótr, and was a great chief; he had to wife Eðnu daughter of Kjarvalr, the Irish king (*Írakonungr*); their son was Sigurðr *digri* . . . [who] took the earldom after him; he was a great chief and wide of lands. He held by main force Caithness against the Scots, and had a host out every summer . . .
>
> Sigurðr went to ask his mother's counsel, for she knew many things . . . She answers: 'I would have reared you in my wool-bag had I known you would like to live forever; and fate rules life, but not where a man is come; it is better to die with honour than to live with shame. Take hold of this banner which I have made for you with all my cunning and I believe it will bring victory to those before whom it is borne, but speedy death to him who bears it.' The banner was made with much needlecraft and famous skill. It was made in a raven's shape; and when the wind blew out the banner, then it was as though the raven spread his wings for flight . . .
>
> Óláfr Tryggvason [king of Norway, c. 995–c. 999] was four years in warfare in the western lands . . . before he let himself be baptised in the Scilly Isles. From there he fared to England and got there to wife Gyða, the daughter of Kváran [Amlaíb Cuarán of Dublin], the Irish king. After that he stayed a while in Dublin until Jarl Hákon sent Þórir the Whiner [to Dublin] to lure him from there. Óláfr sailed from the west with four ships and came first to the Orkneys. There he met Jarl Sigurðr . . .

And when they met, King Óláfr spoke to him, 'It is my will that you let yourself be baptised and all the folk that serve you, else you shall die here at once, but I will fare with fire and flame over all the isles.' ... Then all the Orkneys became Christian ... But after that Jarl Sigurðr yielded no obedience to King Óláfr. He went into a marriage with a daughter of Máel Coluim the king of the Scots, and their son was Jarl Þorfinnr ...

Five [in fact fourteen] winters after the battle at Svöld, Jarl Sigurðr fared to Ireland, to help King Sygtryggr Silkiskeggi [Sitriuc Silkenbeard of Dublin] ... But when Jarl Sigurðr came to Ireland, he and King Sygtryggr marched with that host to meet Brian, the Irish king (*Írakonungr*), and their meeting was on Good Friday. Then it fell out that there was no one left to bear the raven banner, and the earl bore it himself, and fell there, but King Sygtryggr fled. King Brian fell with victory and glory (*Brjánn konungr fell með sigri ok gagni*).[9]

Although the detail on Clontarf is sparse, the background information is extraordinary. As we can see, the *Orkneyinga* story is centred on Sigurðr Hlöðvisson or Sigurðr digri (Sigurðr the Stout), who was the first certain earl of Orkney and who also controlled parts of the northern Scottish mainland, including Caithness (and, *Njáls saga* claims, Sutherland and, rather less likely, Moray and Ross). *Orkneyinga saga* claims that Sigurð's mother was Eðnu, daughter of Kjarvalr *Írakonungr* ('Irish king'), presumably someone named Cerball and his daughter Eithne. The problem with this is that if the writer intends Cerball mac Dúnlainge, the extraordinary king of Osraige who is mentioned in the Icelandic *Landnámabók* and from whom a number of prominent families in later mediaeval Iceland claimed descent, his death in 888 undoubtedly rules him out.[10] A more realistic possibility is Cerball mac Muirecáin, the great Uí Fáeláin king of Leinster who died in 909 (table 4; above, page 147). Even he seems a little early, but what is interesting about him is that he was an ancestor of Sigurð's ally at Clontarf, Máelmórda mac Murchada, who would have been—if there is any truth to the relationship—Sigurð's first cousin once removed. It is just possible, therefore, that such a familial tie accounts for their alliance.

But, to be blunt, in all probability the author invented Sigurð's descent from Kjarvalr *Írakonungr*. The most we can hope for is that he did so for genuine reasons, being aware that Sigurð's mother was Irish but confused about her precise family. And if Sigurð's mother *was* Irish, why should we not expect him to pursue ambitions there?

So, assuming Sigurð's mother was indeed a Leinster princess, it is interesting that *Orkneyinga saga* says that he himself married a daughter of Máel Coluim mac Cineáda, the man who was king of Scotland at the time of Clontarf, because we know from the 'Prophecy of Berchán' that Máel Coluim's mother was also a Leinsterwoman. It is just possible, therefore, that both men were the products of strategic marriages into the same dynasty, perhaps that of Máelmórda mac Murchada of Uí Fáeláin, and that these marriages are part of a broader picture of stable political coalitions in the region, which dictated involvement at Clontarf (table 4).

It is not clear how we should interpret *Orkneyinga saga*'s account of relations between Jarl Sigurðr and Óláfr Tryggvason, who would become king of Norway about 995. The suggestion seems to be that Sigurðr converted to Christianity under some duress applied by Óláfr, and the writer seems anxious to suggest that he was Máel Coluim's man rather than Óláfr Tryggvason's. But from our viewpoint perhaps the most important point is the emphasis placed by the text on yet another marriage into Ireland. We are told that Óláfr Tryggvason had married a sister of Sitriuc of Dublin (table 4). Óláfr, of course, had disappeared from the scene a decade or more before the planning for Clontarf can have begun. The point is that if there is any truth to the marriages that lie behind *Orkneyinga saga*'s narrative we should not be in the least surprised to find these men plotting conquests in a country with which they seem to have been altogether familiar and from whose aristocracy they claimed very recent descent.

As to what *Orkneyinga saga* has on the Battle of Clontarf itself, it is meagre for some reason. What it does do is underline the importance of Sitriuc. Nobody else among Brian's opponents from Ireland is mentioned. Jarl Sigurðr travelled to Ireland to help Sitriuc; together they marched against Brian. The battle that ensued, the author states emphatically, took place on Good Friday. As we have seen, this is the inference to be drawn from Marianus Scottus's account, written in Germany within living memory of the battle, and such diverse sources can hardly have said as much unless it was common belief.

Jarl Sigurð's death in the battle is to be accounted for (although the writer is laconic on the subject) by the fact that he himself ended up holding the raven banner made for him by his Irish mother, which, perversely, brought death to its standard-bearer. A further implication of the brief account, contrary to the version of events portrayed in the Cogadh, is that King Sitriuc personally fought in the battle but fled, implicitly in defeat. The account ends with the widely repeated assertion that 'King Brian fell with victory and glory (*Brjánn konungr fell með sigri ok gagni*).' Brian, therefore, died and yet won.

It is a strange notion. The implications of it are great, and we shall pursue them presently.

NJÁLS SAGA

Icelandic traditions about Clontarf get their fullest treatment in the wonderful *Njáls saga*, or *Brennu-Njáls saga* ('The story of Burnt Njál'), which is later still in date and was put together from earlier materials and folk memory, perhaps in the 1270s or 80s. As ever with Icelandic sagas—especially because of how late they assumed their present form—the problem can be in knowing what to accept as a genuine memory and what to reject as mere storytelling. But these Scandinavian texts have so much of their core story in common with Irish memories of Clontarf, as recorded principally in Cogadh Gáedhel re Gallaibh, that the suspicion must be that they found their way into the Norse world from an Irish source. It is often speculated in fact that a narrative about Brian and Clontarf might have been written in Dublin and eventually found its way to Iceland, and this 'saga'—which may never have existed—has even been given a name, *Brjáns saga*, 'Brian's story'.[11]

If indeed a written account from Ireland lies behind the Icelandic epics it might be worth considering the possibility of a source emanating from Norse Limerick—for two reasons: firstly because of the general similarity between the Scandinavian account of the Battle of Clontarf and that found in the Cogadh, which originated from somewhere under Dál Cais influence in the Limerick area, and secondly because *Njáls saga* portrays a positive image of Brian, where one might have expected a negative picture if it was drawing on a Dublin source.

Either way, at the very least we can say that the preservation of an account of the Battle of Clontarf in Scandinavian sources, which may or may not have originated in Ireland, has much to tell us about how the battle was remembered in the Norse world.

The account of Clontarf in *Njáls saga* begins with a Yuletide feast organised by Sigurðr at the end of 1013, attended by a *jarl* called Gilli from the Hebrides (who had married Sigurð's sister); and the claim being made is that Sigurðr was Gilli's suzerain. The Western Isles were bound up with the Hiberno-Norse enclaves in Ireland, so that the ruler of one sometimes ruled the other. It follows, therefore, that the *overlord* of one might claim overlordship of the other. In other words, we can imagine that when Brian gained the submission of Dublin in 1000 he demanded that all those overseas territories over which the Dubliners had some claim were now ultimately under his jurisdiction, which might include Gilli's supposed Hebridean lordship. But equally, if Gilli really was ruler of the Western Isles—a lordship linked with one or more of the Hiberno-Norse settlements in Ireland, including Dublin—and if Sigurðr really was Gilli's overlord, Sigurðr might well have harboured overlordship ambitions relating to Ireland.

To his Yuletide gathering there also arrived Sygtryggr (Sitriuc) of Dublin, who, the saga tells us, was son of Óláfr Kváran (Amlaíb Cuarán) and Kormlǫð (Gormlaith) (see table 4), the latter 'a most beautiful woman who showed the best qualities in all matters that were not in her own power, but in all those that were, people said she showed herself of an evil disposition.' We are then told:

> She had been married to a king named Brján [Brian], but now they were divorced, for he was a king of the noblest qualities. He lived in Kantaraborg [Cenn Corad] in Ireland. His brother was named Úlfr *hreða*, a great champion and warrior. A foster-son of Brján was named Kerþjálfaðr [Tairdelbach?]. He was the son of King Kylfir [Célechair?] who had fought many battles against King Brján, but who had left the land, fleeing before him, and had entered a monastery. But when King Brján had gone south on a pilgrimage he had met King Kylfir and become reconciled with him; whereupon King Brján took King Kylfir's son Kerþjálfaðr into fosterage and loved him more than his own sons. Kerþjálfaðr was already grown to manhood at the time the events to be told here took place, and was a most valiant man. Dungaðr [Donnchad] was the name of one of King Brján's sons; a

second was named Margaðr [Murchad], and a third Taðkr [Tadc], for which we say Tann. Tann was the youngest, but the elder sons of King Brján were full grown and very brave men. Kormlǫð was not the mother of King Brján's children. She was so filled with hatred for King Brján after her divorce that she would have wished to see him dead. King Brján forgave all whom he had outlawed three times for the same misdeed, but if they transgressed more often, he had them judged in accordance with the law. From this one may gather what kind of king he was. Kormlǫð was forever egging on her own son Sygtryggr to slay King Brján and she sent him to Jarl Sigurðr to ask for his support.[12]

Here we can see the core of the narrative as it ended up in the Scandinavian world: the just king brought low by his former queen with all the fury of a woman scorned. There is a certain amount of confused knowledge about these and the other people and places. The saga's Kantaraborg is presumably the ring-fort at Cenn Corad near Killaloe (borg is Old Norse for stronghold, and Kantara is an easy error for Kancara). The striking thing is that this place, which did become Brian's favourite abode, appears in the historical record only in his later years, suddenly being mentioned in his domestic Annals of Inisfallen as a place to which submitting kings and their hostages are brought in 1010 and 1011 and then as having been built (presumably rebuilt) in 1012. That the Icelandic sources know of it is rather remarkable. Likewise, Brian did have sons called Donnchad, Murchad and Tadc. He also had a grandson called Tairdelbach, who was killed at Clontarf, and this is presumably the Kerþjálfaðr erroneously described as his foster-son (table 3; above, page 100).

Brian's supposed brother named Úlfr hreða is less clear, but it translates as 'troublesome wolf', and it has been pointed out that one of Brian's companions recorded in Irish sources among the dead at Clontarf was Cú Duilig mac Cennétig, whose forename can also translate as 'troublesome wolf';[13] and although he was not Brian's brother he was a family member, being the grandson of Brian's brother Donncuan.

In general, therefore, there are grounds for thinking that some tolerably accurate source of information is feeding into Njáls saga's account of the Battle of Clontarf.

We are then told that at Sigurð's Yuletide feast it was Sitriuc of Dublin (presumably because he was a king) who sat at the centre of the main table, with the jarls Sigurðr and Gilli on either side. Next, when Sitriuc asked Sigurðr 'to go to war with him against King Brján,' Sigurðr hesitated at first but consented on one condition: 'that he was to marry King Sygtrygg's mother Kormlǫð and become a king in Ireland, should Brján be slain.'[14] The Dublin king agreed to these rather extraordinary terms.

The whole thing seems utterly preposterous; but it would not seem preposterous to a writer familiar with the traditions that had grown up in Ireland surrounding a number of women called Gormlaith who became famous for strategic marriages, one of whom was indeed the Gormlaith who was Sitriuc's mother. Only the Scandinavian tradition has it that Brian and Gormlaith had divorced, although it is implicit in Irish sources, which have a salacious preoccupation with her penchant for powerful husbands.

By the twelfth century it was believed that Gormlaith had been married three times, to three famous kings, that she had first been married to Sitriuc's father, Amlaíb Cuarán, then to the king of Tara, Máel Sechnaill mac Domnaill, and then to Brian. There are reasons for believing that all three marriages took place, although evidence for the marriage to Máel Sechnaill is less substantial, and we simply do not know the sequence.[15] But as Amlaíb was ousted from power after his defeat by Máel Sechnaill at the Battle of Tara in 980, and Máel Sechnaill was in turn ousted by Brian in 1002, it is easy to see how the idea might have grown that Gormlaith was a kind of sovereignty figure who gave power to the man whom she married.

Hence the origin of the idea in *Njáls saga* that, when Jarl Sigurðr of Orkney took up King Sitriuc's challenge to go to Dublin, part of the deal was that he would 'marry King Sygtrygg's mother Kormlǫð and become a king in Ireland, should Brján be slain.' The assumption here, despite the text's admission that Brian and Gormlaith were divorced, was that Brian still exercised sovereignty by virtue of his union with Gormlaith, and that if he were slain and Gormlaith married Sigurðr the sovereignty would pass to the latter; and although the phrase used is that he would be 'a king *in* Ireland (*konungr á Írlandi*)', the implication seems to be that he would be king *of* Ireland.[16]

Sigurðr agreed that he would come to Dublin with all his army on the Sunday before Easter (Palm Sunday), and King Sitriuc returned to Dublin to tell his mother the news; but she said that an even larger force was needed, and that there were two commanders of ships, called Úspakr and Bróðir, lying off the west coast of Man who had thirty vessels, and Sitriuc went there to recruit them.

Bróðir had been consecrated a deacon but had lapsed to heathenism. He sported 'a coat of mail no iron could pierce, was tall and strong and his hair was so long that it hung below his belt—it was black.' He similarly agreed to come to Dublin in return for a duplicitous offer from Sitriuc that he too could marry his mother and succeed to a kingdom. Úspakr, on the other hand, was a heathen but now refused to go to war with 'so good a king' as Brian and, taking ten ships with him, instead 'sailed west to Ireland and did not stop till they got to Kankaraborg; Úspakr told King Brján everything he had learned and he was baptised and entrusted himself to the protection of the king.' So Brian then 'made them gather force over all his realm, and the whole host was to come to Dublin in the week before Palm Sunday.'

If, therefore, we ask ourselves why, according to *Njáls saga*, Brian Bóraime marched on Dublin in 1014, the answer it provides is that he did so because he knew of the imminent arrival of a fleet to aid Sitriuc, led by Sigurðr and Bróðir, both of whom were coming to Ireland in expectation of acquiring a kingdom there.

Jarl Sigurðr arrived at Dublin from Orkney with his army on Palm Sunday, Bróðir having already arrived. Bróðir used sorcery to learn how the battle would turn out, the answer being that if it was fought on Friday, Brian would win the victory but die, and that if it was fought before that time, all who were against him would fall. So Bróðir said they should not fight before Friday. Brian 'had come up to the fortified town (*borg*) with his entire army, and on Friday the army issued from the town,' but Brian himself, we are told, refused to fight, because it was Good Friday. Thus *Njáls saga* repeats the assertion of *Orkneyinga saga* regarding the date of the battle, corroborating Marianus Scottus's evidence.

Both hosts arranged themselves in battle array, Bróðir heading one wing with Úlfr *hreða* (Cú Duilig mac Cennétig?) facing him on Brian's side, King Sitriuc on the other wing facing Úspakr and Brian's sons, and

Jarl Sigurðr in the middle facing Kerþjálfaðr (perhaps Brian's grandson Tairdelbach). Sigurð's forces had with them the banner of the black raven made for him by his mother, as described in *Orkneyinga saga*, which brought life to those behind it and death to the man who bore it; and after Sigurðr himself took hold of it he was duly slain.

Soon afterwards King Sitriuc fled before an assault led by Úspakr in which, however, two sons of Brian fell, and with Sitriuc's flight his whole army retreated. Some of Brian's bodyguards went in pursuit, and Bróðir, who had taken refuge in a wood, saw that the king was vulnerable and, rushing past Brian's last few protectors, levelled a blow at him that cut clean through Tadc's arm, severing it and Brian's head, although when Brian's blood spilled on the arm the amputation was reversed. Bróðir was then apprehended and the Irish 'slit open his belly, led him round and round an oak tree, and in this way unwound all his intestines out of his body, and Bróðir did not die before they were all pulled out of him.' When Brian's body was laid out it was found that the head had again grown on the trunk.

There are remarkable parallels here with the Cogadh and with the more embellished Irish annalistic tradition.[17] In *Njáls saga*, Brian is a saintly figure who takes as a foster-child his sworn enemy's son and loves him more than his own offspring, who forgives his outlaws three times, who refuses to do battle on Good Friday, whose blood, falling on his son's amputated arm, can heal it, and whose own head is miraculously rejoined to his body after death. He causes the heathen Úspakr to be baptised, and when Brian is murdered by the apostate Bróðir it is a kind of martyrdom.

The germ of this idea of a saint-king who does not fight but prays and spends Good Friday preparing for Easter is present in Marianus Scottus, the Cogadh and the embellished Annals of Loch Cé. Gormlaith has a small role in the Cogadh in inciting her brother Máelmórda to rebellion, apparently out of shame felt at the subordination of her province of Leinster to Brian's overlordship, and in *Njáls saga* she also helps initiate things but this time incites her son, Sitriuc. The depiction of her is purely misogynistic: she is Brian's jilted ex-wife looking for revenge.

Bródar (Bróðir) is central to things in both traditions. The reference in *Njáls saga* to him having taken refuge in a wood towards the end of the battle is reminiscent of the Cogadh's contention that the Norse forces perished because the incoming tide prevented them from reaching the wood. In *Njáls saga*, Brian meets his death at a remove from the action in the company of his son Tadc; in the Annals of Loch Cé he is with his nephew Conaing. In *Njáls saga*, Bróðir happens upon Brian and Tadc, beheads Brian and chops off Tadc's arm; in the Annals of Loch Cé a lone unnamed Dane escaping from the battle chances upon Brian and Conaing and beheads both. And so on. One can quibble with points of detail throughout, but in general *Njáls saga* presents a record of proceedings at Clontarf that—bearing in mind the distance in time and place from other versions of events—is astonishingly consistent with other reports. And for this reason it is unwise to dismiss it as mere folklore.

Njáls saga and other Scandinavian texts report that in the Hebrides, in Orkney and as far away as Iceland strange visions were seen and miraculous occurrences reported that all who witnessed them knew to be attendant on the shocking events at Clontarf. Before the battle Bróðir and his men were awoken in their ships by a shower of boiling blood falling on their heads, which penetrated even their shields, and a man was found to have died on each one of their vessels. They slept during the day after this but again were woken up by a loud noise and saw their swords leap out of their sheaths, and axes and spears fly about in the air fighting, so that they had to protect themselves; but still many were wounded, and again a man died out of every ship. On the third night they were woken by ravens flying at them, whose beaks and claws were made of iron, and they had to fight them off with their swords. This went on until morning, and again another man had died in every ship. It was eventually explained to him that 'when blood rained on you, therefore shall you shed many men's blood, both your own and others; when you heard a great din, you were shown the crack of doom, and you shall all die speedily; and when weapons fought against you, that must forebode a battle; but when ravens pressed you, that marks the devils in which you put faith, and who will drag you all down to the pains of hell.' In this way the Battle of Clontarf is painted as a contest between Christians and heathens and between good and evil; and it is extraordinary that even in this great Scandinavian epic it is the Irish who are the 'good'.

On Good Friday itself a man in Caithness saw twelve women who had set up a loom, and men's heads were the weights, men's entrails the warp and weft, a sword was the shuttle, and the reeds were arrows. At Svínafell in Iceland blood appeared on a priest's stole on the day of the battle, and on the same day another Icelandic priest saw the ocean beside the altar, and many awful sights occurring in it. In Orkney a man thought he saw Jarl Sigurðr and mounted his horse to ride to meet him, and men saw them meeting under a brae, but they were never seen again. Jarl Gilli in the Hebrides dreamed that a man came to him and told him he had just returned from Ireland and quoted the verses that famously end 'Brian fell and was victorious (*Brjánn fell ok helt velli*),'[18] echoing *Orkneyinga saga*'s summing up of the fateful day with the pithy verdict that 'King Brian fell with victory and glory (*Brjánn konungr fell með sigri ok gagni*).'[19] In doing so they captured the awful contradiction that baffles us to this day: how can we say that Brian was victorious in the Battle of Clontarf when he lost his own life in the act?

Conclusion ∼

THE LEGACY OF BRIAN AND CLONTARF

Whatever his other achievements, Brian Bóraime is remembered today for the Battle of Clontarf, and especially for being the hero-figure who led his people to victory over their would-be Norse conquerors. In some respects, in the generations since Brian's day the Irish have thought of 1014 as the mediaeval equivalent of 1916: if the bloody execution of the leaders of the Easter Rising were lives sacrificed in the cause of Ireland, so the Battle of Clontarf, taking place on Good Friday, had associations with Christian martyrdom, in the form of King Brian's death in his hour of victory over the heathen Norse.

Of course there have long been those with misgivings about this. A full seventy-five years have passed since the influential historian Father John Ryan published his lengthy essay called simply 'The Battle of Clontarf' in which the traditional interpretation of the battle was unceremoniously debunked:

> It is, I think, true to say that no battle in Irish history has impressed itself more deeply on the national imagination than the Battle of Clontarf. Even the dullest schoolboy knows, or fancies that he knows, something of the issue and the consequences. The name of Brian Boruma is more familiar to Irish people than the name of any other Irish King, with the possible exception of Niall of the Nine Hostages. And the situation has been thus since the morrow of Brian's death ...

... In the course of the eleventh century, however, the view seems to have gained universal acceptance that the Battle of Clontarf was the great decisive struggle par excellence of Irish history. Brian in the retrospect was everywhere acclaimed as a national hero and his unique stature as High-King joyfully recognised. He had been in command, at least nominally, at Clontarf. With him were mighty forces. The battle had lasted the livelong day, almost an incredible length for a single uninterrupted encounter in that simple age. Among the princes and nobles in particular the number slain had been extremely high. The Norse were a substantial section of the opposing force, and in the mellow haze of popular imagination the battle tended to be transformed into a clear-cut issue, Irish versus Norse, with the former victorious. Even in the Northern countries the battle passed rapidly from history into saga. And as a crowning feature in a never-to-be-forgotten day was the death of the venerated High-King, a tragedy that lost nothing of its poignant drama in the hands of poet and storyteller.

As in more recent times the question, 'Where were you in 1916?' might mean much to the interrogated, so in the course of the eleventh century the question, 'Where were you in 1014?' meant much to the chroniclers. Thus, when opportunity offered, the names of kings who ruled their states when Clontarf was fought were slipped quietly into Brian's army! ...

National instinct is rarely at fault in matters of such significance. Clontarf was undoubtedly a great battle. All the stronger is the reason why its character should not be misconceived. In the first place it was not simply a battle between the Irish and the Norse. Brian's army was not a national army in the accepted sense, but an army of Munstermen, increased by levies from two small south Connacht states. The opposing force was not an army of Norse, but an army composed of Leinster and Norse troops, in which the former were certainly the predominant element and may have constituted two-thirds of the whole. Nor was the battle a struggle between paganism and Christianity, again because the majority of the troops opposed to Brian were Irish Catholics like himself, whilst a fair proportion of the Norse had already been converted ...

The battle, furthermore, was not a contest for the sovereignty of Ireland, save in a negative sense. Success for the Leinster-Norse allies might mean the beginning of the end of Dalcassian rule, possibly its immediate termination. It does not follow that the Norse or the Leinstermen, or the Norse and Leinstermen combined (should the alliance be permanently maintained), could count the kingship of Ireland among the fruits of victory...

The allies, therefore, while struggling against Brian's hegemony, were not fighting directly for succession to him in the High-Kingship. Still less were the Norse, as distinct from the Leinstermen, waging war for such an objective, which must have lain outside the range of their wildest dreams...

Victory at Clontarf would mean—at any rate for the moment—relief from Munster suzerainty and Munster political pressure. It would result in increased prestige for Dublin and Leinster and possibly secure for both a weightier word in the counsels of the nation. It would not mean that either Sitric or Maelmórda, no matter how far each supported the other, would become King of Ireland, a dignity for which neither showed particular aptitude.

Fundamentally, then, the issue at Clontarf was the age-old determination of the Leinstermen to maintain their independence against the High-King. In this cause they had fought bitterly and stubbornly against the Uí Néill for centuries. Their resolve never to submit to the upstart Munster High-King was, if possible, sterner. One with them in policy were the Norse of Dublin, a state small, indeed, in extent and weak in man power, but rich out of all proportion to its size and skilful in securing mercenary aid from willing kin. This alien challenge, with all that it implied of hostility to the Irish political system and to the Irish people, thus became a secondary issue. In Brian's army there was, it need hardly be said, incomparably more intense feeling against the Foreigners than against the Leinstermen, and this fact, when Clontarf was a glorious memory, was so emphasised that the main issue was overshadowed. By common consent it fell in time completely into the background. Hence the popular tradition of Clontarf as wholly an Irish-Norse struggle.[1]

The result of this and other revisionist readings of the Battle of Clontarf[2] has been that nowadays few 'serious' scholars reckon it as much more than the culmination of a rebellion against Brian by the insubordinate king of Leinster and his Dublin sidekicks. But there are problems with this interpretation of Clontarf as nothing more than an (albeit major) inter-provincial quarrel that came to a bloody head. While of course the traditional belief, that the Vikings were banished for ever from Ireland following defeat at Clontarf, is not true either (as Dublin and the other Norse enclaves were to remain inhabited, wealthy, and powerful), there must surely have been something else to the events of Good Friday 1014.

Clontarf was a victory for Brian, even though he died: that is the almost unanimous view of our sources; and the only way in which that could be true is if, notwithstanding Brian's death, his forces achieved what they wanted to achieve. In this way they could reluctantly accept his loss as the price that had to be paid for what had been secured, or averted, on that perilous day. And it is surely a fact that what Brian secured or averted—or was thought by contemporaries to have secured or averted—is linked to contemporary events that we are inclined to ignore.

SO WHAT REALLY HAPPENED AT CLONTARF?

The most sober contemporary account of Clontarf is the one in the Annals of Inisfallen; but even this says that 'there was a slaughter of the Foreigners of the Western World in the same battle (*ocus ar Gall iarthair domain isi[n] chath chetna*).' The hardly more sensational Annals of Ulster have it that Brian's opponents were the Leinstermen, Dubliners and 'a like number of the Foreigners of Lochlainn (*a coimlin do Ghallaib Lochlainne*).' The more elaborate account in the Annals of Boyle has Brian marching to Dublin 'against the Black Foreigners and Denmarkians (*inagid Gall glas & [D]anmargach*).' The Cogadh was written almost within living memory of the battle, and it too repeatedly includes among Brian's enemies at Clontarf 'the Danars and Denmarkians (*Danair ocus Anmargaigh*).' A poem attributed to Flann Mainistrech (died 1056) and therefore composed within a generation of the battle has Brian's opponents as 'a band of Danars of Denmark (*drong Danar Danmarg*).'[3]

The emergence of this terminology is interesting. The term *Danair* means 'Danes'; and although Vikings had been in and around Ireland since 795 we first find Danair in Irish waters only in the generation leading up to Clontarf.[4] This was what has been called Britain's Second Viking Age, when, from 980 onwards, raids resumed in England after a lull of nearly a hundred years; and although the severest assaults may have been in the east of England, the Irish Sea region was a frantic warzone.[5] Danair or Danes are first mentioned as arriving on the coast of Dál Riata in 986, when they raided Iona—surely from Scandinavia or the Northern Isles—and they attacked the Isle of Man with Gofraid mac Arailt the following year.[6] This was three years after Gofraid and Brian Bóraime had exchanged hostages in Waterford before a planned assault on Dublin, which would make Brian an ally, at least indirectly, of those Danes at this point.

One of the leaders of the Danair was Óláfr Tryggvason, who would go on to rule as king of Norway from about 995 to about 999. One source claims that Óláfr was born in Orkney and another that his wife, Gyða, was a daughter of Amlaíb Cuarán of Dublin, making him the brother-in-law of King Sitriuc (table 4; above, page 147); and we are also told he had a base in Dublin from which his raiding in the Irish Sea region was conducted.[7] If this is true it might explain why it is that when Iona was pillaged in 986 the abbot 'suffered red martyrdom from the Danair in Dublin (*do dul dergmartra lasna Danuroib a n-Ath Clíath*),' as much as to suggest that the raiders transported him south to Dublin.[8]

To begin with, Óláfr was allied with another leader of the Danair, in the person of Sveinn *Tjúguskegg* (Swein Forkbeard), king of Denmark and overlord of Norway. According to Adam of Bremen, when Sveinn was exiled, perhaps in 992 or 993, he took refuge with the king, or *a* king, of the Scoti (*rex Scothorum benigne recepit ibidemque Suein*).[9] It is pointless to speculate on the identity of this king: we just need to remind ourselves that in this period the term Scoti applied to the Irish as much as to the Scots (which is why Brian was *Imperator Scotorum*). In 995, eight years after the strike on the Isle of Man by Brian's ally Gofraid mac Arailt in 987, Sveinn Forkbeard was in the Irish Sea and similarly attacking Man.[10] It is rather extraordinary that the king of the English, Æðelræd II (Ethelred 'the Unready'), also directed an assault on Man in 1000.[11] It is most unlikely that these are casual buccaneering raids: the Isle of Man seems to have been a battleground at this time, ripe for conquest, and Æðelræd's offensive in 1000 suggests it was then in the hands of Danair favourable to Sveinn.

But Sveinn was now about to set his sights on the conquest of England. He led a protracted operation there in 1003, returning to Denmark only in 1005. There were devastating Danish raids on England nearly every year between 1006 and 1012, culminating in Sveinn's full-scale invasion in July 1013. He based himself at Gainsborough in Lincolnshire and rapidly secured the hostages, as a sign of submission, of the inhabitants of northern England, and as he moved south through the east midlands he secured further submissions, and then approached London.

London held out against him for some time, and it was only after he had gone to Bath and secured the submissions and hostages of the south-west that the Londoners finally yielded. By Christmas, King Æðelræd was heading to exile in Normandy, Sveinn was declared king, and England had been conquered.

Perhaps it is only a coincidence that Sitriuc of Dublin, who had been Brian's faithful vassal since 1000, broke out in rebellion at the time of Sveinn's invasion of England. If it is not coincidence, perhaps he did so believing that the time was ripe, now that potential Danish allies were in the ascendant across the Irish Sea. Late that year Brian placed Dublin under a siege, but he abandoned his blockade at Christmas and withdrew home, at the very moment when Sveinn snatched the English crown. Again there may be no connection, or it may be that Brian did so knowing that the triumphant Danes in England were now in a position to help out their Dublin friends.

Sveinn's reign over England ended after a mere five weeks when he died at Gainsborough on 3 February, whereupon the Danes chose his younger son, Knútr, as king of England. But the English sent for Æðelræd, who returned at some time in Lent (10 March to 25 April), and Knútr was banished, withdrawing from England without a fight at some time in April 1014.

At this point Brian was on his march to Dublin, an advance that reached a climax in the great battle on Good Friday, 23 April. We do not know how quickly news passed back and forth across the Irish Sea at this period, but we can be pretty certain that those who gathered for the Battle of Clontarf knew of Sveinn's death ten weeks earlier, and they probably knew that Æðelræd had now been restored and that the attempt to have the young Knútr succeed him had failed (for now). In other words, in late April 1014 there were Danish chieftains and large numbers of Danish warriors who had seen their conquest of England slip away before their eyes. Surely some of them then enlisted with their old partner in crime Sigurðr of Orkney, whose new earldom, it has been credibly argued, was 'a creation of the Danish empire'[12] and who had a great scheme to put their suddenly underemployed conquering talents to good use. Together they would make up for lost English ground in what they were no doubt promised would be a walk-over in Ireland. Instead, of course, their voyage led only to the 'slaughter of the Foreigners of the Western World' at Clontarf. And that slaughter is what earned Brian his lasting reputation; it is because of it that the poet could write: *Brjánn fell ok helt velli,* 'Brian fell and was victorious.'

In other words, it is not the case that the Battle of Clontarf was primarily the climax of Leinster's rebellion again Brian Bóraime. Brian marched on *Dublin* in the autumn of 1013 and laid *Dublin* under a siege, and marched on it again in the spring of 1014—much as he had done before the Battle of Glenn Máma in 999—because Dublin was the focus of resistance to him. Yes, the Leinstermen threw in their lot with the Dubliners, but there is no evidence that the Leinstermen were dominant over them at this juncture. On the contrary, what evidence we have suggests that the Uí Dúnlainge overkingship of Leinster had dwindled away to almost nothing by 1014. Indeed the tripartite rotation of the title 'king of Leinster' between the three branches of Uí Dúnlainge, which had followed a regular enough pattern for three hundred years, went the way of the rotating kingship of Tara between Northern and Southern Uí Néill at that point. It was faltering before Clontarf and collapsed entirely four years after the battle when Sitriuc blinded, in Dublin, the incumbent, Bran, son of his great Clontarf ally (and maternal uncle) Máelmórda, so that within a few decades Uí Dúnlainge were permanently ousted from the overkingship by the long-overshadowed Uí Chennselaig in the south of the province.[13]

It is unlikely, therefore, that we will grasp the full significance of the Battle of Clontarf if we focus on the insubordination of the king of Leinster. There seems to have been a great deal more going on than that, and it is not only later sources that emphasise that it was Sitriuc mac Amlaíb who had the upper hand in the Dublin-Leinster axis in opposition to Brian. But Sitriuc had evidently learnt the lesson of his shocking defeat at Brian's hands in 999–1000, which had led to the unprecedented domination of the town of Dublin—including its military, naval and economic resources—by an unwelcome king of Munster for the next thirteen years. In retrospect, it is not the conspiracy against Brian that burst out in 1013 that is surprising but rather the fact that it took so long.

Sitriuc's father, Amlaíb Cuarán, had been one of the great figures throughout the archipelago in the tenth century who, over a forty-year career, at various times held power in Dublin and a large swathe of adjacent territory, as well as in York and Northumbria, and most probably also in Man and the Western Isles; indeed, when he died in 981 it was in retirement at Iona in the Western Isles, shortly after his defeat by Máel Sechnaill mac Domnaill of the Southern Uí Néill in a major battle at, of all places, Tara.

The Battle of Tara was an important moment. Surely it took place in 980 because that was the year in which the great Northern Uí Néill possessor of the kingship of Tara, Domnall ua Néill, died; and surely too it took place at Tara because succession to the kingship of Tara was at stake. It has been argued that Amlaíb Cuarán sought the kingship himself.[14] That may or may not be so (although it may be relevant that he had slain Domnall ua Néill's son and heir Muirchertach three years earlier).[15] At the very least he was attempting to extend his sway over the eastern half of Uí Néill territory in Brega at the expense of Máel Sechnaill's western half in Mide. Big ambitions were certainly involved at Tara. The numbers embroiled on both sides were great, and the slaughter considerable, the annals listing among the many dead six Irish kings or lords and three Norse chieftains. We are told that Amlaíb sent into battle the forces of both Dublin and the Isles (*for Gallaibh Atho Cliath & na n-Indsedh*).[16] The latter are rarely referred to when the Dublin army is mentioned, even though Amlaíb may have exercised some kind of hegemony there, and so it seems likely that an army from Man or the Western Isles, or both, was specially drafted in in 980 to help Amlaíb achieve his objective.

That is as much as the Annals of Ulster record; but the Four Masters, Tigernach and Chronicon Scotorum have an extraordinary tale to tell of what the victor in the battle, Máel Sechnaill, did next, and they now call him king of Tara for the first time. He did not bear this title going into the Battle of Tara, and the writer (for it is one account, replicated in all three texts) clearly implies that Máel Sechnaill secured the title by his victory over Amlaíb. This very point is made in an elegy ascribed to the poet Flann ua Rónáin, to the effect that 'the Foreigners gave battle at Tara, | a fine musical household went to the attack; | the Irish under slender Máel Sechnaill | make the merry bright well-made king on the spot (*Cath Temra tucsatar Gaill;* | *at-eth teglach bregda binn:* | *Gaídil fá Mael Sechnaill seng,* | *rígait ann in ngelchruinn ngrinn*)', the implication being that it was his leadership on this great occasion that secured him the kingship.[17]

According to the annals, Máel Sechnaill then marched on Dublin, together with the king of Ulaid—who, as the possessor of a considerable fleet, probably blockaded the town from Dublin Bay—and laid siege to the town for three days and nights, whereupon they 'carried from there the hostages of Ireland, including Domnall Clóen, king of Leinster, and the pledges of the Uí Néill likewise.' Obtaining his demand for two thousand cattle, together with jewels and treasures, Máel Sechnaill secured 'the freedom of the Uí Néill, from the Shannon to the sea, from tribute (*cen cháin*) and announced the famous rising: "Let every one of the Irish who is in the Foreigners' territory in bondage and oppression come forth to his own country for peace and comfort." That captivity was the Babylonian captivity of Ireland: it was next to the captivity of Hell (*Is and immorro for-fuacair Mael Sechnaill in eseirghi n-airrdirc: Gach aen do Gaedelaib fuil a crich Gall a n-dairi & docraite tait ass dia tir ar cind sidha & sochair. Ba sí bruit Babilone na h-Erenn in bruit-sin. Ba tanaisti na bruiti ifirn*).'[18]

We have no idea when this was written, and it is so effusive that there is a strong possibility that it was written later and inserted in the annals from a literary-type source written to glorify Máel Sechnaill. But whoever wrote it had an extraordinary conception of the dominance of Amlaíb Cuarán. He was holding the king of Leinster as a hostage, in effect therefore claiming to be his overlord. He had secured too the hostages, or the pledges of the hostages, of the Southern Uí Néill from the Shannon to the Irish Sea. That is presumably the author's rationale for not calling Máel Sechnaill king of Tara until he had triumphed over Amlaíb in the battle of the same name. If Amlaíb was not *de facto* king of Tara himself going into the battle (assuming the incumbent, Domnall ua Néill, had already died), he was the obstacle in the way of Máel

Sechnaill securing the title, and it is remarkable to think what might have happened if Máel Sechnaill had lost and Amlaíb won.

But Amlaíb did not win. The Annals of Ulster say, in a significant statement, that the outcome of the Battle of Tara was the ejection of the 'power of the Foreigners from Ireland (*nert Gall a h-Erinn*),' as a result of which Dublin remained largely quiescent under Máel Sechnaill's overlordship thereafter. Under the terms of the Bleanphuttoge agreement of 997, however, the king of Tara ceded suzerainty over Leth Moga (the southern half of Ireland, including Dublin) to Brian Bóraime, although it was going to be up to Brian to procure Dublin's submission for himself. That presented an opportunity for the reigning king of Dublin, Amlaíb Cuarán's son Sitriuc, to reassert his dynasty's former autonomy; but his hopes were spectacularly crushed by Brian's victory over him at Glenn Máma two years later, another pivotal battle that, had it gone the other way, would surely have put paid to Brian's chances of national dominance.

As it is, this humiliation of Sitriuc meant that the Dubliners had to tolerate Munster domination until such time as an opportunity came to break free. That opportunity did not come until 1013, amidst the upheaval of the Danish conquest of England, when change was in the air, when unparalleled numbers of Scandinavian and Insular troops and warships were at hand, battle-ready and confident of the new possibilities. These are the men—under the raven banner of Jarl Sigurðr of Orkney, manning the vessels of Bróðir of York or the Isle of Man— whom Sitriuc of Dublin recruited to his cause and who lined up on the shores of Dublin Bay in April 2014 to take on his Munster oppressor, as Brian must have seemed.

There is no telling, at this remove, what they hoped to achieve, but if England could be won and lost Ireland surely seemed a sitting duck. And the question that was asked of Brian on that Good Friday was whether he would crumple as Æðelræd the Unready had done in the face of Sveinn Forkbeard the previous summer. That he did not was his claim to fame. That he gave even his own life to the task was his indisputably remarkable achievement.

THE AFTERMATH OF CLONTARF

The after-effects of the death of Brian and of his intended heir, Murchad, were great, although our main sources of information, the annals, are written in such a flavourless way that, on the surface, it is as if life went on as before. But Ireland had lost its dominant political figure, and whatever arrangements he had made for a succession (which, given his age, was inevitable sooner rather than later) were thwarted. All eyes, no doubt, were on Dál Cais to see if it would throw up from among Brian's kindred a worthy heir, but the problem was that Brian had two sons in a position to challenge for the kingship. One was Gormlaith's son Donnchad and the other was Tadc, whose mother was Echrad, daughter of Carlus of Uí Áeda Odba, although Donnchad seems to have been the more senior and therefore immediately sought to rule. Cogadh Gáedhel re Gallaibh never so much as mentions Tadc—despite the fact that his son, Tairdelbach (died 1086), and grandson Muirchertach (died 1119) would later recover the high-kingship, and one or other of them is likely to have been reigning when the Cogadh was composed. Instead the only version of the text that deals with the aftermath of the Battle of Clontarf depicts Donnchad as a kind of Oisín i ndiaidh na Féinne, who picks up the pieces after the destruction of Dál Cais forces at Clontarf, secures the absolute loyalty of his weary, wounded and dying men and shows extraordinary fortitude in leading the survivors home, through the lands of faithless traitors and rebels, to Cenn Corad.[19]

The other problem for Dál Cais was that they had been dominant in Munster only for the previous half century, and their former Eóganacht masters were bound to try to stage a recovery. Therefore, within months if not weeks of the Battle of Clontarf we find the much-depleted army of Donnchad mac Briain again at war with the Eóganacht Raithlind and fighting, and losing, an initial contest with his half-brother Tadc. Although Tadc joined Donnchad at Limerick in 1015 in successfully withstanding an Eóganacht invasion,[20] which may have put paid to their rebellion, internal opposition remained. Donnchad lost his right hand in an attempted assassination in 1019 and was complicit in the murder of Tadc in 1023.[21] This, though, settled the issue of the succession to Brian until Tadc's then teenage son Tairdelbach was in a position to raise the issue again in the next generation (table 3; above, page 100).

For a brief period in the 1020s, therefore, Donnchad mac Briain began to look as if he would re-create his father's ascendancy, obtaining the hostages of Connacht in 1025 and reaching a pinnacle of success the following year when he replicated on a more modest scale one of Brian's great circuits, going north to Mide then eastwards from there to Brega, then succeeding in doing what his forces had failed to do after Clontarf, marching on Dublin and spending three days with no opposition, having his camp beside the *dún* or fortress, and from there marching into Leinster and Osraige and, more to the point, obtaining the hostages of all these five kingdoms in a sign of submission to him.[22] It was probably after this triumph that he commissioned the ornamental shrine of the Stowe or Lorrha Missal on which he is depicted as RIG HEREND ('king of Ireland') (plate 25);[23] but it was a shallow boast, as he had no prospect of securing hegemony over the North, and his fortunes began to dip thereafter (plates 26 and 27).

Donnchad's difficulty was that, although his father had fundamentally changed the rules of Irish kingship, so that men of no great pedigree could look forward to national supremacy if only they were energetic enough and wealthy enough and lucky enough, old habits die hard, and so there was a natural tendency on the part of the Uí Néill to want to resuscitate their wilted paramountcy. Thus, at the same time that Donnchad mac Briain was trying to hold things together following the death of his father and his older brother at Clontarf, the most senior surviving leader in the country, Brian's predecessor Máel Sechnaill mac Domnaill of the Southern Uí Néill, naturally attempted to reassert his dominance.[24] And it may have been Máel Sechnaill's panicky efforts in these years to make the case for his reinstatement that lie behind the contemporary production of so much pseudo-historical propaganda, material that emphasises the Uí Néill's unassailable claim by force of supposed tradition and birthright to an immemorial high-kingship.[25] Furthermore, Brian had discovered how difficult it was to keep the Northern Uí Néill compliant, and they too sought to fill the vacuum left by his departure.

Within a year of the Battle of Clontarf, therefore, Flaithbertach Ua Néill of Cenél nEógain had come south. While the annals remain sympathetic to Máel Sechnaill—the former high-king now trying to turn back the clock—and paint the northern king as his ally, marching with him to Dublin to burn the *dún* and then invading Leinster and Osraige in 1015 to obtain their hostages,[26] there was not an awful lot to be gained by Flaithbertach in propping up the aged high-king. And so a second assault on Leinster that same year is said to have been led by

Ua Néill, having the armies of Mide and Brega at his command,[27] as if *he* was now supreme; and even though Máel Sechnaill could rouse himself to invade Leinster again in 1016, including this time the southern lands of Uí Chennselaig, and twice invaded Osraige that year, as well as marching north to take the hostages of the Ulaid, there is an air of Sisyphus about his new lease of life. True, he defeated the Dubliners in battle in 1017, but it was at Obda in Co. Meath, suggesting that they were closing in on him rather than the reverse, and by the following year he was at war with the Northern Uí Néill (*Coccadh etir Maol Sechlainn & h-Uí Néill an Tuaisceirt*),[28] that word *coccadh* ('war') indicating a major offensive, which can only have been required if his overkingship of the Uí Néill, north and south, had been denied.

This may have bolstered him. In 1020 it is reported that he was joined by Flaithbertach Ua Néill and Donnchad mac Briain of Munster and by Ua Ruairc of Bréifne when they marched to the Shannon and secured the hostages of Connacht, which were then handed over to Máel Sechnaill,[29] a significant acknowledgment of his royal status, if it is to be believed. And yet within a year he is again reported to have been campaigning against the Northern Uí Néill,[30] and within a year of that he was dead, surely aware that he was the last of a line.

While annals favourable to Máel Sechnaill have obits calling him the 'high-king of Ireland (*airdri Erenn*)', the Munster Annals of Inisfallen will stretch only as far as 'king of Tara', and it was to the latter title alone that his fissiparous Southern Uí Néill heirs aspired.[31] This means that the separation Brian had put into effect between the kingship of Ireland and the kingship of Tara proved lasting. A king-list attributed to the eleventh-century historian and poet Gilla Cóemáin ends with the reign of Brian, as if to imply that Máel Sechnaill's supposed restoration after Clontarf was a figment of his propagandists' imaginations.[32] Still, when Máel Sechnaill died in 1022 he was, feasibly, king of Ireland, if we take it that his various campaigns in Leinster and Osraige and against the Dubliners and the Ulaid had secured him their hostages, and that when he led Donnchad mac Briain of Munster, Art Ua Ruairc of Bréifne and Flaithbertach Ua Néill of the Northern Uí Néill to the Shannon in 1020 to accept the hostages of Connacht he had a full set of submissions (map 1). He was also, feasibly, king of Tara, in the sense of being supreme among the Uí Néill. But nobody after him held both those titles. When later Northern Uí Néill dynasts, such as Domnall Mac Lochlainn (died 1121) and his grandson Muirchertach (died 1166), put forward a credible case to be considered king of Ireland, neither bothered claiming the kingship of Tara, which, for what it was worth, was the exclusive property of Máel Sechnaill's descendants. And although Máel Sechnaill himself was shortly to be succeeded as king of Clann Cholmáin of Mide by his underachieving grandson Conchobar (died 1073), who claimed also to be king of Tara, it would have been pointless pretending that he was similarly king of Ireland, and he never did.

The conclusion to be reached, therefore, is that Brian's intrusion into the high-kingship was revolutionary. Indeed at the time when Gilla Cóemáin composed his poem on (as he calculated it) the forty-eight men who were 'in the high-kingship of Ireland (*i n-ardrígi na Herend*)' from the time of St Patrick onwards, he seemed convinced, as we have seen, that Brian was the last of them, as if in the post-Brian age the very institution was no more. He would be proved wrong—and Brian himself was to produce one or two worthy heirs to the title—but we can forgive him perhaps his basic point, which is that Brian was the last of the greats, that if one were to think of the high-kingship as a linear progression from the dawn of Ireland's Christian era onwards it reached its apogee in Brian, and he came closer to making the ideal real than any of his Uí Néill predecessors whose creation it had been.

IRELAND AND ITS NEIGHBOURS AFTER CLONTARF

Shifting our focus to the wider political scene, if the career of Brian and its climax at Clontarf teach us anything it is that we cannot afford to be blind to the broad landscape against which Irish politics in that age were played out. As we have seen, for instance, the titles that annalists give individuals, in their obituary notices in particular, are frequently exaggerated but rarely invented. As the object was to sing the praises of the deceased, there was no room for a claim that bordered on the ridiculous, and there is usually therefore more than a germ of truth in the title used. So when Brian is accorded in his obit, among his lesser titles, that of 'high-king ... of the Welsh (*ardrí ... Bretan*)', it constitutes evidence of interests there, although it is very difficult to know exactly what they might be. The man who ended the efforts of Brian's son Donnchad to secure the high-kingship was Diarmait mac Máel na mBó, who was not from the

Uí Néill but, like Brian, an upstart from the South Leinster lineage of Uí Chennselaig (map 5).[33] He never gained supremacy throughout Ireland, but at his death in 1072, like Brian (and only Brian), he was also described by an Irish annalist as 'king of the Welsh'. What is more, the Welsh annals have a remarkable and unusually glowing obituary notice of this Leinster king. Clearly, therefore, Diarmait mac Máel na mBó, like Brian before him, was heavily involved in Welsh affairs.

It is notable that when Cynan ab Iago, the would-be ruler of Gwynedd (North Wales), fled across the Irish Sea in or after 1039 he married into the dynasty of Sitriuc Silkenbeard of Dublin, and the product of that marriage was his famous son Gruffudd ap Cynan (died 1137), who was later to establish stable rule for his family in North Wales.[34] It is perfectly conceivable that the Irish annals labelled Diarmait mac Máel na mBó 'king of the Welsh' for no greater reason than that he had championed Cynan ab Iago's cause with a view to securing the restoration of his dynastic line in Gwynedd; and we can envisage King Diarmait providing Cynan with sanctuary in Ireland and military resources for coup attempts across the Irish Sea.

Diarmait certainly had a record in this kind of patronage. When they were in exile in Ireland in the winter of 1051/2 it was the king of Leinster who played host to two of the sons of Earl Godwin of Wessex, Leofwine and Harold, and following the latter's death at the Battle of Hastings in 1066 at least two of his sons in turn fled to Ireland. Diarmait again provided a fleet in 1068, which they used in an unsuccessful assault on Bristol and the harrying of Devon and Somerset and in a repeat attempt to recover ground in the West Country in 1069—which met with such resistance that it was all Harold's sons could do to make it back in one piece to Leinster, never to be heard of again.[35]

That the Godwinssons' relationship with King Diarmait was similar to that which he seems to have had with the family of Cynan ab Iago of Gwynedd—what might traditionally have been viewed as the bond between a lord and his clients—is suggested by an event that occurred in 1068. Munster had recently obtained a worthy successor to Brian Bóraime in the person of his grandson Tairdelbach ua Briain (died 1086) (table 3). Although he was a protégé of Diarmait mac Máel na mBó, Toirdelbach's gratitude was short-lived, and in 1068 he led an expedition into Leinster to assert pre-eminence over his erstwhile patron,[36] obtaining as a trophy from Diarmait what the Irish annals call 'the standard of the king of the English'. The most likely identity of this treasured artefact is the battle-standard borne by Harold at Hastings and bestowed by his sons on Diarmait mac Máel na mBó, presumably as some kind of acknowledgement of his overlordship, after they had found refuge in Ireland under his protection.

It was most probably direct domination of the Hiberno-Scandinavian settlement at Wexford that first manoeuvred Diarmait mac Máel na mBó's long-ailing dynasty into a position of prominence and power throughout the south-eastern quadrant of Ireland. But Diarmait's great leap forward, what propelled him to national importance and gave him a recognition factor in England and Wales, was the fact that in 1052 he succeeded in adding Dublin and its hinterland, Fine Gall ('the territory of the Foreigners'), to his personal domain.[37] Its importance lies in the fact that Diarmait expelled the Hiberno-Norse king of Dublin and appropriated the kingship of Dublin to himself. Brian had never done this. What Brian and others had been content with, it seems, was a relatively undemanding assertion of authority, whereby Dublin's ruler merely submitted and handed over hostages and booty but remained on, or soon reappeared, as king. There is therefore under way a process of intensification of Irish lordship over the Hiberno-Norse, which Brian had greatly accelerated but which was now stepping up a gear.

And several consequences flowed from Diarmait's action. Firstly, to all intents and purposes, in 1052 Dublin was transformed from a Viking beachhead on Leinster soil into the capital of that province. Secondly, boosted by its acquisition, Diarmait mac Máel na mBó and his South Leinster dynasty of Uí Chennselaig were able, after three centuries in the wilderness, to displace their North Leinster counterparts, the Uí Dúnlainge, as overkings of all Leinster.[38] Thirdly (in the light of the precedent it set, as we shall see), he then proceeded to bestow Dublin on his favoured son, Murchad, who ruled from Dublin under his father's remote direction.[39] And fourthly, in exploiting the maritime gateway that Dublin provided, Murchad invaded the Isle of Man in 1061 and exacted tribute from its inhabitants, thereby extending the Leinster dynasty's lordship to encompass this transmarine satellite, no doubt emulating long-standing Viking practice and perhaps also a hegemony that lay behind Brian's adoption of the title *Imperator Scotorum*.[40]

Murchad died as 'king of the Foreigners' in 1070, and when his father followed him to the grave two years later the annalists recognised him as king of Dublin and of Innse Gall, the Gaelic term for the Hebrides and Man. Apparently control of Dublin provided a key with the potential to unlock access to specific overseas territory.

It was control of Dublin after 1052 that provided Diarmait mac Máel na mBó with access to the resources to take the war to his rival province-kings beyond Leinster's borders and stake a claim to being king of all Ireland. Like Brian, he was not of Uí Néill stock, but since Brian had exposed the irrelevance of such a prerequisite Diarmait was now to take full advantage of this new equal-opportunities era. By the time of his death in 1072 he had become the most successful Irish king since Brian. He was king of Leinster and of the Hiberno-Norse bases at Wexford and Dublin and, having obtained submissions from neighbouring Osraige and Munster, was ruler of Leth Moga, the southern half of Ireland.

Unfortunately for the Leinstermen's hopes of elevating themselves to a position of paramountcy throughout Ireland, while attempting an offensive into Leth Cuinn (the northern half) by gaining overlordship of the Southern Uí Néill, Diarmait met his end there in the Battle of Odba in 1072.

But it was because of his achievements in emulating Brian in this inter-provincial game of snakes and ladders that Diarmait mac Máel na mBó was described in an (admittedly slightly retrospective) obit as 'king of Ireland with opposition (*rí hÉrend co fressabra*).'[41] This is a term coined after the Uí Néill ascendancy had crumbled, intended to provide a dispassionate depiction—in so far as that could be expected from retained mandarins—of the new style of province-king who bid for, while rarely achieving, unopposed mastery over the whole island. Although the title did not exist in his day, it was in effect what Brian was for most of the dozen years during which he professed to be high-king. In that sense, therefore, the new age that Brian ushered in embodies a new concept of Irish kingship, the age of the *rí hÉrend co fressabra*, 'king of Ireland with opposition', and it was Diarmait mac Máel na mBó's plucky emulation of Brian that won him the title. And, as with the great landmarks in Brian's career, it is remarkable how big a part Dublin played.

It should come as no surprise, therefore, that no sooner had Diarmat met his end at Odba in 1072 than Brian's grandson Tairdelbach ua Briain marched his armies on Dublin and accepted the offer of its kingship from the Hiberno-Norse. The very fact of doing so seems to have secured him a place in posterity as the second *rí hÉrend co fressabra*, 'king of Ireland with opposition'. And, just as Diarmait had appointed his son Murchad to rule the city and its territory under him, by 1075 the annals confirm that Tairdelbach had followed suit, and his son and successor Muirchertach (died 1119) is recorded as having taken over the kingship of Dublin. He was in effect serving an apprenticeship that in time would qualify him to succeed as the third *rí hÉrend co fressabra*.[42]

While Muirchertach Ua Briain—Brian's great-grandson and therefore from the first generation to bear the name Ua Briain (O'Brien) as a surname (table 3; above, page 100)—ruled and probably resided in Dublin, there seems little doubt that Tairdelbach appointed another son, Diarmait (died 1115), to govern the Viking-founded town of Waterford, and that he himself had one of his royal residences in Limerick, the third of the great urban achievements of the Vikings in Ireland. It was Brian who began this after he subsumed Limerick into his domain early on in his reign, and therefore he was undoubtedly the first Irish king to appreciate fully the advantages of urbanisation. And, as the last quarter of the eleventh century began, there must have seemed every reason to suppose that Brian's grandsons and great-grandsons would prove successful in his object of attaining durable rule over Ireland. It is certainly ironic, therefore—given the traditional depiction of Brian as having driven the Vikings out of Ireland—that it was his family that above all others was the champion of the towns, those Trojan horses inherited from the Vikings, making them quintessentially their own for the purpose of familial and dynastic aggrandisement.

As we have seen, at the height of the Viking Age the Uí Néill had been resilient enough to thwart the emergence of permanent Viking bases in Leth Cuinn, while their southern counterparts had had to tolerate what they could not force out. But by the time of Brian's death at Clontarf those footholds were flourishing towns, the greatest concentrations of wealth on the island; and the southern kings prospered through transaction with them, as the Uí Néill, bemoaning perhaps their short-sighted inhospitality, saw their former vigour wither for lack of resources and their ancient primacy scorned.

As with Diarmait mac Máel na mBó before them, the domestic elevation of the Uí Briain consequent on their command of the towns seems to have conferred an immediate international profile. It was to the court of Brian's grandson Tairdelbach, the annals tell us, that a delegation of Jews repaired in 1079, presumably seeking leave to establish themselves there, although they were rapidly sent away.[43] With the profile came responsibilities. When the clergy and people of Dublin came together in 1074 to elect as their bishop Gilla Pátraic, an Irish monk schooled under St Wulfstan at Worcester, Archbishop Lanfranc of Canterbury consecrated him, sending him back to Dublin with a letter for its Hiberno-Norse leader and another for its overlord, Tairdelbach ua Briain.[44] It is a letter of praise for this peace-loving and just ruler (as Gilla Pátraic had described him to Lanfranc) but also an exhortation to Tairdelbach to convene an assembly of clerics for the purposes of prohibiting by edict the many abuses in Ireland of which Lanfranc had heard reports, primarily in the area of marriage customs.[45]

It was long held that this appeal fell on deaf ears and that it was not until the latter part of the reign of Tairdelbach's son, Muirchertach Ua Briain, that the issue of spiritual and structural reform of the Irish church got under way. Indeed this process is almost invariably referred to as 'the twelfth-century reform' of the church, and the council held under Muirchertach's auspices at Cashel in 1101 is perennially cited as its official unveiling. In fact, however, it appears that Tairdelbach presided over a synod held in Dublin in 1080, attended by the most senior cleric in the country, the successor of St Patrick at Armagh, and the leading churchmen of Munster, if not of other provinces.[46] When their deliberations led to a difference of opinion they despatched a letter to Lanfranc at Christmas 1080 asking him to clarify the issues concerned, as he duly did in a letter that, if it arrived while the synod was still in session, shows that the synod must surely have continued into 1081.

Furthermore, in 1085 Tairdelbach again presided over an assembly of the bishops of Ireland and the clergy and people of Dublin, which elected another Irishman, Donngus Ua hAingliu, a monk under Lanfranc at Canterbury, to replace the late Gilla Pátraic, and he too was consecrated by the English primate.[47] Following Donngus's death his nephew Samuel, a monk at St Albans, was consecrated by Archbishop Anselm of Canterbury in 1096, having been chosen in an assembly by the

Dubliners with the assent of Tairdelbach's son Muirchertach. And later that year another Hiberno-Norse town, Waterford, got its first bishop when Muirchertach and his brother Diarmait presided over an assembly of senior clerics and laymen, which chose Máel Ísu Ua hAinmire, an Irish monk trained at Winchester, and sent him too for formal consecration at the hands of the archbishop of Canterbury.[48]

Only when Limerick, the third great Viking-built town—and now the Uí Briain's capital—got a bishop, in the person of the celebrated Gille (Gilbert), was the Canterbury link broken. He was elected some time after the great Council of Cashel in 1101 and before approximately 1107, when the first of his surviving letters was written.[49]

Thus it would appear that for the last quarter of the eleventh century the Uí Briain made no objection to the involvement of Canterbury in the Irish church, over which Lanfranc in particular was vigorous in asserting a primacy that had no historical precedent.[50] On the face of it, it appears odd that a dynasty seeking sovereign authority throughout all Ireland in matters secular would allow and indeed promote the ecclesiastical encroachment of Canterbury. Perhaps this was tolerated while relations with William the Conqueror (died 1087) and his son William Rufus (died 1100) were on an even keel, and the political crises at the outset of Henry I's reign, in which (as we shall see) Muirchertach Ua Briain was implicated, upset the balance and made recourse to Canterbury unworkable. Or perhaps the absence of a resident archbishop of Canterbury during Anselm's exile from April 1103 to August 1106 explains the particular circumstances that denied Gille of Limerick the possibility of a Canterbury consecration, and it may well have occasioned second thoughts about the advisability of reliance on an external superior.

But the most likely explanation is that the Uí Briain had stomached Canterbury's pretensions only for as long as it suited them, in other words while Ireland's *de facto* ecclesiastical capital, Armagh, lay within the compass of the former high-kings, the Uí Néill. However, if a solution could be found whereby an acknowledgement of Armagh's primacy carried no political implications—did not smack of deference to the Uí Néill—then Canterbury could be put aside. And that solution presented itself in 1101.

The site of the council of 1101 was Cashel, the ancient capital of Munster, and the highlight of the gathering was Muirchertach's bestowal of the Rock of Cashel in perpetuity on the Irish church.[51] Two years later he visited Armagh in person and laid an offering of gold on the altar, as his great-grandfather Brian had done almost exactly a century earlier, in 1005. Here was the ground being laid for Muirchertach's solution, as was formally enacted at the council of Ráith Bressail in 1111.[52] This established the territorial diocesan structure that has survived in large part ever since. There would be two ecclesiastical provinces (later increased to four), that of Cashel for the southern half and Armagh for the northern, but with the latter having the primacy. And, possibly taking advantage of the vacancy at Canterbury following Anselm's death in 1109, Canterbury's claims to superior status or to any jurisdiction over the affairs of the Irish church would be repudiated.[53]

The delicate diplomacy required of Brian's descendants, the Uí Briain, in their dealings with the English primate was a consequence of their domination of the towns. This domination also encouraged supranational aspirations.[54] It is worthy of note that in 1073, within a year of Tairdelbach claiming lordship over Dublin, two Uí Briain met violent deaths in the Isle of Man, almost certainly in the act of asserting a claim to it arising from Dublin's acquisition.[55] Similarly, when his son Muirchertach took charge of Dublin in 1075 he became patron of the exiled heirs of Iago of Gwynedd, and the romantic biography of Iago's grandson, Gruffudd ap Cynan, chronicles a long alliance between the two.[56] It began in the very year that Muirchertach took control of Dublin, when he supplied Gruffudd with the city-state's fleet in response to the first of the Welshman's regular pleas for such assistance to establish himself in Gwynedd.[57] As we have seen, another of Tairdelbach's sons, Diarmait Ua Briain, had control of Waterford, and the biography of Gruffudd ap Cynan gives Diarmait's naval aid much of the credit for the success of Gruffudd and of Rhys ap Tewdwr of Deheubarth (South Wales) at the famous Battle of Mynydd Carn the following year, which secured both men in their respective kingships.

After 1066 partisan entanglements in Wales led Irish kings directly to encounters with Normans, and specifically with an Anglo-Norman court alert to Ireland's role in offering asylum and assistance to Insular enemies. William the Conqueror's expedition to St David's in 1081 may be viewed in such a context, as may perhaps a mysterious eulogy in the 'Peterborough' Anglo-Saxon Chronicle that maintains that had the

Conqueror lived but another couple of years beyond 1087 he would have won Ireland by astuteness, without the use of weapons.[58] The observation may be baseless, but it is just conceivable that there is something to it.

In the autumn of 1085 William, alerted to an imminent invasion of England by Knútr IV of Denmark in alliance with the count of Flanders, returned from Normandy to England,[59] and it was amid this crisis that Domesday Book was commissioned.[60] Although the invasion was postponed in 1085, it was expected the following year, and it may be partly against this background that William the Conqueror exacted the 'Oath of Salisbury' from his tenants-in-chief and their major tenants on 1 August 1086.[61] We do not know whether William was aware at that point of the assassination of Knútr in Odense on 10 July, or of the death of Tairdelbach ua Briain four days later at his palace of Cenn Corad, but no doubt such good news travels fast. Be that as it may, William was forced to cross the English Channel soon afterwards to counter raids by Philip I of France and was himself dead within a year. If, therefore, we are to give any credence to the Peterborough chronicler's curious remark about the Conqueror and Ireland, perhaps he is echoing some rumour of Norman aspirations to fill the vacancy in Ireland's high-kingship following Tairdelbach's death.

Recent intervention by the Uí Briain in the affairs of Wales must have been a bone of contention, and the Normans may also have had some antipathy towards the Irish for suspected favouritism to the conquered Anglo-Saxons. But it must also have been known at William's court that, if past performance was anything to go by, forces from Ireland were likely to lend their backing to Scandinavian ambitions in England, as had been made manifest on numerous occasions within living memory, indeed stretching from the time of the Battle of Clontarf onwards.

There is some evidence in the years after Clontarf of King Knútr's influence, if not power, in towns such as Dublin, and perhaps even Sitriuc Silkenbeard's espousal of the Anglo-Danish regime.[62] In 1058 the Dublin fleet had augmented forces drawn from Orkney and the Hebrides in support of the western expedition of Magnús, son of King Haraldr Harðraði of Norway, which an Irish annalist at least believed was intent on the conquest of England.[63] When Haraldr himself invaded England in 1066 Adam of Bremen thought there was an Irish king in his army.[64] And, bearing in mind that two of Harold Godwinsson's sons and his daughter Gyða had fled to Sweden after Hastings, it may not be a coincidence that the Danish invasion of England in 1069, in which the future Knútr IV participated, overlapped with the last attempt by two more of Harold's sons to effect a restoration in England—which, as we have seen, saw them bring from Ireland a fleet of sixty ships acquired from Diarmait mac Máel na mBó.[65] Knútr commanded the Swedish armada of two hundred ships that struck at York in 1075. This was the year in which Muirchertach Ua Briain took the kingship of Dublin, banishing overseas its Hiberno-Norse ruler, who 'died beyond the sea, having assembled a great fleet [to come] to Ireland.'[66] Perhaps the annalist believed that the Swedish fleet bound for England would also provide succour to Dublin's exiled Hiberno-Norse ruler—an episode reminiscent of the context of the Battle of Clontarf.

The demise of Tairdelbach ua Briain in 1086 did not halt the progress of Brian's dynasty, although the ensuing succession contest between his sons unquestionably sowed the seeds of later, and predictable, destabilisation among the Uí Briain.[67] From this dispute, by the late 1080s, Muirchertach Ua Briain emerged the victor and was happy to follow the now time-honoured blueprint. Control of Dublin was essential, and at some unknown date he became the third consecutive *rí hÉrend co fressabra,* high-king 'with opposition', to appoint his heir to the position of king of the city-state.[68] Dublin in turn, we have seen, opened up possibilities in the Isles, and by the mid-1090s not only were members of the Uí Briain again active in the Isle of Man (where Amlaíb, a son of Muirchertach's late brother Tadc, met a violent end in 1096) but, according to the Manx Chronicle, when the king of the Isles died leaving only a minor, the nobles of the Isles sent to Muirchertach requesting a regent until their own royal heir came of age. He responded, we are told, by offering them the services of another of Tadc's sons, Domnall.[69] Like much in this early portion of the Chronicle, this sounds rather far-fetched, but we have confirmatory evidence from the Irish annals (admittedly from a good deal later, in 1111) that this Domnall did indeed take possession of the kingship of the Isles at that point.

Irish expansionism in the region may have been one concern that prompted Haraldr Harðraði's grandson, King Magnús III Barelegs of Norway, to make at least two western expeditions at the turn of the century,[70] although it is quite conceivable that he was only the latest (and, to all intents and purposes, the last) in a long succession of Scandinavian royal figures with territorial ambitions elastic enough to embrace any and all parts of the archipelago. The Irish certainly got off lightly on Magnús's first expedition in 1098, where the targets of his energy were the Western Isles, Man and Britain's western littoral from Galloway to Gwynedd. Almost all sources, on the other hand, are agreed that the primary or at least initial objective of Magnús's 1102 campaign was Ireland, and the Irish annals indicate a successful occupation of Dublin from his Manx base. War with Muirchertach Ua Briain seemed inevitable, and as Dublin's impressive city walls have been dated archaeologically to approximately 1100, quite possibly this was done by directive of Muirchertach in the face of that threat.

As it transpired, both kings seem to have recognised that more was to be achieved by joining forces than by locking horns. A truce gave them time to hammer out an agreement that saw the Norwegian king's son, the future King Sigurðr Jerusalem-farer, married off to a daughter of Ua Briain. King Magnús evidently envisaged a cadet western kingdom ruled by this younger son under the protection of an Irish father-in-law of distinguished pedigree. For Muirchertach, who had striven without success throughout his adult life (like his forefathers back to and including Brian) to wring submission from the recalcitrant rulers of Ireland's far north, the services of dedicated Norwegian and Insular allies stationed to his enemy's flank and rear must have evoked the prospect of ultimate victory. That was not to be. The ignominious demise of the great Magnús Barelegs, slain in a petty ambush on the shores of Ulster in the summer of 1103, all but ended Norway's western dream. And when Muirchertach's family lost their grip on Dublin, soon after he himself fell gravely ill in 1114, the Uí Briain too had to bid farewell to at least forty years of intervention in the north Irish Sea region and quite possibly a history of involvement there stretching all the way back to Brian's assertion of a claim to be *Imperator Scotorum*; but in truth it was always something of a long shot for a dynasty rooted in Ireland's south-west.

Involvement in southern Britain somehow seems much more likely. When we read that Muirchertach's brother Diarmait brought the Waterford fleet across St George's Channel to help secure Rhys ap Tewdwr in the kingship of Deheubarth, it seems entirely credible.[71] When we read that Rhys was driven into exile in Ireland some years later, in 1088, but returned within the year and effected a restoration with Irish aid, it can be believed; as can the statement that when Rhys was killed in battle in 1093 by the Normans, then making heavy inroads into South Wales, his young son Gruffudd was brought for safety to Ireland. Evidently the ruling line of Deheubarth had Irish allies. But to be told that this young boy, Gruffudd ap Rhys ap Tewdwr, remained in his Irish exile for the next twenty years, returning to Wales only as a grown man, and that he nevertheless was greeted with acclaim by his compatriots and in due course managed to secure at least the substance of his ancestral Welsh patrimony—this seems like the stuff of legend. And yet it appears to be true, with all the implications it has, for instance, for cross-channel lines of communication, language use, cultural diversities, and Welsh attitudes to Ireland and the Irish.

Of course the life story of Rhys's now elderly contemporary in Gwynedd, Gruffudd ap Cynan, was far from dissimilar, except that this latter Welsh king was actually born in Ireland and apparently never set foot in his homeland until adulthood. Here too is food for thought.

Hardly less credible, were it not amply corroborated, is Orderic Vitalis's well-known tale of Arnulf de Montgomery, lord of Pembroke, one of the Normans who in the last decade of the eleventh century had annexed so much of South Wales. When Henry I ascended the throne of England in 1100, Arnulf's family were to the fore in rebelling, and when that rebellion began to falter there was nothing for it but to look west and to make contact with the greatest of the Irish, Muirchertach Ua Briain. These contacts led to another of Muirchertach's daughters being given in marriage, this time to Arnulf de Montgomery, who obtained with her substantial naval assistance against King Henry; but it was of little avail. Orderic Vitalis has Arnulf forced to flee to Ireland, sending Norman troops into battle against his father-in-law's enemies and hoping to succeed to Ua Briain's kingdom in right of his new wife but beating a hasty retreat when his treacherous hosts turned against him.

This piece of anti-Irish bias does not stand up to scrutiny: that much is clear from the fact that Muirchertach later sent a letter of thanks to Anselm of Canterbury for his intercession with King Henry on his son-in-law's behalf. The chronicler William of Malmesbury may be closer to the mark when he says that it was only when Henry I instituted a trade embargo between England and Ireland that a rapid cooling occurred in Ua Briain's ardour for intrigue, 'for of what value', he asks, 'would Ireland be if deprived of the merchandise of England?'[72] Whatever the precise course of events, and whatever the driving force behind it all, the Montgomery alliance of 1102 allows us a sneak glimpse at what was by any reckoning a world of strange associations and remarkable possibilities.

Precisely one hundred years link the events of 1102 with those that saw an upstart Irish dynast named Brian Bóraime call the bluff of the straw kings who had postured unchallenged since time immemorial and grasp the high-kingship for himself. The Uí Néill had depended for their ascendancy on the force of tradition and the persuasiveness of their propaganda; Brian and his successors fought their way up, and fought to stay up. And for a century after the Battle of Clontarf all but one of Ireland's would-be kings were men of Brian's blood: his son, his grandson, and his great-grandson. But a century in power can make even an upstart forget: in time he may feel the impulse to convince others, as he has convinced himself, of his *right* to rule.

And so it was that Cogadh Gáedhel re Gallaibh made its appearance, propaganda commissioned to persuade the world of Dál Cais's royal birthright by reason of their assumed role in saving the Gael from the Viking Gall. Was the Cogadh written in celebration of the greatness of Brian and his kin, or is it the product of desperation, written at a time when the memory of the glory days of Brian's reign was beginning to fade, perhaps intended to remind its audience that Dál Cais supremacy deserved a second chance? It is difficult to know, but whatever the case it was probably already too late. Brian's great-grandson Muirchertach rubbed shoulders (and his daughter had shared a marriage bed) with a new type of Gall, a Norman. When, later in the twelfth century, these new Foreigners decided to take a gamble and follow in the Vikings' footsteps to Ireland, they faced an every-man-for-himself polity.

It had been different in the Viking Age, when concerted Irish opposition to the invader was a not uncommon phenomenon. And it was Brian Bóraime who created this new polity. The notion of power he bequeathed to his heirs was one that provided, virtually without exception, only for a 'king of Ireland with opposition.' In other words, when Brian proved that potentially anyone could reign, it meant that there was a built-in incentive to oppose the incumbent, in the hope of taking his place one day. For the same reason that Brian tried but failed to get national backing for his march on Dublin in 1014—that is, because too many had too much to gain from his demise—so after 1169 the incumbent high-king, Ruaidrí Ua Conchobair, rapidly found out that there was no possibility of concerted Irish resistance to the likes of Strongbow. And that was an inevitable consequence of the free-for-all that Brian had helped create.

THE ENDURING REPUTATION OF BRIAN AND CLONTARF

Brian Bóraime was not the first high-king of Ireland to fall in battle. He was not even the first high-king to meet his death at the hands of Norse opponents. Clontarf may perhaps have been the bloodiest battle that Ireland had seen—we simply have no way of knowing—and it is possible that more kings and aristocrats were killed there than in any previous encounter, although some previous battles could give it a run for its money: only a decade earlier, for example, the long-forgotten Battle of Cráeb Tulcha in Ulster left behind nearly as many dead Irish royalty. But it was the Battle of Clontarf that caught the imagination. And even if one believes—as some do—that its hold on the popular imagination is undeserved, to some extent it is pointless trying to modify inherited memory. For it took hold early.

Contemporaneous annalists were more loquacious on the subject of Brian's victory and death at Clontarf than their predecessors had been about the great events they observed. And they portray Clontarf in terms consistent with the later popular tradition: it was an immensely bloody battle, much larger than usual; Brian's principal opponents were the Hiberno-Norse allied to Leinster; and it was notable in particular for the great numbers of overseas Norse forces present, and for the huge losses they incurred by fighting and drowning. And Brian won, even though he died.

Chroniclers in Wales and in south-western France were similarly certain that something significant had occurred, and Marianus Scottus, an Irish historian in exile in Germany, for whom Clontarf was no doubt a dramatic childhood memory, may have been the first to home in on the Good Friday connection: Brian, the venerable king, not engaged in worldly combat but spending the day of battle at prayer and losing his life as he prepared his soul for Easter.

The celebrated epic that tracks the story of Brian and his dynasty's rise to greatness, Cogadh Gáedhel re Gallaibh, can hardly have been written much later and springs from a very different milieu and yet has a similar tale to tell: an elderly king, given over to prayer, losing his life (at the hands of Bródar) in the hour of victory over a largely Norse force, assisted by Leinstermen who had been spurred into rebellion by Brian's chauvinistic former wife, Gormlaith, who reminded her brother Máelmórda, king of Leinster, of his dynasty's own past renown. Implicitly, for the Cogadh's author, two centuries of Irish opposition to Viking invasion, spearheaded by Brian's dynasty, reached a climax at Clontarf.

That picture was imprinted too, with remarkable correspondences, on the minds of those thirteenth-century Icelandic writers who compiled their sagas from folk memories and earlier accounts. Those who did battle with Brian came from the Norse world seeking a kingdom for themselves in Ireland, egged on by Gormlaith, by now only a scorned ex-wife with a hellish fury for vengeance; Brian did not fight, because it was Good Friday, but, his forces having put their enemies to flight, met his death at the hands of Bróðir, a heathen apostate who felled a good and Christian king.

These are the survivals from the many writings generated by Brian's death at the Battle of Clontarf, and we must believe that they are reflective of prevailing opinion. And that being so, it is easy to see how that process of magnification continued thereafter, how grey areas became blacker or whiter, how complications were ironed out and an increasingly one-dimensional narrative took its place, how the contrast between good and evil, right and wrong, Christian and heathen, native and foreign, was accentuated over time. In such a process Brian's very humanity was in danger of losing out, being replaced by the image of a saint, or a superhero, or a saviour.

This is the Brian of the bardic poets. And of the many literary allusions to him in Gaelic verse, no single piece captures Brian the saint, superhero and saviour better than the spirited poem that begins 'Aonar dhuit a Bhriain Bhanba' ('To you alone, Brian of Ireland'), attributed to the celebrated Muiredach Albanach Ó Dálaigh.[73] Possibly written within two centuries of Brian's death, it has all the ingredients of the lore of Brian that are sometimes assumed to be a product of modern nationalist mythologising. Brian's superhero status is established in the poem's opening *caithréim* ('battle-career'), which lists all his great victories, from his youth when he was assisting his brother Mathgamain to his own confrontations as king—in 977 against the Limerick Norse on Inis Cathaig (Scattery) and then at Cathair Cuan against the Uí Chairbre and their Limerick Norse allies; in 978, the Battle of Belach Lechta fought against his bitter enemies, the Eóganacht Raithlind; a successful rebuff of Máel Sechnaill when the latter attacked Mag Adair in 982; Brian's acquisition of the hostages of Leinster and of Osraige in 983; the banishment of the king of Déisi Muman in 985; his victory over the Dubliners at Glenn Máma in 999 and destruction of Dublin thereafter; and his winning of the hostages of Connacht and Mide in 1002. Afterwards 'the peace of all Ireland was established by Brian Bóraime (*Síth Eirionn uile uile | do rinne Brian Bóroime*)'—called here by his famous sobriquet—so that a woman walked from coast to coast without hindrance; and it all culminated in the battle of *Cluain Tairbh air Mhaigh nEalta* ('Clontarf, on [the plain of] Mag Elta').

There follows a long litany of Viking depredations in Ireland. A Viking fleet was on every lough, they had a *longphort* or ship-camp at every *dún* or fort; churches everywhere were destroyed, Armagh going without mass for seven years until Brian came along; Ireland's kings and princes were killed and its women and children enslaved; a Norse soldier billeted on each house, who took even the milk from its cows and levied a tax of an ounce of gold per person on every household.

All this is copied from the Cogadh or a very similar text, and it tells us nothing new. But the poet now begins to get to his point. It was Brian, he tells us, who put an end to this. All the *Danair*—the first time this word, meaning 'Danes', is used in the poem—who engaged in these extortionate practices were felled by Brian. He relieved Ireland's church sanctuaries and instead established a school in every church. There were two pairs of men who had excelled in coming to Ireland's aid: the first two were the legendary Lug Lámfhata and Finn mac Cumaill, the second pair were St Patrick and Brian Bóraime.

This is an extraordinary association to make, as much as to say that what Brian had done for Ireland rivalled the contribution of its patron saint. The reason is his conviction that Brian was a kind of martyr who had devoted his life to defending Ireland from the Gaill, who had been

forced to abandon Ireland for fear of him. The Danair had come to
Dublin to slaughter the youths of the Irish, but Brian, 'the protector
of Ireland (*buachuill Banba*)', had mustered the men of Ireland against
them. In the battle that ensued (Clontarf), the nobles of the Irish fell,
but they killed the royalty of the Gaill who had come from the islands
of Lochlainn. Brian's son Murchad killed a hundred and six before he
himself was slain, and Brian was killed by Bródar in the sidelines of
the battle, 'believing in Christ without sin, sweetly singing his psalter.'
Remarkably, the poet adds:

On Good Friday Brian was killed
Defending the hostaged Irish,
As Christ without sin was killed
Defending the children of Adam.
(*Aoine cásg do marbadh Brian* | *ag díon Gaoidhiol na ngiall,* | *mar do
marbadh Críost gan coir* | *ag diodhan chloinne hAdhamh*).[74]

So, as Jesus gave his life to save humankind, Brian sacrificed his to save
his countrymen. Where earlier the poet had seen Brian as something of
a new patron saint to rival Patrick, he excels himself in equating Brian's
death at Clontarf with that of Christ on Calvary.

The consequence of Brian's act was that for a space of a hundred
and fifty years 'the Foreigners did not inhabit Ireland from then onward
until today, until the Earl came today (*níor aithreabhset Goill Éirinn
ó shoin anuas gusaniodh, go toirriocht an t-iarla anamh*).' The earl in
question is Richard fitz Gilbert de Clare, better known as Strongbow.
And evidently the poet believed that the freedom Brian had secured for
Ireland at Clontarf had been lost again on the arrival of a new kind of
Gaill, the Anglo-Normans, in the late 1160s. From then on, he tells us,
'there comes a fleet of Gaill every year until they captured Ireland of the
peaks, they have possession of the country completely (*Ón ló tháinic in
t-iarla* | *tig loingeas Gall gach bliagain,* | *gur ghabhsad Banba na mbeann,*
| *aca atá an chríoch go coitchend*).'

The poem's pleading message is kept for the last quatrain:

When will there come the like of Brian
South or north, east or west,

Who will protect the Irish against evil
As he alone protected?
(*Cuin thucfas shamhail Briain | theas ná thuaigh, toir ná thiar, | neach fhóirfeas Gaoidhil air ghoimh | mar do fhóir sion a n-aonar?*)[75]

This, then, is what Brian has become. He is a man who selflessly saved the Irish from foreign oppression, and now that oppressors had returned Ireland needed 'the like of Brian (*shamhail Briain*)' to rise up and if necessary similarly sacrifice his life for the sake of his fellow-Irish.

It must be said that the task of depicting Brian as champion of the Gael was complicated by the fact that he had secured the high-kingship by ousting his predecessor, Máel Sechnaill mac Domnaill, and therefore later writers felt the need to blacken Máel Sechnaill's reputation. When Geoffrey Keating (Seathrún Céitinn) compiled his very influential *Foras Feasa ar Éirinn* ('Compendium of knowledge about Ireland'), which he completed about the year 1634, he unashamedly asserted that, because

it was Brian mac Cinnéide who was undergoing the labour and hardship of expelling the Lochlannaigh from Ireland, and that Máel Sechnaill, who was the king of Ireland, gave himself up to luxury and comfort and ease, a line of action that was useless for the defence of Ireland at that juncture, Brian and the nobles who were with him resolved for these reasons to send envoys to Máel Sechnaill, king of Ireland, to inform him that it was not right that anyone should hold the sovereignty of Ireland but one who should devote his energies to banishing the Foreigners from the country, and that, as it was Brian who was undergoing the labour of banishing them, it was right he should get the sovereignty of Ireland for having relieved the country from the oppression of the Foreigners.[76]

Keating then recounts—quite faithfully from the Cogadh or a very similar text—the story of Brian's negotiations with Máel Sechnaill to secure his submission, the conclusion to which was that

Brian sent envoys to Máel Sechnaill asking him to send hostages to him to Áth Luain, and Máel Sechnaill himself came and gave him hostages and sureties. It was then that Brian brought together the main forces of Munster, of Connacht, and of Leinster, and of Mide, and he went with them to Dún Delca where he received the hostages and sureties of all Ulaid. And it was in this way that Brian Bóraime obtained the kingdom of Ireland, by the strength and bravery of his feats of valour and championship, driving the Foreigners and the Danair out of the country, and not by treachery as others assert.[77]

He does not tell us who these others were who asserted that Brian had been a usurper, but it was an allegation he countered as follows:

For it was not the custom in Ireland that the son should succeed the father in the sovereignty of Ireland, as is plain from the history up to this point, but the sovereignty of Ireland was given to him who was the most powerful in action and exploit. And since Brian was the most powerful in action of the Irish in his own time, the majority of the nobles of Ireland chose him to be sovereign of the country, and as many of them as did not consent that the sovereignty of Ireland should be given to him were forced to submit to him against their will, and Máel Sechnaill was obliged to abandon the sovereignty of Ireland and cede it to Brian as we have said . . .

Or if he should be called a usurper for supplanting Máel Sechnaill in the sovereignty of the country, having been chosen by the majority of the Irish nobles, let the reader judge whether it be more just to call him a usurper than to call the majority of the kings of Ireland who sprang from the children of Míl usurpers. For not one in every seven of them gained the sovereignty who did not do so by killing the king who came before him; and since they are not called usurpers, being of the royal blood, for killing the king who came before them, in the same way, since Brian was of the royal blood he should not be called a usurper for having supplanted Máel Sechnaill, whom, though he was in his power, he did not kill, as other kings killed those who came before them in the sovereignty of Ireland, as we have said.[78]

Keating works very hard to exculpate Brian, culminating in the accusation that, although Máel Sechnaill mustered to join Brian in the preparations for Clontarf, he did not participate in the battle because 'he did not wish to help them,'[79] having made a secret deal with the

Dubliners. It is a suggestion borrowed from the Cogadh, which, because of the pervasive influence of Keating's much more widely read work—especially after it began appearing in print in English translation from the early eighteenth century—has been very compelling in casting aspersions on Máel Sechnaill's reputation.

In other ways too we can see the effects of the wide dissemination of Keating's work, the 1723 English translation of which had as its frontispiece, of all the many characters from Irish history and mythology sympathetically portrayed in its pages, a ludicrously armour-clad Brian Bóraime (plate 20).[80] A point made in passing by the author of the Cogadh, having been paraphrased in Keating's Foras Feasa, remained emblazoned in the popular mind, so that Brian the warrior-king became Brian, patron of the arts:

In the first place he restored and built churches, and gave every cleric his own temple according to his rank and his right to it. He built and set in order public schools for the teaching of letters and the sciences in general, and he also gave the price of books and expenses to each one who could not defray the expenses and who desired to devote himself to learning.[81]

And Keating is the source of the oft-repeated notion that Brian invented Irish surnames:

It was Brian, too, who gave the men of Ireland distinct surnames by which each separate sept of them is distinguished from the rest.[82]

It is not true, of course, although one can understand how the idea caught hold. Brian lived through the age when the modern Irish Mac and Ua (later Ó) surnames were indeed beginning to take shape. It was a precocious development, and it is not entirely clear why it happened when it did. The probability is that the use of a fixed patronymic in the form A mac B (A son of B) or C ua D (C grandson of D) was an attempt by those closest to the reins of power to exclude from succession to lordship, and land, more remotely separated segments of the kin-group. And if that is so, it is indicative of a society undergoing major and rapid change. Brian's dynasty managed to concentrate power and land in their own hands to such an extent that individuals like Brian (and his sons and grandsons) and his brothers (and their sons and grandsons) and his cousins (and *their* sons and grandsons) became the eponyms from which a large number of lordly and landed lineages descend and were thus the ancestors of a surprisingly large number of what are common Irish surnames to this day. This fed into the theory that Brian *invented* the whole 'system', as no less a scholar than Eugene O'Curry, in an influential book published in 1861, exaggeratedly put it:

> Previous to the time of the monarch Brian Boroimhé (about the year 1000), there was no general system of family names in Erinn; but every man took the name either of his father or his grandfather for a surname. Brian, however, established a new and most convenient arrangement, namely, that families in future should take permanent names, either those of their immediate fathers, or of any person more remote in their line of pedigree . . .[83]

And he gives an account of Brian's extended family, listing (with a number of inaccuracies) some of the modern surnames that derive from them, as follows:

> Lachtna [Brian's great-grandfather], the son of Corc, had a valiant son, Lorcán (a name now Anglicised 'Lawrence'). Lorcán had three sons, Cinneidigh or Kennedy; Cosgrach; and Bran. From Cosgrach, the second son, descend the O'Lorcans, or Larkins; the O'Sheehans; the O'Cnaimhins (now Bowens); the O'Hogans; the O'Flahertys [those of Thomond, not those of Iar-Chonnacht]; the O'Gloiarns; the O'Aingidys; and the O'Maines. From Bran, the third son, descend the Sliocht Branfinn, in Dufferin in Wexford, a clann who subsequently took, and still retain, the name of O'Brien.
>
> Cinneidigh, or Kennedy, the eldest son of Lorcán, had twelve sons, four only of whom left issue—namely, Mahon, Brian, Donnchuan (or Doncan), and Echtighern.
>
> From Mahon, the eldest son of Kennedy, descend the O'Bolands, the O'Caseys, the O'Siodhachans, the Mac Inirys, the O'Connallys, and the O'Tuomys, in the county of Limerick.

From the great Brian Boroimhé, the second son of Kennedy, descend the O'Briens and the Mac Mahons of Clare.

Donnchuan, third son of Kennedy, had five sons—namely, two of the name of Kennedy, Riagan, Longargan, and Ceileachair. From one of the two Kennedys descend the family of O'Conuing (now Gunning), and from the other the family of O'Kennedy. From Riagan descend the O'Riagans, or O'Regans, of Clare and Limerick. From Longargan descend the O'Longergans, or Lonergans; and from Ceileachair, the fifth son, descend the O'Ceileachairs or Kellehers.

Brian Boroimhé, the second son of Kennedy, had six sons: Murchadh, or Moroch, killed at the battle of Clontarf; Tadhg; Donnchadh, or Donoch; Domhnall, or Donnall; Conor; and Flann;—but two of them only left issue, namely Tadhg, the eldest after Moroch, and Donoch. From Tadhg descend the great family of the O'Briens of Thomond; and from Donoch, the O'Briens of Cuanach and Eatharlagh, in the present counties of Limerick and Tipperary.

Tadhg, the eldest surviving son of Brian Boroimhé, after the battle of Clontarf, had a son, Torloch. Torloch had two sons, Muircheartach, or Mortogh, and Diarmaid, or Dermod. Mortoch, from whom descend the Mac Mahons of Clare, assumed the monarchy of Ireland, and died in the year 1119 . . .[84]

It may be that O'Curry allowed himself to believe Brian's role in the adoption of the surname 'system' because of the conviction with which Geoffrey Keating had stated the case; and he too had a potent effect on other writers. Keating influenced the vernacular tale about Brian's last battle, known as *Cath Cluana Tarbh*, which is known to survive in a remarkable eighty-nine manuscripts from the eighteenth and nineteenth centuries.[85] And the intertwining of traditions apparent by that stage is evident from the fact that Keating had blended elements from the Cogadh with English-language material then beginning to appear in print. One of these accounts, which Keating may have come across indirectly in Meredith Hanmer's *Chronicle of Ireland* (published in 1633), is the sixteenth-century Book of Howth, which has the following curious tale to tell:

There was a merchant in Doubling [Dublin] called the White Merchant, (he was the King of Denmark's son) and had a fair wife, and he, minding to travel in other realms for merchandise, came to Brene Borowe, then chief and principal King of Ireland, and desired the King to take the charge of his wife in his absence, for her beauty was such that he feared all men; which he promised to do in his absence; and so the merchant departed. And while the merchant was in his merchandise, Morcke McBren Borow [Murchad son of Brian Bóraime], the King's son, made suit to her, and won her love, and lay with the merchant's wife. And by chance and fortune the merchant arrived after his long voyage in other realms with seven great ships upon the sudden at Pollbeyeg, by Doubling [Poolbeg near Dublin], in a great fog and mist, in the morning early, and so came to his house, and found ... Morhewe McBreine in bed with his wife ...

The White Merchant went to Bren Boro the King, to complain and declared to him the trust he put him in, and how he was deceived by his son, and demanded judgement; who willed the White Merchant to give what sentence or judgement he would, seeing he was his son. The White Merchant said, this was his judgement, and none other, that he would be in the field of Clontarff by that day twelve-month, to fight there a field with Morhe and all his that would take his part, and there trusted to be revenged on that wrong, and so departed, and went to seek his friends to Denmark, from whence his generation came; and by the day appointed brought a great number of stalworth soldiers out of Denmark, and landed at Clontarff, and there proclaimed a field, and after fought a terrible battle for all the forenoon ...

The Irish won, and drove the strangers to seek aid to their ships, and found them burned to coals. When they saw that they returned again to the battle, and so won the field by very force of fight, and killed both Bren and left his son Morhowe for dead benorth the stinking stream, lying upon his shield; to whom came a priest called Segert Ne Fenemy, and asked for his son ... The priest's son ... did confess the treason done ... And so he was taken, and brought to a hill twelve mile from Dublin, called the Weyn-gatts [Windgates, Co. Wicklow], and there put him in the earth [with stones], standing ... and there doth it rest to this day, a great heap of stones. There was the end of the field of Clontarff, wherein was a soldier of Morhe called Douling of Hertackane [Dúnlaing ua hArtagáin], which that day fought best . . .

The causes that the field was lost. First the haste that Bren the King made to the field, and did not tarry till his friends came to his aid, as his sons and others, which came three days after with 7,000 men. This great haste and worse speed may be an example to all men. Another cause was . . . [Bren] placed his men in this order. The horsemen was put on the right hand of his woward [vanguard] as nigh the sea as might be . . . The left wing was kerne and men with slings, spears, stones, and shields, all naked men . . . These horsemen was the force of the King's army . . . and by reason of the slimy and deep ground towards the sea, the horsemen did nothing, being there placed afore as their ill fortune was . . . The King's horsemen stood him in no stead. By reason thereof the King lost the field and his life and 11,000 men and his son.[86]

The amalgamation of traditions, Gaelic and non-Gaelic, is striking in this work, produced by and on behalf of Christopher St Lawrence, seventh baron of Howth, a member of the Old English gentry of the late sixteenth-century Pale.[87] Clearly Irish material like the Cogadh is feeding in somewhere: hence, for example, the reference to an Otherworld character called Dúnlaing ua hArtagáin, who flits in and out of the Cogadh's account. But it is also a quintessentially Dublin version of events, to the extent that it seems that in the end Brian lost!

This same tradition of a Dublin victory against the Irish occurs in another contemporary work, this time by the Dubliner Richard Stanihurst in his *Description of Ireland* (1577), who has it that the Danes of Oxmantown

discomfitted at Clontarfe, in a skirmish, diverse of the Irishe. The names of the Irish Capitaynes slayne, were Bryanne Borrogh, Miagh mack Bryen, Tadg Okelly, Dolyne Ahertigan, Gylle Barramede. These were Irish potentates, and before their discomfiture they ruled the rest. They were interred at Kilmaynanne over against the great cross.[88]

He too, therefore, imagines Dúnlaing ua hArtagáin as one of the 'Irish Capitaynes' killed alongside Brian, Murchad mac Briain and

Tadc ua Cellaig of Uí Maine, and his unidentified 'Gylle Barramede' is presumably also traceable to Irish tradition, while the belief that they were buried at Kilmainham must have come from Dublin.

Meredith Hanmer, an Anglo-Welsh clergyman who settled in Ireland in the late sixteenth century and wrote a *Chronicle of Ireland* not printed until 1633, expresses doubt about the outcome of the battle, although in the end he opts to follow earlier writers and blame it on (an unnamed) Gormlaith:

> Bernardus, commonly called Brian Bowrow, Monarch of Ireland, and his son Murcath, alias Murchadus Mac Brian, with other Kings of the land subiect onto him, gathered great power, and met at Clantarfe, nigh Dublin, and gave a sore battle unto Sutraic, alias Sutric, the sonne of Abloic, King of Dublin, and unto Moilmordha, King of Leinster. This Sutric, to withstand the monarch, had hired to his aide, all manner of strangers he could get by sea or by land, as Danes, Norwegians, Scots, Britaines, Pirates and sea rovers. The fight was desperate, the field all blood, a horse (they say) was sometimes up to his belly in bloud. There were slaine that day of the one side, Brian the Monarch, and his sonne Murchard; of the other side, Mailmordha King of Leinster, Rodericke the Arch-Pirate, and Captain of the strangers, with others of both sides, innumerable. Sutrick was sore wounded, was brought to Dublin, and shortly after died of his wound. I pray the gentle Reader, who got by the bargain? As farre as ever I could learne, a woman set them together by the eares.[89]

Sir James Ware's *De Hibernia et Antiquitatibus Eius* appeared in 1654 and similarly queries the outcome, presenting the two traditions, of an Irish victory and a Dublin victory, and opting for the latter. His account is also notable for its insistence—which would prove persuasive—that Clontarf was in essence an attempt by Brian to banish the 'Danes' from Ireland:

> About the beginning of the year 1014, or a little before, Brian Boro treated with most of the Kings of Ireland to joyne their Forces with him, and endeavor the expulsion of the Danes as publick enemies

of the Kingdom. Sitricus on the other side understanding the design, neglected nothing that might Contribute to his Defence; and therefore having made his peace with Maelmorrius, Son of Murchad King of Leinster, he procured assistance both from him and from the Danes of the Isle of Man and the Hebrides.[90]

Whatever about the interpretation of Clontarf as a Dublin victory, which seems to have passed from the pages of history at this point, the emphasis on the expulsion of the Danes was firmly fixed. It is there, along with much Keating-inspired detail, in one of the first novels published by an Irish writer, Sarah Butler's *Irish Tales* (1716).[91] And belief in it was, for instance, the motivation behind Daniel O'Connell's decision to follow up his great 'monster meeting' at Tara in 1843 with what was intended to be the climax of his campaign to secure repeal of the Act of Union by one more giant gathering, at Clontarf. As one of his early biographers put it:

After Tara, several other large demonstrations were held, and it was resolved to wind up the series by a final 'monster' at Clontarf. It was at Clontarf that Brian Boroimhe had expelled the Danes from Ireland in 1014. What fitter spot, it was asked, could be found for completing the expulsion of another set of intruders?[92]

The meeting was set for Sunday 8 October 1843. People were beginning to flock towards it from throughout Ireland, and even further afield, when the government issued a surprise proclamation forbidding it late on the Saturday afternoon, because of fears of the explosive cocktail of O'Connell's oratory, a crowd of hundreds of thousands, and a site so potent in popular imagination as the very field of battle on which Brian had fought and won.

For the best part of a century leading to that point Catholic historians had been publishing narrative histories of Ireland that—unlike Protestant historians from an Anglo-Irish background, who tended to deal only with the story of Ireland from the twelfth-century English conquest onwards—displayed a passionate interest in rediscovering, as they saw it, the glories of ancient Ireland. They therefore made much of Brian. But there was no sectarian difference of opinion on the subject of the Vikings,[93] and given the, by then, near-universal belief that Brian had played a part in ending Ireland's Viking tyranny, historians, irrespective of religious persuasion, tended to think well of him for having realised so good a triumph.

Still, it is noticeable that some eighteenth-century historians had commented on the shortcomings of the Irish polity in the aftermath of Brian's appropriation of the high-kingship, which, depending on their viewpoint, they saw as justifying English intervention, or as an unforeseen flaw that led to a tragic consequence for the Irish nation.

And even historians sympathetic to the Irish position could be dismissive of Brian's role.[94] More than a century after Geoffrey Keating strove so hard to refute unnamed authorities who rejected Brian's high-kingship as a usurpation, it is still evident in the pages of the *Dissertations on the Antient History of Ireland* (1753) by Charles O'Conor of Bellanagare, which claimed that Brian 'thrust himself upon the Throne, although incapacitated by the law,' and that the consequence was a period of 'factious Wantonness', so that the Irish 'gave up their Country and Liberties.'[95] O'Conor even anticipated twentieth-century revisionist views of Clontarf by asserting that the great battle was merely the culmination of a 'civil war' that had seen a rebellion against Brian by the Leinstermen, the latter merely aided by the Norse.[96]

But his was virtually a lone voice. By now the mythic Brian predominated; and no historian of the period captured so graphically the image of Brian the Christian king as Sylvester O'Halloran in his *General History of Ireland* (1778). He had got sight of a work written earlier in the century that is sometimes called the 'Dublin Annals of Inisfallen', written at the behest of one of Brian's descendants, John O'Brien, Bishop of Cloyne and Ross (1748–69), with the result that this minor manuscript account has gained immortality in O'Halloran's published words:

Brien rode through the ranks with a crucifix in one hand, and his drawn sword in the other. He exhorted them as he passed along, 'to do their duty as soldiers and Christians, in the cause of their religion and their country.' He reminded them of all the distresses their ancestors were reduced to, by the perfidious and sanguinary Danes, strangers to religion and humanity! That these, their successors, waited impatiently to renew the same scenes of devastation and cruelty, and, by way of anticipation, (says he), 'they have fixed on the very day on which Christ was crucified, to destroy the country of his greatest votaries; but that God, whose cause you are to fight this day, will be present with you, and deliver his enemies into your hands.' So saying, he proceeded towards the centre to lead on his troops to action; but the chiefs of the army with one voice requested he would retire from the field of battle, on account of his great age, and leave to the gallant Morrogh the chief command.[97]

O'Halloran proved stealthily influential as throughout the nineteenth century numerous historians replicated his telling of the story. We see it in such best-sellers as Mary Frances Cusack's *Illustrated History of Ireland* (1868), while A. M. Sullivan's blockbuster *The Story of Ireland* (1869) outrageously plagiarises O'Halloran, including his preposterous tale of Brian, the pious prince on horseback, with a cross in one hand and sword in the other, urging onwards his Christian soldiers.

And, needless to say, the internet age has allowed this and many another yarn to leapfrog over all the scholarship that intervened, into our living-rooms and into our class-rooms, by way of the benign tyranny of the search engine. A web search for 'Brian Boru' claims to offer three-quarters of a million results, and two-thirds of a million for 'Battle of Clontarf'. This battle took place a full thousand years ago. Brian is long, long dead. But the myth of both has never been more alive.

ABBREVIATIONS

AFM   *Annala Rioghachta Eireann: Annals of the Kingdom of Ireland by the Four Masters, from the Earliest Period to the Year 1616*, ed. John O'Donovan (7 vols.), Dublin: Hodges and Smith, 1851.

AI   *The Annals of Inisfallen (MS. Rawlinson B.503)*, ed. Seán Mac Airt, Dublin: Dublin Institute for Advanced Studies, 1951.

ALC   *The Annals of Loch Cé: A Chronicle of Irish Affairs from A.D. 1014 to A.D. 1590* (Rolls Series), ed. W. M. Hennessy (2 vols.), London: Longman, 1871; reprinted Dublin: Irish Manuscripts Commission, 1939.

AT   'Annals of Tigernach,' ed. Whitley Stokes, *Revue Celtique*, 16 (1895), p. 374–419; 17 (1896), 6–33, 119–263, 337–420; 18 (1897), 9–59, 150–97, 267–303; reprinted (2 vols.), Felinfach (Ceredigion): Llanerch Press, 1993.

AU   *Annala Uladh: Annals of Ulster, Otherwise Annala Senait, Annals of Senat: A Chronicle of Irish Affairs from A.D. 431 to A.D. 1540 . . .* ed. W. M. Hennessy and B. Mac Carthy (4 vols.), London: Her Majesty's Stationery Office, 1887–1901; *The Annals of Ulster (to AD 1131)*, ed. Seán Mac Airt and Gearóid Mac Niocaill, Dublin: Dublin Institute for Advanced Studies, 1983.

CGG   *Cogadh Gaedhel re Gallaibh: The War of the Gaedhil with the Gaill, or, The Invasions of Ireland by the Danes and Other Norsemen* (Rolls Series), ed. James Henthorn Todd, London: Longmans, Green, Reader, and Dyer, 1867.

CGH   *Corpus Genealogiarum Hiberniae*, ed. M. A. O'Brien, Dublin: Dublin Institute for Advanced Studies, 1962.

CS   *Chronicum Scotorum: A Chronicle of Irish Affairs, from the Earliest Times to* A.D. *1135* (Rolls Series), ed. W. M. Hennessy, London: Longmans, Green, Reader, and Dyer, 1866.

LL   *The Book of Leinster: Formerly Lebar na Núachongbála*, ed. R. I. Best, Osborn Bergin, M. A. O'Brien and Anne O'Sullivan (6 vols.), Dublin: Dublin Institute for Advanced Studies, 1954–83.

REFERENCES

Preface

1. CGG, p. ccii.
2. Chadwick, 'The Vikings and the Western World,' p. 31.

Introduction

1. McManus, *A Guide to Ogam*; Swift, *Ogam Stones and the Earliest Irish Christians*; Sims-Williams, *The Celtic Inscriptions of Britain*.
2. Patrick, 'Confessio,' in *Libri Epistolarum Sancti Patricii*, chap. 1.
3. See, for example, Sharpe, 'St Patrick and the See of Armagh,' p. 33–59.
4. Herbert, *Iona, Kells, and Derry*.
5. John Bannerman, *Studies in the History of Dalriata*, Edinburgh: Scottish Academic Press, 1974.
6. Kelly, *A Guide to Early Irish Law*, p. 95–7.
7. Gerald of Wales, *Expugnatio Hibernica*, p. 70–71.
8. John [Eoin] MacNeill, 'Early Irish population-groups,' p. 59–109.
9. Ó Corráin, 'Nationality and kingship in pre-Norman Ireland,' p. 10.
10. Byrne, 'Historical note on Cnogba (Knowth),' p. 383–400.
11. Ó Corráin, 'Nationality and kingship in pre-Norman Ireland'.
12. Byrne, *Irish Kings and High-Kings*, chap. 12; Breatnach, 'Ardri as an old compound,' p. 192–3.
13. Carey, *A New Introduction to Lebor Gabála Érenn*; Carey, *The Irish National Origin-Legend*; Ó Corráin, 'Irish origin legends and genealogy,' p. 51–96; Ó Corráin, 'Historical need and literary narrative,' p. 141–58.
14. Kelleher, 'The pre-Norman Irish genealogies,' p. 138–53; Nicholls, 'The Irish genealogies,' p. 256–61; Ó Corráin, 'Creating the past,' p. 177–208.
15. Byrne, *Irish Kings and High-Kings*, chap. 4; Bhreathnach, 'Temoria,' p. 67–88; Carey, 'Tara and the supernatural,' p. 32–48; Binchy, 'The Fair of Tailtiu and the Feast of Tara,' p. 113–38; Jaski, *Early Irish Kingship and Succession*, p. 214–28; Charles-Edwards, *Early Christian Ireland*, chap. 12.

16. Byrne, *The Rise of the Uí Néill and the High-Kingship of Ireland*; Bhreathnach, 'Temoria'; Warntjes, 'The alternation of the kingship of Tara,' p. 394–432.

17. Byrne, *Irish Kings and High-Kings*, chap. 6; Ó Corráin, *Ireland Before the Normans*, p. 17–23; Byrne, 'Certain Southern Uí Néill kingdoms'; O'Flynn, 'The organisation and operation of Uí Néill kingship in the Irish midlands.'

18. Lacey, *Cenél Conaill and the Donegal Kingdoms*.

19. AU.

20. See biographies of the kings of Tara by Ailbhe MacShamhráin in James McGuire and James Quinn (eds.), *Dictionary of Irish Biography*, Cambridge: Cambridge University Press, in collaboration with the Royal Irish Academy, 2009; see also Byrne, *Irish Kings and High-Kings*, chap. 6 and 7; MacShamhráin, 'Cenél nEogain and the Airgialla,' p. 55–84; Ó Corráin, *Ireland Before the Normans*, p. 14–17; Ó Fiaich, 'The church of Armagh under lay control,' p. 75–127.

21. Byrne, *Irish Kings and High-Kings*, chap. 7; Charles-Edwards, *Early Christian Ireland*, p. 54–67.

22. Kelleher, 'Uí Maine in the annals and genealogies,' p. 61–107.

23. Byrne, *Irish Kings and High-Kings*, chap. 10; Jaski, *Early Irish Kingship and Succession*, p. 218–21.

24. Stokes, 'The Borama,' p. 32–124.

25. Walsh, 'Leinster states and kings in Christian times,' p. 47–61; Byrne, *Irish Kings and High-Kings*, chap. 8; Smyth, *Celtic Leinster*; MacShamhráin, *Church and Polity in Pre-Norman Ireland*.

26. AU 744.

27. Ryan, 'The historical content of the "Caithréim Ceallacháin Chaisil"; p. 89–100.

28. Jaski, *Early Irish Kingship and Succession*, chap. 7; Ní Mhaonaigh, 'Cormac mac Cuilennáin,' p. 109–28.

29. de Paor, 'The high crosses of Tech Theille (Tihilly), Kinnitty and related sculpture,' p. 131–58.

30. Casey, 'Studies in the exercise of royal power in Ireland.'

31. *The Annals of St-Bertin*, s.a. 848.

32. *Dicuili Liber de Mensura Orbis Terrae*, p. 74–6; D. R. Howlett, 'Dicuill on the Islands of the North,' *Peritia*, 13 (1999), p. 127–34; John J. Contreni, 'Dícuil,' *Oxford Dictionary of National Biography*, Oxford: Oxford University Press, 2004.

33. *Dicuili Liber de Mensura Orbis Terrae*, p. 74–6.

34. *Anglo-Saxon Chronicle*, s.a. 793.

35. Alcuin of York, Letter to Higbald, trans. by Stephen Allott in *Alcuin of York, c. A.D. 732 to 804: His Life and Letters,* York: William Sessions, 1974.

36. *Anglo-Saxon Chronicle*, s.a. 794.

37. AU, AFM 795; Downham, 'An imaginary Viking raid on Skye in 795?' p. 192–6.

38. AU, 798; AFM 793 = 798.

39. Simpson, 'Viking warrior burials in Dublin,' p. 11–62.

40. Edmond O'Donovan, 'The Irish, the Vikings, and the English: New archaeological evidence from excavations at Golden Lane, Dublin,' in Seán Duffy (ed.), *Medieval Dublin, VIII,* Dublin: Four Courts Press, 2008, p. 36–130.

41. AI 795.

42. AU 821.

43. AU 811.

44. Byrne 'The Viking Age,' p. 610.

45. Kelly, 'Re-evaluation of a supposed inland promontory fort,' p. 485–97.

46. *The Tripartite Life of Patrick*, p. 140.

47. CS 836; Etchingham, 'Evidence of Scandinavian settlement in Wicklow,' p. 113–38.

48. Simpson, 'The longphort of Dublin,' p. 94–112.

49. *The Tripartite Life of Patrick*, p. 192.

50. AU 836; Bhreathnach, 'Saint Patrick, Vikings and Inber Dée,' p. 36–40.

51. Bhreathnach, 'The cultural and political milieu of the deposition and manufacture of the hoard discovered at Reerasta Rath, Ardagh, Co. Limerick,' p. 15–23.

52. See Downham, 'The career of Cearbhall of Osraighe,' p. 1–18; Downham, 'The good, the bad and the ugly,' p. 28–40.

53. *The Annals of St-Bertin*, s.a. 848.

54. See Dumville, 'Old Dubliners and New Dubliners in Ireland and Britain,' p. 78–93; Etchingham, 'Laithlinn, "Fair Foreigners" and "Dark Foreigners",' p. 80–88.

55. Ó Corráin, 'The Vikings in Scotland and Ireland in the ninth century,' p. 296–339.

56. Downham, *Viking Kings of Britain and Ireland.*

57. Woolf, *From Pictland to Alba,* chap. 3.

58. AU 918.

59. Smyth, *Scandinavian York and Dublin.*

60. Oftedal, 'Scandinavian place-names in Ireland,' p. 125–33.

61. Goedheer, *Irish and Norse Traditions about the Battle of Clontarf*, p. 268.

62. Downham, 'The historical importance of Viking-Age Waterford,' p. 71–96; Kelly and Maas, 'The Vikings and the Kingdom of Laois,' p. 123–59.

63. Holm, 'The slave trade of Dublin,' p. 317–45.

64. Jaski, 'The Vikings and the kingship of Tara,' p. 310–51; Downham, 'The Vikings in Southern Uí Néill to 1014,' p. 233–55.

Chapter 1

1. MacNeill, 'The Vita Tripartita of St Patrick,' p. 34–40.

2. Breatnach, 'The ecclesiastical element in the Old Irish legal tract Cáin Fhuithirbe,' p. 36–52.

3. Ní Dhonnchadha, 'The guarantor list of Cáin Adomnáin,' p. 178–215.

4. CGH, p. 240 (153a29–31).

5. AFM 760 = 765; AI 769.

6. For the dynasty's genealogies see Jaski, 'The genealogical section of the Psalter of Cashel,' p. 295–337, p. 308–10.

7. CGH, p. 237 (152b22); Ó Corráin, 'Foreign connections and domestic politics,' p. 214, 220, 225; Ó Riain, *A Dictionary of Irish Saints*, p. 346–9.

8. AU 836.

9. CGH, p. 21.

10. AU, AI 845.

11. *Bethu Phátraic*, p. 123; *The Tripartite Life of Patrick*, vol. I, p. 206.

12. *Fragmentary Annals of Ireland*, §423, p. 150, 160.

13. James Carney, 'The dating of early Irish verse texts,' *Éigse*, 19 (1982–3), p. 179, 187–8; Mac Cana, 'Praise poetry in Ireland before the Normans,' p. 19–20; Meyer, 'A poem by Dallán mac Móre,' p. 210–14.

14. Westropp, 'Magh Adhair, Co. Clare,' p. 55–60; Fitzpatrick, *Royal Inauguration in Gaelic Ireland*.

15. Lucas, 'The sacred trees of Ireland,' p. 16–54.

16. AFM 981, 1051.

17. Westropp, 'Magh Adhair, Co. Clare,' p. 60.

18. Meyer, 'Brian Borumha,' p. 68–73; *Cath Cluana Tarbh*, p. 132.

19. LL, vol. 1, p. 141, line 4361; Edel Bhreathnach, 'Two contributors to the Book of Leinster: Bishops Finn of Kildare and Gilla-na-Náem Ua Duinn,' in Richter and Picard, *Ogma*, p. 105–11.

20. Meyer, 'Mitteilungen aus Irischen handschriften,' p. 21–3; for Cúán see Downey, 'The life and work of Cúán Ua Lothcháin,' p. 55–78.

21. CGH, p. 52, 96, 140.

22. Ó Lochlainn, 'Poets on the Battle of Clontarf', *Éigse*, 4 (1943), p. 42.

23. Fischer, 'Two poets and the legend of Brian Bóraimhe,' p. 91–109.

24. LL, vol. 3, p. 493 (line 15402).

25. AFM 877 = 879.

26. CGH, p. 207 (149b22–3).

27. AFM 1116.

28. O'Kelly, 'Beal Boru,' p. 1–27.

29. R. M. H. Dolley, 'The coins from Beal Boru,' in *Journal of the Cork Historical and Archaeological Society*, 67 (1962), p. 18–27; Ciarán Ó Murchadha (ed.), *County Clare Studies: Essays in Memory of Gerald O'Connell, Seán Ó Murchadha, Thomas Coffey and Pat Flynn*, Ennis: Clare Archaeological and Historical Society, 2000; Damian Bracken and Dagmar Ó Riain-Raedel (eds.), *Ireland and Europe in the Twelfth Century: Reform and Renewal*, Dublin: Four Courts Press, 2006, p. 95.

30. Byrne, *Irish Kings and High-Kings*, p. 211–15.

31. Kelleher, 'The rise of the Dál Cais,' p. 234; Ó Corráin, 'Irish origin legends and genealogy,' p. 70–71.

32. CGG, p. 39.

33. AU; AI 922.

34. CGG, p. 39–43.

35. CGG, p. 53–5, 57.

36. *An Leabhar Muimhneach*, p. 316.

37. AU 934; AFM 932 = 934.

38. *An Leabhar Muimhneach*, p. 126; 'Rém rígraidi Dáil Cais,' fol. 229re20.

39. Dobbs, 'The Ban-shenchus,' *Revue Celtique*, 47 (1930), 314, 338; 48 (1931), 188, 227.

40. Dobbs, 'Ban-shenchus,' *Revue Celtique*, 48 (1931), 186, 187, 226.

41. Kelleher, 'The rise of the Dál Cais,' p. 238–9.

42. Ryan, 'Historical content of the "Caithréim Ceallacháin Chaisil"', p. 89–100; Ó Corráin, 'Caithréim Chellacháin Chaisil,' p. 1–69.

43. AU 944.

44. AFM 942 = 944; CGH, p. 237 (152b37).

45. *An Leabhar Muimhneach*, p. 122; CGG, p. 140.

46. Kelleher, 'The rise of the Dál Cais,' p. 237.

47. See note 11 above.

48. *Caithreim Cellachain Caisil*; Ó Corráin, 'Caithréim Chellacháin Chaisil'; Jaski, *Early Irish Kingship and Succession*, p. 232–6.

49. CGH, p. 207.

50. CGG, p. 54–5.

51. *An Leabhar Muimhneach*, p. 126.

52. Ó Corráin, 'Muirchertach Mac Lochlainn and the circuit of Ireland,' p. 238–50.

53. AFM, CS 948 = 950; *The Book of Lecan*, fol. 226r; *The Book of Uí Maine*, fol. 30v; Pender, 'The O'Clery book of genealogies,' p. 152, §1999.

54. AFM 949 = 951.

55. Ó Corráin, 'Irish regnal succession,' p. 35; Warntjes, 'Regnal succession in early medieval Ireland,' p. 378, n. 3.

56. CGH, p. 360 (320ab27).

57. CGG, p. 44.

58. CGH, p. 237 (152b36); *An Leabhar Muimhneach*, p. 127, 298.

59. See Westropp, 'Types of the ring-forts remaining in eastern Clare,' p. 205–6.

60. AI 990; AFM 1009 = 1010; AU 1010; Ó Corráin, 'Dál Cais,' p. 52–3.

61. Kelleher, 'The rise of the Dál Cais,' p. 238–9.

62. CGH, p. 360; *An Leabhar Muimhneach*, p. 321–4, 333–6.

63. AU 963; AI 963; AFM 961 = 963; CGG, p. 5, 71.

64. AFM 957 = 959.

65. CS, AFM 961 = 963.

66. AI 963.

67. CS, AFM 961 = 963.

68. CS, AFM 961 = 963.

69. *An Leabhar Muimhneach*, p. 127–8.

70. See Ní Mhaonaigh, 'Cogad Gáedel re Gallaib and the annals,' p. 101–26.

71. CGG, p. 69.

72. CGG, p. 71.

73. T. F. O'Rahilly, 'Notes on Irish place-names,' *Hermathena*, 23, no. 48 (1933), p. 205; Kelleher, 'The rise of the Dál Cais,' p. 239.

74. CGH, p. 170 (145d39).

75. CGG, p. 75–7.

76. AFM 965 = 967.

77. CGG, p. 79–81.

78. AU 967.

79. AI 972.

80. For *svartleggja* see Whitley Stokes, 'Irish etymologies,' *Zeitschrift für Celtische Philologie*, 3 (1901), p. 473; Casey, '"A compulsory and burdensome imposition",' p. 193–216.

81. AFM 972 = 974; AI 974, 975.

82. AFM 967 = 969.

83. CGG, p. 83–5.

84. AFM 967 = 969.

85. AI 972.

86. AI 973.

87. AI 974, 975.

88. AFM 974 = 976; AI 976; see also AU, CS, AT 976.

89. CGG, p. 101.

Chapter 2

1. CGG, p. 105.

2. See Meyer, 'Brian Borumha.'

3. Cf. Byrne, *Irish Kings and High-Kings* (2nd edition), p. xv.

4. E. G. Withycombe, *The Oxford Dictionary of English Christian Names* (3rd edition), Oxford: Oxford University Press, 1977.

5. Smith, *Province and Empire*; Cassard, *Le Siècle des Vikings en Bretagne*.

6. F. J. Byrne, 'Ireland before the Battle of Clontarf,' in Dáibhí Ó Cróinín (ed.), *A New History of Ireland, 1: Prehistoric and Early Ireland*, Oxford: Clarendon Press, 2005, p. 852–5; Downham, *Viking Kings of Britain and Ireland*, p. 31.

7. CGG, p. 38–41.

8. CGG, p. 53.

9. AFM 975 = 977; cf. AI, CS, AT 977.

10. CGG, p. 57–9.

11. CGG, p. 61.

12. CGG, p. 69.

13. CGG, p. 75.

14. CGH, p. 238 (152b48); Dobbs, 'Ban-shenchas,' *Revue Celtique*, 48 (1931), p. 228.

15. CGH, p. 174 (145g8).

16. CS; AFM 1013 = 1014.

17. Ní Mhaonaigh, 'Tales of three Gormlaiths in medieval Irish literature,' p. 1–24.

18. Dobbs, 'Ban-shenchus,' *Revue Celtique*, 48 (1931), p. 189, 228; Bhreathnach, 'Columban churches in Brega and Leinster,' p. 11.

19. CGG, p. 101.

20. AFM 975 = 977; AU, AT, CS, AI 977; CGH, p. 238 (153a2).

21. AI 977; AFM 976 = 977; CGG, p. 103.

22. Ó Riain, *Historical Dictionary of Gaelic Placenames*, fasc. 2, p. 111.

23. AI, AU, AT, CS 978; AFM 976 = 978.

24. Kelleher, 'The rise of the Dál Cais,' p. 240.

25. CGG, p. 107.

26. AI 982.

27. O'Flynn, 'The career of Máelsechnaill II,' p. 29–68.

28. AFM 981 = 982; CS, AT 982.

29. Lucas, 'The sacred trees of Ireland,' p. 25.

30. AFM 1051.

31. Ó Corráin, *Ireland Before the Normans*, p. 121.

32. CGG, p. 107–9.

33. AI 984.

34. AI 983.

35. AFM 983 = 984.

36. Etchingham, 'North Wales, Ireland and the Isles,' p. 145–87; Hudson, *Viking Pirates and Christian Princes*, p. 65–74; Woolf, *From Pictland to Alba*, p. 206–8, 212–14, 216–19, 298.

37. AI 983.

38. AI 984.

39. AI 985.

40. CGG, p. 107.

41. AI 986.

42. AI, AU 1011.

43. Karkov and Ruffing, 'The Southern Uí Néill and the political landscape of Lough Ennell,' p. 336–59.

44. AI, AT, SC 988; AFM 987 = 988.

45. AI 990.

46. AU, CS 990; AFM 989 = 990.

47. AI 991.

48. AU, AT, CS 992; AFM 991 = 992.

49. AI 993; AFM 992 = 993.

50. AT, CS; AFM 994.

51. AI 995.

52. AI 996.

53. AI 997.

54. CGG, p. 108–9.

55. AT 1171.

56. AFM 997 = 998; cf. AU, CS 998.

57. AFM 998 = 999; AU, AT, CS 999.

58. AU, AT 999.

59. CGG, p. 111.

60. See MacShamhráin, *Church and Polity in Pre-Norman Ireland*, p. 86–9; Downham, *Viking Kings of Britain and Ireland*, p. 42.

61. AU 999.
62. MacShamhráin, 'The Battle of Glenn Máma, Dublin, and the high-kingship of Ireland: A millennial commemoration,' p. 53–64.
63. LL, vol. 1, p. 98 (line 3146–7).
64. CGG, p. 113.
65. CS 999; AFM 998 = 999.
66. AI 1000; cf. AU, AT, CS 1000; AFM 999 = 1000.
67. CGG, p. 119; AI 1003.

Chapter 3
1. Valante, *The Vikings in Ireland*.
2. CGG, p. 113–19.
3. AU 1013; cf. Ó Súilleabháin, 'Nótaí ar thrí fhocal ó na hAnnála,' p. 22–3.
4. CGG, p. 113.
5. LL, vol. 1, line 6362.
6. Halpin, *Weapons and Warfare in Viking and Medieval Dublin*.
7. AU, CS, AT 1000; AFM 999 = 1000.
8. CGG, p. 119–33.
9. CS, AT 1001.
10. AU, CS, AT 1001; AFM 1000 = 1001.
11. Joyce, *The Origin and History of Irish Names of Places*, vol. I, p. 374.
12. AU, CS, AT 1002.
13. AFM 1001 = 1002
14. CGG, p. 133.
15. AFM 1002 = 1003.
16. CGG, p. 133–5.
17. AT, CS, AU, AI 1002; AFM 1001 = 1002.
18. CGG, p. 135.
19. AI 1003.
20. CGG, p. 135.
21. AU 1004; AFM 1003 = 1004.
22. Byrne, *Irish Kings and High-Kings*, p. 127.
23. AI, CS, AU 1005; AFM 1004 = 1005.
24. Aitchison, *Armagh and the Royal Centres in Early Medieval Ireland*; Chris J. Lynn, *Excavations at Navan Fort, 1961–71, by D. M. Waterman*, Belfast: Stationery Office, 1993.
25. See Gwynn, 'Brian in Armagh,' p. 35–50; MacShamhráin, 'Brian Bóruma, Armagh and High Kingship,' p. 1–21; Woolf, *From Pictland to Alba*, p. 225.

26. AI; AFM 1031.
27. AU 1006, 1012.
28. *The Patrician Texts in the Book of Armagh.*
29. O'Curry, *Lectures on the Manuscript Materials of Ancient Irish History,* p. 654.
30. AFM 1006 = 1007; Gwynn, 'Brian in Armagh,' p. 49; MacShamhráin, 'Brian Bóruma, Armagh and High Kingship,' p. 16.
31. AU 1014; CGG, p. 205.
32. Gwynn, 'Brian in Armagh,' p. 42–6.
33. See, for example, Flachenecker, *Schottenklöster*; Ó Riain-Raedel, 'Irish Benedictine monasteries on the Continent,' p. 25–63.
34. *Anglo-Saxon Chronicle,* s.a. 972; Thornton, 'Edgar and the eight kings,' p. 49–79; Williams, 'An outing on the Dee,' p. 229–43.
35. 'Ælfric of Eynsham,' in David C. Douglas et al. (eds.), *English Historical Documents* (14 vols.), London: Eyre and Spottiswoode, 1955–77, vol. I, p. 853.
36. AFM 972 = 974.
37. Etchingham, 'North Wales, Ireland and the Isles,' p. 180–83.
38. AI 972.
39. O'Rahilly, *Early Irish History and Mythology,* p. 386, n. 2.
40. Kenney, *The Sources for the Early History of Ireland,* p. 615, n. 316.
41. AU 989. See Herbert, *Iona, Kells, and Derry,* p. 84 and n. 24, p. 120 and n. 38.
42. AU, AFM, ALC 1064.
43. CS, AT 1148.
44. AFM 1169.
45. AU 1005.
46. CS 1005.
47. Woolf, *From Pictland to Alba,* p. 225–30.
48. Anderson, 'The prophecy of Berchan,' p. 1–56, st. 181–2; *The Prophecy of Berchán,* p. 52–3, 90.
49. AU 999; LL, vol. 1, line 5469–70.
50. *The Metrical Dindshenchas,* vol. 4, p. 152–3.
51. AI 1013; CGG, p. 149.
52. AU 1006.
53. CGG, p. 137.
54. AFM 1001 = 1002.
55. AU 870, 871.
56. *The Prophecy of Berchán,* p. 90; Woolf, *From Pictland to Alba,* p. 225–6.
57. AFM 772 = 774; AI 974; Woolf, *From Pictland to Alba,* p. 212–13; Downham, *Viking Kings of Britain and Ireland,* p. 49.

58. *Brut y Tywysogyon: Peniarth* MS. 20 *Version*; *Brut y Tywysogyon: Red Book of Hergest Version*, s.a. 980, 982.

59. AI 984.

60. AU 987; *Brut y Tywysogyon: Red Book of Hergest Version*, s.a. 987.

61. CS, AU 1005; AI 1004.

62. Etchingham, 'North Wales, Ireland and the Isles,' p. 180.

63. 'Cottonian annals'; CS, AFM, AU, ALC 1014.

64. CGG, p. 135.

65. AFM 1005 = 1006.

66. AU 941; AFM 939 = 941. See Ó Corráin, 'Muirchertach Mac Lochlainn and the circuit of Ireland,' p. 238–50.

67. CGG, p. 137.

68. CGG, p. 137–9.

69. CGG, p. 139.

70. AU 1006.

71. AU 1008.

72. AU, CS 1008, 1009; AFM 1007 = 1008, 1008 = 1009.

73. AI 1010; cf. AU; CS 1010; AFM 1009 = 1010.

74. See Westropp, 'Types of the ring-forts remaining in eastern Clare,' p. 203.

75. Ó Corráin, 'Muirchertach Mac Lochlainn and the circuit of Ireland'.

76. AFM 1091.

77. Hogan, *Onomasticon Goedelicum*.

78. CGG, p. 139.

79. CGG, p. 139–41.

80. AI 990; AFM 1009 = 1010; AU 1010; Ó Corráin, 'Dál Cais'.

81. Ó Carragáin, 'Patterns of patronage,' p. 23–41.

82. Madden, *Holy Island / Inis Cealtra*.

83. CS 966.

84. AI 1011.

85. AU, CS 1011; AFM 1010 = 1011.

86. Katharine Simms, *From Kings to Warlords: The Changing Political Structure of Gaelic Ireland in the Later Middle Ages* (Studies in Celtic History, 7), Woodbridge (Suffolk): Boydell Press, p. 178.

87. AI 1011; AFM 1010 = 1011.

Chapter 4

1. AU 1011; AFM 1010 = 1011.

2. AU 1012; AFM 1011 = 1012.

3. AU 1013.

4. AU 1013; AFM 1012 = 1013.

5. AI 1012; AU 1013; AFM 1012 = 1013.

6. AU, CS 1013; AFM 1012 = 1013.

7. Ní Mhaonaigh, 'Bréifne bias in Cogad Gáedel re Gallaib,' p. 135–58.

8. CGG, p. 147.

9. AT 977.

10. AU, CS, AI 1013; AFM 1012 = 1013; CGG, p. 149.

11. AU, CS, AI 1013; AFM 1012 = 1013.

12. CGG, p. 151.

13. CGG, p. 151.

14. Ó Lochlainn, 'Poets on the Battle of Clontarf'; Fischer, 'Two poets and the legend of Brian Bóraimhe.'

15. Ó Corráin, 'Dál Cais,' 54.

16. CGG, p. 185.

17. Marstrander, 'Lochlainn,' p. 250–51; Ó Corráin, 'The Vikings in Scotland and Ireland in the ninth century'; Colmán Etchingham, 'The location of historical Laithlinn/Lochla(i)nn: Scotland or Scandinavia?' in *Proceedings of the Seventh Symposium of Societas Celtologica Nordica*, ed. Mícheál Ó Flaithearta, Uppsala: Uppsala Universitet, 2007, p. 11–31; Ní Mhaonaigh, 'Literary Lochlann,' p. 25–37.

18. CGG, p. 207.

19. See Marstrander, *Bidrag til det Norske Sprogs Historie i Irland*; Stokes, 'On the linguistic value of the Irish annals,' p. 56–132; Ó Corráin, 'The Vikings in Scotland and Ireland in the ninth century.'

20. *Brennu-Njáls Saga*, p. 440–44, 448–51; *Orkneyinga Saga: The History of the Earls of Orkney*, p. 36–8, 225; Sayers, 'Clontarf and the Irish destinies of Sigurðr Digri, Earl of Orkney, and Þorsteinn Síðu-Hallsson,' p. 164–86.

21. AU 989.

22. AFM 1142.

23. CS 883; AU 918; AFM 916 = 918.

24. CGG, p. 39.

25. Marstrander, *Bidrag til det Norske Sprogs Historie i Irland*, p. 89.

26. Meyer, 'Altirisch Erulb n. pr. m.,' p. 108; Thornton, 'Clann Eruilb,' p. 161–6.

27. Landnámabók Íslands.

28. AFM 960 = 962; 972 = 974; CGG, p. 207; Ó Murchadha, 'Lagmainn, Lögmenn,' p. 136–40.

29. Lönnroth, *Njals Saga*, p. 226–36; Sveinnson, *Brennu-Njáls Saga*, p. 445–8; *Njal's Saga*, p. 344–6.

30. CGG, p. 150, 167, 207; AU 980.

31. ALC 1014; AFM 1013 = 1014.

32. *Lebor Gabála Érenn*, p. 404–5.

33. For a full discussion see Casey, 'Historical and literary representations of Brian Boru's burial in Armagh,' p. 29–44.

34. Gwynn, 'Were the Annals of Inisfallen written at Killaloe?' p. 20–33.

35. CGG, p. 211–13.

36. AU 935, 980, 1064.

37. CGG, p. 201–3.

38. CGG, p. 211.

39. The Annals of Boyle are printed in Freeman, 'The annals in Cotton. MS Titus A XXV.'

40. P. [George Petrie], 'Ancient monument in the Hospital Fields, Dublin,' p. 68–9.

41. Stanihurst, 'A description of Ireland,' p. 582.

42. See MacShamhráin, *Church and Polity in Pre-Norman Ireland*, p. 89; AFM 1029, 1050, 1051; CGH, p. 11 (117b10).

43. CGG, p. 193.

44. Cf. O'Flynn, 'The career of Máelsechnaill II.'

45. Alex Woolf, 'Amlaíb Cuarán and the Gael,' p. 34–43.

46. Duffy, 'The royal dynasties of Dublin and the Isles in the eleventh century,' p. 51–65.

47. AFM 975 = 977; AU, AT, CS 977.

48. AFM 972 = 974; AI 974, 975.

49. Mac Cionnaith, *Díoghluim Dána*, p. 321–5.

Chapter 5

1. Casey, 'A reconsideration of the authorship and transmission of Cogadh Gáedhel re Gallaibh,' p. 1–23.

2. CGG, p. 151–3.

3. AU, CS, AT, AFM 1034.

4. Duffy, 'Ostmen, Irish and Welsh in the eleventh century,' p. 378–96.

5. Duffy, 'Ostmen, Irish and Welsh in the eleventh century'; Davies, *Patterns of Power in Early Wales*, p. 57–9; Etchingham, 'North Wales, Ireland and the Isles.'

6. AU 960; AFM 958 = 960; see O'Flynn, 'The Dublin Vikings and the Clann Cholmáin kings of Southern Uí Néill.'

7. *The Annals of Clonmacnoise*, 988 = 995; AFM 994 = 995; CS 993 = 995; AT 995; see also AU, CS, AT, AFM 1029.

8. CGG, p. 155.

9. CGG, p. 155; for Mag Elta see Ryan, 'Battle of Clontarf,' p. 33–4.

10. CGG, p. 155.

11. Ní Mhaonaigh, 'Bréifne bias in Cogad Gáedel re Gallaib.'

12. CGG, p. 159.

13. CGG, p. 161–3.

14. CGG, p. 163–5.

15. TCD ms. 1298 (formerly H.2.7), fol. 254.

16. CGG, p. 167–9.

17. CGG, p. 171.

18. CGG, p. 175; on the *mormaer* see Kenneth Jackson, *The Gaelic Notes in the Book of Deer* (Osborn Bergin Memorial Lecture, 1970), Cambridge: Cambridge University Press, 1972, p. 102–10; Woolf, *From Pictland to Alba*, p. 342–4.

19. CGG, p. 175–7.

20. CGG, p. 209.

21. Ní Mhaonaigh, 'Bréifne bias in Cogad Gáedel re Gallaib.'

22. CGG, p. 181.

23. CGG, p. 185.

24. AFM 1112.

25. AFM, vol. 2, 1013 = 1014, note.

26. CGG, p. 189.

27. CGG, p. 191.

28. CGG, p. 193.

29. CGG, p. 207–9.

30. Duffy, 'Ostmen, Irish and Welsh in the eleventh century.'

31. CGG, p. 191–3.

32. AI 1000.

33. CGG, p. 197, 199.

34. Cf. Ryan, 'The Battle of Clontarf,' p. 31–7.

35. Samuel Haughton, 'On the time of high water in Dublin Bay,' p. 495–511.

36. CGG, p. xxv–xxvii.

37. O'Gorman, 'On the site of the Battle of Clontarf,' p. 169–82; Traynor, 'Where was the battle of Clontarf fought?' p. 106; Clery [Ua Clérigh], 'Early Irish history,' p. 31–43, 87–97; Lloyd, 'Earl Sigurd's forlorn hope,' p. 35–54, 87–99; Westropp, *King Brian, the Hero of Clontarf.*

38. CGG, p. 193.

39. CGH, p. 360–61 (LL 320ab33–6).

40. CGG, p. clxxxiv, n. 3.
41. Aidan O'Sullivan, 'Place, memory and identity among estuarine fishing communities: Interpreting archaeology of early medieval fish weirs,' *World Archaeology*, 35 (2003), p. 449–68.
42. Cosgrave, *North Dublin: City and Environs*, p. 125–31.
43. CGG, p. 203–5.
44. Ní Mhaonaigh, *Brian Boru*, p. 59.
45. Biblioteca Apostolica Vaticana, MS Pal. lat. 830; MacCarthy, *The Codex Palatino-Vaticanus*, p. 8.
46. Casey, 'A reconsideration of the authorship and transmission of Cogadh Gáedhel re Gallaibh.'
47. CGG, p. 211.

Chapter 6
1. 'Þorsteins Saga Síðu Hallssonar,' p. 301–2.
2. See Duffy, 'Ostmen, Irish and Welsh in the eleventh century'; Etchingham, 'North Wales, Ireland and the Isles,' p. 180–83.
3. *Brut y Tywysogyon or the Chronicle of the Princes: Peniarth MS 20 Version*, p. 11.
4. *Annales Cambriae*, p. 22.
5. Gillingham, 'Ademar of Chabannes and the history of Aquitaine in the reign of Charles the Bald,' p. 3–14.
6. Picard, *Aquitaine and Ireland in the Middle Ages*.
7. Michel Dillange, *Les Comtes de Poitou, Ducs d'Aquitaine (778–1204)*, Poitiers: Geste Éditions, 1995, p. 61.
8. Adémar of Chabannes, *Chronicon Aquitanicum et Francicum*, p. 177.
9. *Orkneyinga Saga, Legenda de Sancto Magno*, p. 25–7.
10. Downham, 'The career of Cearbhall of Osraighe,' p. 1–18.
11. See, for example, Ó Corráin, 'Viking Ireland: Afterthoughts,' p. 447–52; Ní Mhaonaigh, *Brian Boru*, p. 83–90; DuBois, 'Juxtaposing Cogadh Gáedel re Gallaib with Orkneyinga Saga,' p. 267–96.
12. *Brennu-Njáls Saga*, p. 445.
13. Sayers, 'Clontarf and the Irish destinies of Sigurðr Digri, Earl of Orkney, and Þorsteinn Síðu-Hallsson,' p. 174.
14. *Brennu-Njáls Saga*, p. 445.
15. See, for example, Ní Mhaonaigh, 'Tales of three Gormlaiths in medieval Irish literature,' p. 1–24.
16. *Pace* Goedheer, Irish and Norse Traditions about the Battle of Clontarf, p. 106–7.

17. See Goedheer, *Irish and Norse Traditions about the Battle of Clontarf*, p. 87–102; Ní Mhaonaigh, *Brian Boru*, p. 83–90.
18. *Brennu-Njáls Saga*, p. 459–60.
19. *Orkneyinga Saga, Legenda de Sancto Magno*, p. 27.

Conclusion

1. Ryan, 'The Battle of Clontarf,' p. 47–9.
2. See, for example, Goedheer, *Irish and Norse Traditions about the Battle of Clontarf*, chap. III; Young, 'A note on the Norse occupation of Ireland,' p. 20–21; Ó Corráin, *Ireland Before the Normans*, p. 130. In contrast see Hudson, *Viking Pirates and Christian Princes*, p. 96–106.
3. *The Book of Leinster*, vol. 3, p. 514 (line 15966–9).
4. Hudson, *Viking Pirates and Christian Princes*, p. 74–8; Woolf, *From Pictland to Alba*, p. 94, 217–18, 298; Downham, *Viking Kings of Britain and Ireland*, p. 60, 128–9, 195–6, 224.
5. Keynes, 'The historical context of the Battle of Maldon,' p. 81–113.
6. AU 986, 987.
7. Hudson, 'Knútr and Viking Dublin,' p. 323.
8. CS 984 = 986.
9. Adam of Bremen, *Gesta Hammaburgensis Ecclesiae Pontificum*, vol. 2, p. 32.
10. *Brut y Tywysogyon*, s.a. 995.
11. *Anglo-Saxon Chronicle*, s.a. 1000.
12. Woolf, *From Pictland to Alba*, p. 300–308.
13. Ó Corráin, 'The career of Diarmait mac Máel na mBó, King of Leinster.'
14. Woolf, 'Amlaíb Cuarán and the Gael.'
15. AU 977.
16. AU 980.
17. Carney, 'The Ó Cianáin miscellany,' p. 144, 146 (stanza 4).
18. AT 979 = 980; CS 978 = 980; AFM 979 = 980.
19. CGG, p. 211–17.
20. AFM 1014 = 1015.
21. AT; AFM 1023.
22. AI; AFM; AT; AU; CS 1026.
23. Ó Riain, 'The shrine of the Stowe Missal redated,' p. 285–95.
24. O'Flynn, 'The career of Máelsechnaill II.'
25. Ó Riain, 'The Psalter of Cashel,' p. 107–30; Downey, 'The life and work of Cúán ua Lothcháin,' p. 55–78.
26. AFM 1014 = 1015; CS 1013 = 1015.

27. AFM 1014 = 1015.
28. AFM 1017 = 1018.
29. AT 1020 p. 358; CS 1018 (= 1020) p. 259; AFM 1019 (= 1020) p. 795.
30. AT; AFM 1021.
31. Walsh, 'The Ua Maelechlainn Kings of Meath,' p. 165–83.
32. LL, vol. 3, p. 493.
33. Ó Corráin, 'The Uí Chennselaig kingship of Leinster.'
34. *Historia Gruffudd vab Kenan; Vita Griffini Filii Conani.*
35. Ben Hudson, 'The family of Harold Godwinson and the Irish Sea province,' *Journal of the Royal Society of Antiquaries of Ireland,* vol. 109 (1979), p. 92–100.
36. Seán Duffy, '"The western world's tower of honour and dignity",' p. 56–73.
37. Byrne, *Irish Kings and High-Kings,* p. 271.
38. Ó Corráin, 'The Uí Chennselaig kingship of Leinster.'
39. Duffy, 'Irishmen and Islesmen in the kingdoms of Dublin and Man.'
40. Duffy, 'The royal dynasties of Dublin and the Isles in the eleventh century,' p. 51–65.
41. LL, vol. 1, p. 98.
42. Candon, 'Muirchertach Ua Briain, politics and naval activity in the Irish Sea'; Duffy, '"The western world's tower of honour and dignity".'
43. AI 1079.
44. Martin Holland, 'Dublin and the reform of the Irish church in the eleventh and twelfth centuries'; Holland, 'The Synod of Dublin in 1080.'
45. Clover and Gibson, *The Letters of Lanfranc, Archbishop of Canterbury,* nos. 9 and 10.
46. Holland, 'The Synod of Dublin in 1080.'
47. Gwynn, *The Irish Church in the Eleventh and Twelfth Centuries;* Bethell, 'English monks and Irish reform in the eleventh and twelfth centuries.'
48. Michael Richter (ed.), *Canterbury Professions, with Palaeographical Notes by T. J. Brown,* Torquay: Canterbury and York Society, 1973.
49. Fleming, *Gille of Limerick;* Flanagan, *The Transformation of the Irish Church in the Twelfth Century.*
50. Martin Brett, 'Canterbury's perspective on church reform and Ireland, 1070–1115.'
51. Martin Holland, 'Cashel, Synod of (1101),' in Duffy, *Medieval Ireland: An Encyclopedia,* p. 65–6.
52. Martin Holland, 'Ráith Bressail, Synod of,' in Duffy, *Medieval Ireland: An Encyclopedia,* p. 397–8.
53. Flanagan, *Irish Society, Anglo-Norman Settlers, Angevin Kingship,* chap. 1.

54. Candon, 'Muirchertach Ua Briain, politics and naval activity in the Irish Sea.'

55. Duffy, 'Irishmen and Islesmen in the kingdoms of Dublin and Man,' p. 109.

56. *Historia Gruffudd van Kenan*, passim; *Vita Griffini Filii Conani*, passim.

57. Duffy, 'Ostmen, Irish and Welsh in the eleventh century.'

58. Hudson, 'William the Conqueror and Ireland.'

59. Maddicott, 'Responses to the threat of invasion.'

60. Higham, 'The Domesday survey.'

61. Holt, '1086,' p. 41–4.

62. Benjamin Hudson, 'Cnut and Viking Dublin' and 'Cnut and the Scottish kings,' reprinted in Hudson, *Irish Sea Studies*, chap. 2 and 3.

63. Etchingham, 'North Wales, Ireland and the Isles.'

64. Adam of Bremen, *Gesta Hammaburgensis Ecclesiae Pontificum*, vol. 3, p. 51.

65. Ben Hudson, 'The family of Harold Godwinson and the Irish Sea province,' *Journal of the Royal Society of Antiquaries of Ireland*, vol. 109 (1979), p. 92–100.

66. Duffy, 'Irishmen and Islesmen in the kingdoms of Dublin and Man,' p. 102.

67. Ryan, 'The O'Briens in Munster after Clontarf.'

68. Duffy, 'Irishmen and Islesmen in the kingdoms of Dublin and Man.'

69. *Cronica Regum Mannie et Insularum*.

70. Power, 'Magnus Barelegs' expeditions to the west'; Power, 'Meeting in Norway.'

71. Duffy, 'The 1169 invasion as a turning-point in Irish-Welsh relations.'

72. Curtis, 'Murchertach O'Brien, high king of Ireland, and his Norman son-in-law, Arnulf de Montgomery'; Victoria Chandler, 'The last of the Montgomerys: Roger the Poitevin and Arnulf,' *Historical Research*, 62 (1989), p. 1–14; Kathleen Thompson, 'Note de recherche: Arnoul de Montgommery,' *Annales de Normandie*, 45 (1995), p. 49–53.

73. Ní Mhaonaigh, *Brian Boru*, p. 53–4, 82–3, 119–20.

74. Goedheer, *Irish and Norse Traditions about the Battle of Clontarf*, p. 50, 55 (quatrain 47).

75. Goedheer, *Irish and Norse Traditions about the Battle of Clontarf*, p. 45–59.

76. Keating, *Foras Feasa ar Éirinn*, vol. III, p. 247–9.

77. Keating, *Foras Feasa ar Éirinn*, vol. III, p. 255–7.

78. Keating, *Foras Feasa ar Éirinn*, vol. III, p. 257.

79. Keating, *Foras Feasa ar Éirinn*, vol. III, p. 275, 285–7.

80. O'Connor, *The General History of Ireland*.

81. Keating, *Foras Feasa ar Éirinn*, vol. III, p. 261.

82. Keating, *Foras Feasa ar Éirinn*, vol. III, p. 263.

83. O'Curry, *Lectures on the Manuscript Materials of Ancient Irish History*, p. 214.

84. O'Curry, *Lectures on the Manuscript Materials of Ancient Irish History*, p. 210–11.

85. *Cath Cluana Tarbh*, p. 1.

86. J. S. Brewer and William Bullen (eds.), *Calendar of the Carew Manuscripts Preserved in the Archiepiscopal Library at Lambeth*, London: Longmans, Green, Reader, and Dyer, vol. 5, p. 24–5; Fischer, 'How Dublin remembered the Battle of Clontarf.'

87. Valerie McGowan-Doyle, *The Book of Howth: The Elizabethan Re-conquest and the Old English*, Cork: Cork University Press, 2011.

88. Stanihurst, 'A description of Ireland,' p. 582.

89. Hanmer, *The Chronicle of Ireland*, p. 91.

90. Ware, *Antiquities and History of Ireland*, p. 63.

91. Butler, *Irish Tales*.

92. Dunlop, Robert, *Daniel O'Connell and the Revival of National Life in Ireland*, New York: G. P. Putnam's Sons, 1900, p. 350.

93. O'Halloran, *Golden Ages and Barbarous Nations*, p. 92–3.

94. O'Halloran, 'The triumph of "virtuous liberty"', p. 151–63.

95. O'Conor, Charles, *Dissertations on the Antient History of Ireland* (1st edition), Dublin: 1753, p. 83–4.

96. O'Conor, Charles, *Dissertations on the Antient History of Ireland* (2nd edition), 1766, p. 264.

97. O'Halloran, *A General History of Ireland*, vol. III, p. 263–7.

BIBLIOGRAPHY

PRIMARY SOURCES

Adam of Bremen, *Gesta Hammaburgensis Ecclesiae Pontificum*, ed. Bernhard Schmeidler (Monumenta Germaniae Historica, Scriptores Rerum Germanicarum), Hannover and Leipzig: Hahnsche Buchhandlung, 1917.

Adémar of Chabannes, *Chronicon Aquitanicum et Francicum* or *Historia Francorum*, ed. Jules Chavanon, Paris: Alphonse Picard et Fils, 1897.

Anderson, A. O., 'The prophecy of Berchan,' *Zeitschrift für Celtische Philologie*, 18 (1930), p. 1–56.

The Anglo-Saxon Chronicle, ed. Michael Swanton, London: J. M. Dent, 1996.

The Anglo-Saxon Chronicle, ed. Dorothy Whitelock, London: Eyre and Spottiswoode, 1961; revised edition, 1965.

Annala Rioghachta Eireann: Annals of the Kingdom of Ireland, by the Four Masters, from the Earliest Period to the Year 1616, ed. John O'Donovan (2nd edition), 7 vols., Dublin: Royal Irish Academy, 1856.

Annales Cambriae, ed. John Williams ab Ithel (Rolls Series), London: Longman, Green, Longman and Roberts, 1860.

Annales Cambriae, A.D. 682–954: Texts A–C in Parallel, ed. David N. Dumville, Cambridge: Cambridge University Press, 2002.

Annales de Saint-Bertin, ed. Félix Grat et al., Paris: Klincksieck, for the Société de l'Histoire de France, 1964.

The Annals of Clonmacnoise, Being Annals of Ireland from the Earliest Period to A.D. 1408, ed. Denis Murphy, Dublin: Royal Society of Antiquaries, 1896; facsimile reprint, Felinfach (Ceredigion): Llanerch Press, 1993.

The Annals of Inisfallen (MS Rawlinson B503), ed. Séan Mac Airt, Dublin: Dublin Institute for Advanced Studies, 1951.

The Annals of Loch Cé: A Chronicle of Irish Affairs from A.D. 1014 to A.D. 1590, ed. William M. Hennessy (Rolls Series), 2 vols., London: Longman, 1871.

The Annals of St-Bertin, trans. Janet L. Nelson, Manchester: Manchester University Press, 1991.

The Annals of Tigernach, ed. Whitley Stokes (2nd edition), 2 vols., Felinfach (Ceredigion): Llanerch Press, 1993.

The Annals of Ulster (to A.D. *1131),* ed. Seán Mac Airt and Gearóid Mac Niocaill, Dublin: Dublin Institute for Advanced Studies, 1983.

Baile in Scáil: 'The Phantom's Frenzy,' ed. Kevin Murray, London: Irish Texts Society, 2004.

Bede's Ecclesiastical History of the English People, ed. Bertram Colgrave and R. A. B. Mynors, Oxford: Clarendon Press, 1969; revised edition, 1991.

Bergin, Osborn, 'A dialogue between Donnchad son of Brian and Mac Coisse,' *Ériu,* IX (1921–3), p. 175–80.

Best, R. I., 'The Leabhar Oiris,' *Ériu,* 1 (1904), p. 74–112.

Bethu Brigte, ed. Donncha Ó hAodha, Dublin: Dublin Institute for Advanced Studies, 1978.

Bethu Phátraic: The Tripartite Life of Patrick, I: Text and Sources, ed. Kathleen Mulchrone, Dublin: Royal Irish Academy, 1939.

'The Book of Howth,' in J. S. Brewer and William Bullen (eds.), *Calendar of the Carew Manuscripts Preserved in the Archiepiscopal Library at Lambeth,* V, London: Longmans, Green, Reader, and Dyer, 1871.

The Book of the Icelanders: Íslendingabók by Ari Thorgilsson, ed. Halldór Hermansson, *Islandica,* vol. 20, Ithaca (NY): Cornell University Press, 1930.

The Book of Lecan: Leabhar Mór Mhic Fhir Bhisigh Leacáin (Facsimiles in Collotype of Irish Manuscripts, 2), introd. Kathleen Mulchrone, Dublin: Stationery Office, for the Irish Manuscripts Commission, 1937.

The Book of Settlements: Landnámabók, ed. Hermann Pálsson and Paul Edwards (University of Manitoba Icelandic Studies, 1), Winnipeg: University of Manitoba Press, 1972.

The Book of Uí Maine, Otherwise Called the Book of the O'Kellys (Facsimiles in Collotype of Irish Manuscripts, 4), introd. R. A. S. Macalister, Dublin: Stationery Office, for the Irish Manuscripts Commission, 1941.

Brenhinedd y Saesson or The Kings of the Saxons, ed. Thomas Jones (Board of Celtic Studies, University of Wales, History and Law Series, 25), Cardiff: University of Wales Press, 1971.

Brennu-Njáls Saga, ed. Einar Ól. Sveinsson (Íslenzk Fornrit, 12), Reykjavík: Íslenzka Fornritafélag, 1954.

Brut y Tywysogyon: Peniarth MS. 20, ed. Thomas Jones (Board of Celtic Studies, University of Wales, History and Law Series, 6), Cardiff: University of Wales Press, 1941.

Brut y Tywysogyon or The Chronicle of the Princes: Peniarth MS 20 *Version*, trans. Thomas Jones (Board of Celtic Studies, University of Wales, History and Law Series, 11), Cardiff: University of Wales Press, 1952.

Brut y Tywysogyon or The Chronicle of the Princes: Red Book of Hergest Version, ed. Thomas Jones (Board of Celtic Studies, University of Wales, History and Law Series, 16), Cardiff: University of Wales Press, 1955; second edition, 1973.

Butler, Sarah, *Irish Tales, or Instructive Histories for the Happy Conduct of Life*, London: Edmund Curll and John Hooke, 1716.

Butler, Sarah, *Irish Tales, or Instructive Histories for the Happy Conduct of Life* [1716], ed. Ian Campbell Ross et al., Dublin: Four Courts Press, 2010.

Caithreim Cellachain Caisil: The Victorious Career of Cellachan of Cashel, or the Wars between the Irish and the Norsemen in the Middle of the Tenth Century, ed. Alexander Bugge (Norske Historiske Kildeskriftfonds Skrifter), Christiania [Oslo]: J. C. Gundersens Bogtrykkeri, 1905.

Carney, James, 'The Ó Cianáin miscellany,' *Ériu*, 21 (1969), p. 122–47.

Cath Cluana Tarbh: 'The Battle of Clontarf,' ed. Meidhbhín Ní Úrdail, London: Irish Texts Society, 2011.

Charlemagne and Louis the Pious: Lives by Einhard, Notker, Ernoldus, Thegan, and the Astronomer, trans. Thomas F. X. Noble, University Park (Pa.): Pennsylvania State University Press, 2009.

Chronicles of the Vikings: Records, Memorials and Myths, trans. R. I. Page, London: British Museum Press, 1995.

Chronicum Scotorum: A Chronicle of Irish Affairs, from the Earliest Times to A.D. *1135, with a Supplement Containing the Events from* A.D. *1114 to* A.D. *1150*, ed. William M. Hennessy (Rolls Series), London: Longman, 1866.

Clover, Helen, and Gibson, Margaret (eds.), *The Letters of Lanfranc, Archbishop of Canterbury*, Oxford: Oxford University Press, 1979.

Cogadh Gaedhel re Gallaibh: The War of the Gaedhil with the Gaill; or, the Invasions of Ireland by Danes and Other Norsemen, ed. James Henthorn Todd (Rolls Series), London: Longmans, Green, Reader, and Dyer, 1867.

Corpus Genealogiarum Hiberniae, ed. M. A. O'Brien, Dublin: Dublin Institute for Advanced Studies, 1962.

Corpus Iuris Hibernici: Ad Fidem Codicum Manuscriptorum, ed. D. A. Binchy, 6 vols., Dublin: Dublin Institute for Advanced Studies, 1978.

Críth Gablach, ed. D. A. Binchy (Medieval and Modern Irish Series, 11), Dublin: Stationery Office, 1941.

Cronica Regum Mannie et Insularum: Chronicles of the Kings of Man and the Isles: BL *Cotton Julius Avii*, ed. George Broderick, Douglas (Isle of Man): Manx National Heritage, 1995.

Dicuili Liber de Mensura Orbis Terrae, ed. J. J. Tierney (Scriptores Latini Hiberniae, 6), Dublin: Dublin Institute for Advances Studies, 1967.

Dobbs, Margaret E., 'The Ban-Shenchus,' *Revue Celtique*, 47 (1930), p. 283–339; 48 (1931), p. 163–234; 49 (1932), p. 437–89.

Early Sources of Scottish History, A.D. 500 to 1286, trans. Alan Orr Anderson, 2 vols., Edinburgh: Oliver and Boyd, 1922; reprinted with corrections, Stamford (Lincs): Paul Watkins, 1990.

Egils Saga Skalla-grímssonar, ed. Sigurður Nordal (Íslenzk Fornrit, 2), Rejkjavík: Íslenzka Fornritafélag, 1933.

English Historical Documents, c. 500–1042, trans. Dorothy Whitelock (2nd edition), London: Methuen, 1979.

Fagrskinna: Nóregs Kononga Tal, ed. Finnur Jónsson, København: S. L. Mollers Bøgtrykkeri, 1902–3.

Flateyjarbók: En Samling af Norske Konge-sagaer, ed. Guðbrandr Vígfusson and C. R. Unger, 3 vols., Christiania [Oslo]: P. T. Mallings Forlagsboghandel, 1860–68.

Fragmentary Annals of Ireland, ed. Joan Radner, Dublin: Dublin Institute for Advanced Studies, 1978.

Freeman, A. M., 'The annals in Cotton. MS Titus A XXV,' *Revue Celtique*, 41 (1924), p. 301–30; 42 (1925), p. 283–305; 43 (1926), p. 358–84; 44 (1927), p. 336–61.

Gerald of Wales, *Expugnatio Hibernica: The Conquest of Ireland, by Giraldus Cambrensis*, ed. A. B. Scott and F. X. Martin, Dublin: Royal Irish Academy, 1978.

Gerald of Wales, *The History and Topography of Ireland*, trans. John J. O'Meara, Harmondsworth (Middx): Penguin Classics, 1982.

Hanmer, Meredith, *The Chronicle of Ireland*, Dublin: 1633.

Historia Gruffudd vab Kenan, ed. D. Simon Evans, Caerdydd: Gwasg Prifysgol Cymru, 1977.

Hudson, Benjamin T., 'The Scottish Chronicle,' *Scottish Historical Review*, 77 (1998), p. 129–61.

Keating, Geoffrey, *Foras Feasa ar Éirinn: The History of Ireland* [c. 1634], ed. David Comyn and P. S. Dineen, 4 vols., London: Irish Texts Society, 1902–14.

Landnámabók Íslands, ed. Einar Arnórsson, Reykjavik: Helgafell, 1948.

Laxdœla Saga: Halldórs Þættir: Snorrasonar Stúfs Þáttr, ed. Einar Ól. Sveinsson (Íslenzk Fornrit, 5), Reykjavík: Íslenzka Fornritafélag, 1934.

Leabhar Mór na nGenealach: The Great Book of Irish Genealogies, compiled (1645–66) by Dubhaltach Mac Fhirbhisigh, ed. Nollaig Ó Muraíle, 5 vols., Dublin: de Búrca, 2003–4.

An Leabhar Muimhneach maraon le Suim Aguisíní, ed. Tadhg Ó Donnchadha, Dublin: Irish Manuscripts Commission, 1941.

Lebor Gabála Érenn: The Book of the Taking of Ireland, ed. R. A. S. Macalister, 5 vols., London: Irish Texts Society, 1938–56.

Lebor na Cert: The Book of Rights, ed. Myles Dillon, London: Irish Texts Society, 1962.

Liber Ardmachanus: The Book of Armagh, ed. John Gwynn, Dublin: Hodges, Figgis; London: Williams and Norgate; for the Royal Irish Academy, 1913.

Libri Epistolarum Sancti Patricii Episcopi. Part 1: Introduction, Text and Commentary, ed. Ludwig Bieler, Dublin: Stationery Office, 1952.

MacCarthy, Bartholomew (ed.), *The Codex Palatino-Vaticanus, No. 830* (Todd Lecture Series, 3), Dublin: Hodges, Figgis, for the Royal Irish Academy, 1892.

Mac Cionnaith, Láimhbheartach (ed.), *Díoghluim Dána*, Dublin: Oifig an tSoláthair, 1938.

MacNeill, John [Eoin], 'Poems by Flann Mainistrech on the Dynasties of Ailech, Mide and Brega,' *Archivium Hibernicum*, 2 (1913), p. 37–100.

Mariani Scotti Chronicon, ed. Georg Waitz (Monumenta Germaniae Historica, Scriptores [in folio], V), Hannover: 1844, p. 481–564.

A Mediaeval Prince of Wales: The Life of Gruffudd ap Cynan, trans. D. Simon Evans, Felinfach (Ceredigion): Llanerch Press, 1990.

The Metrical Dindshenchas, ed. Edward Gwynn, 5 vols., Dublin: Royal Irish Academy, 1903–35; reprinted Dublin: Dublin Institute for Advanced Studies, 1991.

Meyer, Kuno, 'Mitteilungen aus Irischen handschriften: Aus dem buch der Huí Maine fo. 112b.1: Drei berümte bäume Irlands,' *Zeitschrift für Celtische Philologie*, 5 (1904), p. 21–3.

Meyer, Kuno, 'A poem by Dallán mac Móre,' *Revue Celtique*, 29 (1908), p. 210–14.

Ní Bhrolcháin, Muireann, 'An Banseanchas Filíochta' (MA dissertation, National University of Ireland, Galway), 1977.

Ní Bhrolcháin, Muireann, 'The Prose Banshenchas' (PhD dissertation, National University of Ireland, Galway), 1980.

Njal's Saga, trans. Magnus Magnusson and Hermann Pálsson, Harmondsworth (Middx): Penguin Classics, 1960.

O'Connor, Dermod, *The General History of Ireland . . . Collected by the Learned Jeoffrey Keating, D.D.: Faithfully Translated from the Original Irish Language, with Many Curious Amendments Taken from the Psalters of Tara and Cashel, and Other Authentic Records*, Dublin: 1723.

O'Keefe, J. G., 'On Mael Shechlainn, King of Ireland, †1022, and his contemporaries,' in James Fraser, Paul Grosjean and J. G. O'Keefe (eds.), *Irish Texts*, fasiculus IV, London: Sheed and Ward, 1934, p. 30–33.

Ó Lochlainn, Colm, 'Poets on the Battle of Clontarf,' *Éigse*, 3 (1941–2), p. 208–18; 4 (1943–4), p. 33–47.

Orkneyinga Saga, Legenda de Sancto Magno, Magnúss Saga Skemmri, Magnúss Saga Lengri, Helga Þáttr ok Úlfs, ed. Finnbogi Guðmundsson (Íslenzk Fornrit, 34), Reykjavík: Íslenzka Fornritafélag, 1965.

Orkneyinga Saga: The History of the Earls of Orkney, trans. Hermann Pálsson and Paul Edwards, Harmondsworth (Middx): Penguin Classics, 1981.

The Patrician Texts in the Book of Armagh, ed. Ludwig Bieler (Scriptores Latini Hiberniae, 10), Dublin: Dublin Institute for Advanced Studies, 1979.

Pender, Séamus (ed.), 'The O'Clery Book of Genealogies,' *Analecta Hibernica*, 18 (1951).

The Prophecy of Berchán: Irish and Scottish High-Kings of the Early Middle Ages, ed. Benjamin T. Hudson, Westport (Conn.): Greenwood Press, 1996.

'Rém rígraidi Dáil Cais,' in *The Book of Lecan*, fol. 229re20.

Smith, Peter J., 'Mide Maigen Clainne Cuind: A medieval poem on the kings of Mide,' *Peritia*, 15 (2001), p. 108–44.

Smith, Peter (ed.), *Three Historical Poems Ascribed to Gilla Cóemáin: A Critical Edition of the Work of an Eleventh-Century Irish Scholar* (Studien und Texte zur Keltologie, 8), Münster: Nodus, 2007.

Snorri Sturluson, *Heimskringla*, ed. Bjarni Aðalbjarnarson (Íslenzk Fornrit, 26–8), 3 vols., Reykjavík: Íslenzka Fornritafélag, 1941–51.

Stanihurst, Richard, 'A description of Ireland,' in Raphael Holinshed, *Chronicles*, vol. 3, London: 1577.

Stokes, Whitley, 'The Borama,' *Revue Celtique*, 8 (1892), p. 32–124.

Stokes, Whitley, 'On the deaths of some Irish heroes,' *Revue Celtique*, 23 (1902), p. 303–48.

'Þorsteins Saga Síðu Hallssonar,' in Jón Jóhannesson (ed.), *Austfirðinga Sögur* (Íslenzk Fornrit, 11), Reykjavík: Íslenzka Fornritafélag, 1950.

The Tripartite Life of Patrick: With Other Documents Relating to That Saint, ed. Whitley Stokes (Rolls Series), 2 vols., London: HM Stationery Office, 1887.

Two of the Saxon Chronicles Parallel, with Supplementary Extracts from the Others, ed. Charles Plummer, 2 vols., Oxford: Clarendon Press, 1892–9; revised impression, ed. Dorothy Whitelock, 1952.

Venerabilis Baedae Opera Historica, ed. Charles Plummer, 2 vols., Oxford: Clarendon Press, 1896.

Vita Griffini Filii Conani: The Medieval Latin Life of Gruffudd ap Cynan, ed. Paul Russell, Cardiff: University of Wales Press, 2005.

Ware, James, *Antiquities and History of Ireland*, trans. Walter Harris, Dublin: 1705.

SECONDARY STUDIES

Abrams, Lesley, 'The conversion of the Scandinavians of Dublin,' *Anglo-Norman Studies*, 20 (1997), p. 1–29.

Abrams, Lesley, 'Conversion and assimilation,' in Dawn M. Hadley and Julian D. Richards (eds.), *Cultures in Contact: Scandinavian Settlement in England in the Ninth and Tenth Centuries*, Turnhout: Brepols, 2000, p. 135–53.

Abrams, Lesley, 'England, Normandy and Scandinavia,' in Christopher Harper-Bill and Elizabeth van Houts (eds.), *A Companion to the Anglo-Norman World*, Woodbridge (Suffolk): Boydell and Brewer, 2003, p. 43–62.

Aitchison, Nicholas B., *Armagh and the Royal Centres in Early Medieval Ireland*, Woodbridge (Suffolk): Boydell and Brewer, 1994.

Andersen, Per Sveaas, 'Norse settlement in the Hebrides: What happened to the natives and what happened to the immigrants?' in Ian Wood and Niels Lund (eds.), *People and Places in Northern Europe, 500–1600: Essays in Honour of Peter Hayes Sawyer*, Woodbridge (Suffolk): Boydell and Brewer, 1991, p. 131–47.

Anderson, Marjorie Ogilvie, *Kings and Kingship in Early Scotland* (2nd edition), Edinburgh: Scottish Academic Press, 1980.

Andersson, Theodore M., 'The Viking policy of Ethelred the Unready in Anglo-Saxon England,' in John D. Niles and Mark Amodio (eds.), *Anglo-Scandinavian England: Norse-English Relations in the Period Before the Conquest*, Lanham (Md): University Press of America, 1989, p. 1–11.

Barrow, Julia, 'Chester's earliest regatta?: Edgar's Dee-rowing revisited,' *Early Medieval Europe*, 10 (2001), p. 81–93.

Bartlett, Robert, *The Making of Europe: Conquest, Colonization and Cultural Change, 950–1350*, London: Allen Lane, 1993.

Bates, David, *Normandy Before 1066*, London: Longman, 1982.

Bethell, Denis, 'English monks and Irish reform in the eleventh and twelfth centuries,' in T. D. Williams (ed.), *Historical Studies*, 8 (1971), p. 111–35.

Bhreathnach, Edel, *Tara: A Select Bibliography* (Discovery Programme Reports, 3), Dublin: Royal Irish Academy, 1995.

Bhreathnach, Edel, 'Temoria: Caput Scotorum?' *Ériu*, 47 (1996), p. 67–88.

Bhreathnach, Edel, 'The documentary evidence for pre-Norman Skreen, County Meath,' *Ríocht na Midhe*, 9, no. 2 (1996), p. 37–45.

Bhreathnach, Edel, 'Saint Patrick, Vikings and Inber Dée: Longphort in the early Irish literary tradition,' *Wicklow Archaeology and History*, 1 (1998), p. 36–40.

Bhreathnach, Edel, 'Columban churches in Brega and Leinster: Relations with the Norse and the Anglo-Normans,' *Journal of the Royal Society of Antiquaries of Ireland*, vol. 129 (1999), p. 5–18.

Bhreathnach, Edel, 'The cultural and political milieu of the deposition and manufacture of the hoard discovered at Reerasta Rath, Ardagh, Co. Limerick,' in Mark Redknap et al. (eds.), *Pattern and Purpose in Insular Art*, Oxford: Oxbow Books, 2001, p. 15–23.

Biddle, M., and Kjølbye-Biddle, B., 'Repton and the "Great Heathen Army," 873–4,' in James Graham-Campbell et al. (eds.), *Vikings and the Danelaw: Select Papers from the Proceedings of the Thirteenth Viking Congress*, Oxford: Oxbow Books, 2001, p. 45–96.

Binchy, D. A., 'The Fair of Tailtiu and the Feast of Tara,' *Ériu*, 18 (1958), p. 113–38.

Binns, Alan, 'The York Vikings: Relations between Old English and Old Norse culture,' in Alan Small (ed.), *The Fourth Viking Congress, York, August 1961*, Edinburgh: Oliver and Boyd, for the University of Aberdeen, 1965, p. 179–89.

Blackburn, Mark, and Pagan, Hugh, 'A revised checklist of coin hoards from the British Isles, c. 500–1100,' in M. A. S. Blackburn (ed.), *Anglo-Saxon Monetary History: Essays in Memory of Michael Dolley*, Leicester: Leicester University Press, 1986, p. 291–313.

Bradley, John, 'The interpretation of Scandinavian settlement in Ireland,' in John Bradley (ed.), *Settlement and Society in Medieval Ireland: Studies Presented to F. X. Martin, O.S.A.*, Kilkenny: Boethius Press, 1988, p. 49–78.

Bradley, John, and Halpin, Andrew, 'The topographical development of Scandinavian and Anglo-Norman Waterford city,' in T. W. Nolan and T. P. Power (eds.), *Waterford: History and Society*, Dublin: Geography Publications, 1992, p. 105–29.

Breatnach, Liam, 'Ardri as an old compound,' *Ériu*, 37 (1986), p. 192–3.

Breatnach, Liam, 'The ecclesiastical element in the Old Irish legal tract Cáin Fhuithirbe,' *Peritia*, 5 (1986), p. 35–50.

Breatnach, Liam, *A Companion to the Corpus Iuris Hibernici* (Early Irish Law Series, 5), Dublin: Dublin Institute for Advanced Studies, 2005.

Breese, Lauren Wood, 'The persistence of Scandinavian connections in Normandy in the tenth and eleventh centuries,' *Viator*, 8 (1977), p. 47–61.

Brett, Martin, 'Canterbury's perspective on church reform and Ireland, 1070–1115,' in Damian Bracken and Dagmar Ó Riain-Raedel (eds.), *Ireland and Europe in the Twelfth Century: Reform and Renewal*, Dublin: Four Courts Press, 2006, p. 13–35.

Broderick, George, 'Irish and Welsh strands in the genealogy of Godred Crovan,' *Journal of the Manx Museum*, 8 (1980), p. 32–8.

Brooke, Daphne, 'Gall-Gaidhil and Galloway,' in Richard D. Oram and Geoffrey P. Stell (eds.), *Galloway: Land and Lordship*, Edinburgh: Scottish Society for Northern Studies, 1991, p. 97–116.

Brooke, Daphne, *Wild Men and Holy Places: St Ninian, Whithorn, and the Medieval Realm of Galloway*, Edinburgh: Canongate, 1994.

Broun, Dauvit, 'Dunkeld and the Origins of Scottish Identity,' *Innes Review*, 48 (1997), p. 112–24.

Broun, Dauvit, 'Pictish kings, 761–839: Integration with Dál Riata or separate development?' in Sally Foster (ed.), *The St Andrews Sarcophagus: A Pictish Masterpiece and Its International Connections*, Dublin: Four Courts Press, 1998, p. 71–83.

Broun, Dauvit, *The Irish Identity of the Kingdom of the Scots in the Twelfth and Thirteenth Centuries* (Studies in Celtic History, 18), Woodbridge (Suffolk): Boydell and Brewer, 1999.

Broun, Dauvit, 'The Welsh identity of the kingdom of Strathclyde, ca 900–ca 1200,' *Innes Review*, 55 (2004), p. 111–80.

Brown, Phyllis R., 'The Viking policy of Ethelred: A response,' in John D. Niles and Mark Amodio (eds.), *Anglo-Scandinavian England: Norse-English Relations in the Period Before the Conquest*, Lanham (Md): University Press of America: 1989, p. 13–15.

Bugge, Alexander, *Contributions to the History of the Norsemen in Ireland* (Videnskabsselskabets Skrifter, II, Historisk-filosofisk Klasse, no. 4–5), 3 parts, Christiania [Oslo]: J. Dybwad, 1900.

Byock, Jesse, *Viking Age Iceland*, London: Penguin, 2001.

Byrne, F. J., 'Historical note on Cnogba (Knowth),' *Proceedings of the Royal Irish Academy*, 66C (1968), p. 383–400.

Byrne, F. J., *The Rise of the Uí Néill and the High-Kingship of Ireland*, Dublin: National University of Ireland, 1970.

Byrne, F. J., *Irish Kings and High-Kings*, London: Batsford, 1973; 2nd edition, Dublin: Four Courts Press, 2001.

Byrne, F. J., 'Heads of churches to c. 1200,' in T. W. Moody, F. X. Martin and F. J. Byrne (eds.), *A New History of Ireland, IX: Maps, Genealogies, Lists*, Oxford: Clarendon Press, 1984, p. 237–63.

Byrne, F. J., 'High-kings and provincial kings,' in T. W. Moody, F. X. Martin and F. J. Byrne (eds.), *A New History of Ireland, IX: Maps, Genealogies, Lists*, Oxford: Clarendon Press, 1984, p. 189–210.

Byrne, F. J., 'The Viking Age,' in Dáibhí Ó Cróinín (ed.), *A New History of Ireland, I: Prehistoric and Early Ireland*, Oxford: Clarendon Press, 2005, p. 609–34.

Byrne, F. J., and Nicholls, K. W., 'Genealogical tables,' in T. W. Moody, F. X. Martin and F. J. Byrne (eds.), *A New History of Ireland, IX: Maps, Genealogies, Lists*, Oxford: Clarendon Press, 1984, p. 125–74.

Byrne, Paul, 'The community of Clonard, sixth to twelfth centuries,' *Peritia*, 4 (1985), p. 157–73.

Byrne, Paul F., 'Certain Southern Uí Néill kingdoms' (PhD thesis, University College, Dublin), 2000.

Cahill, Mary, and Ó Floinn, Raghnall, 'Two silver kite brooches from near Limerick city,' *North Munster Antiquarian Journal*, 36 (1995), p. 65–82.

Candon, Anthony, 'Muirchertach Ua Briain, politics and naval activity in the Irish Sea, 1075–1119,' in Gearóid Mac Niocaill and Patrick F. Wallace (eds.), *Keimelia: Studies in Medieval Archaeology and History in Memory of Tom Delaney*, Galway: Galway University Press, 1988, p. 397–415.

Carey, John, *A New Introduction to Lebor Gabála Érenn*, London: Irish Texts Society, 1993.

Carey, John, *The Irish National Origin-Legend: Synthetic Pseudohistory*, Cambridge: University of Cambridge, 1994.

Carey, John, 'Tara and the supernatural,' in Edel Bhreathnach (ed.), *The Kingship and Landscape of Tara*, Dublin: Four Courts Press, for the Discovery Programme, 2005, p. 32–48.

Casey, Denis, 'Studies in the exercise of royal power in Ireland, c. 650–c. 1200' (PhD thesis, University of Cambridge), 2009.

Casey, Denis, 'Historical and literary representations of Brian Boru's burial in Armagh, 1014 AD,' *North Munster Antiquarian Journal*, 50 (2010), p. 29–44.

Casey, Denis, '"A compulsory and burdensome imposition": Billeting soldiers in medieval and early modern Ireland,' in Albrecht Classen and Nadia Margolis (eds.), *War and Peace: Critical Issues in European Societies and Literature, 800–1800*, Berlin: De Gruyter, 2011, p. 193–216.

Casey, Denis, 'A reconsideration of the authorship and transmission of Cogadh Gáedhel re Gallaibh,' *Proceedings of the Royal Irish Academy*, 113C (2013), p. 1–23.

Cassard, Jean-Christophe, *Le Siècle des Vikings en Bretagne*, Paris: Éditions Gisserot, 1996.

Chadwick, N. K., 'The Vikings and the Western World,' in Brian Ó Cuív (ed.), *Proceedings of the International Congress of Celtic Studies*, Dublin: Dublin Institute for Advanced Studies, 1962, p. 13–42.

Charles, B. G., *Old Norse Relations with Wales*, Cardiff: University of Wales Press Board, 1934.

Charles-Edwards, T. M., *Early Irish and Welsh Kinship*, Oxford: Clarendon Press, 1993.

Charles-Edwards, T. M., 'Irish warfare before 1100,' in Thomas Bartlett and Keith Jeffery (eds.), *A Military History of Ireland*, Cambridge: Cambridge University Press, 1996, p. 26–51.

Charles-Edwards, T. M., *Early Christian Ireland*, Cambridge: Cambridge University Press, 2000.

Chédeville, André, and Guillotel, Hubert, *La Bretagne des Saints et des Rois, Ve–Xe Siècle* (Histoire de la Bretagne, 4), Rennes: Éditions Ouest-France, 1984.

Christiansen, Eric, *The Norsemen in the Viking Age*, Oxford: Blackwell, 2002.

Clarke, Howard B., 'The bloodied eagle: The Vikings and the development of Dublin, 841–1014,' *Irish Sword*, 18 (1990–92), p. 91–119.

Clarke, Howard B., 'Proto-towns and towns in Ireland and Britain in the ninth and tenth centuries,' in Howard B. Clarke et al. (eds.), *Ireland and Scandinavia in the Early Viking Age*, Dublin: Four Courts Press, 1998, p. 331–80.

Clarke, Howard B., 'Christian cults and cult centres in Hiberno-Norse Dublin and its hinterland,' in Ailbhe Mac Shamhráin (ed.), *The Island of St Patrick: Church and Ruling Dynasties in Fingal and Meath, 400–1148*, Dublin: Four Courts Press, 2004, p. 140–58.

Clery [Ua Clérigh], Arthur, 'Early Irish history: Brian Boru: Clontarf,' *New Ireland Review*, 24 (September–October 1905), p. 31–43, 87–97.

Connon, Anne, 'The Banshenchas and the Uí Néill queens of Tara,' in Alfred P. Smyth (ed.), *Seanchas: Studies in Early Medieval Irish Archaeology, History and Literature in Honour of Francis J. Byrne*, Dublin: Four Courts Press, 2000, p. 98–108.

Cosgrave, Dillon, *North Dublin: City and Environs* (2nd edition): Dublin: M. H. Gill and Son, 1938.

Crawford, Barbara E., *Scandinavian Scotland: Studies in the Early History of Britain*, Leicester: Leicester University Press, 1987.

Crawford, Barbara E., *Earl and Mormaer: Norse-Pictish Relationships in Northern Scotland* (Groam House Lecture Series, 6), Rosemarkie (Ross and Cromarty): Groam House Museum, 1995.

Curtis, Edmund, 'Murchertach O'Brien, high king of Ireland, and his Norman son-in-law, Arnulf de Montgomery, c. 1100,' *Journal of the Royal Society of Antiquaries of Ireland*, 6th series, 11 (1921), p. 116–24.

Davies, Wendy, *Patterns of Power in Early Wales* (O'Donnell Lectures, 1983), Oxford: Clarendon Press, 1990.

de Paor, Liam, 'The Viking towns in Ireland,' in Bo Almqvist and David Greene (eds.), *Proceedings of the Seventh Viking Congress, Dublin, 15–21 August 1973*, Dublin: 1976, p. 29–38.

de Paor, Liam, 'Viking Dublin,' *Dublin Historical Record*, 31 (1978), p. 142–5.

de Paor, Liam, 'The high crosses of Tech Theille (Tihilly), Kinnitty and related sculpture,' in Etienne Rynne (ed.), *Figures from the Past: Studies on Figurative Art in Christian Ireland in Honour of Helen M. Roe*, Dublin: Glendale Press, for the Royal Society of Antiquaries of Ireland, 1987, p. 131–58.

Doherty, Charles, 'Exchange and trade in early medieval Ireland,' *Journal of the Royal Society of Antiquaries of Ireland*, 110 (1980), p. 67–89.

Doherty, Charles, 'The Vikings in Ireland: A review,' in Howard B. Clarke et al. (eds.), *Ireland and Scandinavia in the Early Viking Age*, Dublin: Four Courts Press, 1998, p. 288–330.

Doherty, Charles, 'Cluain Dolcáin: A brief note,' in Alfred P. Smyth (ed.), *Seanchas: Studies in Early Medieval Irish Archaeology, History and Literature in Honour of Francis J. Byrne*, Dublin: Four Courts Press, 2000, p. 182–8.

Dolley, R. H. M., *The Hiberno-Norse Coins in the British Museum* (Sylloge of Coins of the British Isles, 8), London: British Museum, 1966.

Dolley, Michael, 'The palimpsest of Viking settlement on Man,' in Hans Bekker-Nielsen et al. (eds.), *Proceedings of the Eighth Viking Congress, Aarhus, 24–31 August 1977* (Mediaeval Scandinavia Supplements, 2), Odense: Odense University Press, 1981, p. 173–81.

Dolley, R. H. M., and Ingold, J., 'Viking Age coin-hoards from Ireland and their relevance to Anglo-Saxon studies,' in R. H. M. Dolley (ed.), *Anglo-Saxon Coins: Studies Presented to F. M. Stenton on the Occasion of his 80th Birthday, 17 May 1960*, London: Methuen, 1961, p. 241–65.

Downey, Clodagh, 'The life and work of Cúán ua Lothcháin,' *Ríocht na Midhe*, 19 (2008), p. 55–78.

Downham, Clare, 'An imaginary Viking raid on Skye in 795?' *Scottish Gaelic Studies*, 20 (2000), p. 192–6.

Downham, Clare, 'The chronology of the last Scandinavian kings of York,' *Northern History*, 40 (2003), p. 25–51.

Downham, Clare, 'England and the Irish Sea zone in the eleventh century,' *Anglo-Norman Studies*, 26 (2003), p. 55–73.

Downham, Clare, 'The Vikings in Southern Uí Néill to 1014,' *Peritia*, 17 (2003–4), p. 233–55.

Downham, Clare, 'The career of Cearbhall of Osraighe,' *Ossory, Laois and Leinster*, 1 (2004), p. 1–18.

Downham, Clare, 'The Battle of Clontarf in Irish history and legend,' *History Ireland*, 13, no. 5 (2005), p. 19–23.

Downham, Clare, 'The good, the bad and the ugly: Portrayals of Vikings in "The Fragmentary Annals of Ireland",' *Medieval Chronicle*, 3 (2005), p. 28–40.

Downham, Clare, 'The historical importance of Viking-Age Waterford,' *Journal of Celtic Studies*, 4 (2005), p. 71–96.

Downham, Clare, 'Irish chronicles as a source for inter-Viking rivalry, A.D. 795–1014,' *Northern Scotland*, 26 (2006), p. 51–63.

Downham, Clare, 'Living on the edge: Scandinavian Dublin in the twelfth century,' in Beverley Ballin-Smith et al. (eds.), *West over Sea: Studies in Scandinavian Sea-Borne Expansion and Settlement Before 1300: A Festschrift in Honour of Dr Barbara E. Crawford*, Leiden: Brill, 2007, p. 33–52.

Downham, Clare, *Viking Kings of Britain and Ireland: The Dynasty of Ívarr to A.D. 1014*, Edinburgh: Dunedin Academic Press, 2007.

Downham, Clare, '"Hiberno-Norwegians" and "Anglo-Danes": Anachronistic ethnicities in Viking-Age England,' *Mediaeval Scandinavia*, 19 (2009), p. 139–69.

Doyle, Ian W., 'The early medieval activity at Dalkey Island, Co. Dublin: A re-assessment,' *Journal of Irish Archaeology*, 9 (1998), p. 89–103.

DuBois, Thomas A., 'Juxtaposing Cogadh Gáedel re Gallaib with Orkneyinga Saga,' *Oral Tradition*, 26, no. 2 (2011), p. 267–96.

Duffy, Seán, 'Irishmen and Islesmen in the kingdoms of Dublin and Man, 1052–1171,' *Ériu*, 43 (1992), p. 93–133.

Duffy, Seán, 'Ostmen, Irish and Welsh in the eleventh century,' *Peritia*, 9 (1995), p. 378–96.

Duffy, Seán, 'The 1169 invasion as a turning-point in Irish-Welsh relations,' in Brendan Smith (ed.), *Britain and Ireland, 900–1300: Insular Responses to Medieval European Change*, Cambridge: Cambridge University Press, 1999, p. 98–113.

Duffy, Seán, 'Ireland and Scotland, 1014–1169: Contacts and caveats,' in Alfred P. Smyth (ed.), *Seanchas: Studies in Early and Medieval Irish Archaeology, History and Literature in Honour of Francis J. Byrne*, Dublin: Four Courts Press, 2000, p. 348–56.

Duffy, Seán (ed.), *Medieval Ireland: An Encyclopedia*, New York: Routledge, 2005.

Duffy, Seán, 'A reconsideration of the site of Dublin's Viking thing-mót,' in Tom Condit and Christiaan Corlett (eds.), *Above and Beyond: Essays in Memory of Leo Swan*, Bray: Wordwell, 2005, p. 351–60.

Duffy, Seán, 'The royal dynasties of Dublin and the Isles in the eleventh century,' in Seán Duffy (ed.), *Medieval Dublin, VII: Proceedings of the Friends of Medieval Dublin Symposium, 2005*, Dublin: Four Courts Press, 2006, p. 51–65.

Duffy, Seán, '"The western world's tower of honour and dignity": The career of Muirchertach Ua Briain in context,' in Damian Bracken and Dagmar Ó Riain-Raedel (eds.), *Ireland and Europe in the Twelfth Century: Reform and Renewal*, Dublin: Four Courts Press, 2006, p. 56–73.

Duffy, Seán (ed.), *Atlas of Irish History* (3rd edition), Dublin: Gill & Macmillan, 2011.

Dumville, David N., *The Churches of North Britain in the First Viking-Age* (Whithorn Lecture, 5), Whithorn (Dumfries and Galloway): Friends of the Whithorn Trust, 1997.

Dumville, David N., *Three Men in a Boat: Scribe, Language, and Culture in the Church of Viking-Age Europe*, Cambridge: Cambridge University Press, 1997.

Dumville, David N., 'The Chronicle of the Kings of Alba,' in Simon Taylor (ed.), *Kings, Clerics and Chronicles in Scotland, 500–1297: Essays in Honour of Marjorie Ogilvie Anderson on the Occasion of Her Ninetieth Birthday*, Dublin: Four Courts Press, 2000, p. 73–86.

Dumville, David N., 'Images of the Viking in eleventh-century Latin literature,' in Michael Herren et al. (eds.), *Latin Culture in the Eleventh Century: Proceedings of the Third International Conference on Medieval Latin Studies, Cambridge, 9–12 September 1998* (2 vols.), Turnhout: Brepols, 2002, vol. 1, p. 250–63.

Dumville, David N., 'Vikings in the British Isles: A question of sources,' in Judith Jesch (ed.), *The Scandinavians from the Vendel Period to the Tenth Century: An Ethnographic Perspective* (Studies in Historical Archaeoethnology, 5), San Marino: Centre for Interdisciplinary Research on Social Stress, 2002, p. 209–50.

Dumville, David N., 'Old Dubliners and New Dubliners in Ireland and Britain: A Viking-Age story,' in Seán Duffy (ed.), *Medieval Dublin, VI*, Dublin: Four Courts Press, 2004, p. 78–93.

Duncan, A. A. M., *Scotland: The Making of the Kingdom*, Edinburgh: Edinburgh University Press, 1975; revised edition, 1979.

Duncan, A. A. M., 'The Battle of Carham, 1018,' *Scottish Historical Review*, 55 (1976), p. 20–28.

Edwards, Nancy, 'A possible Viking grave from Benllech, Anglesey,' *Transactions of the Anglesey Antiquarian Society and Field Club* (1985), p. 19–24.

Etchingham, Colmán, 'Evidence of Scandinavian settlement in Wicklow,' in Ken Hannigan and William Nolan (eds.), *Wicklow: History and Society*, Dublin: Geography Publications, 1994, p. 113–38.

Etchingham, Colmán, *Viking Raids on Irish Church Settlements in the Ninth Century: A Reconsideration of the Annals* (Maynooth Monographs, Series Minor, 1), Maynooth: Department of Old and Middle Irish, St Patrick's College, 1996.

Etchingham, Colmán, *Church Organisation in Ireland, AD 650 to 1000*, Maynooth: Laigin Publications, 2000.

Etchingham, Colmán, 'North Wales, Ireland and the Isles: The Insular Viking Zone,' *Peritia*, 15 (2001), p. 145–87.

Etchingham, Colmán, 'Laithlinn, "Fair Foreigners" and "Dark Foreigners": The identity and provenance of Vikings in ninth-century Ireland,' in John Sheehan and Donnchadh Ó Corráin (eds.), *The Viking Age: Ireland and the West: Papers from the Proceedings of the Fifteenth Viking Congress, Cork, 18–27 August 2005*, Dublin: Four Courts Press, 2010, p. 80–88.

Fellows-Jensen, Gillian, 'Scandinavian settlement in the Isle of Man and North-West England: The place-name evidence,' in Christine Fell et al. (eds.), *The Viking Age in the Isle of Man: Select Papers from the Ninth Viking Congress*, London: Viking Society for Northern Research, 1983, p. 37–52.

Fellows-Jensen, Gillian, 'Scandinavian settlement in Cumbria and Dumfries-shire: The place-name evidence,' in John R. Baldwin and Ian D. Whyte (eds.), *The Scandinavians in Cumbria* (Scottish Society for Northern Studies Publications, 3), Edinburgh: Scottish Society for Northern Studies, 1985, p. 65–82.

Fellows-Jensen, Gillian, 'Scandinavian place-names of the Irish Sea province,' in James Graham-Campbell (ed.), *Viking Treasure from the North West: The Cuerdale Hoard in Its Context: Selected Papers from the Vikings of the Irish Sea Conference, Liverpool, 18–20 May 1990*, Liverpool: National Museums and Galleries on Merseyside, 1992, p. 31–42.

Fischer, Lenore, 'The sack of Viking Limerick,' *Old Limerick Journal*, 39 (2003), p. 25–30.

Fischer, Lenore, 'Two poets and the legend of Brian Bóraimhe,' *North Munster Antiquarian Journal*, 49 (2009), p. 91–109.

Fischer, Lenore, 'How Dublin remembered the Battle of Clontarf,' in Seán Duffy (ed.), *Medieval Dublin, XIII*, Dublin: Four Courts Press, 2013.

Fitzpatrick, Elizabeth, *Royal Inauguration in Gaelic Ireland, c. 1100–1600: A Cultural Landscape Study*, Woodbridge (Suffolk): Boydell and Brewer, 2004.

Flachenecker, Helmut, *Schottenklöster: Irische Benediktinerkonvente im Hochmittelalterlichen Deutschland*, Paderborn: Ferdinand Schoningh, 1995.

Flanagan, Marie Therese, *Irish Society, Anglo-Norman Settlers, Angevin Kingship: Interactions in Ireland in the Late Twelfth Century*, Oxford: Clarendon Press, 1989.

Flanagan, Marie Therese, *The Transformation of the Irish Church in the Twelfth Century*, Woodbridge (Suffolk): Boydell and Brewer, 2010.

Fleming, John, *Gille of Limerick (c. 1070–1145): Architect of a Medieval Church*, Dublin: Four Courts Press, 2001.

Foote, Peter, and Wilson, David M., *The Viking Achievement: The Society and Culture of Early Medieval Scandinavia*, London: Sidgwick and Jackson, 1970.

Forte, Angelo, et al. (eds.), *Viking Empires*, Cambridge: Cambridge University Press, 2005.

Gibbons, Erin, and Kelly, E. P., 'A Viking-Age farmstead in Connemara,' *Archaeology Ireland*, 17, no. 1 (2003), p. 28–32.

Gillingham, John, 'Ademar of Chabannes and the history of Aquitaine in the reign of Charles the Bald,' in Margaret Gibson and Janet Nelson (eds.), *Charles the Bald: Court and Kingdom*, Oxford: Oxford University Press, 1981, p. 3–14.

Gillingham, John, '"The most precious jewel in the English crown": Levels of Danegeld and Heregeld in the early eleventh century,' *English Historical Review*, 104 (1989), p. 373–84.

Gillingham, John, 'Chronicles and coins as evidence for levels of tribute and taxation in late tenth and early eleventh-century England,' *English Historical Review*, 105 (1990), p. 939–50.

Goedheer, Albertus Johannes, *Irish and Norse Traditions about the Battle of Clontarf*, Haarlem: H. D. Tjeenk Willink en Zoon, 1938.

Grabowski, Kathryn, and Dumville, David, *Chronicles and Annals of Mediaeval Ireland and Wales: The Clonmacnoise-Group Texts* (Studies in Celtic History, 4), Woodbridge (Suffolk): Boydell and Brewer, 1984.

Graham-Campbell, James (ed.), *Cultural Atlas of the Viking World*, New York: Facts on File, 1994.

Graham-Campbell, James, 'The early Viking Age in the Irish Sea area,' in Howard B. Clarke et al. (eds.), *Ireland and Scandinavia in the Early Viking Age*, Dublin: Four Courts Press, 1998, p. 104–30.

Graham-Campbell, James, and Batey, Colleen E. (eds.), *Vikings in Scotland: An Archaeological Survey*, Edinburgh: Edinburgh University Press, 1998.

Greene, David, 'The influence of Scandinavian on Irish,' in Bo Almqvist and David Greene (eds.), *Proceedings of the Seventh Viking Congress, Dublin, 15–21 August 1973*, Dublin: 1976, p. 75–82.

Griffiths, David, 'Settlement and acculturation in the Irish Sea region,' in John Hines et al. (eds.), *Land, Sea and Home: Proceedings of a Conference on Viking-Period Settlement at Cardiff, July 2001* (Society for Medieval Archaeology Monograph, 20), Leeds: Maney Publishing, for the Society for Medieval Archaeology, 2004, p. 125–38.

Griffiths, David, *Vikings of the Irish Sea: Conflict and Assimilation, AD 790–1050*, Stroud (Glos.): History Press, 2010.

Gwynn, Aubrey, 'Brian in Armagh (1005),' *Seanchas Ard Mhacha*, 9, no. 1 (1978), p. 35–51.

Gwynn, Aubrey, *The Irish Church in the Eleventh and Twelfth Centuries*, ed. Gerard O'Brien, Dublin: Four Courts Press, 1992.

Gwynn, Aubrey, 'Were the Annals of Inisfallen written at Killaloe?' *North Munster Antiquarian Journal*, 8 (1958), p. 20–33.

Hadley, Dawn, '"Cockle among the wheat": The Scandinavian settlement in England,' in William O. Frazer and Andrew Tyrell (eds.), *Social Identity in Early Medieval Britain* (Studies in the Early History of Britain), London: Leicester University Press, 2000, p. 111–36.

Hadley, Dawn, *The Vikings in England: Settlement, Society and Culture*, Manchester: Manchester University Press, 2006.

Haliday, Charles, *The Scandinavian Kingdom of Dublin* (2nd edition), Dublin: M. H. Gill, 1884.

Hall, R. A., 'A check-list of Viking Age coin finds from Ireland,' *Ulster Journal of Archaeology*, 36–7 (1974), p. 71–86.

Hall, R. A., *Exploring the World of the Vikings*, London: Thames and Hudson, 2007.

Hall, R. A., 'The five boroughs of the Danelaw: A review of present knowledge,' *Anglo-Saxon England*, 18 (1989), p. 149–206.

Hall, R. A. (ed.), *Viking Age York and the North* (CBA Research Report, 27), London: Council for British Archaeology, 1978.

Halpin, Andrew, *Weapons and Warfare in Viking and Medieval Dublin* (Medieval Dublin Excavations, 1962–81, series B, vol. 9), Dublin: National Museum of Ireland, 2008.

Hart, Cyril, *The Danelaw*, London: Hambledon Press, 1992.

Haughton, Samuel, 'On the time of high water in Dublin Bay, on Good Friday, the 23rd April, 1014, the day of the Battle of Clontarf: With observations on the battle by Rev. J. H. Todd,' *Proceedings of the Royal Irish Academy*, ser. 1, 7 (1857–61), p. 495–511.

Henry, Françoise, *Irish Art during the Viking Invasions (800–1020 A.D.)*, Ithaca (NY): Cornell University Press, 1967.

Henry, Françoise, *Irish Art in the Romanesque Period (1020–1170 A.D.)*, London: Methuen, 1965.

Herbert, Máire, *Iona, Kells, and Derry: The History and Hagiography of the Monastic Familia of Columba*, Oxford: Clarendon Press, 1988.

Higham, N. J., 'The Domesday survey: Context and purpose,' *History*, 78 (1993), p. 7–21.

Higham, N. J., *The Kingdom of Northumbria, A.D. 350–1100*, Stroud (Glos.): Alan Sutton, 1993.

Higham, Nick, 'The Scandinavians in north Cumbria: Raids and settlements in the later ninth to mid tenth centuries,' in John R. Baldwin and Ian D. Whyte (eds.), *The Scandinavians in Cumbria* (Scottish Society for Northern Studies, 3), Edinburgh: Scottish Society for Northern Studies, 1985, p. 37–51.

Hill, David, *An Atlas of Anglo-Saxon England*, Oxford: Blackwell, 1981.

Hines, John, *Old Norse Sources for Gaelic History* (Quiggin Pamphlets on the Sources of Mediaeval Gaelic History, 5), Cambridge: University of Cabridge, 2002.

Hodkinson, Brian, 'Summary report of the excavations at St Mary's Cathedral, Limerick, 1992,' *North Munster Antiquarian Journal*, 37 (1996), p. 37–64.

Hodkinson, Brian, 'The topography of pre-Norman Limerick,' *North Munster Antiquarian Journal*, 42 (2002), p. 1–6.

Hogan, Edmund I. (ed.), *Onomasticon Goedelicum Locorum et Tribuum Hiberniae et Scotiae*, Dublin: Hodges, Figgis, 1910.

Holland, Martin, 'Dublin and the reform of the Irish church in the eleventh and twelfth centuries,' *Peritia*, 14 (2000), p. 111–60.

Holland, Martin, 'The Synod of Dublin in 1080,' in Seán Duffy (ed.), *Medieval Dublin, III: Proceedings of the Friends of Medieval Dublin Symposium, 2001*, Dublin: Four Courts Press, 2002, p. 81–94.

Holm, Poul, 'The slave trade of Dublin, ninth to twelfth centuries,' *Peritia*, 5 (1986), p. 317–45.

Holm, Poul, 'Between apathy and antipathy: The Vikings in Irish and Scandinavian history,' *Peritia*, 8 (1994), p. 151–69.

Holm, Poul, 'Viking Dublin and the city-state concept: Parameters and significance of the Hiberno-Norse settlement,' in Mogens Herman Hansen (ed.), *A Comparative Study of Thirty City-State Cultures: An Investigation Conducted by the Copenhagen Polis Centre* (Kongelige Danske Videnskabernes Selskab, Historiske-Filosofiske Skrifter, 21), Copenhagen: Royal Danish Academy of Sciences and Letters, 2000, p. 251–62.

Holt, J. C., '1086,' in *Domesday Studies: Papers Read at the Novocentenary Conference of the Royal Historical Society and the Institute of British Geographers, Winchester, 1986,* Woodbridge (Suffolk): Boydell and Brewer, 1987, p. 41–64.

Hore, Herbert Francis, 'The Scandinavians in Leinster,' *Journal of the Kilkenny and South-East of Ireland Archaeological Society,* 1 (1856–7), p. 430–43.

Hudson, Benjamin T., 'Cnut and the Scottish Kings,' *English Historical Review,* 107 (1992), p. 350–60.

Hudson, Benjamin T., *Kings of Celtic Scotland* (Contributions to the Study of World History, 43), Westport (Conn.): Greenwood Press, 1994.

Hudson, Benjamin T., 'William the Conqueror and Ireland,' *Irish Historical Studies,* 29 (1994), p. 145–58.

Hudson, Benjamin T., 'Knútr and Viking Dublin,' *Scandinavian Studies,* 46 (1994), p. 319–35.

Hudson, Benjamin T., 'The changing economy of the Irish Sea province,' in Brendan Smith (ed.), *Britain and Ireland, 900–1300: Insular Responses to Medieval European Change,* Cambridge: Cambridge University Press, 1999, p. 39–66.

Hudson, Benjamin, *Viking Pirates and Christian Princes: Dynasty, Religion, and Empire in the North Atlantic,* New York: Oxford University Press, 2005.

Hudson, Benjamin, *Irish Sea Studies, 900–1200,* Dublin: Four Courts Press, 2006.

Hughes, Kathleen, *The Church in Early Irish Society,* London: Methuen, 1966.

Hughes, Kathleen, *Early Christian Ireland: Introduction to the Sources,* London: Hodder and Stoughton, 1972.

Hull, Eleanor, *The Gael and the Gall: Notes on the Social Condition of Ireland during the Norse Period* (Saga Book of the Viking Society for Northern Research, 5), London: Viking Society, 1907–8, p. 363–92.

Hunter Blair, Peter, *An Introduction to Anglo-Saxon England* (2nd edition), Cambridge: Cambridge University Press, 1977.

Jaski, Bart, 'Additional notes to the Annals of Ulster,' *Ériu,* 48 (1997), p. 103–52.

Jaski, Bart, *Early Irish Kingship and Succession,* Dublin: Four Courts Press, 2000.

Jaski, Bart, 'The genealogical section of the Psalter of Cashel,' *Peritia*, 17–18 (2003–4), p. 295–337.

Jaski, Bart, 'The Vikings and the kingship of Tara,' *Peritia*, 9 (1995), p. 310–53.

Jesch, Judith, 'Norse historical traditions and Historia Gruffudd vab Kenan: Magnús Berfœttr and Haraldr Hárfagri,' in K. L. Maund (ed.), *Gruffudd ap Cynan: A Collaborative Biography* (Studies in Celtic History, 16), Woodbridge (Suffolk): Boydell and Brewer, 1996, p. 117–48.

Jesch, Judith, 'Scaldic verse in Scandinavian England,' in James Graham-Campbell et al. (eds.), *Vikings and the Danelaw: Select Papers from the Proceedings of the Thirteenth Viking Congress*, Oxford: Oxbow Books, 2001, p. 314–27.

Jesch, Judith, 'Scandinavian Wirral,' in Paul Cavill et al. (eds.), *Wirral and Its Viking Heritage*, Nottingham: English Place-Name Society, 2000, p. 1–10.

Johnson, Ruth, 'An archaeological and art historical investigation into the supposed hiatus in Irish art during the tenth century AD, with particular reference to excavations carried out in Dublin City (1962–81) and Ballinderry Crannog No. 1 (1936)' (3 vols., PhD dissertation, University of Dublin, Trinity College), 1997.

Johnson, Ruth, *Viking Age Dublin*, Dublin: Townhouse, 2004.

Jones, Bedwyr Lewis, 'Gwriad's heritage: Links between Wales and the Isle of Man in the early Middle Ages,' *Transactions of the Honourable Society of Cymmrodorion* (1990), p. 29–44.

Joyce, P. W., *The Origin and History of Irish Names of Places* (3 vols.), Dublin: Phoenix, 1869–1913.

Karkov, Catherine E., and Ruffing, John, 'The Southern Uí Néill and the political landscape of Lough Ennell,' *Peritia*, 11 (1997), p. 336–59.

Kehnel, Annette, *Clonmacnois: The Church and Lands of St Ciarán: Change and Continuity in an Irish Monastic Foundation* (6th to 16th century), Münster: Lit, 1997.

Kelleher, John V., 'Early Irish history and pseudo-history,' *Studia Hibernica*, 3 (1963), p. 113–27.

Kelleher, John V., 'The pre-Norman Irish genealogies,' *Irish Historical Studies*, 16 (1968), p. 138–53.

Kelleher, John V., 'The rise of the Dál Cais,' in Etienne Rynne (ed.), *North Munster Studies: Essays in Commemoration of Monsignor Michael Moloney*, Limerick: Thomond Archaeological Society, 1967, p. 230–41.

Kelleher, John V., 'Uí Maine in the annals and genealogies to 1225,' *Celtica*, 9 (1971), p. 61–107.

Kelly, Eamonn P., 'Re-evaluation of a supposed inland promontory fort: Knoxpark, Co. Sligo: Iron Age fortress or Viking stronghold?' in Gabriel Cooney et al. (eds.), *Relics of Old Decency: Archaeological Studies in Later Prehistory: Festschrift for Barry Raftery*, Dublin: Wordwell, 2009, p. 485–97.

Kelly, Eamonn P., and Maas, John, 'The Vikings and the Kingdom of Laois,' in P. G. Lane and William Nolan (eds.), *Laois: History and Society*, Dublin: Geography Publications, 1999, p. 123–59.

Kelly, Eamonn P., and Maas, John, 'Vikings on the Barrow: Dunrally Fort, a possible Viking longphort in County Laois,' *Archaeology Ireland*, 9, no. 3 (1995), p. 30–32.

Kelly, Eamonn P., and O'Donovan, Edmond, 'A Viking longphort near Athlunkard, Co. Clare,' *Archaeology Ireland*, 12, no. 4 (1998), p. 13–16.

Kelly, Fergus, *Early Irish Farming* (Early Irish Law Series, 4), Dublin: Dublin Institute for Advanced Studies, 1997.

Kelly, Fergus, *A Guide to Early Irish Law* (Early Irish Law Series, 3), Dublin: Dublin Institute for Advanced Studies, 1988.

Kenney, James F., *The Sources for the Early History of Ireland: Ecclesiastical: An Introduction and Guide*, New York: Columbia University Press, 1929; revised edition by Ludwig Bieler, 1966.

Keynes, Simon, 'Apocalypse then: England, A.D. 1000,' in Przemysław Urbańczyk (ed.), *Europe Around the Year 1000*, Warsaw: Institute of Archaeology and Ethnology, Polish Academy of Sciences, 2001, p. 247–70.

Keynes, Simon, 'The declining reputation of King Æthelred the Unready,' in David Hill (ed.), *Ethelred the Unready: Papers from the Millenary Conference* (British Series, 59), Oxford: British Archaeological Reports, 1978, p. 227–53.

Keynes, Simon, 'The historical context of the Battle of Maldon,' in Donald Scragg (ed.), *The Battle of Maldon, AD 991*, Oxford: Blackwell, 1991, p. 81–113.

Keynes, Simon, 'The Vikings in England, c. 760–1016,' in Peter Sawyer (ed.), *The Oxford Illustrated History of the Vikings*, Oxford: Oxford University Press, 1997, p. 48–82.

Lacey, Brian, *Cenél Conaill and the Donegal Kingdoms, AD 500–800*, Dublin: Four Courts Press, 2006.

Larsen, A. C. (ed.), *The Vikings in Ireland*, Roskilde: Viking Ship Museum, 2001.

Lawson, M. K., 'Danegeld and Heregeld once more,' *English Historical Review*, 105 (1990), p. 951–61.

Lawson, M. K., '"Those stories look true": Levels of taxation in the reigns of Æthelred II and Cnut,' *English Historical Review*, 104 (1989), p. 385–406.

Leech, Roger H., 'Cogadh Gaedhel re Gallaibh and the Annals of Inisfallen,' *North Munster Antiquarian Journal*, 11 (1968), p. 13–21.

Lloyd, J. H., 'Earl Sigurd's forlorn hope,' *New Ireland Review*, 28 (September–October 1907), p. 35–54, 87–99.

Logan, F. Donald, *The Vikings in History* (2nd edition), London: Harper-Collins, 1991.

Lönnroth, Lars, *Njals Saga: A Critical Introduction*, Berkeley (Calif.): University of California Press, 1970.

Loyn, Henry, *The Vikings in Wales* (Dorothea Coke Memorial Lecture, 1976), London: Viking Society for Northern Research, 1976.

Lucas, A. T., 'The plundering and burning of churches in Ireland, 7th to 16th century,' in Etienne Rynne (ed.), *North Munster Studies: Essays in Commemoration of Monsignor Michael Moloney*, Limerick: Thomond Archaeological Society, 1967, p. 172–229.

Lucas, A. T., 'The sacred trees of Ireland,' *Journal of the Cork Historical and Archaeological Society*, 68 (1963), p. 16–54.

Lund, Niels, 'The armies of Swein Forkbeard and Cnut: Leding or lið?' *Anglo-Saxon England*, 15 (1986), p. 105–19.

Lund, Niels, 'King Edgar and the Danelaw,' *Mediaeval Scandinavia*, 9 (1976), p. 181–95.

MacAlister, R. A. S., 'A runic inscription at Killaloe Cathedral,' *Proceedings of the Royal Irish Academy*, 33 C (1916–17), p. 493–8.

Mac Cana, Proinsias, 'Praise poetry in Ireland before the Normans,' *Ériu*, 54 (2004), p. 11–40.

Mac Giolla Easpaig, Dónall, 'L'influence scandinave sur la toponymie irlandaise,' in Élisabeth Ridel (ed.), *L'Héritage Maritime des Vikings en Europe de l'Ouest*, Caen: Presses Universitaires de Caen, 2002, p. 441–82.

McGrail, Sean, *Medieval Boat and Ship Timbers from Dublin* (Medieval Dublin Excavations, 1962–81, series B, vol. 3), Dublin: National Museum of Ireland, 1993.

McManus, Damian, *A Guide to Ogam*, Maynooth: An Sagart, 1991.

Mac Mathúna, Liam, 'The Vikings in Ireland: Contemporary reaction and cultural legacy,' in Folke Josephson (ed.), *Celts and Vikings: Proceedings of the Fourth Symposium of the Societas Celtologica Nordica*, Göteborg: Göteborgs Universitet, 1997, p. 41–65.

MacNeill, Eoin, 'Chapters of Hebridean history, I: The Norse kingdom of the Hebrides,' *Scottish Review*, new series, 39 (1916), p. 254–76.

MacNeill, Eoin, 'The Vita Tripartita of St Patrick,' *Ériu*, 11 (1932), p. 1–41.

MacNeill, John [Eoin], 'Early Irish population-groups: Their nomenclature, classification, and chronology,' *Proceedings of the Royal Irish Academy*, 29C (1911), p. 59–109.

Mac Niocaill, Gearóid, *The Medieval Irish Annals* (Medieval Irish History Series, 3), Dublin: Dublin Historical Association, 1975.

MacShamhráin, Ailbhe, 'The Battle of Glen Máma, Dublin and the high-kingship of Ireland,' in Seán Duffy (ed.), *Medieval Dublin, II*, Dublin: Four Courts Press, 2000, p. 53–64.

MacShamhráin, Ailbhe, 'Brian Bóruma, Armagh and high kingship,' *Seanchas Ardmhacha*, 20, no. 2 (2005), p. 1–21.

MacShamhráin, Ailbhe, 'Cenél nEogain and the Airgialla from the sixth to the eleventh centuries,' in Charles Dillon and H. J. Jefferies (eds.), *Tyrone: History and Society*, Dublin: Geography Publications, 2000, p. 55–84.

MacShamhráin, Ailbhe, *Church and Polity in Pre-Norman Ireland: The Case of Glendalough*, Maynooth: An Sagart, 1996.

MacShamhráin, Ailbhe, *The Vikings: An Illustrated History*, Dublin: Wolfhound Press, 2002.

Madden, Gerard, *Holy Island / Inis Cealtra: Island of the Churches: Pilgrimage, Folklore, Graveyard Inscriptions*, Mountshannon (Co. Clare): Holy Island Tours, 2008.

Maddicott, J. R., 'Responses to the threat of invasion, 1085,' *English Historical Review*, 122, no. 498 (September 2007), p. 986–97.

Marstrander, Carl, 'Lochlainn,' *Ériu*, 5 (1911), p. 250–51.

Marstrander, Carl J. S., *Bidrag til det Norske Sprogs Historie i Irland* (Videnskapsselskapets Skrifter, II, Historisk-Filosofiske Klasse, 5), Kristiania [Oslo]: J. Dybwad, 1915.

Maund, K. L., 'Dynastic segmentation and Gwynedd, c. 950–c. 1000,' *Studia Celtica*, 32 (1998), p. 155–67.

Maund, K. L., *Ireland, Wales, and England in the Eleventh Century* (Studies in Celtic History, 12), Woodbridge (Suffolk): Boydell and Brewer, 1991.

Megaw, Basil, 'Norseman and native in the Kingdom of the Isles: A re-assessment of the Manx evidence,' *Scottish Studies*, 20 (1976), p. 1–44.

Meyer, Kuno, 'Altirisch Erulb n. pr. m.,' *Zeitschrift für Celtische Philologie*, 13 (1921), 108.

Meyer, Kuno, 'Brian Borumha,' *Ériu*, 4 (1910), p. 68–73.

Moody, T. W., et al. (eds.), *A New History of Ireland, IX: Maps, Genealogies, Lists*, Oxford: Clarendon Press, 1984.

Moore, A. W., *A History of the Isle of Man* (2 vols.), London: T. Fisher Unwin, 1900.

Morris, Christopher D., 'Raiders, traders and settlers: The Early Viking Age in Scotland,' in Howard B. Clarke et al. (eds.), *Ireland and Scandinavia in the Early Viking Age*, Dublin: Four Courts Press, 1998, p. 73–103.

Musset, Lucien, *Nordica et Normannica: Recueil d'Études sur la Scandinavie Ancienne et Médiévale, les Expéditions des Vikings et la Fondation de la Normandie*, Paris: Société des Études Nordiques, 1997.

Nelson, Janet L., *Charles the Bald: The Medieval World*, Harlow (Essex): Longman, 1992.

Nelson, Janet L., 'England and the Continent in the ninth century, II: The Vikings and others,' *Transactions of the Royal Historical Society*, 13 (2003), p. 1–28.

Nelson, Janet L., 'Inauguration rituals,' in Peter Sawyer and I. N. Wood (eds.), *Early Medieval Kingship*, Leeds: School of History, University of Leeds, 1977, p. 50–71; reprinted in *Politics and Ritual in Early Medieval Europe*, London: Hambledon, 1986, p. 283–307.

Nicholls, Kenneth, 'The Irish genealogies: Their value and defects,' *Irish Genealogist*, 2 (1975), p. 256–61.

Ní Dhonnchadha, Máirín, 'The guarantor list of Cáin Adomnáin,' *Peritia*, 1 (1982), p. 178–215.

Ní Mhaonaigh, Máire, 'Bréifne bias in Cogad Gáedel re Gallaib,' *Ériu*, 43 (1992), p. 135–58.

Ní Mhaonaigh, Máire, 'Cogad Gáedhel re Gallaib: Some dating considerations,' *Peritia*, 9 (1995), p. 354–77.

Ní Mhaonaigh, Máire, 'Cogad Gáedhel re Gallaib and the annals: A comparison,' *Ériu*, 48 (1996), p. 101–26.

Ní Mhaonaigh, Máire, 'Friend and foe: Vikings in ninth and tenth-century Irish literature,' in Howard B. Clarke et al. (eds.), *Ireland and Scandinavia in the Early Viking Age*, Dublin: Four Courts Press, 1998, p. 381–402.

Ní Mhaonaigh, Máire, 'Tales of three Gormlaiths in medieval Irish literature,' *Ériu*, 52 (2002), p. 1–24.

Ní Mhaonaigh, Máire, 'Literary Lochlann,' in Wilson McLeod, James E. Fraser and Anja Gunderloch (eds.), *Cànan agus Cultar / Language and Culture* (Rannsachadh na Gàidhlig, 3), Edinburgh: Dunedin Academic Press, 2006, p. 25–37.

Ní Mhaonaigh, Máire, *Brian Boru: Ireland's Greatest King?* Stroud (Glos.): Tempus, 2008.

Ní Mhaonaigh, Máire, 'Cormac mac Cuilennáin: King, bishop and "wondrous sage",' *Zeitschrift für Celtische Philologie*, 58 (2011), p. 109–28.

Ní Mhaonaigh, Máire, 'A neglected account of the Battle of Clontarf,' *Zeitschrift für Celtische Philologie*, 59 (2012), p. 143–167.

O'Brien, A. P., 'Commercial relations between Aquitaine and Ireland, 1000 to 1550,' in Jean-Michel Picard (ed.), *Aquitaine and Ireland in the Middle Ages*, Dublin: Four Courts Press, 1995, p. 31–80.

O'Brien, Elizabeth, 'A reassessment of the "great sepulchral mound" containing a Viking burial at Donnybrook, Dublin,' *Medieval Archaeology*, 36 (1992), p. 170–73.

O'Brien, Elizabeth, 'A reconsideration of the location and context of Viking burials at Kilmainham/Islandbridge, Dublin,' in Conleth Manning (ed.), *Dublin and Beyond the Pale: Studies in Honour of Patrick Healy*, Bray: Wordwell, in association with Rathmichael Historical Society, 1998, p. 35–44.

O'Brien, Richard, Quinney, R. P., and Russell, Ian, 'Preliminary report on the archaeological excavation and finds retrieval strategy of the Hiberno-Scandinavian site of Woodstown 6, Co. Waterford,' *Decies*, 61 (2005), p. 13–122.

O'Brien, Richard, and Russell, Ian, 'The Hiberno-Scandinavian site at Woodstown 6, Co. Waterford,' in Jerry O'Sullivan and Michael Stanley (eds.), *Recent Archaeological Discoveries on National Road Schemes, 2004: Proceedings of a Seminar for the Public, Dublin, September 2004*, Dublin: National Roads Authority, 2005, p. 111–24.

Ó Carragáin, Tomás, 'Patterns of patronage: Churches, round towers and the Dál Cais kings of Munster (c. 950–1050),' in Roger Stalley (ed.), *Limerick and South-West Ireland: Medieval Art and Architecture*, Leeds: Maney, for the British Archaeological Association, 2011, p. 23–41.

Ó Corráin, Donnchadh, 'The career of Diarmait mac Máel na mBó, King of Leinster,' *Journal of the Old Wexford Society*, 3 (1970–71), p. 26–35; 4 (1972–3), p. 16–24.

Ó Corráin, Donnchadh, 'Irish regnal succession: A reappraisal,' *Studia Hibernica*, 11 (1971), p. 7–39.

Ó Corráin, Donnchadh, *Ireland Before the Normans*, Dublin: Gill & Macmillan, 1972.

Ó Corráin, Donnchadh, 'Dál Cais: Church and dynasty,' *Ériu*, 24 (1973), p. 52–63.

Ó Corráin, Donnchadh, 'Caithréim Chellacháin Chaisil: History or propaganda?' *Ériu*, 25 (1974), p. 1–69.

Ó Corráin, Donnchadh, 'The Uí Chennselaig kingship of Leinster,' *Journal of the Old Wexford Society*, 5 (1974–5), p. 26–31; 6 (1976–7), p. 45–53.

Ó Corráin, Donnchadh, 'High-kings, Vikings and other kings,' *Irish Historical Studies*, 21 (1978–9), p. 283–323.

Ó Corráin, Donnchadh, 'Nationality and kingship in pre-Norman Ireland,' in T. W. Moody (ed.), *Historical Studies, XI: Nationality and the Pursuit of National Independence: Papers Read at the 12th Irish Conference of Historians, Held at Trinity College, Dublin, 28–31 May 1975*, Belfast: Appletree Press, for the Irish Committee of Historical Sciences, 1978, p. 1–35.

Ó Corráin, Donnchadh, 'Foreign connections and domestic politics: Killaloe in twelfth-century hagiography,' in Dorothy Whitelock et al. (eds.), *Ireland in Early Mediaeval Europe: Studies in Memory of Kathleen Hughes*, Cambridge: Cambridge University Press, 1982, p. 213–34.

Ó Corráin, Donnchadh, 'Irish origin legends and genealogy: Recurrent aetiologies,' in Tore Nyberg et al. (eds.), *History and Heroic Tale: A Symposium*, Odense: Odense University Press, 1985, p. 51–96.

Ó Corráin, Donnchadh, 'Brian Boru and the battle of Clontarf,' in Liam de Paor (ed.), *Milestones in Irish History*, Cork: Mercier Press, in collaboration with Raidió Teilifís Éireann, 1986, p. 31–40.

Ó Corráin, Donnchadh, 'Historical need and literary narrative,' in D. Ellis Evans (ed.), *Proceedings of the Seventh International Congress of Celtic Studies*, Oxford: Oxbow Books, 1986, p. 141–58.

Ó Corráin, D., 'Vikings, I–III,' *Peritia*, 10 (1996), p. 224, 236, 273.

Ó Corráin, Donnchadh, 'Ireland, Wales, Man, and the Hebrides,' in Peter Sawyer (ed.), *The Oxford Illustrated History of the Vikings*, Oxford: Oxford University Press, 1997, p. 83–109.

Ó Corráin, Donnchadh, 'Creating the past: The early Irish genealogical tradition,' *Peritia*, 12 (1998), p. 177–208.

Ó Corráin, Donnchadh, 'Viking Ireland: Afterthoughts,' in Howard B. Clarke et al. (eds.), *Ireland and Scandinavia in the Early Viking Age*, Dublin: Four Courts Press, 1998, p. 421–52.

Ó Corráin, Donnchadh, 'The Vikings in Scotland and Ireland in the ninth century,' *Peritia*, 12 (1998), p. 296–339.

Ó Corráin, Donnchadh, 'Muirchertach Mac Lochlainn and the circuit of Ireland,' in Alfred P. Smyth (ed.), *Seanchas: Studies in Early and Medieval Irish Archaeology, History and Literature in Honour of Francis J. Byrne*, Dublin: Four Courts Press, 2000, p. 238–50.

Ó Cróinín, Dáibhí, *Early Medieval Ireland, 400–1200*, London: Longman, 1995.

Ó Cróinín, Dáibhí, 'Three weddings and a funeral: Rewriting Irish political history in the tenth century,' in Alfred P. Smyth (ed.), *Seanchas: Studies in Early and Medieval Irish Archaeology, History and Literature in Honour of Francis J. Byrne*, Dublin: Four Courts Press, 2000, p. 212–24.

Ó Cuív, Brian, 'Personal names as an indicator of relations between native Irish and settlers in the Viking period,' in John Bradley (ed.), *Settlement and Society in Medieval Ireland: Studies Presented to F. X. Martin*, O.S.A., Kilkenny: Boethius Press, 1988, p. 79–88.

O'Curry, Eugene, *Lectures on the Manuscript Materials of Ancient Irish History: Delivered at the Catholic University of Ireland* . . . Dublin: James Duffy, 1861.

Ó Fiaich, Tomás, 'The church of Armagh under lay control,' *Seanchas Ard Mhacha*, 5, no. 1 (1969), p. 75–127.

Ó Floinn, Raghnall, 'The archaeology of the Early Viking Age in Ireland,' in Howard B. Clarke et al. (eds.), *Ireland and Scandinavia in the Early Viking Age*, Dublin: Four Courts Press, 1998, p. 131–65.

Ó Floinn, Raghnall, 'Two Viking burials from Co. Wicklow,' *Wicklow Archaeology and Society*, 1 (1998), p. 29–35.

O'Flynn, Eoin, 'The career of Máelsechnaill II,' *Ríocht na Midhe*, 20 (2009), p. 29–68.

O'Flynn, Eoin, 'The Dublin Vikings and the Clann Cholmáin kings of Southern Uí Néill,' in Seán Duffy (ed.), *Medieval Dublin, XIII*, Dublin: Four Courts Press, 2013.

O'Flynn, Eoin, 'The organisation and operation of Uí Néill kingship in the Irish midlands: Clann Cholmáin, c. 550–916' (PhD thesis, University of Dublin, Trinity College), 2012.

Oftedal, Magne, 'Scandinavian place names in Ireland,' in Bo Almqvist and David Greene (eds.), *Proceedings of the Seventh Viking Congress, Dublin, 15–21 August 1973*, Dublin: 1976, p. 125–33.

O'Gorman, Thomas, 'On the site of the Battle of Clontarf,' *Journal of the Historical and Archaeological Association of Ireland*, series 4, vol. V, part 1 (1879), p. 169–82.

O'Halloran, Clare, *Golden Ages and Barbarous Nations: Antiquarianism and Cultural Politics in Eighteenth-Century Ireland, c. 1750–1800*, Cork: Cork University Press, 2004.

O'Halloran, Clare, 'The triumph of "virtuous liberty": Representations of the Vikings and Brian Boru in eighteenth-century histories,' *Eighteenth-Century Ireland / Iris an Dá Chultúr*, 22 (2007), p. 151–63.

O'Halloran, Sylvester, *A General History of Ireland, from the Earliest Accounts to the Close of the Twelfth Century, Collected from the Most Authentic Records* . . . London: 1778.

O'Kelly, M. J., 'Beal Boru,' *Journal of the Cork Historical and Archaeological Society*, 67 (1962), p. 1–27.

O'Leary, Aideen M., 'The identities of the poet(s) Mac Coisi: A reinvestigation,' *Cambrian Medieval Celtic Studies*, 38 (1999), p. 53–71.

Ó Murchadha, Diarmuid, 'Lagmainn, Lögmenn,' *Ainm: Bulletin of the Ulster Place-Name Society*, 2 (1987), p. 136–40.

O'Rahilly, Thomas F., *Early Irish History and Mythology*, Dublin: Dublin Institute for Advanced Studies, 1946.

Ó Riain, Pádraig, 'The Psalter of Cashel: A provisional list of contents,' *Éigse*, 23 (1989), p. 107–30.

Ó Riain, Pádraig, 'The shrine of the Stowe Missal redated,' *Proceedings of the Royal Irish Academy*, 91C (1991), p. 285–95.

Ó Riain, Pádraig, et al. (eds.), *Historical Dictionary of Gaelic Placenames*, London: Irish Texts Society, 2005–.

Ó Riain, Pádraig, *A Dictionary of Irish Saints*, Dublin: Four Courts Press, 2011.

Ó Riain-Raedel, Dagmar, 'Irish Benedictine monasteries on the Continent,' in Martin Browne and Colmán Ó Clabaigh (eds.), *The Irish Benedictines: A History*, Blackrock (Co. Dublin): Columba Press, 2005, p. 25–63.

Ó Súilleabháin, Pádraig, 'Nótaí ar thrí fhocal ó na hAnnála,' *Éigse*, 15 (1973–4), p. 22–3.

P. [George Petrie], 'Ancient monument in the Hospital Fields, Dublin,' *Dublin Penny Journal*, 1, no. 9 (25 August 1832), p. 68–9.

Page, R. I., *'A most vile people': Early English Historians on the Vikings* (Dorothea Coke Memorial Lecture in Northern Studies, 1986), London: Viking Society for Northern Research, 1987.

Perennec, Ronan, 'Les Vikings à Landavennec: Les traces du "passage" des Normands en 913,' *Chronique de Landévennec*, 85 (1996), p. 32–40.

Picard, Jean-Michel (ed.), *Aquitaine and Ireland in the Middle Ages*, Dublin: Four Courts Press, 1995.

Picard, Jean-Michel, 'Early contacts between Ireland and Normandy: The cult of Irish saints in Normandy before the Conquest,' in Michael Richter and Jean-Michel Picard (eds.), *Ogma: Essays in Celtic Studies in Honour of Proinséas Ní Chatháin*, Dublin: Four Courts Press, 2002, p. 85–93.

Power, Rosemary, 'Magnus Barelegs' expeditions to the west,' *Scottish Historical Review*, 66 (1986), p. 107–32.

Power, Rosemary, 'Meeting in Norway: Norse-Gaelic relations in the Kingdom of Man and the Isles, 1090–1270,' *Saga-Book: Viking Society for Northern Research*, 29 (2005), p. 5–66.

Price, Neil S., 'The Vikings in Brittany,' *Saga-Book of the Viking Society*, 22 (1986–9), p. 323–440.

Quin, E. G., et al. (eds.), *Dictionary of the Irish Language: Based Mainly on Old and Middle Irish Materials* (compact edition): Dublin: Royal Irish Academy, 1983.

Randsborg, Klavs, 'Offensive armies and navies,' *Acta Archaeologica*, 69 (1998), p. 163–74.

Redknap, Mark, *Vikings in Wales: An Archaeological Quest*, Cardiff: Llyfrau Amgueddfa Cymru / National Museum of Wales Books, 2000.

Roesdahl, Else, *The Vikings*, London: Penguin, 1991.

Ross, Ian Campbell, '"One of the principal nations in Europe": The representation of Ireland in Sarah Butler's Irish Tales,' *Eighteenth-Century Fiction*, 7, no. 1 (1994), p. 1–16.

Ryan, John, 'The Battle of Clontarf,' *Journal of the Royal Society of Antiquaries of Ireland*, vol. 68 (1938), p. 1–50.

Ryan, John, 'The historical content of the "Caithréim Ceallacháin Chaisil",' *Journal of the Royal Society of Antiquaries of Ireland*, vol. 71 (1941), p. 89–100.

Ryan, John, 'The O'Briens in Munster after Clontarf,' *North Munster Antiquarian Journal*, 2 (1941), p. 141–52; 3 (1942), p. 1–52.

Ryan, John, 'Pre-Norman Dublin,' *Journal of the Royal Society of Antiquaries of Ireland*, vol. 79 (1949), p. 64–83.

Ryan, John, 'Brian Boruma, King of Ireland,' in Etienne Rynne (ed.), *North Munster Studies: Essays in Commemoration of Monsignor Michael Moloney*, Limerick: Thomond Archaeological Society, 1967, p. 355–74.

Sawyer, P. H., *The Age of the Vikings* (2nd edition), London: Edward Arnold, 1971.

Sawyer, Peter, 'Conquest and colonisation: Scandinavians in the Danelaw and in Normandy,' in Hans Bekker-Nielsen et al. (eds.), *Proceedings of the Eighth Viking Congress, Aarhus, 24–31 August 1977* (Mediaeval Scandinavia Supplements, 2), Odense: Odense University Press, 1981, p. 123–45.

Sawyer, Peter, *Kings and Vikings: Scandinavia and Europe*, A.D. 700–1100, London: Routledge, 1982.

Sawyer, Peter, 'The Vikings and Ireland,' in Dorothy Whitelock et al. (eds.), *Ireland in Early Mediaeval Europe: Studies in Memory of Kathleen Hughes*, Cambridge: Cambridge University Press, 1982, p. 345–61.

Sawyer, Peter, 'Ethelred II, Olaf Tryggvason and the conversion of Norway,' in John D. Niles and Mark Amodio (eds.), *Anglo-Scandinavian England: Norse-English Relations in the Period Before the Conquest*, Lanham (Md): University Press of America, 1989, p. 17–24.

Sawyer, Peter, 'The last Scandinavian kings of York,' *Northern History*, 31 (1995), p. 39–44.

Sayers, William, 'Clontarf and the Irish destinies of Sigurðr Digri, Earl of Orkney, and Þorsteinn Síðu-Hallsson,' *Scandinavian Studies*, 63 (1991), p. 164–86.

Scragg, Donald (ed.), *The Battle of Maldon, A.D. 991*, Oxford: Blackwell, 1991, p. 1–36.

Sharpe, Richard, 'St Patrick and the see of Armagh,' *Cambridge Medieval Celtic Studies*, 4 (1982), p. 33–59.

Sheehan, John, 'Early Viking-Age silver hoards from Ireland and their Scandinavian elements,' in Howard B. Clarke et al. (eds.), *Ireland and Scandinavia in the Early Viking Age*, Dublin: Four Courts Press, 1998, p. 166–202.

Sheehan, John, 'Viking Age hoards from Munster: A regional tradition?' in Michael A. Monk and John Sheehan (eds.), *Early Medieval Munster: Archaeology, History and Society*, Cork: Cork University Press, 1998, p. 147–63.

Sheehan, John, 'Ireland's early Viking-Age silver hoards: Components, structure and classification,' *Acta Archaeologica*, 71 (2000), p. 49–63.

Sheehan, John S., Hansen, Stumann, and Ó Corráin, Donnchadh, 'A Viking Age maritime haven: A reassessment of the island at Beginish, Co. Kerry,' *Journal of Irish Archaeology*, 10 (2001), p. 93–119.

Sigurðsson, Gísli, 'Gaelic influence in Iceland: Historical and literary contacts: A survey of research,' *Studia Islandica*, 46, 1988.

Simpson, Linzi, 'Forty years a-digging: A preliminary synthesis of archaeological investigations in medieval Dublin,' in Seán Duffy (ed.), *Medieval Dublin, I*, Dublin: Four Courts Press, 2000, p. 11–68.

Simpson, Linzi, 'Viking warrior burials in Dublin: Is this the longphort?' in Seán Duffy (ed.), *Medieval Dublin, VI*, Dublin: Four Courts Press, 2005, p. 11–62.

Simpson, Linzi, 'The longphort of Dublin: Lessons from Woodstown, Co. Waterford, and Annagassan, Co. Louth,' in Seán Duffy (ed.), *Medieval Dublin, XII*, Dublin: Four Courts Press, 2012, p. 94–112.

Sims-Williams, Patrick, *The Celtic Inscriptions of Britain: Phonology and Chronology, c. 400–1200*, Oxford: Blackwell, 2003.

Skyum-Nielsen, Niels, 'Nordic slavery in an international setting,' *Mediaeval Scandinavia*, 11 (1978–9), p. 126–48.

Smith, J. M. H., *Province and Empire: Brittany and the Carolingians*, Cambridge: Cambridge University Press, 1992.

Smyth, Alfred P., 'The Black Foreigners of York and the White Foreigners of Dublin,' *Saga-Book of the Viking Society*, 19 (1974–7), p. 101–17.

Smyth, Alfred P., *Scandinavian York and Dublin: The History and Archaeology of Two Related Viking Kingdoms* (2 vols.), Dublin: Templekieran Press, 1975–9.

Smyth, Alfred P., *Scandinavian Kings in the British Isles, 850–880*, Oxford: Oxford University Press, 1977.

Smyth, Alfred P., *Celtic Leinster: Towards an Historical Geography of Early Irish Civilization, A.D. 500–1600*, Blackrock (Co. Dublin): Irish Academic Press, 1982.

Smyth, Alfred P., *Warlords and Holy Men: Scotland, A.D. 80–1000*, London: Edward Arnold, 1984.

Smyth, Alfred P., 'The effect of Scandinavian raiders on the English and Irish churches: A preliminary assessment,' in Brendan Smith (ed.), *Britain and Ireland, 900–1300: Insular Responses to Medieval European Change*, Cambridge: Cambridge University Press, 1999, p. 1–38.

Stenton, F. M., *Anglo-Saxon England* (3rd edition), Oxford: Oxford University Press, 1971.

Stokes, Whitley, 'On the linguistic value of the Irish annals,' *Bezzenbergers Beiträge zur Kunde der Indogermanischen Sprachen*, 18 (1892), p. 56–132.

Swift, Catherine, 'Forts and fields: A study of "monastic towns" in seventh and eighth century Ireland,' *Journal of Irish Archaeology*, 9 (1998), p. 105–25.

Swift, Catherine, *Ogam Stones and the Earliest Irish Christians*, Maynooth: Department of Old and Middle Irish, St Patrick's College, 1997.

Thornton, David E., 'Clann Eruilb: Irish or Scandinavian?' *Irish Historical Studies*, 30, no. 118 (1996), p. 161–6.

Thornton, David E., 'The genealogy of Gruffudd ap Cynan,' in K. L. Maund (ed.), *Gruffudd ap Cynan: A Collaborative Biography* (Studies in Celtic History, 16), Woodbridge (Suffolk): Boydell and Brewer, 1996, p. 79–108.

Thornton, David E., 'Hey Macc!: The name Maccus, tenth to fifteenth centuries,' *Nomina*, 20 (1997), p. 67–94.

Thornton, David E., 'Maredudd ab Owain (d. 999): The most famous king of the Welsh,' *Welsh History Review*, 18 (1996–7), p. 567–91.

Thornton, David E., 'Edgar and the eight kings, A.D. 973: Textus et dramatis personae,' *Early Medieval Europe*, 10 (2001), p. 49–79.

Traynor, Patrick, 'Where was the Battle of Clontarf fought?' *Irish Builder*, 39, no. 899 (1 June 1897), p. 106.

Trindade, W. A., 'Irish Gormlaith as a sovereignty figure,' *Études Celtiques*, 23 (1986), p. 143–56.

Valante, Mary A., 'Reassessing the Irish "monastic town",' *Irish Historical Studies*, 31 (1998–9), p. 1–18.

Valante, Mary, 'Dublin's economic relations with hinterland and periphery in the later Viking Age,' in Seán Duffy (ed.), *Medieval Dublin, I*, Dublin: Four Courts Press, 2000), p. 69–83.

Valante, Mary A., *The Vikings in Ireland: Settlement, Trade and Urbanization*, Dublin: Four Courts Press, 2008.

Wallace, Patrick F., 'The archaeology of Viking Dublin,' in H. B. Clarke and Anngret Simms (eds.), *The Comparative History of Urban Origins in Non-Roman Europe: Ireland, Wales, Denmark, Germany, Poland, and Russia from the Ninth to the Thirteenth Century*, Oxford: British Archaeological Reports, 1985, p. 103–45.

Wallace, Patrick F., 'The English presence in Viking Dublin,' in M. A. S. Blackburn (ed.), *Anglo-Saxon Monetary History: Essays in Memory of Michael Dolley*, Leicester: Leicester University Press, 1986, p. 201–21.

Wallace, Patrick F., *The Viking Age Buildings of Dublin* (2 vols.) (Medieval Dublin Excavations, 1962–81, series A, vol. 1), Dublin: National Museum of Ireland, 1992.

Wallace-Hadrill, J. M., *The Vikings in Francia* (Stenton Lecture, 1974), Reading: University of Reading, 1975.

Walsh, Paul, 'Leinster states and kings in Christian times,' *Irish Ecclesiastical Record*, 53 (1939), p. 47–61.

Walsh, Paul, 'The Ua Maelechlainn Kings of Meath,' *Irish Ecclesiastical Record*, 57 (1941), p. 165–83.

Warntjes, Immo, 'The alternation of the kingship of Tara, 734–944,' *Peritia*, 17–18 (2003–4), p. 394–432.

Warntjes, Immo, 'Regnal succession in early medieval Ireland,' *Journal of Medieval History*, 30 (2004), p. 377–410.

Westropp, Thomas J., *King Brian, the Hero of Clontarf*, Dublin: Talbot Press, 1914.

Westropp, Thomas Johnson, 'Magh Adhair, Co. Clare: The place of inauguration of the Dalcassian kings,' *Proceedings of the Royal Irish Academy*, 4 (1896–8), p. 55–60.

Westropp, Thomas Johnson, 'Types of the ring-forts remaining in eastern Clare: Killaloe, its royal forts, and their history,' *Proceedings of the Royal Irish Academy*, 29C (1911–12), p. 186–212.

Williams, Ann, *Kingship and Government in Pre-Conquest England, c. 500–1066* (British History in Perspective), Basingstoke: Macmillan, 1999.

Williams, Ann, 'An outing on the Dee: King Edgar at Chester, A.D. 973,' *Mediaeval Scandinavia*, 14 (2004), p. 229–43.

Wilson, P. A., 'On the use of the terms "Strathclyde" and "Cumbria",' *Transactions of the Cumberland and Westmorland Antiquarian and Archaeological Society,* new series, 66 (1966), p. 57–92.

Wood, Michael, 'The making of Aethelstan's empire: An English Charlemagne?' in Patrick Wormald et al. (eds.), *Ideal and Reality in Frankish and Anglo-Saxon Society: Studies Presented to J. M. Wallace-Hadrill,* Oxford: Blackwell, 1983, p. 250–72.

Woolf, Alex, 'Amlaíb Cuarán and the Gael, 941–81,' in Seán Duffy (ed.), *Medieval Dublin, III,* Dublin: Four Courts Press, 2002, p. 34–44.

Woolf, Alex, *From Pictland to Alba, 789–1070,* Edinburgh: Edinburgh University Press, 2007.

Woolf, Alex, 'The "Moray question" and the Kingship of Alba in the tenth and eleventh centuries,' *Scottish Historical Review,* 79 (2000), p. 145–64.

Woolf, Alex, 'The origins and ancestry of Somerled: Gofraid mac Fergusa and "the Annals of the Four Masters",' *Mediaeval Scandinavia,* 15 (2005), p. 199–213.

Wormald, C. Patrick, 'Viking studies: Whence and whither?' in R. T. Farrell (ed.), *The Vikings,* London: Phillimore, 1982, p. 128–53.

Yorke, Barbara, *Wessex in the Early Middle Ages* (Studies in the Early History of Britain), London: Leicester University Press, 1995.

Young, Jean I., 'A note on the Norse occupation of Ireland,' *History,* new series, 35 (1950), p. 11–33.

INDEX

Act of Union 277
Adam of Bremen 243, 260
Adémar of Chabannes 225–6
Adomnán of Iona 42
Áed Allán, king of Tara 16, 21, 23–4, 41, 117, 178
Áed Findliath, king of Tara 23, 24, 54
Áed, Mathgamain's son 112–13
Áed Oirnide, king of Tara 24, 34–5
Áed Sláine, king of Tara 18, 42
Æðelræd (Ethelred the Unready), king of the English 243–4, 248
Aíbinn of Craicliath, fairy-woman 197, 219
Ailech 21, 80, 86, 131, 134, 136, 137, 156–7, 210
Ailill Ólum 71
Aindlid 62
Ainéislis, of Dál Cais 65, 66–7
Airgialla 21–2, 23, 24, 26, 30, 125, 136, 139, 168, 185, 192
Airthir Liphe (Eastern Liffey Plain) 34
Alan II, Duke of Brittany 94
Alcuin 46–7
Amlaíb Cuarán, king of Dublin 20, 25, 54, 80, 199, 234, 246–7
  defeated by Máel Sechnaill II 247–8
  son Sitriuc 120, 212, 232
  wife Gormlaith 99–101, 170, 212, 232, 234
Amlaíb Find, king of Dublin 24
Amlaíb mac Lagmainn 184
Amlaíb, son of Sitriuc Silkenbeard 173

Amond mac Duibginn, 'king of Waterford' 181
Anglesey 54, 109, 149, 150, 200
Anglo-Normans 34, 268
Anglo-Saxon Chronicle 46
Anlón, Brian's ancestor 62
Annagassan 53
Annales Cambriae 225
annals 23–4, 26, 39, 49, 62–4, 71, 74, 81, 118
  of Boyle 188, 191
  on Brian 115, 148
  of the Four Masters 56, 65, 76, 85, 87, 89, 91–2, 95, 106
    on Áed Ua Néill 136
    on Brian 109, 119–20, 122, 124, 134–5, 138, 152–4, 158
    on Flaithbertach Ua Néill 151–2, 156
    on invasion of Cenél Conaill 163
    on Máel Sechnaill II 133, 156, 246
    on revolt against Brian 170
  Fragmentary Annals of Ireland 65
  of Inisfallen 39, 42, 56, 70, 81, 87, 89, 91, 104–8
    on Brian 108, 111–14, 116, 122–3, 130, 134–6, 138, 151–4, 157–8, 233
    on invasion of Cenél Conaill 162–4
    on Máel Sechnaill II 133–4, 251
    on revolt against Brian 170, 173–4
  of Loch Cé 180, 188, 191–2, 194–8, 202, 219, 236–7
    on Máel Sechnaill II 133
  of St-Bertin 44, 52

of Tigernach 69, 115, 122, 124, 133, 246
of Ulster 31, 41–2, 47, 56, 76, 81, 88, 92,
    152, 246
    on Armagh 169, 179–80
    on battle of Tara 248
    on Brian 119, 121–2, 130, 138, 142, 151,
        155, 157–8, 163, 224
    on Gilla Mo-Chonna mac Fogartaig
        127
    on revolt against Brian 170, 172–4
    see also Clontarf
Anrath mac Elbric, 'son of the king of
    Lochlainn' 200, 218
Anselm, Archbishop of Canterbury 257,
    258–9, 263
Antrim 54
Ardagh (Co. Limerick) 51
Ards Peninsula 169
Argyll 3
Armagh 2–4, 23, 43, 52, 56, 138–43, 145,
    150, 151, 158
    abbot of (comarba Pátraic) 3, 64, 90,
        140–41, 145, 155, 187–8
    and Annals of Ulster 179–80
    Book of 140–42, 144
    Brian brings Munster army to 157–8
    burials 180, 185–9, 195
    primacy over Irish church 3, 139, 142,
        257–8
    and the Vikings 267
    visit of Muirchertach Ua Briain 259
Arnaill Scot, at Clontarf 210
Artrí mac Finguine,, king of Munster 41
Ath in Cháerthainn 174
Áth Luain (Athlone) 120, 133
Áth Senaig (Ballyshannon, Co. Kildare)
    23–4, 178
Augaire mac Tuathail, king of Leinster
    107, 108
Auisle, Viking leader 54
Aurchad, king of Iar-Chonnachta 74, 93

baile 154, 169, 210
Baile Dubgaill (Baldoyle, Co. Dublin)
    210
Banshenchas 75
battles
    against Donnubán mac Cathail 103
    against Norse 103, 104
    Ballaghmoon see Belach Mugna
    on banks of Tyne 54
    Belach Lechta (Co. Cork) 37, 92–3,
        103–4, 267
    Belach Mugna (Ballaghmoon, Co.
        Carlow) 19–20, 42, 65
    Bithlann 190
    Carlingford Lough 53
    Cathair Cuan 103, 267
    Catinchi 84–5
    Cell Mo-shamhóc 24, 56
    in Co. Limerick 30
    Cráeb Tulcha 27, 138, 265
    Déis Tuaiscirt against Vikings 62–4
    Faughart 23
    Glenn Máma 102, 120–24, 129, 171, 175,
        185, 212, 245, 267
    Gort Rotacháin 76–7
    Hastings 253–4
    Mag Dúin 76, 92
    Mag Léna 19, 42
    Muine Broccáin 25
    Mynydd Carn 259
    Odba 255
    Skreen 52
    Sulchóit (Solloghod, Co. Tipperary) 87
    Tara 110, 184, 234, 246–8
    Tigh-mic-nEthach 56
    Vikings against Osraige army 50
    see also Clontarf
Bébinn, Brian's mother 74–5, 93
Bébinn, Brian's daughter 99, 102, 138, 162
Bél Bóraime (Béal Boru, ringfort, near
    Killaloe) 66–9
Birr, Synod of 61

Blat, father of Cáirthenn Finn 71
Bleanphuttoge accord 116–19, 120, 122, 123, 124, 248
Book of Armagh 140–42, 144
Book of Howth 273–5
Book of Leinster 69, 82, 128, 146, 218
Bórama 65, 66–70, 82, 160
Bórama Laigen 31, 43
Bran mac Máelmórda, king of Leinster 34, 245
Brega 18, 39, 41, 127, 157, 246, 250–51
Brehon laws 4, 9–11
Bréifne 115, 202, 209
Brian Bóraime
  in battle of Clontarf 29–30, 38, 67, 150–51, 167–279
  beginning to make his mark 26
  birth and early years 1, 95–8
  building blitz 158–62
  death 176, 179–80, 194, 268
  dynasty 39, 40, 51
  emperor of the Gael (Scoti) 125–64
  enduring reputation 265–79
  family 20–21, 61–91, 161, 272–3
    breakthrough of 71–4
    earliest known family members 65
    father 74–82, 91, 94
    grandfather 62, 64, 65, 74, 85, 97
    known and conjectural relationships 147
    mother 74–5, 93
  final push 162–4
  high-king of Ireland 135–8, 141–2, 156–64, 167, 185, 269, 278
  internal opposition 110–13
  invasion of Déisi territory 111
  invasion of Leinster 103, 110, 114, 118, 119–20
  joint king of Ireland 119–20
  king of Dál Cais 103–4, 108, 110, 112, 114
  king of Munster 101, 104–6, 167

  legacy 239–79
  name 93–5
  overking of Leth Moga 106–8, 125–6, 128
  overlord of Leinster 124
  revolt of Dublin and Leinster 169–74, 241–2
  rise to power 92–124
  and the Scots 144–51
  seizure of high-kingship 129–35
  Slógad Timceall Érenn 151–6
  undermining of Brian's hegemony 168–9
  victory over Dublin 123–4, 232
  wives and children 99–102
Brian mac Máelruanaid, king of Iar-Chonnachta 93
Brigit, St 3
Brión (a quo Uí Briúin) 93
Brjánsorrosta (Brian's Battle) 223
Brogarbán mac Conchobair, king of Uí Failgi 190
Bródar (Bróðir) 184, 219–20, 225, 235–7, 248, 266, 268
Bronze Age 13
Brooking, Charles 210
Butler, Sarah 277

Caill Tomair 214–15
Cáin Adomnáin 61
Cáin Fhuithirbe 61
Cáirthenn Finn, son of Blat 62, 64, 71
Caithness 237–8
Caithréim Chellacháin Chaisil 77–9
Cambrensis, Giraldus 5, 113
Canterbury 257–9
Carlus mac Amlaíb, of Dublin 201
Carlus, Sword of 201
Carlus son of Ailill Fiach of Uí Áeda Odba 102, 249
Carlus, 'son of the king of France' 199, 200, 205

Carlus, grandson of Donnchad Donn of Clann Cholmáin 201
Carman 35
Cashel 38, 78, 83, 85–91, 257–9
Cath Cluana Tarbh 273
Cathair Cuan 103, 267
Cathal mac Conchobair, king of Connacht 102, 131, 133
Cathal mac Finguine, king of Munster 24, 37, 39, 41, 42, 117
Célechair, Dál Cais abbot of Terryglass 180
Cellachán Caisil, king of Munster 20, 76, 77–8, 83
Cell Mo-shamhóc (near Islandbridge, Dublin) 24, 56
Cenél Conaill 21, 23, 25, 136, 153–4, 158, 170
    and Flaithbertach Ua Néill 169
    submits to Brian 162–3, 168
Cenél Fermaic 8
Cenél Lugdach 163
Cenél nEógain 21–7, 43, 54–5, 102, 131–2, 136–40, 152, 154
    and Armagh 187
    humbling of 156–8, 168
    inauguration site burned 169
Cenn Abrat/Febrat 160
Cenn Corad (Kincora) 67, 69, 158–9, 171, 233, 249
Cennétig, Brian's father 74–82, 91, 94
    achievement 79–81
    other sons 80–81
Cerball mac Dúnlainge, king of Osraige 52, 229
Cerball mac Muirecáin, king of Leinster 65, 229
Charlemagne 44–5, 47, 49
Christianity in Ireland 2–3
    and church politics 111–12
    and Irish churchmen abroad 44–7
    reform of church 257

Chronicle of Ireland 273, 276
Chronicon Scotorum 56–7, 75, 81, 92, 119–20, 122, 124, 133
    on Brian 138, 151, 152, 154, 158
    on Clontarf 188–91
    on Flaithbertach Ua Néill 156
    on Máel Sechnaill 246–7
    on Muirchertach mac Liacc 159
    churches and cathedrals 161–2
Cian, son of Máel Muad mac Brain, Brian's son-in-law 102
Ciannachta 8
Ciarraige 27
Ciarraige Luachra 38, 179, 186
Cináed II, king of Scotland 146
Cláenloch of Sliab Fuait 157
Clann Cholmáin 18, 19, 34, 43, 65, 79–80, 132
    kings of Mide 84, 252
Cléirech of Uí Fiachrach Aidne 99
Clonmacnoise 19, 43, 71, 76, 84
Clonmore (Co. Carlow) 50–51
Clontarf 29–30, 38, 67, 150–51, 167–222
    aftermath of 248–52
    Annals of the Four Masters 190–91, 220
    Annals of Inisfallen 174–7, 184, 191, 214, 233, 242
    Annals of Loch Cé 180, 188, 192, 195–7, 198, 202, 219, 236–7
    Annals of Ulster 177–90, 191–2, 225, 227, 242
    and Aquitaine 225–8
    arrival of Scandinavian fleet 214, 235
    Chronicon Scotorum 190–91
    Cogadh Gáedhel re Gallaibh 180–81, 184, 191, 197–222, 227, 231, 236, 266, 273, 275
    enduring reputation 265–79
    Ireland and its neighbours after 252–65
    Irish annals 167–97
    later annal collections 189–97

Clontarf (*continued*)
  legacy of 239–79
  Njáls saga 227, 231–7
  Orkneyinga Saga 228–31
  revisionist readings 239–42, 278
  through others' eyes 223–38
  tide 21–6
  visions 196–7, 219, 237–8
  Welsh *Brut* 223–5
  what really happened? 242–8
cocad ('war') 170, 175, 176
Coccarán, Brian's messenger 104, 171
Cogadh Gáedhel re Gallaibh 64, 67, 71–3,
    78–9, 82–3, 95–6, 148–9, 249
  on Brian 96–8, 104, 107, 111, 116–17,
    120–24, 126–8, 130–34, 137–8, 142,
    151, 153–6, 164
  on Flaithbertach Ua Néill 172
  on fortifications and churches 159–62
  on Gormlaith and Máelmórda 101
  on Máel Sechnaill II 131–2, 136, 146
  on Mathgamain 85–91, 96, 97–8, 103
  on Murchad 92–3
  on Óttarr 94, 183
  as propaganda 264, 267
  on revolt against Brian 170–74
  see also Clontarf
Colmán Már (a quo Clann Cholmáin)
    18
Colum Cille, St 3, 23, 48
Columbanus, St 44
comarba Pátraic see Armagh, abbot of
Conailli Muirthemne 25, 135, 152, 169
Conaing, Brian's nephew 171, 176, 179,
    189, 195, 202, 237
Conall Corc 35–6
Conall Cremthainne, son of Niall
    Noígiallach 18
Conall Echluaith 39
Conall Gulban, son of Niall Noígiallach
    21
Conchobar, Brian's son 99

Conchobar mac Nessa, legendary king of
    Ulster 139
Conchobar, Máel Sechnaill II's grandson
    252
Congalach Cnogba, king of Tara 18,
    20–21, 25, 26, 80–81
Congalach, son of Lorcán (Brian's uncle)
    74
Conmael 184
Conmaicne 209
Conn Cétchathach 14, 15, 27, 30, 71
Connacht 27–30, 85, 109, 111, 114–15,
    119–20, 249, 267
  army 174, 186, 210
  invaded by Máel Ruanaid Ua Máel
    Doraid 170
  and Máel Sechnaill II 125, 129, 134, 136
Connadar 65
Connemara 49
Corcc 62
Corco Baiscind 8, 38, 55, 179, 186
Corco Mruad 62, 109
Cork 173
Cormac Cass 39, 71
Cormac mac Airt, ancestor of Uí Néill
    and Connachta 3
Cormac mac Cuilennáin, king of
    Munster 19, 38, 42, 65, 70
Cormac, son of Fáelán of the Déisi 90
Coscrach, son of Lorcán (Brian's uncle)
    109
Cú Chulainn 136
Cú Duilig mac Cennétig mic Donncuain,
    Brian grandnephew 233
Cusack, Mary Frances 279
Cynan ab Iago 254

Dál Cais 1, 7–8, 20–21, 37, 39, 40, 70–71,
    73, 221–2
  after Brian 177, 249
  against Viking enemy 95–8
  and battle of Belach Lechta 92–3

and battle of Mag Dúin 76–7
Brian as king of 103–4, 108, 110, 112, 114
claims to kingship 83, 86, 89, 105–6
and the Eóganachta 79–80
and meic Arailt of the Isles 149–50
and the Norse 86–7
rival branches of 82
source for Loch Cé annalist 195–6
territory raided by Fergal ua Ruairc
85
and Ulaid 157
Dál Fiatach 26–7, 49, 138, 139, 151, 153,
156, 169
Dál nAraidi 27, 138, 139, 151, 153
Dál Riata 3, 26–7, 150, 153, 243
Dallán mac Móire, poet 64, 66–7
Danair (Danes) 242–4, 248, 267–8, 276–7
De Hibernia et Antiquitatibus Eius 276
De mensura orbis terrae 45
Deheubarth (South Wales) 143, 259,
262–3
Déis Tuaiscirt 7, 51, 61
Déisi 38–9, 55–6, 61, 76
Déisi Muman 90, 111, 185, 267
Delbna, king of 87
Denmark 242–4, 248, 261, 267–8, 276–7
Derry 3
Description of Ireland 189, 275
Desmumu 77, 89, 112, 221
Diarmait mac Cerbaill, king of Tara 18,
42
Diarmait mac Máel na mBó, king of
Leinster 252–7, 261
Dícuil 44–5
Dissertations on the Antient History of
Ireland 278
Domesday Book 260
Domnall, Brian's son 163, 164, 176, 207–8
Domnall Clóen, king of Leinster 107–8,
116, 247
Domnall mac Diarmata, king of Corco
Bascind 179

Domnall mac Eimin mic Cainnich Móir,
mormaer of Mar 150–51, 178, 186,
207–8
Domnall mac Ragallaig, of Bréifne 209
Domnall Midi, king of Tara 16
Donegal 163
Donnchad, Brian's son 93, 101, 144, 171,
197, 202, 212, 233, 249
after battle of Clontarf 220–22, 249–52
Donnchad Donn, king of Tara 20, 56, 75,
79–80, 201
Donnchad mac Cellacháin, king of
Munster 83, 84, 85–6
Donnchad Midi, king of Tara 16, 18, 34
Donnchad of Eóganacht Glendamnach
78
Donnchad, son of Domnall Clóen, king
of Leinster 116, 120–21, 123–4, 136–7
Donncuan, Brian's brother 179
Donnubán mac Cathail of Uí Chairbre
(a quo Uí Dhonnubáin) 87, 89, 91,
103
Dubcenn mac Ímair, of Limerick 172
Dub Choblaig, Brian's fourth wife 102,
134, 157, 171
Dub Gilla mac Rebacháin 74
Dub-dá-Bairenn, king of Munster 84, 114
Dub-dá-leithe, abbot of Armagh 145
Dubgall mac Amlaíb, Sitriuc's brother
182, 184, 199, 210, 211
Dubgall's bridge (on the Tolka?) 210, 213,
215, 218
Dubgenti 53, 54
Dublin 20, 24, 70, 109–10, 119, 128, 150,
243
after battle of Clontarf 250–51, 254–7,
259, 261–2
and battle of Glenn Máma 267
with Brian in invasion of Leth Cuinn
129
Brian's victory over 123–4, 232, 246,
248

Dublin (continued)
  Norse of 26, 80, 102, 105, 107, 109,
    120–22, 130, 170–75, 242
  revolt against Brian 169–74, 241–2
  siege of 114, 244–5, 247
  synod 257
  Vikings in 48, 50, 52, 53, 54–5, 56
  see also Clontarf
Dubthach Albanach 145
Dún Cliath (Áine Cliach, Co. Limerick)
  160
Dún Crot (Dungrud, Glen of Aherlow)
  160
Dún Cuirc (Rock of Cashel, Co.
  Tipperary?) 86
Dún Delca (Dundalk, Co. Louth) 135–6
Dún Echdach (Duneight, Co. Down)
  168–9
Dún Eochair Maige (Bruree, Co.
  Limerick) 160
Dúnchad (a quo Uí Dúnchada) 33–4
Dúnlaing mac Tuathail, king of Leinster
  107, 108, 172, 209
Dúnlaing, son of Dub-dá-Bairenn, of
  Eóganacht Raithlind 114
Dunseverick 54
Durrow 3

early Ireland 1–6
Ebric/Elbric, 'son of the king of France'
  199, 200, 205
Echmarcach mac Ragnaill, king of
  Dublin and the Isles 144
Echrad, Brian's third wife 101–2, 249
Edgar, king of the English 143–4
Eðnu (Eithne), daughter of Kjarvalr
  Írakonungr 229
Edward the Elder, king of the English 94
Eiden mac Cléirig, king of Uí Fiachrach
  Aidne 99
Eithne Thóebfhota, daughter of king of
  Leinster 33

Éli, north Tipperary 90
Emain Macha 26, 138–9
Emly 83, 90, 112
England 143, 223, 243–5, 248, 254, 260–61
Eochaid mac Ardgail, king of Ulaid 131,
  136, 138
Eochu Ballderg 62, 64, 71
Eógan, son of Niall Noígiallach 21, 30
Eógan Már (a quo the Eóganachta) 35,
  39, 71
Eóganachta 8, 30, 31, 35–8, 39, 42, 49, 61,
  65, 70–71, 73, 77–9, 83, 86–7, 90, 98,
  104, 110, 112, 159, 168, 177, 249
  Áine 70, 89
  Airthir Chliach 70
  Chaisil 37, 42, 52, 65, 76, 77, 83, 84, 88
  Glennamnach 37, 39, 78, 185
  Locha Léin 37, 49, 178, 185
  Raithlend 37, 84, 87, 89, 90, 91, 102,
    103, 104, 114, 249, 267
  Brian's dominance over 110
  Mathgamain at war against 98, 104
Éremón and Éber, sons of Míl 30
Ethelred the Unready see Æðelræd

Fáelán (a quo Uí Fáeláin of Leinster)
  33–4
Fáeláin (a quo Uí Fáeláin of Déisi
  Muman) 90
Fedelmid mac Crimthainn, king of
  Munster 24, 35, 38, 41–2, 70
Fergráid, king of Munster 84
Ferns 50
Ferta Nemed 130
Findgenti 53
Fine Gall (C. Dublin) 173, 199, 202, 210,
  254
Finn mac Cumaill, leader of the Fianna
  11, 267
Finn, son of Dubchrón of Uí Fhidgeinti
  109
Fir Umaill 49

flaith Érenn ('sovereignty of Ireland') 14
Flaithbertach, king of Iar-Chonnachta 74
Flaithbertach mac Inmainén, king of
    Munster 70
Flaithbertach, Áed Ua Néill's nephew *see*
    Ua Néill, Flaithbertach 138
Flann, Brian's son 99
Flann, Máel Sechnaill's son 173
Flann Mainistrech, poet and historian
    242
Flann Sinna, king of Tara 19, 42, 65, 69
Flannán, St 62, 161
fleets 52–6, 64, 71, 72, 81, 94, 109, 110,
    113–4, 115, 124, 126, 128, 134, 146,
    148–9, 150, 163, 164, 178, 184, 199,
    205, 214, 226, 247, 253, 259, 260, 261,
    262, 267, 268
Foras Feasa ar Éirinn 269–71
fortifications 158–62
Fortriu 54
Fortuatha Laigen 50
France 225–8, 260, 265

Garbthamnach 172
General History of Ireland 278
Germany 143, 220–21, 230, 265
Gilla Ciaráin mac Glún Iairn, nephew of
    King Sitriuc 182–3
Gilla Cóemáin, historian and poet 69,
    251, 252
Gilla Mo-Chonna mac Fogartaig, king of
    Southern Brega 127
Gilla Pátraic, bishop of Dublin 257
Gilla Pátraic, king of Osraige 106, 110
Gille, bishop of Limerick 258
Gilli, Jarl 234, 238
Giraldus *see* Cambrensis
Glendalough 34, 50, 174
Glenn Máma 102, 120–24, 129, 171, 175,
    185, 212, 245, 267
Glún Iairn, son of Amlaíb Cuarán 182
Godwin, Earl 253

Godwinsson, Harold, king of the English
    253, 260–61
Godwinsson, Leofwine 253
Gofraid mac Arailt, king of the Isles
    149–50, 243
Goistilin Gall 181
Gormlaith, Brian's second wife 93, 101–2,
    108, 146, 170–71, 236, 249
    and battle of Clontarf 266, 276
    previous marriage to Amlaíb Cuarán
        99–101, 170, 212, 232, 234
Griséne 183
Gruffudd ap Cynan of Gwynedd 213, 253,
    259, 263
Gruffudd ap Rhys ap Tewdwr of
    Deheubarth 263
Guaire Aidne, king of Connacht 30
Gwynedd (North Wales) 54, 143, 150, 213,
    253, 259, 262, 263
Gyða, Óláfr Tryggvason's wife 243

Hanmer, Meredith 273, 276
Haraldr, king of Norway 260
Haughton, Samuel 215–17
Hebrides 50, 55, 89, 109, 122, 144, 145,
    149–50, 183, 184, 196, 199, 200,
    228–9, 232, 237–8, 243, 246, 260–62
Helgi 71
Henry I, king of England 258, 263
Hiberno-Norse 254–6, 265
high-kingship 42–4
Horm 54
hostages 19, 20, 23, 42, 43, 73, 76, 81, 89,
    90, 102, 104, 106, 109, 111, 115, 116–7,
    119–20, 123–4, 130–1, 132, 134, 135–7,
    148, 150, 151, 157, 158, 167, 233, 244
Howth 49, 126, 127, 173, 202, 214
Hróaldr 94
Hródolfr 55

Iago of Gwynedd 259
Iar-Chonnachta 74, 93

Iarmumu 37

Iarthar Liphe (Western Liffey Plain) 33, 107, 115, 206

Iceland 54, 183, 195, 221, 228–37, 237–8, 266

Illustrated History of Ireland 279

Ímar of Limerick 103, 109, 149

Imperator Scotorum 138–44, 150, 187, 254, 262

In Fochlae ('The North') 168

Indéirge mac Uradáin, Brian's *fer gráda* 196

Indrechtach, king of Ciannachta 8

Inis Cathaig (Scattery Island) 89, 103, 144, 149, 172, 196, 267

Inis Celtra (Holy Island, Lough Derg) 30, 51, 71, 83, 161, 220

Inis Gaill Duib 159

Inis Sibthonn (King's Island, Limerick) 62, 64, 71, 86

Inishbofin 48

Inishmurray 48–9

introduction 1–57

Iona 3, 45, 48–9, 243

Irish language and literature 11–12

Irish Monthly 217

Irish Tales 277

Iron Age 1–2, 13, 15

Isle of Man *see* Man, Isle of

Isles *see* Hebrides

Ívarr, joint king of Dublin 53–4

John Scottus Eriugena 44

Keating, Geoffrey 269–71, 273, 277–8

Kildare monastery 3, 51

Killaloe (Co. Clare) 62, 67, 69, 83, 158, 160, 161, 172, 186–7, 197, 233

Kincora *see* Cenn Corad

King Brian, the Hero of Clontarf 217

kingship among the Irish 7–9

Knowth 18

Knútr, king of Denmark and England 244

Knútr IV of Denmark 260–61

Knút's conquest of England 228

Lachtna, Brian's brother 62, 64, 82, 83, 95, 99

Láegaire, son of Niall Noígiallach 43

Lagmainn (Old Norse *lögmenn*) 89, 149, 177, 184, 196, 205

Laidainn, Brian's attendant at Clontarf 219

Laigin 2, 31, 33, 41, 105
  see also Leinster

Landnámabók 184, 229

Lanfranc, Archbishop of Canterbury 257, 258

Leabhar Muimhneach, An 74, 76, 82, 85

Lebor Gabála Érenn 11, 13

Leinster 31–5, 106–7, 120, 162, 178, 250, 255
  armies 202
  Book of 69, 82, 128, 146, 218
  Brian deposes king of 136–7
  with Brian in invasion of Leth Cuinn 129
  hostages 123–4, 137, 250, 267
  invaded 103, 108, 110–11, 114, 119–20, 250–51
  overkingship of 24, 101, 107, 245
  revolt against Brian 169–74, 241–2
  and Scotland 145–6

Leth Cathail (Lecale, Co. Down) 156

Leth Cuinn 19, 25, 30–31, 34, 43, 81, 117, 168, 186
  early moves against 108–10
  invaded 129–35, 255
  resumption of raids against 113–16
  and the Vikings 256

Leth Moga 30–31, 34–5, 39, 41, 43, 80, 105, 107, 114, 168, 186
  Brian's claim to overlordship of 125–6, 128, 248
  and Diarmait mac Máel na mBó 255

Lex Innocentium 61
Lia Fáil 14
Liber Angeli 141
Limerick 62, 71, 86–8, 90, 98, 110, 144, 256
  first bishop of 258
  Norse of 90, 144, 149, 181, 196, 208, 231, 267
Lindisfarne 46
Lloyd, J.H. 217
Loch Cend 160
Lochlainn 53, 177, 178, 181, 184, 190, 199, 200, 205, 208, 218, 242, 268
Lochlainn mac Maíl Shechnaill, of Corco Mruad 109
Loígis 222
Lorcán, Brian's grandfather 62, 64, 65, 74, 85, 97
Lough Derg 30, 51, 64, 71, 81, 83, 97, 113, 114, 220
Lough Ree 71–2
Louth 8, 18, 23, 25, 26, 52, 152, 153, 169, 173, 185, 187
Lug, Celtic god 14
Lug Lámfhata 267
Luimne, at Clontarf 178, 184
Luimnech (Shannon Estuary) 51, 51, 55, 64, 71–2, 149, 179, 196, 218

mac Arailt *see* Gofraid, Maccus, *and* Ragnall
mac Cennétig, Brian *see* Brian Bóraime
mac Cennétig, Lachtna *see* Lachtna, Brian's brother
mac Cennétig, Mathgamain *see* Mathgamain, Brian's brother
Maccus mac Arailt, king of the Isles 89, 144, 149, 196
mac Domnaill, Máel Sechnaill *see* Máel Sechnaill II
Mac Gilla Mo-Cholmóc, king of Uí Dúnchada 34

Mac Lochlainn, Domnall, king of Cenél nEógain 210, 252
Mac Lochlainn, Muirchertach, king of Ireland 142, 232
Mac Bethad mac Muiredaig, king of Ciarraige Luachra 179
Mac Murchada, Diarmait, king of Leinster 33
Máel Coluim mac Cineáda (Máel Coluim II), king of Scotand 145–6, 149, 230
Máel Gualae, king of Munster 19, 31
Máel Muad mac Brain, king of Munster 37, 87, 89, 90, 91, 102, 103, 104
Máel Sechnaill I, king of Tara 18–19, 31, 43, 44, 52, 97, 117
Máel Sechnaill II, king of Tara 16, 67, 79, 102, 105–9, 111, 113–14, 116, 122, 137, 269
  after battle of Clontarf 250–51
  in battle of Clontarf 185, 190, 191, 202, 209, 224, 270–71
  in battle of Tara 246
  and the Bleanphuttoge accord 116–19, 116–20
  Brian turns against 129–30
  Brian's ally 163, 173–4, 185
  death 251
  invasion of Connacht 115, 119–20
  king of Tara 105, 125, 135, 157, 168–9, 184–5, 234, 246–8, 251–2
  and Óenach Tailten 146, 156
  rebuff of 267
  war resumes against 123–4, 125, 129–34
Máel Suthain, Brian's *anmchara* 140–41, 142–3
Máelmórda mac Murchada, king of Leinster 34, 101, 108, 120–21, 123, 137, 146, 170, 171–3, 176, 190
  in battle of Clontarf 180, 185, 212, 224–5, 229–30, 236, 245, 266
Mag Adair 65–6, 105–6, 108, 267

Mag Corainn 163
Mag mBreg 130, 132
Mag Muirthemne 169
Mag nAilbe 107
Magnús III Barelegs, King of Norway
    261–2
Magnús, son of King Haraldr of Norway
    260
Mainchín (Munchin), St 62, 64
Maircc Lagen 110
Maistiu (Mullaghmast) 33
Malachy, St 145
Man, Isle of 27, 150, 184, 200, 243, 254,
    259, 261
Manx Chronicle 261
maps 10, 17, 22, 28, 32, 36, 68, 203
Mar(r), mormaer of 150–51, 178, 186,
    207–8
Marcán, Brian's brother 83, 95, 161
Marianus Scottus 220, 230, 235, 236, 265
Mathgamain, Brian's brother 37, 62, 67,
    82–5, 95–8, 99, 144, 162
    assassination 98, 102, 103, 104, 112, 135,
        149, 196
    and the kingship of Cashel 85–91
    son Áed 112–13
    victory over Vikings 98
Medb 136
meic Arailt (Haraldssons) 89, 109, 110,
    144, 149–50, 196, 243
Meic Carthaig 77, 79, 83
Mide 39, 72, 80, 113–14, 115, 132, 185,
    250–51
    invasion of 173, 267
Milesians 11–12, 13–14
Montgomery, Arnulf de, lord of
    Pembroke 263–4
Mór, Brian's first wife 99
mormaer 150, 172, 207–8, 295
Mothla mac Domnaill mic Fáeláin, king
    of Déisi Muman 178, 185–6, 206
Mug Nuadat 30, 96, 168

Muirchertach, Brian's great-grandson
    249, 256
Muirchertach mac Liacc, poet 69, 159
Muirchertach na Cochall Craicinn
    mac Néill Glúnduib, king of Cenél
    nEógain 20, 25, 80, 152
Muirchú 15, 16, 43, 141
Muiredach (a quo Uí Muiredaig of
    Leinster) 33
Muiredach Muillethan (a quo Síl
    Muiredaig of Connacht) 29
Muirgius son of Conchobar, of
    Connacht 114
Mungret, church of 51
Munster 35–9, 77, 80–81, 107, 114–15, 129,
    142, 255
    army 157–8, 162, 174, 185–6, 212, 220
    aspirations 39–42
    Brian as king of 101, 104–6, 167
    churches of 111–12
    churchmen at synod of Dublin 257
    and Fergal ua Ruairc 84–5
    hostages 19, 89, 104, 111
    and Tairdelbach ua Briain 253–4
Murchad, Brian's son 92, 99, 123, 132, 157,
    163, 171–2, 174, 197, 233
    in battle of Clontarf 224–5
    death of 176, 179, 189, 191, 202, 207,
        218–19, 225, 248, 268, 275
    eulogy in Cogadh 210–11
Murchad, king of Iar-Chonnachta 74, 93
Murchad mac Finn, king of Leinster 90,
    101, 146
Murchad, son of Diarmait mac Máel
    na mBó (a quo Meic Murchada,
    MacMurroughs) 254–6
Múscraige 70, 86
Múscraige Tíre, king of 114
myth of national origin 11–12

Naas 34
national consciousness 9–13, 57

Nenagh 115
Niall Caille, king of Tara 24, 35, 41
Niall Frossach, king of Tara 16
Niall Glúndub, king of Tara 20, 24, 25, 56, 80, 178
Niall Noígiallach 15–16, 18, 23, 29, 43
Njáls saga 227, 231–7
Normans 259–60, 263, 264
Norse
    battles against 85–90, 102, 126–7, 181
    and communities of Norse extraction 126
    of Dublin 26, 80, 102, 105, 107, 109, 120–22, 130, 170–75, 181, 242
    of Limerick 90, 144, 149, 181, 196, 231
    plunder of monastery of Rosscarbery 114
    warriors become Brian's vassals 128
    of Waterford 90, 107–8, 181
    see also Clontarf
North Sea monastery 47
Northumbria 46, 54, 246
Norway 260–62

O'Brien, John, Bishop of Cloyne and Ross 278
Ó Cléirigh, Micheál 220
O'Connell, Daniel 277
O'Conor, Charles 278
O'Curry, Eugene 142, 272–3
Ó Dálaigh, Muiredach Albanach 221, 266–9
Óebinn of Craicliath *see* Aíbinn
óenach 35, 66, 105, 134
Óenach Carmain 35, 41
Óenach Colmáin 20
Óenach Conaille 153
Óenach Maige Adair 66, 105, 106
Óenach Tailten 14, 24, 39, 134, 138, 146, 156
Óengus son of Cáirthinn Finn (a quo Uí Óengusso) 62, 64, 71

Óengus son of Donnchad Donn, of Clann Cholmáin 75
Óengus Tírech, ancestor of Dál Cais 40, 73, 96
ogham 1–2, 33, 161
O'Gorman, Thomas 217
O'Halloran, Sylvester 278–9
Oileán Chléire (Cape Clear) 173
Óláfr Tryggvason, king of Norway 230, 243
Óláfr the White, king of Dublin 53, 54
Ólchobor mac Cináeda, king of Munster 44, 70
O'Neills of Ulster 24
Orderic Vitalis 263
Orkneys 182, 193, 194, 200, 229, 237, 260
Orkneyinga saga 228–31
Órlaith, Brian Bóraime's sister 20, 75–6, 92
Osli, son of Dubcenn mac Ímair, Brian's mormaer 172
Osraige 19, 31, 38, 43, 50, 52, 55, 76, 118, 222
    with Brian in invasion of Leth Cuinn 129
    Brian's assault on 101, 105–7, 110
    and Brian's claim to Leth Moga 125–6
    invaded 90, 106, 110, 174, 250–51, 255, 267
    king of 229
Óttarr the Black 72, 94, 183
Otto III, German king 143

Patrick, St 2–3, 5, 15–16, 38, 139–41, 145, 169, 267
    Confessio 141
    Tripartite Life of 50, 51, 64, 77
Petrie, George 188–9
Philip I of France 260
poems quoted 131, 155, 268–9

Quin (Co. Clare) 65

Ragnall mac Arailt, king of the Isles 150
Ráith Bressail, council of 259
Ráith Mór (Rathmore, Co. Antrim) 139
Rawlinson B502 69, 78
Rebachán mac Mothla, king of Dál Cais
    70, 73, 74
Rechru (Lambay?) 47
Rhain, Irish king in Wales 200
Rhodri Mawr of Gwynedd 54
Rhys ap Tewdwr of Deheubarth 259,
    262–3
rígdamna ('material of a king', 'heir-
    designate') 81, 108, 112, 114, 136, 176,
    182, 190
Rome 2, 44, 52, 101, 143, 144
Roscam, monastery of 49
Rosscarbery, monastery of 114
Ruarc (a quo Uí Ruairc) 29
Ryan, Father John 239–41

Sadb, Brian's daughter 99, 102, 104
Sadb, daughter of Conn Cétchathach
    71
St Flannán's Oratory 161
St Lawrence, Christopher 275
Saint-Michel-en-l'Herm 226
St Mullins (Co. Carlow) 56
Samuel, Bishop of Dublin 257
Scannlán mac Cathail, king of Eóganacht
    Locha Léin 185
Scattery Island see Inis Cathaig
Scotland 3–4, 12, 27, 47, 50, 54–5, 62,
    143–51, 154, 173, 178, 186, 200, 207,
    210, 223, 228–30, 243, 276
Scottish Isles see Hebrides
Sedulius Scottus 44
Senán, St 196
Senlis Abbáin (Co. Laois) 172
Shannon, river 52, 79, 80, 81, 84, 85, 105,
    109, 113, 115, 117, 120, 133, 134, 152,
    163
Shannon Estuary see Luimnech

Sigurðr (Siucraid), earl of Orkney 182,
    184, 193, 218, 228–31, 232, 234–8, 245,
    248
Sigurðr Jerusalem-farer, King of Norway
    262
Síl Muiredaig 29, 84
Síl nAedo Sláine 18
Síl nAnmchada 157
Sitriuc (Sigtryggr Silkiskegg,
    'Silkenbeard'), Norse king of Dublin
    102, 120–23, 148–9, 170, 173, 243,
    245–6
  after battle of Clontarf 253, 260
  and battle of Clontarf 182, 185, 194,
    199–200, 210–12, 221, 224–5,
    230–31, 232–6, 244
  and battle of Glenn Máma 248
  family ties to Brian 212–13
Sláine, Brian's daughter 99, 102, 213
Slane 20
slavery 5, 6, 46, 47, 72, 88, 89, 127, 154,
    182, 226, 267
Sliab Fuait (South Armagh) 137, 152, 157
Sliab Luachra 87, 155
Sliab Maircce (Slievemargy, Co. Laois)
    110, 174
Slógad Timceall Érenn 51–6
Stanihurst, Richard 189, 275
Stone Age 13
Story of Ireland, The 279
Stowe Missal, shrine of 250
Strangford 54–5
Strongbow 265, 268
Suartgair (Old Norse svartleggja) 89, 90,
    144, 183
Sulchóit (Solloghod) 87, 98
Sullivan, A.M. 279
surnames 271–2
Sveinn Forkbeard, king of Denmark
    243–4, 248
Sweden 160–61
Sword of Carlus 201

Table 1: Brian's remote ancestors 40
Table 2: Brian's immediate kinsmen 63
Table 3: Brian's wives and offspring 100
Table 4: Brian's known and conjectural familial relationships 147
Tadc, Brian's son 101, 233, 236–7, 249
Taghmon monastery 50
Tailtiu 13–14, 24, 39, 113, 134, 138
Táin Bó Cúailgne 136, 139
Tairdelbach ua Briain, Brian's grandson 10, 99, 176, 189, 191, 218, 233, 235
   after battle of Clontarf 249, 253–7, 259, 260, 261
Tara 13–15, 18, 20, 24–6, 30–31, 33, 35, 66, 138, 245
   battle of 110, 184, 184–5, 234, 246–8
   Brian marches on 129–30, 132
   and claim to high-kingship 42–3
   Daniel O'Connell's monster meeting 277
   invasion of Brega 39
   king Áed Allán 41
   king Congalach Cnogba 80
   king Donnchad Donn 75–6, 79–80
   king Flann Sinna 42, 65, 69, 75
   king Máel Sechnaill I 44, 102
   king Máel Sechnaill II 105, 125, 135, 168–9, 184–5, 246–8, 251–2
   king Niall Caille 24, 35, 41
   king Niall Glúndub 24, 56, 178
Terryglass 83, 180
Thomond *see* TuadmumuTír Conaill 21, 25, 153
Tír nEógain 21
Tírechán, Bishop 141
Tlachtga (Ward), hill of 39–41, 113
Todd, James Henthorn 215, 217, 218
Tomrar (Þórormr), Jarl of Luimnech 55
Tomrar (Þórormr), son of Helgi, at Limerick 71
Torolb (Þórólfr), Jarl, on Lough Neagh 55

Torpaid, king of Déis Tuaiscirt 62
Traynor, Patrick 217
Trinity College, Dublin 15, 140, 206, 215
Tuadmumu 35, 76, 77, 80, 81, 84, 97, 112, 114, 201, 224
Tuamgraney (Tuaim Gréne) church 30, 70, 73, 161, 162, 186
tuarastal ('stipend', 'ceremonial wages') 132, 164, 171, 221
tuath(a) ('a people', 'a territory') 7, 8, 11, 23, 26, 72
Túatha Dé Danann 11, 12, 13
Tuathal (a quo Uí Thuathail of Leinster) 33
Tuathal mac Augaire, son of the king of Leinster 190
Tulach Óc (Tullaghogue, Co. Tyrone) 21, 169
Tulla (Co. Clare) 65, 105

Ua Brain (of Leinster) 34
Ua Briain, Diarmait 256, 258, 259, 262
Ua Briain, Domnall Mór 161
Ua Briain, Muirchertach 249, 256–8, 261–4
ua Briain, Tairdelbach *see* Tairdelbach ua Briain, Brian's grandson
ua Canannáin, Ruaidrí 25, 80
Ua Cellaig, Murchad 186
Ua Cellaig, Tadc 67, 179, 186, 202, 210, 276
Ua Ciarda, Uallgarg 172–3
ua Cillín 162
Ua Clérig, Arthur 217
Ua Conchobair (of Connacht) 29, 84
Ua Conchobair, Áed in Gaí Bernaig, king of Connacht 66
Ua Conchobair, Ruaidrí, king of Ireland 145, 265
Ua Conchobair, Tadc in Eich Gil, king of Connacht 192, 202
Ua Conchobair, Tairdelbach, king of Ireland 69, 142

ua Crichidéin, abbot of Movilla 157

Ua Dálaigh, Gofraid Fionn, poet 197

ua Dubagáin, Géibennach, king of Fer Maige 185

Ua Duinn, Gilla na Náem, historian and poet 67

ua Eruilb, Donnchad 183

ua Fergail, Gilla na Náem (of Bréifne) 209

Ua hAingliu, Donngus, Bishop of Dublin 257

Ua hAinmire, Máel Ísu, Bishop of Waterford 258

ua hArtagáin, Dúnlaing, otherworld figure 189, 275

ua hEidin, Máel Ruanaid, king of Uí Fiachrach Aidne 30, 99, 186

ua hÍmair, Ímar, king of Limerick 86, 87, 89, 91

Ua Longacháin, Dubchrón, king of Uí Chuanach 109

ua Lothcháin, Cúán, poet and historian 67, 146

Ua Máel Doraid, Máel Ruanaid, king of Cenél Conaill 163–4, 169, 170

ua Máelmacha, Tuathal, steward of Armagh in Munster 142

ua Mugthigirn, Cenn Fáelad, king of Munster 70

Ua Néill, Áed, king of Ailech 131–2, 134, 136–8

ua Néill, Domnall, king of Tara 23, 25–6, 55, 187, 246–7

Ua Néill, Flaithbertach, king of Ailech 102, 138, 139, 151–2, 156–8, 162–3, 172
　　invades Leinster 250–51
　　invades Ulaid 168–9
　　secures hostages of Connacht 251

ua Rónáin, Flann, poet 247

Ua Ruairc of Bréifne 202

Ua Ruairc, Art, king of Bréifne 251

ua Ruairc, Fergal, king of Bréifne 26, 84–5, 172, 208–9

ua Slebinn, Gilla Comgaill, poet 131

Ua Tuathail (of Leinster) 33

Uí Áeda Odba 102

Uí Bairrche Tíre 56

Uí Briain 77, 79, 258, 259, 261

Uí Briúin (Connacht) 29, 109

Uí Briúin Bréifne 29

Uí Briúin Seóla 29

Uí Buide 172

Uí Cháim 37

Uí Chairbre (of Uí Fhidgeinti) 267

Uí Chaissíne 8

Uí Chellacháin 83

Uí Chennselaig 33, 50, 108, 110, 115, 209, 253, 254

Uí Chernaig (of Dál Cais) 73, 82

Uí Chléirig 99

Uí Chonaill Gabra 97

Uí Chuanach 109

Uí Dúnchada 34, 101, 107, 108, 116

Uí Dúnlainge 24, 33–4, 101, 107, 245, 254

Uí Eidin 99

Uí Énda of Eóganacht Áine 89

Uí Fáeláin 34, 65, 101, 107, 108

Uí Failgi 171

Uí Fhidgeinti 38, 51, 89, 103, 109

Uí Fhlaithbertaig 74

Uí Fiachrach 29–30

Uí Fiachrach Aidne 99, 117, 186

Uí Flaind (of Dál Cais) 82

Uí Liatháin 38

Uí Maine 27–8, 67, 117, 176, 186

Uí Muiredaig 33, 34, 101, 108, 115–16, 171

Uí Néill 8, 14, 33, 39, 54, 79, 264
　　emergence of 15–16
　　and the high-kingship 42–4, 118–19, 250
　　invasion of Munster 76
　　and Leith Cuinn 30–31
　　and Máel Sechnaill 129, 247, 250
　　and monastery of Clonmacnoise 76

northern 16, 21–6, 35, 55, 80, 125, 152,
      156, 250–52, 256
rotating kingship of Tara 245
southern 16–21, 24–5, 34, 42, 79–80,
      102, 105, 113, 125, 157, 163, 169, 172,
      251
territory in Brega 246
territory in Mide 72, 246
Uí Óengusso (of Dál Cais) 40, 62, 64, 65,
      71, 73–4
Uí Ruairc 84
Uí Thairdelbaig (of Dál Cais) 1, 62–4, 65,
      73, 77
Uisnech, hill of 113–14
Ulaid 21, 24, 26–7, 30, 54, 55, 123, 125, 136,
      153
and Áed Ua Néill 137–8
and Cenél nEógain 152, 156–8
Flaithbertach Ua Néill invades 168–9
hostages 137, 151, 154, 157, 251
kings of 18, 131–2, 139, 247
Úlfr *hreða*, against Brian at Clontarf 235
Ulster Cycle 39
Úspakr, with Brian at Clontarf 235–6

Vikings 5, 18–20, 24–5, 27, 29–30, 37–8,
      43, 71, 242, 278
archaeological evidence 48, 50, 51
in Brittany 94
and Cellachán 78
colonists in Iceland 183
depredations 267
in Dublin 48, 50, 52, 53–4, 56
impact of 51–7
in Leth Moga 126
in Limerick 62, 82, 159, 256
mass expulsion of 56
onslaught 44–51, 96
opposition to 264–5
runic inscription 161
second Viking Age 243
ships 64, 85, 128, 267
in Waterford 54, 256

Wales 2, 37, 54, 143, 150, 200, 213, 253–4,
      260
and the Normans 263
Welsh writers on Clontarf 223–5, 265
see also Deheubarth, Gwynedd
Ware, Sir James 276
Waterford 24, 51, 109, 150, 243, 256,
      257–8, 259, 262
Norse of 90, 107, 113, 181
Vikings in 54–6, 72, 94, 110
Western Isles *see* Hebrides
Westropp, Thomas Johnson 66, 82, 217
Wexford 51, 56, 254–5
William the Conqueror, king of England
      258, 259–60
William of Malmesbury 263
William Rufus, king of England 258

York 20, 53, 54, 101, 184, 192–4, 199,
      219–20, 246, 248, 261
Youghal 55